Hacking
Photoshop® CS2

Shangara Singh

WILEY

Wiley Publishing, Inc.

Hacking Photoshop® CS2

Published by
Wiley Publishing, Inc.
10475 Crosspoint Boulevard
Indianapolis, IN 46256
www.wiley.com

Copyright © 2005 by Wiley Publishing, Inc., Indianapolis, Indiana

Published simultaneously in Canada

ISBN-13: 978-0-7645-9788-6
ISBN-10: 0-7645-9788-4

Manufactured in the United States of America

10 9 8 7 6 5 4 3 2 1

IK/SZ/QZ/QV/IN

For general information on our other products and services or to obtain technical support, please contact our Customer Care Department within the U.S. at (800) 762-2974, outside the U.S. at (317) 572-3993 or fax (317) 572-4002.

Wiley also publishes its books in a variety of electronic formats. Some content that appears in print may not be available in electronic books.

Library of Congress Cataloging-in-Publication Data: Available from Publisher

About the Author

Shangara Singh has written and designed exam study aids for the Adobe Certified Expert product proficiency exams for Adobe Photoshop and co-authored exam study aids for Adobe Illustrator and Macromedia Dreamweaver (www.examaids.com). He regularly answers Photoshop questions on various lists, forums, and from his Photoshop ACE Web site. He has also served as technical editor for books on the use of Photoshop in Web site design and digital photography. He brings his extensive experience as a director of photography, a lighting designer, a photographer, and a Web and print designer to bear on all his visual work.

Credits

Executive Editor
Chris Webb

Senior Development Editor
Kevin Kent

Technical Editor
David Creamer

Copy Editor
Susan Christophersen

Production Manager
Tim Tate

Editorial Manager
Mary Beth Wakefield

Vice President and Executive Group Publisher
Richard Swadley

Vice President and Publisher
Joseph B. Wikert

Project Coordinator
Kristie Rees

Graphics and Production Specialist
Clint Lahnen
Stephanie D. Jumper
Heather Ryan

Quality Control Technician
Brian H. Walls

Book Designer
Elizabeth Brooks

Proofreading and Indexing
TECHBOOKS Production Services

Cover Design
Anthony Bunyan

To all my friends who have given me shelter,
encouragement, and spiritual sustenance
over the years.

Introduction

A great number of people come to Photoshop to fix their images and end up being married to it, doing a thesis on it or, at the very least, pulling out their hair and swearing never to go near a computer ever again. Photoshop is a tough beast to tame by using logic or clicking here, there, and everywhere in the hope of breaking it in, throwing a saddle on it, and riding into the sunset.

Sadly, there is no magic spell for mastering or taming Photoshop. If there were, there would be less need for books such as this one, *Hacking Photoshop® CS2*. No, the only sure formula that seems to work involves learning the basics and then adding to your base knowledge some of the secret handshakes known to the experts . . . and that's the *raison d'être* of this book. It's written with the sole intention of imparting insider knowledge that will help you to understand what Photoshop is capable of and help you speed up your workflow by revealing some of these "secret handshakes."

Whom This Book Is For

This book is for people who have a working knowledge of Photoshop and wish to expand it exponentially. It delves into the nooks and crannies of the interface, the tools, commands, filters, and their employment. It covers the different ways that a task can be performed in Photoshop and invites you to make connections and to discover your own techniques for solving problems. Although squarely aimed at Photoshop CS2 users, people using older versions of Photoshop can make use of the majority of the hacks and tips contained in the book.

How This Book Is Organized

The book has 18 chapters full of "hacks"—tips, tricks, mods, and customizations designed to help you get the most out of Photoshop.

- **Chapter 1, "Optimizing Performance"**—This chapter deals with managing your resources and squeezing the maximum performance out of Photoshop.

- **Chapter 2, "Hacking the Work Area"**—This chapter is all about customizing your entire work area and saving the changes for future use.

- **Chapter 3, "The Fine Art of Using Palettes"**—This chapter provides insights into Photoshop's palettes, some of the secrets that they hold and ways for you to enhance your productivity.

- **Chapter 4, "Browsing with Bridge"**—This chapter helps put Bridge's viewing modes and file-sifting capabilities to work for you.

- **Chapter 5, "Hacking Preferences and Documents"**—The hacks in this chapter show you how to handle Preferences and how to increase your productivity and streamline your workflow when working with documents.

- **Chapter 6, "Working with Layers"**—To work effectively in Photoshop, it pays to learn as much about layers as you can. This chapter has the insights into creating, managing, and editing layers that will help.

- **Chapter 7, "Creating and Applying Layer Styles"**—This chapter discusses how you can make the most of layer styles to create, save, apply and organize styles.

- **Chapter 8, "Hacking Layer Masks"**—Layer masks are incredibly useful devices for hiding underlying content without affecting the values of the pixels that make up the content, and this chapter helps you wield that power.

- **Chapter 9, "Hacking Selection Masks"**—With the techniques, hints, and tips included in this chapter, you should be well armed for creating selection masks for almost any image-editing assignment.

- **Chapter 10, "Drawing and Painting"**—This chapter helps you to use the drawing tools and related commands productively and ingeniously to draw and to paint.

- **Chapter 11, "Editing, Transforming, and Retouching Images"**—This chapter is about taking full advantage of the simple, everyday tasks (editing, transforming, and retouching images) that form the backbone of most Photoshop work.

- **Chapter 12, "Adjusting and Correcting Colors"**—Adjusting and correcting colors in Photoshop is an art form, and this chapter gives you some of the ins and outs that can help you master this fine art.

- **Chapter 13, "Creating and Editing Type"**—Type attributes can now be changed in Photoshop to such an extent that you very rarely have a need to use a page layout program for every job that requires superimposed type. This chapter helps you take control over that power.

- **Chapter 14, "Hacking Camera Raw"**—For something classed as a plug-in, Camera Raw is a very deep application, and this chapter enables you to dig into its depths.

- **Chapter 15, "Automating Tasks"**—Using actions to automate tasks is one key way to optimize your use of Photoshop. This chapter shows you how.

- **Chapter 16, "Outputting to Print"**—Outputting to print can be a tricky business. All the hard work you put into color correcting, adjusting, and editing could turn into frustration if your project doesn't print out as expected. This chapter gives some precautions that you can take to defend yourself and your creations as you get ready to print.

- **Chapter 17, "Outputting to the Web"**—This chapter helps you grapple with some of the limitations of outputting images to the Web.

- **Chapter 18, "Exploiting Filters and Photoshop Flexibility"**—Compared to other image editors on the market, Photoshop does not include too many auto commands or walkthrough wizards. However, it makes up for it by giving the user the flexibility to perform almost any task in numerous ways. The hacks discussed in this final chapter give an indication of what is possible with this flexibility.

- **Appendix, "Troubleshooting"**—This appendix includes some general and specific troubleshooting advice to apply when dealing with Photoshop.

Conventions Used In This Book

Throughout the book, you'll find four icons calling some text to your attention.

CAUTION Gives you valuable information that can help you avoid trouble. Read all of these carefully.

CROSS-REFERENCE These are pointers to other areas in the book or on the Internet where you can find more information on the subject at hand.

NOTE Notes contain information pertaining to items of interest related to the subject at hand.

TIP This icon recommends best-practice methods, techniques, or tools.

Companion Web Site

Finally, you can check out this book's companion Web site at www.wiley.com/go/ extremetech. Point your browser there and you'll find links to Web sites that offer some cool and useful things for the Photoshop user—tutorials, scripts, keyboard shortcuts, color management, plug-ins, and so forth—as well as other great ExtremeTech titles.

Contents at a Glance

Contents

· ·

Contents

Contents

Chapter 13: Creating and Editing Type 311

Contents

chapter **1**

Optimizing Performance

T he hourglass in Windows and the watch and spinning beach ball in Mac OS are icons that most people would prefer not to see when working in Photoshop. Although eliminating them is not always possible, you can go some way toward doing that. You can do this by managing your resources wisely. To that end, it's worth spending a few minutes fine-tuning Photoshop to squeeze the maximum performance out of it.

Reducing Startup Time

What better place to start fine-tuning than by reducing the time it takes to launch Photoshop? The following sections show you several ways to launch Photoshop more quickly.

Disabling Plug-ins

Each time you launch Photoshop, it loads plug-ins and presets into memory. The problem is that you may or may not need many of the plug-ins during the course of a session, but they eat into the memory allocation regardless. So, how do you alleviate this problem? Well, if you find there are some plug-ins that you use rarely, if ever, during your Photoshop sessions, you can disable them temporarily and enable them on the rare occasions when you do need them. The tradeoff in faster loading and more free memory may be worth the odd occasion when you may need to quit Photoshop, enable the plug-in, and relaunch Photoshop.

To disable a plug-in, navigate to the Plug-Ins folder inside the Photoshop install folder and then insert a ~ (tilde) in front of the plug-in name, folder, or directory. For example, a good candidate to start with is the Digimarc plug-in, used to read and write watermarks. If your workflow never makes use of watermarking, loading it into memory each time you launch Photoshop is pointless.

You can also install or move the infrequently used plug-ins out of the plug-ins folder and into a new folder (it cannot be a subfolder because Photoshop will still see it and load into memory any plug-ins that it finds). Plug-ins are easier to move around on Mac OS than they are on the PC (though some do require an install or simply their serial number to be entered after they are launched).

If you do move the infrequently used plug-ins into this secondary folder, you can load them all in one go, as you need them; doing so, however, still requires a relaunch of Photoshop, unfortunately. To load a plug-in, hold down Ctrl+Shift (Windows), ⌘+Shift (Mac OS) *immediately* after you launch Photoshop and then specify the additional plug-ins folder when asked.

CROSS-REFERENCE Photoshop can also follow any shortcuts (Windows) or aliases (Mac OS) that it finds in the plug-ins folder. To take advantage of this little trait, see Chapter 5.

While you're in the Plug-Ins folder, you can safely disable some of the files in the File Formats folder that have been gathering dust because you have rarely, if ever, used them since you installed Photoshop. Some of the prime candidates to consider are as follows:

- **FilmStrip**—Animation file format used by Adobe Premiere and After Effects
- **PCX**—PC Paintbrush file developed by Zsoft
- **PhotoCD**—A file format developed by Kodak for storing images on a CD
- **Pixar**—A file format designed specifically for exchanging files with PIXAR image computers
- **Targa**—Used widely by high-end paint programs and ray tracing packages

Managing Fonts

If you are a font lover, you may have too many fonts enabled at any one time. That can add considerably to the launch time while Photoshop scans the fonts folders. Chances are, you use a font management utility to activate fonts as you need them, but if you don't, they can hog precious resources. Look at the splash screen in Figure 1-1 to see how long Photoshop is taking to scan for available fonts; if it's taking an inordinate amount of time, that's a good indicator that you need to manage your fonts. There are several font management utilities on the market: Suitcase for Window and Mac OS and FontAgent for Mac OS are very popular. If you cannot afford a good font management utility, look into disabling at least some of the infrequently used fonts in the system's fonts folder by using the font management utility that comes with your operating system.

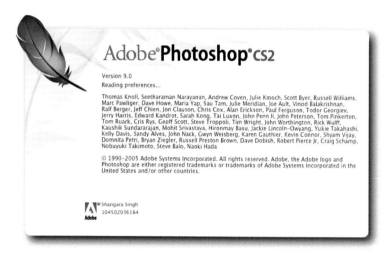

FIGURE 1-1: Watch the splash screen for signs of items' taking too long to load.

Managing Presets

When you launch Photoshop, in addition to fonts it loads brushes, swatches, gradients, styles, patterns, contours, custom shapes, and tool presets into memory. If you have gone to town and loaded all the weird and wonderful sets you can find—and there are plenty of freebies out there to tempt you—don't have them sitting in the background eating resources just in case you may need them one fine day. Be strong willed and use the Preset Manager (Figure 1-2) to ferret out the infrequently used items in the preset libraries and then either delete them one by one, en masse by selecting multiple items, or by choosing Reset from the palette menu (see Chapter 2). You can access the Preset Manager from the Edit menu.

TIP Make sure you save the set with another name when you delete items and do not overwrite the original set. That way, you can always revert to the original by using the Load button.

Managing Profiles

Many devices install ICC color profiles that you will never use, or will use rarely. Over time, they can add up and not only affect launch time but also eat into your precious resources. The thing to do is to move them so that the OS cannot see them and, by association, neither can Photoshop.

If you are not sure where color profiles reside on your system, you can easily find the folders by doing a Search (Windows) or a Find (Mac OS) for .icm and .icc. When you find the folder(s), move the infrequently used color profiles into a backup folder. Do not create the backup folder inside the folder in which you found the files. If you do, the system will still see them, and, by association, so will Photoshop.

3

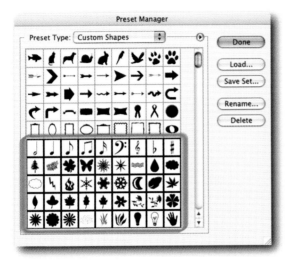

Figure 1-2: You can select multiple items in the Preset Manager by Shift-clicking, or add and subtract from a selection by holding down Ctrl (Windows), ⌘ (Mac OS), and then clicking an item.

Setting Preferences

Photoshop ships with factory settings, known more popularly as Preferences, sometimes shortened to Prefs, that you have the option of accepting or rejecting and, in their place, specifying your own.

Naturally, the settings in Preferences affect your resources. To ration your resources, especially if they are on the meager side, you can tell Photoshop how you would like it to display and save files, how many history states you would like to keep, and other preferences. Most of the settings you want to affect can be found in one dialog box (Figure 1-3).

Windows users can access the Preferences dialog box from Edit ➜ Preferences (Ctrl+K), whereas Macintosh users can access it from Photoshop ➜ Preferences (⌘+K).

TIP   The options that you elect in the Preferences dialog are saved each time you exit Photoshop and loaded when you launch Photoshop. Sometimes the file that they are saved in can become corrupted. If that happens, hold down Ctrl+Alt+Shift (Windows), ⌘+Opt+Shift (Mac OS) a split second after you launch Photoshop and elect to delete the Preferences when prompted. You will have to reset the options by entering the Preferences dialog box, but that can be a small price to pay for curing Photoshop's erratic behavior.

FIGURE 1-3: **The Preferences dialog box can be accessed using the keyboard shortcut Ctrl+K (Windows), ⌘+K (Mac OS).**

Cache Settings for Image Cache Levels

When you view an image in the document window at anything less than 100% magnification, Photoshop can use downsampled, low-resolution cached versions of the 100% view for speedier redraws. This can be helpful if you constantly work on large images and you need to zoom out frequently. However, it will take longer to open files while Photoshop creates the low-resolution previews.

You can specify the number of cache levels in the Preferences ➔ Image & Memory Cache screen (Figure 1-4). Needless to say, the higher the number of cache levels, the more resources Photoshop needs to consume. If you have limited RAM, or scratch disk space, you may wish to set the level to 1 or 2; the default is 4 levels. You can go as high as 8 levels, which will give you cached views at 66.67, 50, 33.33, 25, 16.67, 12.5, 8.33, and 6.25%. Setting the cache level to 1 is the same as turning it off because only the current view is cached at that setting.

NOTE Although the cached views can help with speedier redraws, you'll do well to remember that any reading that you take based on a cached view will be misleading; for example, when you sample a color or use a cached view to judge the effect of a filter, such as USM, it will not be based on actual pixels. For critical readings, always view the image at 100% magnification (View ➔ Actual Pixels).

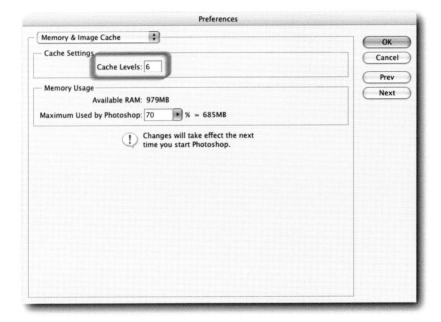

FIGURE 1-4: **Specifying high cache levels can help with redraws but also consumes more resources; Level 2 is a good compromise.**

Pixel Doubling for Faster Screen Redraws

When you use tools or commands to move pixel data, you can force Photoshop to create faster redraws if you have the option Pixel Doubling selected in Preferences ➜ Display & Cursors (Figure 1-5). The feature works by doubling the size of the pixels temporarily (effectively halving the resolution) and, after the tool or command has been applied, restoring them to how they were before the tool or command was applied.

This is not so useful on small files or when plenty of RAM is still available to Photoshop, but when you're working on large files and Photoshop is making use of the scratch disk, you may wish to select the option. Selecting this option has no effect on the actual pixels in the image; it affects only the preview.

Reducing Overheads by Reducing Histories

The Histories feature has become one of the most widely used and "can't-do-withouts" in Photoshop. Its major downside is that it's another resource hog, and it's by no means a small-time operator but one that steals and hordes resources big time; imagine a congregation of Friar Tucks descending after Lent on a pantry stocked with finite provisions and you should get the picture!

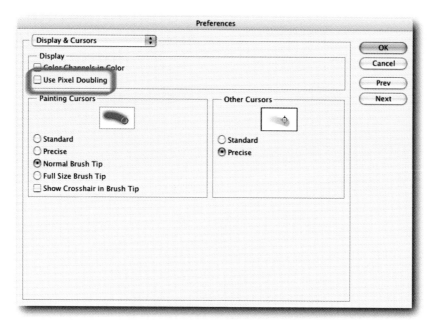

FIGURE 1-5: **To help speed up screen redraws, you can select "Pixel Doubling" in the Display & Cursors section of the Preferences dialog.**

You can change several options to conserve and stretch your provisions. The first one is the number of History states that Photoshop saves in RAM or on your scratch disk. The higher the number, the more resources are eaten up. However, the higher the number, the more undos available to you should you need to step back to a previous state. You need to strike a good balance between a fallback position and the ability to cruise faster.

By default, Photoshop saves 20 history states. You can change this number at any time in the Preferences ➔ General screen, under History States (Figure 1-6). If you find that you rarely, if ever, go back beyond, say, 5 to 10 history states, then reducing the number will allow the saved resources to be used elsewhere. If you find yourself constantly trying to find states that have disappeared from the History palette, then increase the default number and just put up with slower performance, which may not be noticeable on small files or if you have large reserves of RAM and fast, independent scratch disks.

FIGURE 1-6: You can control the number of history states that Photoshop saves in RAM, or in the scratch disk temporary file, from the General section of the Preferences dialog.

Reducing Palette Thumbnail Size

Leaving the Preferences dialog for the time being, the palettes also have options that can affect performance. For example, the Layers, Channels, and Paths palettes all store thumbnails by default, and these thumbnails are continually updated as you work on the image. However, to draw and update the thumbnails, Photoshop uses resources that may be gainfully employed elsewhere. If your resources are painfully low, you may like to select None or the smallest thumbnail size. To customize the palette previews, select Palette Options from the palette's menu and then choose an option that suits your needs (Figure 1-7).

Do You Really Need That Snapshot?

Apart from the maximum number of saved histories, which you can specify in the Preferences dialog, you can set other history options that affect performance by selecting History Options from the History palette menu (Figure 1-8).

The first two options in the History Options dialog box, "Automatically Create First Snapshot" and "Automatically Create New Snapshot When Saving," are the ones that consume extra resources.

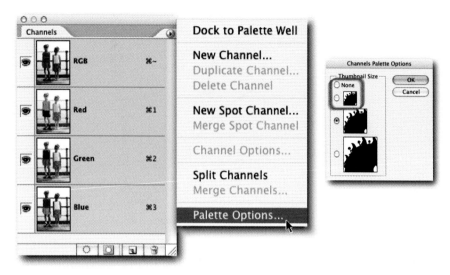

FIGURE 1-7: Palette previews can consume resources. Select "None" or the smallest thumbnail size to conserve resources.

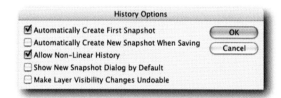

FIGURE 1-8: Histories, though indispensable, can consume resources. You can set the number of saved histories in Preferences and set snapshot preferences in History Options.

Of the two, the first option is actually quite handy, even if it does consume extra resources. It can get you out of a tight spot if you accidentally flattened a multilayered file or pressed Ctrl+S (Windows), ⌘+S (Mac OS)—easily done—when you meant to press another keyboard shortcut and don't discover your mistake until well into the editing session, by which time the earlier history states have been overwritten, including the open, first state. When you click the snapshot, the document will revert back to the state it was in when it was first viewed in Photoshop, which may not be the same as the version on disk if you changed its color profile in any way when the document was opened.

The second option (Automatically Create New Snapshot When Saving) is one that you can probably live without, but again, you'll just have to decide whether to take advantage of it. Just remember that it will consume extra resources if enabled.

NOTE Snapshots are not saved with a document, nor are they kept in memory. After the document is closed, snapshots are purged from memory, along with the document's history states.

The RAM Connection

A Photoshop legend goes, "If you need to test your RAM, use Photoshop." It will root out any inherent problems, as a good farmer roots out weeds. Photoshop will put your RAM under stress, thus revealing any flaws, as few applications will do—or so the legend goes. The legend has spread because it's probably rooted in equal amounts of truth and folklore.

You may ask, where's the connection between this legend and Photoshop performance? Well, if any of your RAM chips have gone south, as it were, Photoshop performance will degrade, and corrupted data may follow in its wake. Photoshop relies very heavily on two things for good performance: masses of RAM and a fast scratch disk (which basically is hard disk space used to temporarily page data out of RAM). A dual processor can make a difference, but not all processes in Photoshop can take advantage of dual processors.

Therefore, you come back to RAM, and the more RAM you can allocate to Photoshop, the more it will use in order to process your images faster, relying less on the scratch disk, which can slow it down (as is discussed later in this chapter). However, Photoshop currently can make use of only 4GB of RAM. Because of the limitation, the less you can waste in allocating to functions that you may not use, the more will be available for tools and commands before Photoshop starts to page data to the scratch disk.

There is good reason for Photoshop's being probably one of the most RAM-hungry programs. Continuous tone images are made of pixels (picture elements). An average image can contain millions of pixels. When you open a file or manipulate it in any way, Photoshop has to keep track of and update the information required to describe each pixel's color, luminosity, and location, among other things.

What's more, because of the method used for storing information about each pixel, as soon as you duplicate the pixels in order to work on an image, the resources required to keep track of the extra data have to be similarly multiplied. Furthermore, now that Photoshop supports most operations on 16-Bits/Channel files, the resources needed to simply open a file in 16-bit mode need to be doubled. Then there are the files in Large Document Format (PSB), 32-bit files in High Dynamic Range (HDR) files, and on and on. So, anything you can do to speed the workflow will help you accomplish your tasks in Photoshop that much quicker.

Assigning RAM for Optimal Performance

If the processor in your computer is the brain, the RAM can be likened to its heart. All the software on your computer, from the operating system to applications to widgets, relies heavily on it for their speed and efficiency. As mentioned previously, Photoshop can guzzle RAM as a Mercedes G500 5L guzzles gasoline. So, you need to give it as much RAM as you can possibly afford. The key word here is *afford* because the operating system also needs a plentiful supply of RAM; therefore, it's a bad idea to starve it while indulging Photoshop.

Photoshop gets its share of RAM from the figure allocated to it in Preferences. When it has used up that allocation, it pages out the data to the hard disk (allocated to it as the scratch disk in Preferences), and the end result is it runs more slowly. Knowing that, you may be tempted to max out the RAM allocation to 100% in order to make it run faster. Not a good idea! If anything, allocating too much memory to Photoshop may slow down the performance by forcing the operating system and Photoshop to swap pages in and out of memory. So, what amount of available RAM should you allocate? Well, as with all things in nature, that depends.

Photoshop can use a maximum of only 4GB of RAM. This limitation is imposed by hardware and the operating systems, among other things that only geeks and engineers with degrees in astrophysics understand fully. Suffice it to say, if you have 4GB of RAM installed, or more, you can safely increase the RAM allocation to 70%. Doing so will ensure that Photoshop uses as much RAM as it possibly can, up to the 3.7GB limit (or thereabouts, because the OS will reserve some of the 4GB for itself). If you do not have more than 4GB of RAM installed, you should reduce the allocation to something like 50–60%, especially if you are experiencing slow performance in Photoshop, which includes Camera Raw. To allocate RAM, go to Preferences ➜ Memory & Image Cache and specify a percentage in the Memory Usage section of the dialog box (Figure 1-9).

NOTE You will need to restart Photoshop before the revised allocation can have an effect.

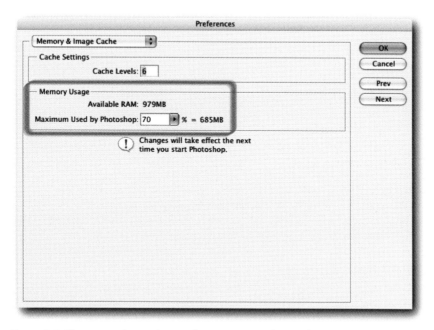

FIGURE 1-9: If you experience slow performance, try reducing the RAM allocation to 50–60% in the Memory Usage section of the Memory & Image Cache section of the Preferences dialog box.

Assigning Scratch Disks

Photoshop uses a temporary file for storing data and performing computations when there is insufficient RAM. It places this temporary file, commonly referred to as a *scratch disk*, on your hard disk, or it can spread it across several hard disks. When you exit Photoshop, this temporary file is deleted, and a fresh one is created the next time you launch Photoshop.

By default, Photoshop uses your primary, startup hard drive as the scratch disk. This is something to be avoided because it can hinder performance if your OS also uses it to for its virtual memory needs. Because Mac OS uses the primary hard drive to place its paging file, you are almost guaranteed conflict on a Mac. To overcome this potential conflict of interests, you can tell Photoshop which hard disk to place its scratch disk on, provided, of course, that you have more than one hard disk installed in your computer. If you have just the one disk but it's partitioned, selecting a different partition to the one containing the OS virtual memory files won't speed up performance. In fact, performing some operations may even take longer because the read/write heads will have to travel farther.

Although Windows users have a choice of easily assigning different hard disks for the paging file, thus avoiding conflict between the Photoshop scratch disk and the system's paging file, Mac OS users will find it a lot harder to assign a different hard drive for its virtual memory (in fact, you have to be an advanced user of Terminal to do it!) and may find it easier to assign a different hard drive for Photoshop to use as a scratch disk.

You can assign scratch disk(s) from the Preferences ➡ Plug-Ins & Scratch Disks screen (Figure 1-10). It's possible to assign up to four hard disks, or partitions, and Photoshop will see them as one large storage space for the temporary file. Photoshop supports up to 64EBs (an exabyte is equal to 1 billion gigabytes) of scratch disk space—more than sufficient for most needs!

Regardless of the number of hard disks you assign, make sure the minimum size is three to five times the RAM allocated to Photoshop. Furthermore, it should be a fast hard drive and, if that hard disk is partitioned, the first partition should be assigned. Do not assign removable media, such as a Zip drive, or a network drive as a scratch disk. If you assign dedicated partitions that do not store any other files, defragging should not be required.

Needless to say, the more space you can spare, the lower the likelihood that you will encounter the dreaded "Scratch disk is full" error at the crucial moment.

Single Scratch Disks vs. RAID

If you work on large files and have maxed out on the amount of RAM you can allocate to Photoshop, you can increase Photoshop performance by investing in a RAID 0 array (Redundant Array of Individual Disks) and assigning it as a scratch disk. Because all the disks in an array can read and write simultaneously, the striped data can be accessed much more quickly than it would be from a single large disk.

There are several types of RAID arrays on the market. The configuration in a RAID 0 level array, sometimes called a striped array, allows two or more disks to be combined into one larger volume and the activity shared over all the disks for improved performance. However, it's not a true RAID, because it does not offer redundancy; in other words, the failure of just one drive in the array will result in all data's being lost. Although such a shortcoming may defeat the whole purpose for creating a true RAID array, the raw speed gained by sacrificing fault tolerance to backup data makes it ideally suited for storing temporary, swap files.

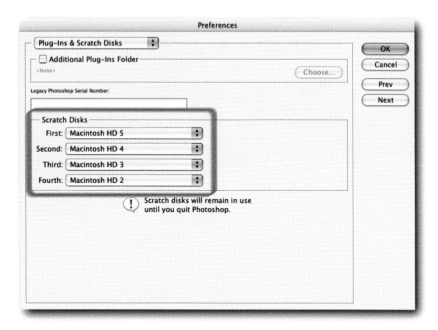

FIGURE 1-10: **Photoshop stores its temporary file on a scratch disk. You can specify in the Plug-Ins & Scratch Disks section of the Preferences dialog box which hard drive, and how many, to use as a scratch disk or disks.**

A RAID array can be composed of two or more Serial ATA drives, SCSI drives, or FireWire 800 drives. Although a software RAID array made of two serial, fast ATA drives will be much faster than a single drive, for speed, a fast SCSI disk array will be hard to beat; however, it will also cost much more. The third possibility, a multichannel FireWire 800 array, devised by adding extra controllers, can even exceed a SCSI disk array for speed and is now a viable alternative.

16-Bits/Channel vs. 8-Bits/Channel

A debate is raging on the benefits of using 16-Bits/Channel files, also known as high-bit, as opposed to the more traditional 8-Bits/Channel files. Basically, and speaking in nutshells, a 16-BPC image can contain 65,536 levels, whereas an 8-BPC image can contain only 256 levels. (In fact, Photoshop shows only 32,768 levels for images in 16-BPC, which is closer to 15-BPC; it also sees any file above 8-BPC as 16-BPC.) Therefore, it seems natural to assume that because 16-BPC images contain more bits, they must contain more information and be superior in every way to images in 8-BPC mode.

Based on the "more bits = more information" theory, the advocates of 16-BPC maintain that you can achieve superior results if you work in high-bit mode. However, the advocates of a 8-BPC workflow maintain that although for a very limited number of images that may be true, for the majority of the images the extra overheads in file size, RAM, larger and faster scratch disks, slower workflow, and so forth do not justify the end results, which are very hard to discern when images are output to print.

Both camps agree that there is more flexibility during image editing in 16-BPC because of fewer quantization errors and, therefore, less banding and overall image degradation, though some of this banding may not actually translate to print. Quantization errors are attributed to the rounding off of numbers when fractions are recalculated to the nearest binary number; only binary numbers, not fractions, can represent digital values. But to benefit from editing in 16-BPC, you must start with a file in 16-BPC mode.

You may have noticed that Photoshop gives you the option of changing from 8-BPC mode *to* 16-BPC mode. If you fall for this option, don't be fooled into thinking you will somehow increase the detail. Changing modes upward can be likened to changing a file in a small color space to a larger color space, or a family of four moving from a small apartment to a large mansion. Though they may find that they have more space to move around, they ostensibly remain the same width and height and have maintained the same number of members. In other words, you will have more space between the colors but not necessarily more colors (more space between the family members but no additional offspring). If anything, you will increase the chance of degradation by having to make larger adjustment moves and introducing quantization errors.

There is a middle way being adapted by digital photographers who work in Raw mode:

1. Process the raw file in Camera Raw and then open it in Photoshop in 16-BPC mode.

2. Do any major tonal and color corrections.

3. Save the file as a master file.

4. Duplicate the document.

5. Convert it down to 8-BPC.

6. Do any major edits that require hefty resources, such as multiple adjustment layers, duplicate blending layers, layer styles, multiple type layers, and so on.

7. Optimize the 8-BPC version for output.

NOTE Printers, overall, can handle only 8-BPC files. If you send a 16-BPC file to a printer, it will be converted on the fly to 8-BPC before output.

While this debate is raging, you may wish to do your own tests, which are easy to perform:

1. Duplicate a 16-BPC file.

2. Convert the copy to 8-BPC (Image ➜ Mode ➜ 8-Bits/Channel).

3. Perform the same edits on the original and the copy (use adjustment layers and drag them into the other file).

4. Send the files to your desktop printer, or convert the 16-BPC to 8-BPC and then send both to a four-color offset printer and a photographic printer for good measure, such as a Fuji Frontier or a LightJet.

If you find no discernible difference between the prints, or the difference is insignificant, you will be in the best position to decide whether to work in 16-BPC or only in 8-BPC mode from the get-go and enjoy cruising through your workload.

Saving Files

When you save your files, you have another prime opportunity to save time and optimize Photoshop performance. The following sections discuss how, where, and when you can save time and space as you save your files.

Saving Files in 16-Bits/Channel Mode

Not only can working on files in 16-Bits/Channel mode slow down many of the processes, such as applying filters, using the Extract command, rotating content, and so forth (as was discussed previously in the chapter) but also saving files can take considerably longer. If you have finished correcting the image and optimizing it for output, there's no benefit in keeping it in 16-Bits/Channel mode, other than keeping the option open for editing it again at some future date. Convert it to 8-Bits/Channel mode before saving it or sending it to your printer if speed and space are a higher priority for you.

Saving Files in CMYK Mode

After you have optimized and purposed a CMYK document, you can remove the embedded profile, which can reduce file size and help speed the saving process. This can amount to a considerable saving of disk space and time if you are purposing hundreds of files. To remove a profile, choose Image ➜ Mode ➜ Assign Profile. In the Assign Profile dialog box (Figure 1-11), select Don't Color Manage This Document.

TIP If a special recipe was used to do the conversion to CMYK, it's usually a good idea to keep notes of the settings used in case you need to match conversions or you are asked to edit the file.

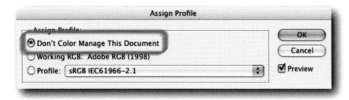

FIGURE 1-11: **You can remove a profile from a document by choosing Image ➜ Mode ➜ Assign Profile and then "Don't Color Manage This Document."**

Reducing Layers and Channels

The number of layers and alpha channels in your file can also impact on the size of the file and consequently the time it takes to save it. You can minimize the file size and the time it takes to save the file by deleting any empty layers, merging others that do not benefit from being standalone layers, and deleting alpha channels that you no longer require.

Maximizing File Compatibility

When you save a file in the native Photoshop file format (PSD), you can include a flattened, composite version, as well as all the layers, layer sets, adjustment layers, blend modes, and styles that go to make up your file. The flattened version can then be used by older versions of Photoshop and applications that do not support all the Photoshop features used to create the file. However, the downside is that it can take considerably longer to save the file and can increase the file size unacceptably, especially if you are working on very large files.

If you feel your workflow is unlikely to benefit from a file that also includes a flattened version, you can elect never to include a flattened version, or to do so always, or sometimes (Figure 1-12). To tell Photoshop how you would like to save PSD files, open the Preferences dialog, choose File Handling from the pop-up menu at the top of the dialog box, and then select an option for Maximize PSD File Compatibility.

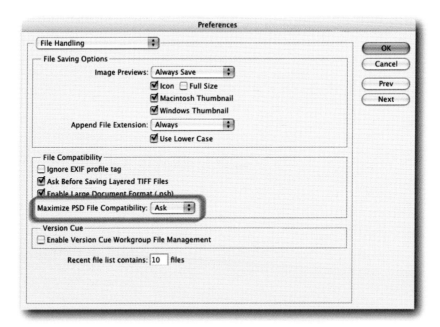

FIGURE 1-12: You can save time and disk space by electing not to save a flattened version with your PSD file automatically or to do it on a case-by-case basis.

16

CAUTION   It has to be said that Adobe has been putting out couched warnings about the blend modes "possibly" changing in a future version of Photoshop and hinting (almost insisting with Photoshop 7.0) that you should include a flattened version. The company says that the composite version may be the only true representation you will see when you open your file. If you choose never to include a flattened version when you save in the PSD format, you may like to factor that veiled warning into your decision-making process. However, many people are ignoring it, especially people who work on very large files, because Photoshop can take a considerable time to generate a composite when the file is saved to disk.

Faster Access When Switching Applications

When you switch from Photoshop to another application, if there is data on the clipboard, Photoshop can "export" it to the system clipboard for pasting into the other application. However, because Photoshop files can be extremely large, it can cause a delay while it "exports" the data on the clipboard. What happens, in fact, is that the data is converted to WMF or PICT format, depending on the OS, and that's what can cause the delay.

If you find yourself waiting more often than you actually use the data on the clipboard, you can tell Photoshop not to export the data on the clipboard, thus ensuring speedier handovers. To turn off the option for exporting clipboard data—the option is turned on by default—go to Preferences ➜ General and deselect the checkbox for "Export Clipboard." Regardless of whether this option is selected, it has no effect on Photoshop's performance while you are working inside Photoshop; only when you have a large amount of data on the clipboard, have forgotten to purge it (Edit ➜ Purge ➜ Clipboard), and then try to exit Photoshop will you notice the difference (Figure 1-13).

You can always select the Export Clipboard option again on the rare occasions when you actually need to use the data on the clipboard in the other application. If you want to cover all bases, you can leave the option selected in Preferences and, before you make the switch to another application, purge the data from the clipboard—but chances are you will forget in your excitement. To purge data on the clipboard, go to Edit ➜ Purge and select Clipboard from the submenu.

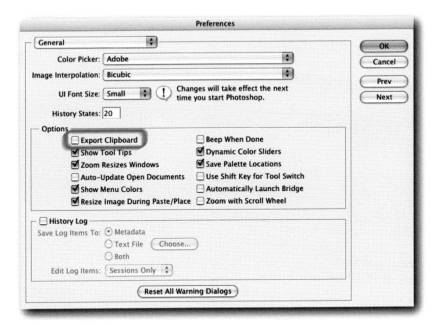

FIGURE 1-13: **To ensure speedier switches between applications, make sure "Export Clipboard" is not selected.**

Summary

That about wraps it up as far as optimizing your system performance is concerned. Applying the suggestions in this chapter should help to cut down the time you spend waiting for Photoshop to do something. Of course, it goes without saying that how well you look after your OS by doing general housekeeping required by a Unix-based OS will have a direct effect on Photoshop's performance. Furthermore, it's always a good policy to check the condition of your hard drives by using the various utilities. Some of these utilities are bundled with your OS, whereas others can be purchased or downloaded for free from the Internet. Two good places to begin your search are www.versiontracker.com and www.tucows.com.

chapter 2

Hacking the Work Area

Photoshop comes with an abundance of commands, tools, and palettes. At first sight, even second, third, and umpteenth sight, it can be quite daunting trying to find the right menu item, tool, or palette in order to carry out a simple task. Even when you do find the right command, you can find it grayed out or find commands that weren't there the last time you looked at a menu! If you want to master the behemoth that is Photoshop, you must memorize where each menu item is, where you can find the tools, and what each palette contains. Some of that happens naturally as you work in Photoshop on a regular basis. However, you can speed up the process if you don't look at the interface on a need-to-know basis but rather with an open mind, which is capable of holding unimaginable amounts of information if you just open the doors and let the information glide in and make itself at home.

So, assuming that you know approximately where each command and tool can be found and what each palette contains, you might ask, "What need is there for a chapter devoted to the interface?" The short answer is this: What you see when you look at the interface is only the tip of the iceberg. The commands, tools, and palettes are capable of hiding many secrets, just as the sea hides the major part of a floating iceberg. This chapter is all about looking under Photoshop's surface to see how the mass of information that lies there can be used to handle documents, to customize your entire work area, and to save the changes for future use.

Dealing with Documents

You may have occasionally wondered what the term *document* has to do with a file or an image being edited in Photoshop. Generally speaking, a file is something that exists on a hard drive or on removable media. When a file is opened in Photoshop, it transforms itself into a document. So, where does the term *image* come into the equation? *Image* refers to the content in the document. Unfortunately, the terms *file*, *document*, and *image* are often used interchangeably, leading to confusion when exchanging information. It's something to be aware of when you deal with the outside world. Anyway, now that you are fully armed in the usage of correct terminology, here are a few short, sharp hacks on how to handle *documents*.

Accessing Opened Documents in ImageReady

If you have a document open in Photoshop and you wish to open it in ImageReady to use its features, you don't need to close it and then open it in ImageReady. Instead, you can access it easily from the ImageReady Window menu. Any changes you make to the document in ImageReady are reflected in Photoshop when the document is accessed again from Photoshop's Window menu, unless, of course, the changes are not supported by Photoshop, such as applying Image Maps or Rollovers.

TIP If you wish to save features that are unsupported by Photoshop, save the file in ImageReady.

Bringing a Document to the Forefront

When you have several open documents and want to work on a particular one, selecting it can soon become a chore if you go about it haphazardly by, for example, moving them out of the way one by one or minimizing the ones at the front of the stack. It's even more tiresome if they are new documents and you have not named them (resolutions to save new documents before beginning work on them tend to take a backseat before that third cup of coffee of the morning). Here are no fewer than three ways to bring a document to the forefront:

- If you know the title, select it from the Window menu.
- If you don't know the title, choose Window ➜ Arrange ➜ Tile Horizontally or Vertically and then select it from the tiled view.
- Hold down the Ctrl key and then Tab until the document you are after comes to the forefront.

The last method is probably the best of the bunch.

Closing All Open Documents

If you have many documents open and wish to close them in one go, press Ctrl+Alt+W (Windows), ⌘+Opt+W (Mac OS). If any of the documents need saving, Photoshop will prompt you.

The only way to bypass the prompt is by using a script. Trevor Morris has such a script, called "Close ALL Without Saving," that you can download from `http://user.fundy.net/ morris/redirect.html?photoshop28.shtml`. To use it from the File → Scripts submenu, move it to the Adobe Photoshop CS2 → Presets → Scripts folder (you will need to restart Photoshop before you can see it) or use the Browse command in the Scripts submenu.

Finding the Location of the Currently Open Document

This hack is really for Macintosh users, but Windows users needn't feel left out (see the upcoming Note). To find the location of the currently open document on your hard drive, ⌘-click the *title* and then view the pop-up menu (Figure 2-1).

FIGURE 2-1: **Navigating to a source folder from the title bar (Mac OS).**

To navigate to the folder in which the document is located, just select the folder below the document title, and a Finder window will open to show you the contents of the selected folder. Of course, for this method to work, the document must be saved (just in case you try it on an unsaved document and decide that you need to reinstall Photoshop!).

NOTE Windows users can see the location only if they hover the mouse pointer over the document title; also, they can't navigate to it automatically. However, if you right-click the title, you can access a pop-up menu containing the following document-related items: Duplicate, Image Size, Canvas Size, File Info, and Page Setup.

Opening and Saving with a Mouse Click (Windows)

Here are some neat, combined mouse and keyboard shortcuts for creating, opening, and saving documents that do away with the need for the File menu—okay, *almost* do away with it.

- **New**—Ctrl+double-click in the program window.
- **Open**—Double-click in the program window.
- **Open As**—Alt+double-click in the program window.
- **Save As**—Alt+Shift+double-click in the program window.
- **Save a Copy**—Ctrl+Shift+double-click in the program window.

Changing the Canvas Border Color

The workspace surrounding the visible image area is commonly referred to as the canvas. This canvas area is filled with a gray color by default (equal amounts of RGB 192), which is a good, neutral choice suitable for optimizing images. However, you are not restricted to this color. You can change it to a custom color if you wish. Changing the color can help to make a decision about the contrast in the image or to simulate the environment in which the image may be eventually presented (Figure 2-2).

To change the canvas area color, take the following steps:

1. Make sure that an area around your image is visible by enlarging the document window or reducing the magnification percentage.
2. Click the Foreground color box in the Toolbox to access the Color Picker.
3. Select a color and close the Color Picker by clicking the OK button.
4. Select the Paint Bucket tool (it's hidden behind the Gradient tool).
5. Hold down the Shift key and click in the canvas area.

Unfortunately, there is no preference to set the color back to the default gray. If you want to revert to it, you will have to choose equal amounts of RGB 192 and repeat the preceding steps.

TIP If you change canvas area color frequently, create a custom swatch from equal amounts of RGB 192 and then you can easily select the default color before applying it (see Chapter 3).

FIGURE 2-2: You can change the canvas area color to a custom color of choice by Shift-clicking with the Paint Bucket tool in the areas surrounding the image.

Customizing the Checkerboard Background

When you open a document that contains transparency, or when you create a document and select the Transparent option for Background Content in the New document dialog box, Photoshop has to show something where there is transparency in the document. By default, it shows a checkerboard as a background.

So, just how do you customize the checkerboard display if you do not like the default display? It's not too difficult when you know where to look. As always, a good place to start looking is in the Preferences dialog box. You can call the dialog box from either the Edit menu (Windows) or the Photoshop menu (Mac OS), or you can use the keyboard shortcut Ctrl+K (Windows), ⌘+K (Mac OS).

23

There are a couple of ways of changing the colors for the checkerboard. Either you can select a preset color from the Grid Colors pop-up menu, or you can click the color boxes and define a custom color. You can do this for either one of the squares that make up the grid by clicking the appropriate swatch (Figure 2-3).

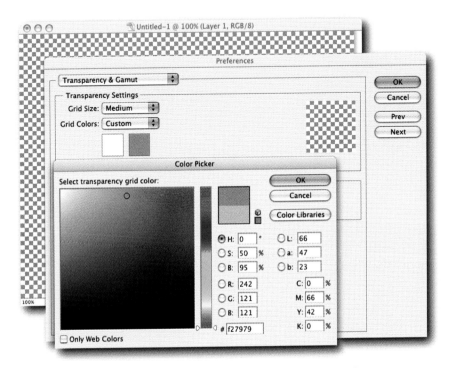

FIGURE 2-3: The Transparency & Gamut screen of the Preferences dialog box. Here you can change the checkerboard display to a custom color; you can also hide the checkerboard altogether by selecting None from the Grid Size pop-up menu.

Customizing the checkerboard is neat, but at times you do not want to see a checkerboard at all; granted, those times may be rare, but they do come around occasionally. So, just how do you turn off the checkerboard display? In the Transparency & Gamut screen of the Preferences dialog box, select None from the Grid Size pop-up menu in the Transparency Settings section of the dialog box. Take note that when this option is selected, transparent areas display as white.

Lording Over the Rulers

Among the arsenal of image editing aids in Photoshop at your disposal, rulers are perhaps the unsung heroes. They can help you to align content down to a pixel, help create guides, and help control the unit of measure globally—all without so much as a peep. If the rulers aren't visible, you can view them by choosing View ➔ Rulers or pressing Ctrl+R (Windows), ⌘+R (Mac OS); the keyboard shortcut is a toggle.

24

Resetting the Zero Origin

By default, the ruler's zero origin is set to 0*x*, 0*y* coordinates (top-left corner of the visible image for us simple folks). However, when you absolutely must set it elsewhere in the document, it's a quick and painless operation. Just click in the box where the two rulers intersect and drag diagonally into the image (Figure 2-4). As you drag, you will see a crosshair temporarily superimposed over the image to help you set the new ruler zero origin. Position the pointer where you would like to set the new ruler zero origin; then let go. That's all there is to it! You can, if you wish, set the new zero origin anywhere in the canvas area and not just the visible image area.

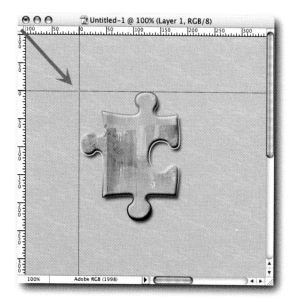

FIGURE 2-4: Dragging inward from the ruler box intersection sets the new ruler zero origin.

The rulers do not move from their locked position when you drag from the ruler intersection box, but if you look at the zero markers on the rulers, you will see that they have been set to the new position. In the example shown in Figure 2-4, the new ruler zero origin is being set to 100 px horizontal (*x*) and 100 px vertical (*y*) from the top-left corner of the image.

To reset the zero origin to the default top left-hand corner, double-click the box intersection.

NOTE The zero origin affects the grid's *x, y* coordinates and, therefore, also the *x, y* readings in the Info palette.

TIP To make it easier to set the new ruler zero origin, you can snap it to Document Bounds, Grids, Guides, Layers, or Slices (these options can be set in the View ➜ Snap To submenu).

Specifying Ruler Units in the Document Window

When working on an image, sometimes you need to change the ruler units from their current setting to something more appropriate to help you create or line up an element. Fortunately, you don't need to make a trip to the Preferences dialog box each time you want to make a change. You can do it from much closer: right inside the document window, in fact. Just right-click (Windows), Ctrl-click (Mac OS) the rulers and, from the contextual menu, choose an item (Figure 2-5). Save your energy for something more strenuous—such as making that third cup of coffee of the morning!

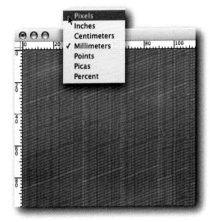

FIGURE 2-5: Specifying ruler units from the contextual menu.

Just for the sake of completeness, you can also change the ruler units by double-clicking the rulers to call up the Preferences dialog box; or, in the Info palette, you can click the cross icon in the mouse coordinates section and select an item from the pop-up menu (Figure 2-6).

FIGURE 2-6: Selecting ruler units from the Info palette.

Using Guides and Grids

Guides and grids are nonprinting visual aids that can help you place or move image content more precisely. They can also help you create selections and paths by providing visual markers for the start or end of a selection or path segment.

Creating

You have two ways of creating guides in Photoshop:

- You can have the rulers showing (View ➜ Rulers) and drag with the mouse pointer into the document window from the horizontal or vertical ruler (to make the guide snap to an increment on the ruler, hold down the Shift key).

- Alternatively, you can choose View ➜ Create Guide and, in the New Guide dialog box, specify whether you would like to create a horizontal or a vertical guide; also specify where you would like to place it. You can enter a value in another unit of measure by adding an abbreviated form of the unit after the number; for example, rather than 2 cm, just type **2 in** for inches. Furthermore, if you prefer to work in percentages, you can use a percentage sign (Figure 2-7).

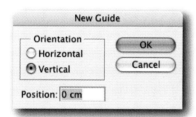

FIGURE 2-7: **To position a new guide, you can enter values in any of the supported units.**

In ImageReady, the Create Guides dialog box (View ➜ Create Guides) gives you many more options for creating guides (Figure 2-8).

TIP You can't create diagonal guides in Photoshop or ImageReady. The workaround is to create a path with the Pen tool and show/hide it by choosing View ➜ Show ➜ Target Path, or clicking in an empty area of the Paths palette to hide it and clicking the path tile to show it. Alternatively, use the keyboard shortcut assigned to it; the default is Ctrl+Shift+H (Windows), ⌘+Shift+H (Mac OS).

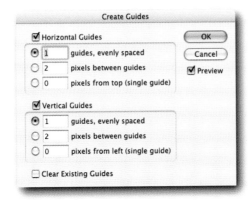

FIGURE 2-8: **The Create Guides dialog box in ImageReady gives you more options than the one in Photoshop.**

Moving

After a guide has been created, you can move it around as much as you like (even onto the canvas, the area outside the visible image). To move a guide, hold down Ctrl (Windows), ⌘ (Mac OS), hover the pointer over the guide, and when it turns into a double-headed arrow, drag the guide. Note that if you have the slice tools selected, this shortcut won't work. You need to select the Move tool, or one of the other tools, first.

Clearing

You can clear guides by selecting View → Clear Guides or simply by grabbing them and dragging them out of the document window (see the preceding section on how to move a guide). If you accidentally move or delete a guide, you can choose Edit → Step Backward or press Ctrl+Z (Windows), ⌘+Z (Mac OS). In ImageReady, choose Edit → Undo Delete Guide.

Hiding

Because guides and grids are considered extras, you can hide them temporarily and show them again when required. To show/hide guides or grids, use the View → Show submenu. To hide guides using a keyboard shortcut, press Ctrl+; (Windows), ⌘+; (Mac OS). The keyboard shortcut works as a toggle; so, to show them again, just press the same combination one more time. To show/hide a grid with a keyboard shortcut, just substitute the apostrophe for the semicolon; like so: Ctrl+' (Windows), ⌘+' (Mac OS).

Locking

When you are moving data around the document window with the Move tool, it's easy to accidentally move a guide. Fear not! You can lock guides by choosing View ➜ Lock Guides or by pressing Ctrl+Alt+; (Windows), ⌘+Opt+; (Mac OS). In fact, if you find that you cannot move a guide, chances are you pressed that key combo accidentally in the editing session.

Customizing

If you don't like the default color of the guides and grids (it may clash with image content or your jumper), you can select a preferred color in the Guides, Grid & Slices screen of the Preferences dialog box. There's the usual route to get to Preferences, but a quicker one, if you have guides showing, is to simply double-click one and be taken directly to the Guides, Grid & Slices screen. When in the screen, you can change the color and the style for both your guides and grid. For your grid, you can also specify the space between each gridline and the number of subdivisions (Figure 2-9).

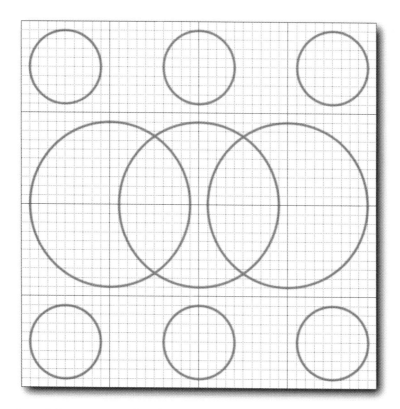

FIGURE 2-9: A custom grid used to snap circular paths to the gridlines and then the paths stroked with a soft brush.

Smart Guides

When you have to align objects on different layers, or even on the same layer, Smart Guides can help to find the edges and the centers of the visible objects (Figure 2-10). Smart guides work equally well on pixel-based objects, selections, shapes, paths, and slices. If you cannot see Smart Guides when you move objects, make sure that View → Show → Smart Guides is selected.

FIGURE 2-10: Smart Guides highlighting the center and sides of objects being moved.

Showing/Hiding Extras by Using Keyboard Shortcuts

Photoshop includes various aids to help you modify your documents. They are all listed under View → Extras for convenience, though it may be argued that Selection Edges and Target Paths are much more than just Extras. Hair splitting apart, you can customize the Extras command by selecting View → Show → Show Extras Options and then choosing which of the Extras you would like to show/hide when you press the default keyboard shortcut Ctrl+H (Windows), ⌘+H (Mac OS).

If you are a long-time user of Photoshop and are used to Ctrl+H (Windows), ⌘+H (Mac OS) for hiding only the selection edges, try assigning the following keys (see Table 2-1) in Edit → Keyboard Shortcuts → View → Extras. This way, you can hide all the Extras individually or collectively and keep your preferred shortcut for hiding only selection edges.

Table 2-1: Suggested Keyboard Shortcuts for Extras

Extras	Windows	Mac OS
Extras	Ctrl+Alt+Shift+H	⌘+Opt+Shift+H
Selection Edges	Ctrl+H	⌘+H
Target Path	Ctrl+Shift+H	⌘+Shift+H
Annotations	Ctrl+Shift+A	⌘+Shift+A
Layer Edges	Ctrl+Shift+,	⌘+Shift+,
Grid	Ctrl+'	⌘+'
Guides	Ctrl+;	⌘+;
Smart Guides	Ctrl+Shift+.	⌘+Shift+.
Slices	Ctrl+Shift+'	⌘+Shift+'

NOTE If an extra is not included in View ➜ Show ➜ Show Extras Options, the shortcut assigned to Extras cannot hide it (Figure 2-11).

FIGURE 2-11: The Show Extras Options dialog box (not available in ImageReady).

Viewing

Although a beginner and an experienced user of Photoshop do not have a lot in common, they do share one thing: They each need to view the document in order to work on it. However, there the shared experience ends because, whereas a beginner may be content to view only the image and drag the document window around occasionally, an experienced user makes use of the available document information and the many ways that the image itself may be viewed. The following sections lay bare the knowledge an experienced user utilizes on a daily basis.

Viewing Actual Pixels, Not Interpolated

Each time you zoom in or out, Photoshop shows an interpolated display. For most editing decisions, it's not a problem and, indeed, it may be the only way that you can make some editing decisions. For example, the image dimensions may be too big to display the image in its entirety on your monitor, or the image detail may be too small to place a tool precisely. So, how do you stop Photoshop from interpolating the display? The short answer is, you can't. That being said, when Photoshop displays an image at 100% magnification, the display is not based on interpolation, and you can take advantage of that setting by always returning to it. Photoshop gives you several ways of doing that, as usual:

- Choose View ➜ Actual Pixels.
- Double-click the Zoom tool in the Toolbox.
- Select either the Hand or the Zoom tool and click the Actual Pixels button on the options bar.
- Enter 100% in the status bar text field, located at the bottom of the document window.
- Press Ctrl+Alt+0 (Windows), ⌘+Alt+0 (Mac OS).

If viewing at a higher than 100% magnification, use even increments, such as 200%, 400%, 800%, or 1600%. That way, Photoshop will display one image pixel accurately over 4 "monitor" pixels, 16 monitor pixels, 64 monitor pixels, or 256 monitor pixels, respectively.

TIP The current document magnification is always displayed in the document's title bar as well as the status bar.

Alpha/Spot Channel Info

After you have created an alpha channel, you can view its options at any time by double-clicking its tile in the Channels palette (Figure 2-12), and likewise for any spot channels (Figure 2-13). Note: The Solidity value specified in the Spot Channel Options dialog box affects only the preview in Photoshop and not the separations. However, if the image is output to a composite printer, then it will have an effect, and the spot color will print at the opacity level specified in the Solidity text box.

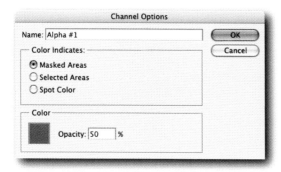

FIGURE 2-12: The Channel Options dialog box.

FIGURE 2-13: The Spot Channel Options dialog box.

Document Information

A wealth of document information is available for the taking if you know where to find it, and not only document information but also other, related information, such as the current tool being used and how efficiently Photoshop is carrying out an allotted task. So where do you find this buried treasure? Fortunately, no complicated treasure maps are required. The information is yours for the taking by clicking the triangle in the status bar and then choosing an item from the Show submenu (Figure 2-14). Here's a quick rundown of the menu items:

- **Current Tool**—Indicates the name of the currently active tool.

- **Document Dimensions**—Indicates the dimensions, displayed in the currently selected ruler units.

- **Document Profile**—Indicates the name of the profile describing the document's current color space—probably the most useful information to display on a regular basis.

- **Document Sizes**—The figure on the left indicates the current size of the file on disk. The figure on the right indicates the estimated size based on the current state of the document, including layers, alpha channels, and so forth, and saved in PSD format.

- **Efficiency**—Indicates whether Photoshop is running at its optimum efficiency or having to page data to the scratch disk. If the figure is less than 100%, Photoshop is paging information in and out of RAM.

- **Scratch Sizes**—The figure on the left indicates how much of the scratch disk is being used, whereas the figure on the right indicates how much RAM has been assigned to Photoshop. In Windows, if the figure on the left is greater, it means Photoshop is making extensive use of the scratch disk and therefore is not running at 100% efficiency.

- **Timing**—Indicates the time taken to execute the last command.

- **Version Cue**—When you have Photoshop CS installed as part of the Creative Suite and you select Enable Version Cue Workgroup File Management from Preferences ➜ File Handling, this option shows the status of the current document within the group.

- **32-bit Exposure**—When you work on 32-bit images, selecting this option gives you control over the exposure.

NOTE The Info palette can also now show the same information plus hints on how to use the current tool.

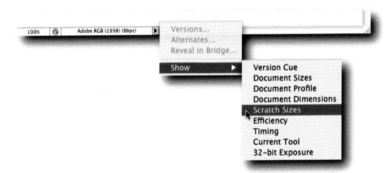

FIGURE 2-14: **The menu items available from the status bar in the document window.**

Wait, there's more—you can access some of the information available in the Image Size dialog box without going through all the steps required to first of all open it and then, having viewed the info, to close it.

- To display document information (Figure 2-15), hold down Alt (Windows), Opt (Mac OS) and click the status bar.

- To display document tile information (Figure 2-16), hold down Ctrl (Windows), ⌘ (Mac OS) and click the status bar.

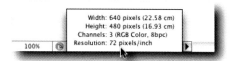

FIGURE 2-15: Document information displayed by holding down Alt (Windows), Opt (Mac OS) and clicking the status bar.

FIGURE 2-16: Document tile information displayed by holding down Ctrl (Windows), ⌘ (Mac OS) and clicking the status bar.

TIP To reset the Efficiency or the Timing values, hold down Alt (Windows), Opt (Mac OS) and then select Efficiency or Timing.

Using an Action to View Full Screen Mode

There is no command or keyboard shortcut for opening a document in full screen mode. However, you can create an action that gives you access to the Open dialog box, lets you select a filename, and then displays the document in full screen mode (see Chapter 15 for more on actions). Unfortunately, creating a successful action is not always as straightforward as it appears. Here are the steps you need to take:

1. Select an existing set in the Actions palette or create a new one by clicking the Create New Set icon.

2. Start recording a new action by clicking the Create New Action icon.

3. Name it and assign a function key (optional).

4. Choose Insert Menu Item from the palette menu.

5. Choose File ➔ Open.

6. Choose Insert Menu Item from the palette menu.

7. Choose View ➔ Screen Mode ➔ Full Screen Mode, or Full Screen Mode With Menu Bar.

8. Stop recording.

9. Save the action set by selecting it and then choosing Save Actions from the palette menu.

When you run the action, the file should open in the screen mode you selected in Step 7. If it doesn't, review the steps in the action or delete it and start again.

Using Keyboard Shortcuts to View Full Screen

You can quickly view opened documents in full screen modes by pressing the F key and then either adding the Shift key or using the Tab key to hide/show palettes, Toolbox, and menus. Table 2-2 contains a quick rundown of the available permutations.

Table 2-2: Keyboard Shortcuts for Full Screen Mode

Key Press	Result
F	Full screen with gray background, Toolbox, palettes, options bar, and menu.
F again	Full screen with black background, Toolbox, and options bar.
Shift+F	Show/Hide menu.
Tab	Hide/Show palettes, Toolbox, and options bar.
Shift+Tab	Hide/Show palettes.

Using the Zoom Tool

There are two ways to use the Zoom Tool. One, by clicking in the document window and, two, by clicking and then dragging to form a marquee around the image content that you would like to fill the window with. Clicking magnifies or diminishes the view by preset percentage amounts; it also centers the clicked image area in the window.

Clicking with the Zoom tool always magnifies unless you hold down Alt (Windows), Opt (Mac OS) at the same time, or select the Zoom Out icon on the options bar. By contrast, creating a marquee gives you more freedom to define the content that you would like to magnify or diminish.

By default, the document window does not change size when you zoom in and out. However, should you want to, you can make it do so by selecting Resize Windows To Fit from the options bar. If you use keyboard shortcuts to zoom in and out, the default behavior is the opposite: The window resizes to fit. If you prefer that the window did not resize, you can deselect Zoom Resizes Window in the General screen of the Preferences dialog box. To force the window to resize, add Alt (Windows), Opt (Mac OS) to the shortcut. So, holding down Ctrl+Alt+Plus (Windows), ⌘+Opt+Plus (Mac OS) zooms in and resizes the window to fit, whereas Ctrl+Alt+Minus (Windows), ⌘+Opt+Minus (Mac OS) zooms out and resizes the window to fit.

Using the Hand Tool

When the image magnification is too high for the document window to display in its entirety, you can use the Hand tool to scroll the image, which is much neater than using the scroll bars. You can switch to the Hand tool by either pressing H or by holding down the Spacebar. The latter is much preferred because it lets you return to the currently active tool after you let go of the Spacebar. The one downside is you cannot use this method while in Type mode.

TIP To quickly fit the document window between the Toolbox and palettes, double-click the Hand tool icon in the Toolbox, or press Ctrl+0 (Windows), ⌘+0 (Mac OS). If you do not want the image to be hidden behind the Toolbox and the palettes when you double-click the icon, make sure that the options Resize Windows to Fit and Ignore Palettes are not selected for the Zoom tool.

Working on the Edges of a Document

If you like to work in full screen mode and find working on the edge of a document difficult, and you find yourself leaving full screen mode, zooming in to the edge, working on it, and then returning to full screen mode, you may be relieved to learn of a little frustration-busting feature.

You remember how you can scroll in the document window with the Hand tool when the image is displayed at a high enough magnification to overspill the document window bounds? Well, the same method works in full screen mode. Just select the Hand tool (press H, or press the Spacebar and hold it down), drag the edge that you want to work on into the workable area of the screen and, after you have finished working on the edge, press Ctrl+0 (Windows), ⌘+0 (Mac OS) to center the image.

Multiple Views

When retouching or color correcting an image, you may like to make use of a feature that can help you become more proficient in executing your job. The feature populates multiple views of the active document. You can use the populated window(s) to zoom and scroll freely, without affecting the display of the parent window. Furthermore, you can use View ➜ Proof Setup to view the duplicate window in another color space. For instance, you can preview how your image will print on your desktop printer while you adjust it in your working space. To do so, simply select the profile for the printer from Proof Setup in the duplicate window—much neater than turning View ➜ Proof Colors on and off while you make the adjustments. In the same vein, if you are retouching, instead of zooming in and out you can zoom in once in the duplicate window while you retouch in the parent window. To access the feature, choose Window ➜ Arrange ➜ New Window.

Scrolling and Zooming Multiple Views

After you have created a duplicate window(s), you can synchronize both the zooming and the scrolling between the parent and the populated windows. You can do this in two ways: one, by selecting the appropriate options for the Zoom and Hand tools and, two, by using a keyboard shortcut.

To use tool options, select the tool and then, for the Hand tool, select Scroll All Windows and, for the Zoom tool, Zoom All Windows. If you prefer not to set the tool options permanently, you can modify their behavior temporarily by holding down the Shift key as you drag with the Hand tool or click with the Zoom tool. Note: When you click with the Zoom tool, the display always centers on the clicked area.

You are not confined to using the tools to scroll and zoom. You can use the usual keyboard shortcuts assigned to them but, to synchronize the windows, add the Shift key. For instance:

- To scroll, use Spacebar+Shift.
- To zoom in, use Ctrl+Spacebar+Shift (Windows), ⌘+Spacebar+Shift (Mac OS).
- To zoom out, substitute Alt for Control (Windows), Opt for Command (Mac OS).

Tiling Multiple Windows

If you have gone to town and have lots of documents open but now want to home in on one, you can use the tiling feature by choosing Window → Arrange → Tile Horizontally/Vertically. If need be, you can use the methods described previously for scrolling and zooming multiple views in synch.

Colorizing and Hiding Menu Items for Easier Scanning

Photoshop and ImageReady contain a huge number of menu items. Although possibly you can remember where frequently used items are located, you can now highlight them to make them stand out for easier scanning. For instance, if you find yourself always scanning the Filter → Blur submenu for Gaussian Blur (there are no fewer than 11 blur filters to choose from in this submenu), just highlight it to make it stand out from the infrequently used filters (Figure 2-17). To highlight menu items:

1. Choose Edit → Menus or press Ctrl+Alt+Shift+M (Windows), ⌘+Opt+Shift+M (Mac OS).

2. In the Keyboard Shortcuts and Menus dialog box, unfurl the menu that you wish to modify.

3. Click the item below the Color heading that you wish to colorize.

4. From the pop-up menu, select a preset color.

5. Save the modified set of menus by clicking the floppy disk icon.

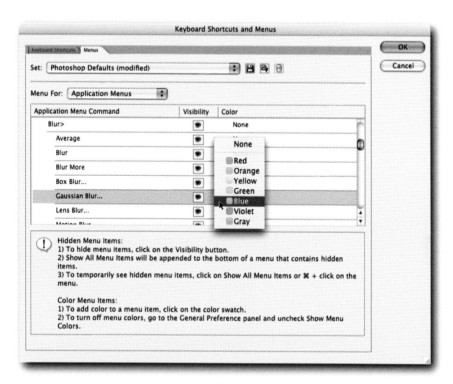

FIGURE 2-17: **In the Keyboard Shortcuts and Menus dialog box, you can colorize a menu item for applications or palette menus.**

You can modify the current set and save the changes or you can create a new set based on it and then save that with a new name. The two icons next to the Set pop-up dialog box let you save changes to the current set and create a new set based on the current set, respectively. One thing you cannot do is modify the default set and then save the changes. If you try to, you will be prompted to save the set as a copy.

At any time, you can turn off menu colors by selecting the default set in the Edit → Keyboard Shortcuts and Menus dialog box, or you can deselect Edit → Preferences → General → Show Menu Colors.

NOTE You are not restricted to colorizing and hiding application menu items alone; you can also customize palette menus. To do so, select Palette Menus from the Menu For pop-up menu and then follow the preceding Steps 2 to 5.

TIP Photoshop ships with predefined sets of colored menus. If you have just upgraded, you may find the What's New – CS2 set particularly helpful. Depending on your workflow, you may also find the other sets useful.

Hiding Menu Items

Over the years, as new features have been added or imported from ImageReady, the number of commands has grown to an overwhelming extent. Because not everyone makes use of all the features, you can now truncate the menus by hiding items that you do not use, or use infrequently enough to warrant hiding them and showing them on a need-to basis.

If you followed the preceding modus operandi for colorizing menu items, you will have noticed the eye icons under the Visibility heading. Simply click one to hide the item. Back in the application or palette menu, the menu in question will be appended with a Show All Menu Items command. If you select it, the hidden items will be shown temporarily. When you reenter the menu, the items will be hidden again.

Managing the Palettes

Including the Toolbox and options bar, Photoshop has no fewer than 19 palettes to help you edit your images. Managing them in a limited screen real estate can be challenging, to put it mildly. Ideally, you have a two-monitor setup, with the image you are trying to edit on the main screen and the palettes on the second screen. However, if your budget or desk space won't allow that, here are some hacks to help you claim back some of the real estate.

Regrouping and Docking

To regroup palettes, decide which one will be the foremost palette in the group and drag it by the tab out of the present group. Next, grab a palette by the tab that you would like to group, hover it over the previous one, and drop it when the outline turns black (Figure 2-18). Apart from grouping the palettes this way, you can also group them vertically. To do so, drag the palette by the *grabber bar*, position it below another palette, and let it snap to it.

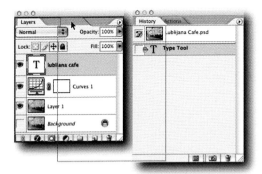

FIGURE 2-18: Drag and drop palette tabs to create new custom groups.

Here are some suggested groupings (Figure 2-19). The most often used palettes are arranged at the forefront of the groups, and the remainder of the palettes are docked in the well to conserve screen real estate. Having grouped the palettes, when you come to align them next to the edge of the screen, hold down the Shift key to make the groups snap against the edge.

FIGURE 2-19: One suggestion for collapsed palette groups.

TIP You can arrange your favorite palettes at the bottom of the screen in collapsed groups (to collapse, double-click the grabber bar) and then double-click their tabs to expand them as required.

Reordering in the Palette Well

When you dock the palettes in the well by either dragging them by their tabs and dropping them into the well or by selecting Dock to Palette Well from the palette menu, the palettes always assume a position at the end of the well. If you do not like the assumed position, you can move it left or right by right-clicking (Windows), Ctrl-clicking (Mac OS) the tab and then choosing an item from the contextual menu (Figure 2-20).

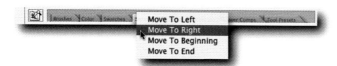

FIGURE 2-20: Reordering palettes in the well.

Hiding/Showing Quickly

When you work in full screen mode, the palettes can obscure the image. If you have only the odd palette open, it's not that big a deal to close and to open it again, but if, as most people do, you have grouped and lined your palettes, there are quicker ways of hiding/showing all the palettes, and doing so in combination with and without the Toolbox.

- To hide/show all the palettes, including the Toolbox but not the options bar, press the Tab key.

- To show the options bar after hiding all the palettes, press Enter (Windows), Return (Mac OS).

- To hide/show all the palettes, excluding the Toolbox and options bar, press Shift+ Tab.

Organizing Content in the Preset Palettes

As you work in Photoshop and use its various tools and commands, you are presented with the opportunity of creating your very own new brushes, contours, custom shapes, gradients, patterns, preset tools, styles, and swatches. Furthermore, you can add to your collection by loading *sets*, also called *libraries*, created by other kind, generous folk. You can find some of these sets by taking a look at the links to related Web sites offered on the companion Web site for this book at www.wiley.com/go/extremetech.

Photoshop keeps track of any new additions to the palettes, lets you save them to disk for safekeeping, and loads them into memory when you launch it. However, the palettes that keep track of the preset items do not let you rearrange the items. Wouldn't it be nice if you could organize a palette's content just the way you prefer to see it? Enter the Preset Manager. Its only *raison d'être* is to let you organize all the libraries in one convenient place.

To open the Preset Manager, choose Edit → Preset Manager. When the dialog box opens, select a library from the Preset Type pop-up menu at the top of the dialog box (Figure 2-21) that you would like to reorganize.

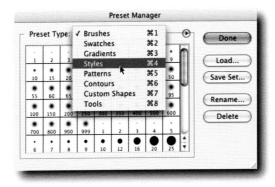

FIGURE 2-21: **You can organize eight sets of libraries in the Preset Manager.**

You can elect to view a library as text only, list, or thumbnails from the Preset Manager palette menu (click the triangle button to access the palette pop-up menu). Whichever viewing method you use, you may find the following hacks handy in helping you with your housekeeping:

- **Selecting**—You can select thumbnails in the usual manner by Ctrl-clicking to add/subtract from a selection (Windows), ⌘-clicking (Mac OS). Shift-clicking selects multiple contiguous items.

- **Moving and Deleting**—After you've selected them, you can move thumbnails around or delete them. To move, simply select and then drag and drop. To delete single thumbnails, hold down Alt (Windows), Opt (Mac OS) and click the thumbnail when the cursor icon turns to a scissors. To delete multiple items, select and then click the Delete button. The contextual menu may also be used to delete items.

- **Creating New Libraries**—You can also create new libraries by selecting items and then saving them with the Save Set button. Make sure that you save them in the default Color Swatches folder located inside the Photoshop program folder if you want Photoshop to see the set and to give you the option of loading it from the palette menu.

NOTE You must quit and launch Photoshop again before the new set appears as an item in the palette pop-up menu.

- **Renaming Libraries**—To rename any of the preset items, double-click the thumbnail, or its name if you're viewing in text or list mode, and enter the new name in the Brush Rename pop-up dialog box. Alternatively, select the item, click the Rename button, and then rename it in the Brush Rename dialog box. If you want to rename multiple items, select them and then click the Rename button; Photoshop will cycle through them all one by one. The contextual menu may also be used to rename items.

- **Storing/Loading Presets**—Photoshop stores the presets in the ~\Adobe Photoshop CS2\Presets folders. You can rename sets or drop custom sets or files into the appropriate folder that you may have downloaded from the Internet. When you relaunch Photoshop, you will be able to select the renamed or added sets from the corresponding palette menu. For example, drop an .atn file into the Photoshop Actions folder, relaunch Photoshop, and then load the action set from the Actions palette menu.

Changing the Location of the Options Bar

When Photoshop is installed, the options bar is placed at the top of the screen. Overall, it's the most logical place for it. However, suppose that you want to place it at the bottom of the screen or, if working on a large monitor, even temporarily in the middle of the screen? Not a problem! You can move the options bar at any time by simply clicking the grabber bar and dragging it to a new position (Figure 2-22).

FIGURE 2-22: **Click the grabber bar and drag to reposition the options bar.**

What you cannot do is dock the options bar to the left or right of the screen, as you can do with the Taskbar (Windows), Dock (Mac OS). On the plus side, you can collapse it and expand it by double-clicking the grabber bar.

Entering Values in Text Fields

Text fields are almost everywhere you look in Photoshop and ImageReady. Indeed, working without them would be impossible. Almost all dialog boxes, palettes, and tool options support one or several for inputting values. Probably because of their numbers and importance, both Photoshop and ImageReady provide a couple of nifty little features for increasing and decreasing the values.

Increasing and Decreasing Values by Using Keys

It's fairly obvious that one can enter a new value in the text fields (Figure 2-23), but what's not so obvious is the fact that you can click in most text fields and then use the Up and Down Arrow keys to change the values. Pressing the Shift key while using the Up or Down Arrow keys will increase the values by a factor of ten.

FIGURE 2-23: Values in text fields can be increased or decreased by clicking in them and then using the arrow keys by the numeric keypad.

Increasing and Decreasing Values by Scrubbing

If you see a text field for entering a value, it's very likely that you can change the value by scrubbing (not all text fields can be scrubbed). First, click in the text field. Next, click to the left of the text field and then drag the mouse pointer to the right to increase or to the left to decrease the values (Figure 2-24). Pressing the Shift key while you drag the mouse pointer will increase the values by a factor of ten.

FIGURE 2-24: Scrubbing feature used to increase or decrease values in the text fields.

TIP To access the scrubbing feature in order to change the display magnification percentage in the text box of the status bar, press Ctrl (Windows), ⌘ (Mac OS).

Working with the Color Picker

The Color Picker is commonly used to define foreground, background, or text color. In Photoshop, the Color Picker is also used to define the color for a fill layer, a shape layer, and some layer styles. Furthermore, it's used to define the target colors for some of the color and tonal adjustments, such as the black, gray, and white points in the Curves and Levels dialog boxes and the targets in the Auto Color Correction Options dialog box. Its usage doesn't just stop there! It's also used to define the stop points that make up a gradient and to specify a color in the Fill, Stroke, and Canvas Size dialog boxes and the color in the Photo Filter dialog box. Overall, this little feature can cover an awful lot of miles over just a short period.

Selecting a Color Picker

Because the Color Picker is used so extensively throughout Photoshop, you may want to select another type rather than the default Adobe Color Picker. As usual, Adobe gives you a number of choices. You can choose from the Adobe Color Picker, the version employed by the operating system, or even a third-party plug-in. To define the default color picker, open the Preferences dialog box to the General screen and then make your choice in the Color Picker pop-up menu (Figure 2-25). However, the Adobe Color Picker is highly recommended.

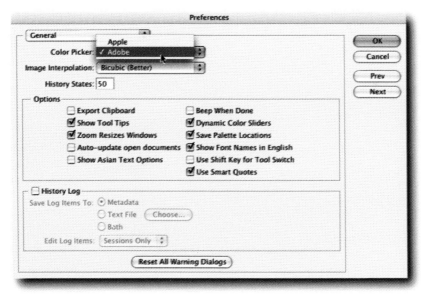

FIGURE 2-25: The General screen of the Preferences dialog box. Here you can select another available Color Picker or stay with the default Color Picker.

NOTE From this point on, assume that this text refers to the Adobe Color Picker whenever it mentions Color Picker.

Choosing a Color Picker Mode

The Color Picker works on the HSB model (Hue, Saturation, Brightness) by default. When you have the dialog box open, you can either choose a color from the color spectrum or define it numerically by entering the values in the text boxes (Figure 2-26).

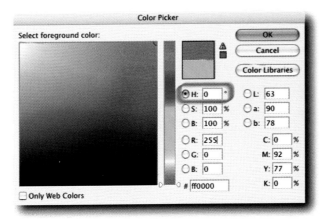

FIGURE 2-26: The Color Picker in HSB mode, showing saturated red.

However, you are not restricted to working with the default HSB model. If you prefer another model, you can alter the display to suit your workflow. For instance, you can set it so that it works on the RGB color model or the Lab color model. The radio buttons to the left of the text fields define which model and how that model affects the behavior of the slider and the color field (Figures 2-27 and 2-28).

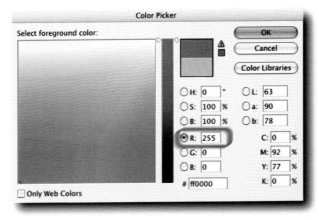

FIGURE 2-27: The Color Picker in RGB mode, showing saturated red.

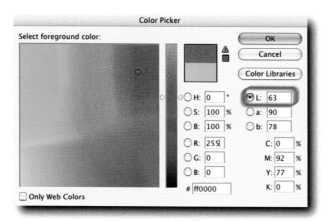

FIGURE 2-28: **The Color Picker in Lab mode, showing saturated red.**

Selecting Colors from Libraries

As well as being able to define custom colors in the Color Picker, you can also select from preset process books and swatches if you are familiar with their usage. You can choose from the following color systems:

- **ANPA-Color**—A color scheme used primarily in newspaper printing. ANPA (American Newspaper Publishers Association) in 1992 became the Newspaper Association of America (NAA).

- **DIC Color Guide**—A color scheme devised by the Japanese chemical group Dainippon Ink and Chemicals, Inc., which also produces printing inks. It's primarily used in Japan for matching process color (CMYK) to spot color.

- **Focoltone**—A color system that specifies Cyan, Magenta, Yellow, and Black components for each color tone, as opposed to a specific ink formulation, enabling the color to be reproduced systematically.

- **HSK swatches**—A color system used in Europe. You can select from the following scales: HKS E, for continuous stationery; HKS K, for gloss art paper; HKS N, for natural paper; HKS Z, for newsprint.

- **Pantone**—A system of standard colors used worldwide. It assigns a specific Pantone color name or number (or both) to identify thousands of spot and process colors, and it provides the exact ink formula to achieve consistency of color, regardless of the printer.

- **TOYO Color Finder 1050**—A system based on the most commonly used inks in Japan, designed for matching spot colors to Toyo's product line. It can also determine whether a selected color can be reproduced with process ink combinations.

- **Trumatch**—A system designed to take some of the guesswork out of 4-color selection and matching. It divides the spectrum into 50 hue families with 40 tints and shades of each hue, plus 4-color grays.

To access the Color Libraries screen (Figure 2-29), click a color box in the Toolbox or use your favorite method for calling the dialog box, and when the Color Picker dialog box appears, click the Color Libraries button.

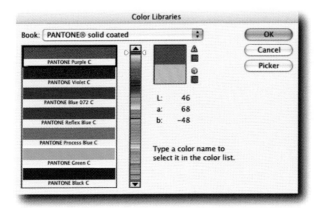

FIGURE 2-29: The Color Picker, showing the Color Libraries screen.

CAUTION The preset colors available do not guarantee a matched print. To ensure closer matching between computer display and printed output, the use of the appropriate type of color swatch (for instance, using Pantone solid colors in a CMYK file is not a good idea), an up-to-date printed color swatch, and consultation with your printer are highly recommended.

TIP If you select a color in Color Libraries and then click the OK button, the next time you access the Color Picker it will go straight to the Color Libraries screen, instead of the Color Picker dialog box. To have the Color Picker appear each time you call it, click the Picker button in the Color Libraries dialog box, select a color in the Color Picker, and click OK to exit.

Viewing a Color Gamut Warning

The range of colors that an output device can display or print is commonly referred to as the color gamut. Photoshop can automatically detect when a color you have selected is out of gamut. It bases the warning on the settings in the Color Settings dialog box or the profile selected in the View ➜ Proof Setup submenu. For example, if you have selected the U.S. Web Uncoated v2 profile for your CMYK working space, Photoshop can warn you if any color in your file is unlikely to print when the file is output to an offset printer that purports to support the color space described by the U.S. Web Uncoated v2 profile.

When you use the Color Picker to select a color, an out-of-gamut warning triangle for print colors and a warning cube for Web-safe colors appears automatically in the dialog box (see next Tip). However, this method of selecting in-gamut colors can be hit or miss. Here is another method that you can employ, and it takes the guesswork out of establishing which color is in gamut: Select the appropriate profile in the working space or in the View → Proof Setup submenu before you enter the Color Picker dialog box. Next, select View → Gamut Warning. Now when you enter the Color Picker dialog box, the colors that are out of gamut will be overlaid with the default gamut warning color (Figure 2-30).

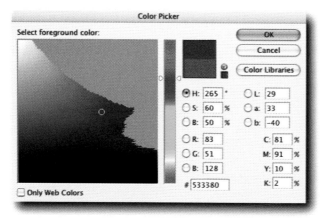

FIGURE 2-30: **The Color Picker showing the out-of-gamut colors for the selected output device.**

If you forget to select Gamut Warning or simply want to turn it off while in the Color Picker dialog box, you can still access the View menu or you can press Ctrl+Shift+Y (Windows), ⌘+Shift+Y (Mac OS) to toggle it. What you cannot do from within the dialog box is select another profile for the working space in Color Settings or in the Proof Setup menu, so make sure that you have the correct profile selected before you open the dialog box.

TIP When the selected color is out of the gamut of the CMYK working space, a small warning triangle appears next to the before and after color boxes. To automatically bring the color back into gamut, you can click the warning triangle or the color box below it. Similarly, when the selected color is out of the gamut of the Web-safe palette, a small warning cube appears. To automatically bring the color back into gamut, you can click the warning cube or the color box below it.

Working with Color Samplers

The Color Sampler tool, hidden under the Eyedropper tool, is too often overlooked when a user is making color corrections. Next time you need to match colors or remember before and after colors, take it for a drive. However, before you do, you might like to read up on some of its dark secrets.

Color samplers used on their own aren't particularly useful. They really shine when used in conjunction with the Info palette. Fortunately, when you place a color sampler, the Info palette is brought to the front automatically. What's more, you can also select it from the Window menu at any time (even if you are in a modal dialog box).

Creating, Moving, and Deleting Color Samplers

Creating color samplers is very easy. All you need to do is select the Color Sampler tool and click in the image. You can embed up to four color samplers per document. However, deleting single samplers is not so obvious and, as usual, there are several ways of going about it:

- Make sure that the Color Sampler tool is active, grab the color sampler that you want to delete, and drag it out of the document window.

- A bit more elegant method is to right-click (Windows), Ctrl-click (Mac OS) the color sampler and then select Delete from the contextual menu.

- If the Color Sampler tool is not active, press Ctrl (Windows), ⌘ (Mac OS) and then drag the sampler out of the document window.

- If the Color Sampler tool is active, you can hold down Alt (Windows), Opt (Mac OS), hover over the sampler, and click when the icon turns to a scissors. If a tool other than the Color Sampler is active, add the Shift key to the above keyboard shortcut.

To delete more than one sampler, select the Color Sampler tool and then click the Clear button on the options bar.

So, is that all there is to creating, moving, and deleting color samplers? Well, not quite. Believe it or not, you can place color samplers without the Color Sampler tool! Photoshop just seems to know when you may need them. For example, when you use some of the adjustment commands, such as Curves, Levels, Hue/Saturation, Selective Color, and Color Balance, the active tool changes to the Eyedropper, which in turn allows you to temporarily access the Color Sampler tool by pressing the Shift key. When you step out of the active dialog box and into the document window, just hold down the modifier key and click to place a color sampler (Figure 2-31).

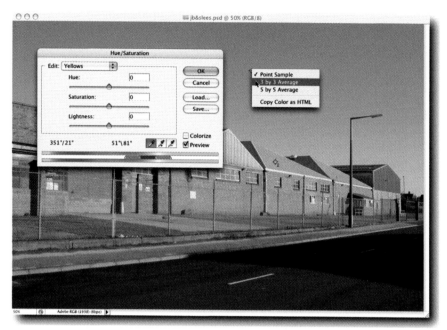

Figure 2-31: **Placing color samplers and changing sample size while working in a color adjustment dialog box.**

When you have an adjustment command's modal dialog box open, such as Curves or Levels, you can still move and delete the color samplers. To delete, press Alt+Shift (Windows), Opt+Shift (Mac OS), hover over the color sampler, and click when the icon changes to a scissors. To move a color sampler, press the Shift key by itself. One other useful shortcut is the right-click (Windows), Ctrl-click (Mac OS). You can use it on a color sampler to change the sample size between Point Sample, 3 by 3 Average, or 5 by 5 Average.

Hiding and Showing Color Samplers

You can also temporarily hide/show the color samplers from the View menu by selecting Extras. By default, Extras has the Ctrl+H (Windows), ⌘+H (Mac OS) keyboard shortcut assigned to it, and you may use that to hide/show any placed color samplers.

Specifying Color Sampler Info Display Option

You have two ways of specifying how the information gathered by a color sampler is displayed. You can either right-click (Windows), Ctrl-click (Mac OS) on the color sampler and then select an item from the contextual menu, or you can click the Eyedropper icon in the Info palette and select an item from the pop-up menu (Figure 2-32).

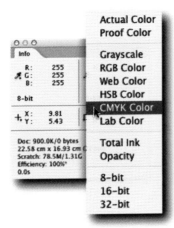

FIGURE 2-32: Specifying a color sampler display option in the Info palette.

One last cherry on the sundae: The placed color samplers are saved with your document. You can refer to them each time you open the document in Photoshop.

Changing the Quick Mask Color Overlay Options

When you create a complex selection by using the various selection tools, they are very rarely perfect or even near perfect. Panic not! There is a special mode dedicated to modifying selections (and can also be used for creating irregular selections). It's called Quick Mask mode and can be invoked by, one, clicking on the Quick Mask mode icon in the Toolbox (Figure 2-33) or, two, by pressing Q on your keyboard (the keyboard shortcut is a toggle). When you enter Quick Mask mode, a rubylith color overlay indicates masked areas and the clear areas indicate the selected areas.

NOTE If you have entered Quick Mask mode and do not see a rubylith overlay, it's because a selection was not active when you invoked the mode. Create a selection and then try again.

Masks created in Quick Mask mode must be saved from the Channels palette or by choosing Select ➔ Save Selection after exiting Quick Mask mode.

When in Quick Mask mode, you can paint with black to contract the selection or white to expand it. However, should you need to, you can reverse the default options. To do so, double-click the Quick Mask icon in the Toolbox and then choose Selected Areas in the Quick Mask Options dialog box (Figure 2-34). You can also choose a custom overlay color if the default rubylith clashes with image content. Furthermore, just for good measure, you can specify an opacity level. Figure 2-35 shows an image viewed in Quick Mask mode.

FIGURE 2-33: Left—Default icons in the Toolbox for entering Quick Mask mode; the depressed icon signifies that color overlay indicates Masked Areas. Right—The depressed icon has changed to signify that color overlay indicates Selected Areas.

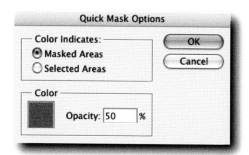

FIGURE 2-34: The Quick Mask Options dialog box, accessed by double-clicking the Quick Mask icon in the Toolbox.

TIP To reverse the options for seeing Masked Areas or Selected Areas without having to enter the Quick Mask Options dialog box, Alt-click (Windows), Opt-click (Mac OS) either one of the Quick Mask icons in the Toolbox.

FIGURE 2-35: **Image viewed in Quick Mask mode showing the color overlay for Selected Areas, instead of the default Masked Areas.**

Specifying Tool Cursors

The default cursors that accompany a tool can be very handy for identifying the tool that you are using, but from a practical point of view, they present a problem because you cannot do any precise work with them. Fortunately, you can choose between five types of cursors for the painting tools and two for the other tools, and the place to choose them is once again the Preferences dialog box.

You probably know the drill for accessing the Preferences dialog box, but here are the keyboard shortcuts for good measure: Ctrl+K (Windows), ⌘+K (Mac OS). When you have the dialog box open (Figure 2-36), select Display & Cursors from the pop-up menu at the top of the dialog box. Next, under Painting Cursors, select Normal Brush Tip or Full Size Brush Tip and then Precise under Other Cursors. Click the OK button for the changes to take effect.

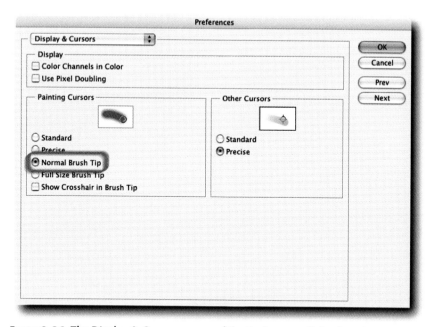

FIGURE 2-36: **The Display & Cursors screen of the Preferences dialog box. Here you can select cursors for painting and other tools.**

TIP If you select Normal Brush Tip or Full Size Brush Tip for the Painting Cursors, you can have the best of both worlds: When you use the painting tools, you can press the Caps Lock key to change the cursor temporarily to a precise cursor. Just remember to take the Caps Lock off!

NOTE When you choose Normal Brush Tip or Full Size Brush Tip for Painting Cursors and use a very large brush tip (anything over 2000 or 1212 pixels, respectively), cursors may not display a true brush size and instead revert to displaying Precise cursors.

Specifying Gamut Warning's
Overlay Color and Opacity

When you use the command Gamut Warning (View ➜ Gamut Warning), Photoshop overlays your image with a nonprinting color to indicate which colors are out of gamut (Figure 2-37), as described by the working color space or the profile selected in the Proof Setup submenu.

FIGURE 2-37: Top: Gamut warning overlaid with the default color, not so visible. Bottom: Gamut warning overlaid with a custom color chosen in the Preferences ➜ Transparency & Gamut screen, very much visible.

By default, the overlay color is slightly lighter than a mid-gray but you can change it to any color you like; a garish purple or green might be good contenders. To do so, take the following steps:

1. Open Preferences: Choose Edit → Preferences (Windows), Photoshop → Preferences (Mac OS).

2. In the dialog box, select Transparency & Gamut from the pop-up menu in the General screen.

3. In the Gamut Warning section of the dialog box, click the color box (Figure 2-38), choose a color from the Color Picker, and click OK.

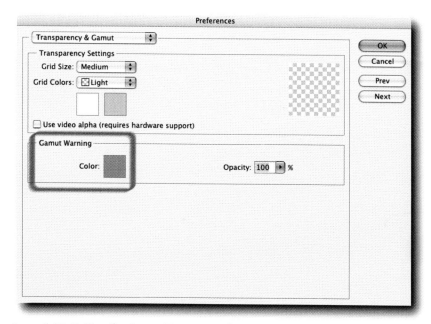

FIGURE 2-38: Setting the Gamut Warning overlay color in Preferences → Transparency & Gamut dialog box.

NOTE While in the Gamut Warning section, you can also set the opacity of the gamut warning overlay, but it's best to leave it at 100% unless you have a specific need to lower it.

Noting the Magic Wand Tool and Eyedropper Connection

One of the most disappointing tools in Photoshop has to be the Magic Wand tool. It just does not do what you expect it to: grant your wishes! Most people get over that when they learn it's actually a tool for making selections and not for granting wishes (you wish!). However, at times it seems to change its behavior, even though you haven't changed any of its options. The explanation lies in its relation to the Eyedropper tool. If you change the Sample Size for the Eyedropper tool, it also affects how the Magic Wand tool samples pixels when you click in the image.

So, next time you click with the Magic Wand tool and find unexpected behavior, check the options for the Eyedropper tool. It could be that you changed its Sample Size to read Point Sample, and consequently, the Magic Wand tool based the selection on the exact pixel that you clicked, which may have been just noise, instead of sampling from an averaged area of 3 by 3 or 5 by 5 pixels (Figure 2-39). Note: Deleting the Prefs can also reset Sample Size to the default Point Sample.

Figure 2-39: **Modifying the Magic Wand tool's behavior by altering the behavior of the Eyedropper tool.**

Image Interpolation Methods

When you resize an image, Photoshop and ImageReady have to recalculate the number of pixels and their color values based on the existing pixels in the image. To preserve the quality and the detail contained in the original image, both applications use complicated math in the background to achieve the best result. Although knowing the math intimately is not necessary, knowing which method to use and when helps to achieve the best result. There are no fewer than five interpolation methods. The following list looks at each very briefly:

- **Bicubic**—This method determines the values of new pixels by calculating the weighted average of the closest 16 pixels (a 4 × 4 array) based on distance. It preserves detail from the original image while endeavoring to create the smoothest tonal gradations.

- **Bicubic Smoother**—A relative of Bicubic, recommended for enlarging images.

- **Bicubic Sharper**—A relative of Bicubic, recommended for downsizing images. It adds some sharpening; if you wish to avoid it, you can use Bicubic.

- **Bilinear**—This method determines the values of new pixels by calculating a weighted average of the 4 closest pixels (a 2×2 array) based on distance. The quality is not as good as Bicubic but the process takes less time.

- **Nearest Neighbor**—This method does not use an algorithm; instead, new pixels are created by using the values of the nearest neighbor. It's used mainly on images that contain hard edges, such as illustrations and screenshots. When an image is enlarged using this method, it can appear noticeably jagged. When an image is reduced in size, it can appear noticeably grainy.

Setting the Default Image Interpolation Method

Regardless of which of the five interpolation methods you use on a per-image basis, you can set one of them in Preferences as your default choice. Setting this preference can be very useful because the interpolation method is employed not only when an image is resized—which includes resizing content on a layer—but also when it is rotated (other than 90 degrees) or transformed. To set the default, open Preferences and in the General screen select a method from the Image Interpolation pop-up dialog box (Figure 2-40).

FIGURE 2-40: **Setting a default image interpolation method in the General screen of the Preferences dialog box.**

Resetting Default Settings in Dialog Boxes

When you are working inside a dialog box, you can easily get carried away and make lots of moves. Sometimes you just need to tear down all your adjustments and start again. Well, instead of canceling out of the dialog box and then launching it again, press Alt (Windows), Opt (Mac OS) and see whether the Cancel button turns into a Reset button (it does in the majority of the dialog boxes). If it does, click it to restore the default values. Make sure that you do not let go of the modifier key before you have clicked the button; if you let go too early, you will invoke Cancel and be thrown out of the dialog box unceremoniously.

Resetting All Warnings in Dialog Boxes

As you use Photoshop, you'll occasionally encounter a warning dialog box. Some of these warning dialog boxes give you the option of never seeing them again or not seeing them again in the current session. Most people choose to not see the warning dialog box again, and move on. However, in some circumstances you do need to see the warning dialog boxes again, for example, if you happen to be a trainer. Fortunately, you can reset all warning dialog boxes back to their default settings (Figure 2-41). To do so, open the Preferences dialog box and in the General screen click Reset All Warning Dialogs.

FIGURE 2-41: All warning dialog boxes can be reset in the General screen of the Preferences dialog box.

Resetting Foreground and Background Colors to Default

The foreground and background colors are widely used by the painting tools, commands, and special effects filters. Consequently, they are continuously being changed during the course of a typical Photoshop session from the default black foreground and white background (Figure 2-42). What to do when you need to restore them to the default colors? As usual, you have several possible ways:

- The obvious way is to click on the foreground color in the Toolbox and then define a color in the Color Picker, and repeat the steps for the background color.

- The other equally obvious but slightly more lateral methods involve the use of the Eyedropper tool, the Color palette, or the Swatches palette.

- The not-so-obvious method, and one that involves fewer steps, is to use the Toolbox but, rather than click the large color boxes, click the small foreground/background default icon directly underneath (Figure 2-42).

Foreground
color box

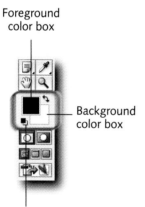

Background
color box

Icon for restoring
the default setting

FIGURE 2-42: Section of the Toolbox showing the foreground and background color boxes and the icon for restoring the default setting.

- Probably the quickest method is to press the D key. This method also just happens to be the coolest!

The preceding little cool keyboard shortcut, along with pressing X to swap the foreground and background colors, is indispensable when it comes to working with masks and alpha channels and when working in Quick Mask mode, refining selections. Easy to remember, too: D for Default.

TIP   When you sample a color with the Eyedropper tool and you find that the background color rather than the expected foreground color is being set, see which color box is highlighted in the Color palette. When the background color box is highlighted, the expected behavior changes, and the Eyedropper will select the background color and not the foreground color.

Customizing Keyboard Shortcuts

If you are an avid user of keyboard shortcuts—and just about everyone from intermediate- to advanced-level user relies heavily on them—then you should take a foray into the Keyboard Shortcuts dialog box (Figure 2-43). There you can assign your own choice of keys to the majority of the commands and to the regularly used commands that do not include keyboard shortcuts—such as Duplicate, Rotate Canvas, Assign Profile, Convert to Profile, adjustment layers, and a host of others.

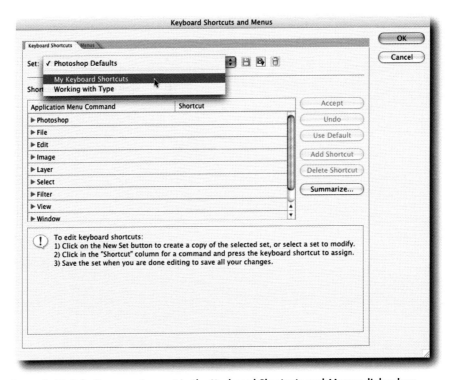

FIGURE 2-43: Selecting a custom set in the Keyboard Shortcuts and Menus dialog box.

Most users are already familiar with calling the adjustment commands via keyboard shortcuts, for example, calling the Curves dialog box with Ctrl+M (Windows), ⌘+M (Mac OS). By simply adding a modifier key to the existing keyboard shortcut, users can make it easy to remember the new shortcuts for creating a new Curves Adjustment layer. Table 2-3 contains a few keyboard shortcuts to get you started.

Table 2-3: Adding Keyboard Shortcuts to Adjustment Layers

Windows		Mac OS		
Original Shortcut	Add	Original Shortcut	Add	Resulting Adjustment Layer
Ctrl+M	Alt+Shift	⌘+M	Opt+Shift	Curves
Ctrl+L	Alt+Shift	⌘+L	Opt+Shift	Levels
Ctrl+U	Alt+Shift	⌘+U	Opt+Shift	Hue/Saturation
Ctrl+B	Alt+Shift	⌘+B	Opt+Shift	Color Balance

Assigning Ctrl+Alt+[or] (Windows), ⌘+Opt+[or] (Mac OS) to Rotate Canvas is also a good idea because you may already be used to Ctrl+[or] (Windows), ⌘+[or] (Mac OS) for rotating thumbnails in Bridge.

The preceding shortcuts are only suggestions and may not suit you. In which case, just assign the keys you feel most comfortable using. Don't forget to save the changes and to back up the file for good measure if you spend valuable time assigning keys.

One more thing—there is a keyboard shortcut to open the Keyboard Shortcuts dialog box: Ctrl+Alt+Shift+K (Windows), ⌘+Opt+Shift+K (Mac OS). The keen-eyed may have noticed that the shortcut is a close cousin to the ones used for Preferences and Color Settings.

TIP One way to memorize keyboard shortcuts is by printing them and carrying them with you to drum them into your brain when you have some time to spare, say, on your daily commute to and from work. Unfortunately, you will find no Print button in the Keyboard Shortcuts dialog box (Figure 2-43). Not a problem! You see the button labeled Summarize? When you click it, it creates an HTML file from the current set. It then lets you save it to your hard disk and, once saved, automatically opens it in your default browser. When the file is open, you can print it from the File menu or, if you are a Mac OS user, also save it as a PDF from the Print dialog box.

Finding the Install Folder's Location Quickly

Many times when you are working on a document you need to get to the folder in which Photoshop is installed in order to check something or other. If you are Mac based, rather than drill down through your hard drive, you can use a cool shortcut to get to it in next to no time: ⌘-click the Photoshop icon in the Dock. A new Finder window opens and displays the contents of the install folder.

If you are Windows based and you have a shortcut on the desktop for Photoshop, you can right-click the icon, choose Properties from the contextual menu, and then click the Find Target button.

Customizing and Saving Your Very Own Workspace

If you have to share your workstation and find yourself constantly having to reset the palettes the way you like them each time you follow a colleague, chances are you either haven't discovered custom workspaces or have forgotten about the feature. Either way, workspaces are very easy to save and load and, once discovered, can save you a great deal of time and frustration. Photoshop ships with preset workspaces that you can either accept or customize and save with another name. Just follow these steps to workspace heaven:

1. Arrange your palettes just the way you like them (including the ones in the palette well).

2. Select the keyboard shortcuts set to go with this workspace (see the section "Customizing Keyboard Shortcuts," earlier in this chapter).

3. Colorize menu items and set their visibility (see the section "Colorizing and Hiding Menu Items for Easier Scanning," earlier in this chapter).

4. Choose ➜ Window ➜ Workspace ➜ Save Workspace.

5. In the Save Workspace dialog box (Figure 2-44), give the workspace a memorable name, check the Capture options that you would like to include, and click Save.

FIGURE 2-44: Check the options that you would like to include in a custom workspace.

To load a workspace, choose Window ➜ Workspace and from the submenu select a workspace. If you are into keyboard shortcuts, you can now assign each workspace a keyboard shortcut. To do so, open the Keyboard Shortcuts dialog box (Edit ➜ Keyboard Shortcuts). Under Application Menu Command, select Window ➜ Workspace ➜ Workspace name and then press the keys that you want to assign (see the section "Customizing Keyboard Shortcuts," earlier in this chapter).

Accessing Tutorials, Tips and Tricks from the Welcome Screen

And in case all the options discussed in this chapter so far aren't enough for you, be assured that the Photoshop Welcome Screen—not to be confused with the splash screen that you see each time you launch Photoshop—contains some very useful links to what's new in Photoshop CS2 and to online tutorials (Figure 2-45). If, as most folks did, you deselected the Show This Dialog at Startup option after installation, you can still gain access to the Welcome Screen from the Help menu at any time during a session.

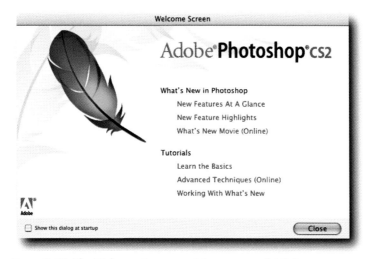

FIGURE 2-45: **The Welcome Screen contains some useful links.**

Summary

By using the techniques you learned in this chapter, you should be able to find your way around Photoshop easily and know quite a number of back alleys for dealing with documents, and working with, customizing, and getting in and out of the various dialog boxes. Additionally, you should know how to customize, save, and revert to your personal workspace whenever you like.

It goes without saying, the more comfortable you feel with the work area, the more easily you'll be able to concentrate on the task of adjusting, manipulating, and optimizing images—and isn't that the main reason you invested in Photoshop?

chapter **3**

The Fine Art of Using Palettes

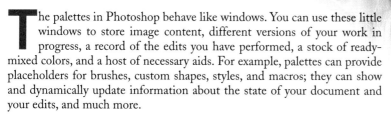

The palettes in Photoshop behave like windows. You can use these little windows to store image content, different versions of your work in progress, a record of the edits you have performed, a stock of ready-mixed colors, and a host of necessary aids. For example, palettes can provide placeholders for brushes, custom shapes, styles, and macros; they can show and dynamically update information about the state of your document and your edits, and much more.

You can do most things to palettes that you can to windows. You can hide them and show them, a common windows behavior. You can also expand, contract, float, dock, or group palettes into clusters (though you cannot contract the Character, Paragraph, Histogram, and Color palettes). About the only thing you cannot do with palettes is eat off them!

Finding screen space for the plethora of palettes used to be a problem for many people. However, now that larger monitors, formerly the preserve of high-end graphics houses, have become more common, the issue is becoming less of a concern. The use of two monitors is also still quite popular, with one monitor being used to view the image and the other to store the palettes.

Regardless of the way you arrange your palettes or whichever method you use to store them, the following hacks should provide insights into some of the secrets that they hold—insights that you can use to enhance your productivity.

Brushes

While working in Photoshop, you will be hard put not to use the brush tools in an editing session. Most tasks require some form of painting, even if it's not your usual Leonardo or Hockney type of painting. For example, creating masks, making selections, burning, and dodging all make use of the brush tools. To assist you with your painting, the Brushes palette is used not only to store brush presets but also to define and modify any existing brush presets (Figure 3-1).

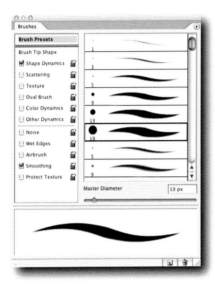

FIGURE 3-1: The Brushes palette, used to store and define new brush presets.

Preserving New Brush Presets

When you create custom brush presets in the Brushes palette, there is no obvious way of saving them and, until you save them, you will likely lose them should Photoshop take a dive. Having invested time in creating new presets, you should make sure to save them, just in case the worse happens. To do so, choose Save Brushes from the palette menu. Make sure that you save the preset in the `~\Adobe Photoshop CS2\Presets\Brushes` folder so that you easily load it again from the palette menu or from the Preset Manager. You will have to quit and relaunch Photoshop before the saved preset becomes available to you in the palette menu and the Preset Manager palette menu.

Previewing a Brush Stroke in Brush Presets

The window at the bottom of the Brushes palette provides a dynamic preview of the selected brush tip shape. If you need to preview the strokes for other brush tip shapes, you have a couple of options.

- One, select Brush Presets in the left pane and then hover the pointer over one of the brush presets. When you see the preview change, you can hover over the other presets to see their previews. This method is a bit clunky because as soon as you scroll more presets into view, you have to wait again while the brushes in the pane are cached.

- Two, use the full stop/period key to cycle downward through the presets, or use the comma key to cycle upward. To jump between the first and the last preset, add the Shift key to the full stop/period or comma key.

Figure 3-2 shows the Brushes palette previewing a brush stroke while the brush tip shape is being modified.

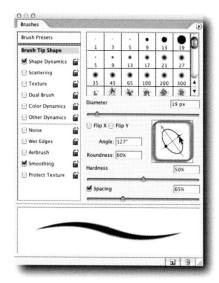

FIGURE 3-2: The previews of the brush tip shapes in the Brushes palette change dynamically when you select another brush or as you modify a tip.

Rearranging Brushes in the Brushes Palette

Unfortunately, you cannot rearrange the brush tip shapes or the brush presets in the Brushes palette or in the pop-up Brushes palette. Although it would be nice to be able to do so directly in the Brushes palette, all is not lost. Select the Preset Manager from the Brush palette menu or call it from the Edit menu. If you select it from the palette menu, it will open showing the brush presets window (Figure 3-3).

You can move the presets one by one or by selecting them in multiples. To rearrange, simply drag and drop singularly or collectively. The changes will be reflected immediately in the Brushes palette.

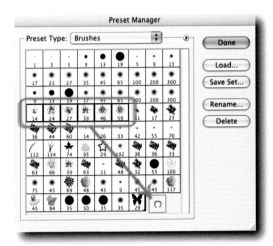

FIGURE 3-3: **Rearranging the brush tip shapes in the Preset Manager.**

CAUTION Do remember to save the library after you have modified it and before you exit the Preset Manager.

Showing the Pop-Up Brushes Palette Temporarily

When you are working in the document window with a painting task, you can show the cutdown version of the Brushes palette right next to the brush tip (Figure 3-4) by right-clicking (Windows), Ctrl-clicking (Mac OS).

As usual, there are several ways of doing anything in Photoshop, and that precept applies to dismissing the palette. To do so, you can start to use the brush that you have just selected, press Esc, or press Enter (Windows), Return (Mac OS).

NOTE If you alter the diameter of the brush tip in the pop-up palette, the effect is only temporary. The next time you select the same brush, it will revert to the preset size.

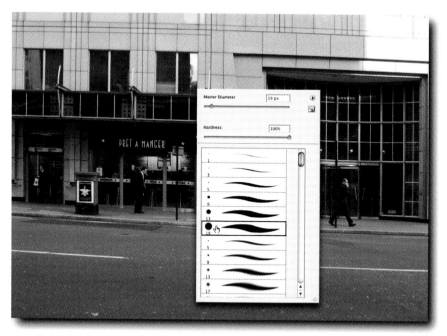

FIGURE 3-4: **Selecting a new brush from the cut-down, pop-up version of the Brushes palette.**

Channels

The Channels palette acts as a sort of container for the pixels in a layer. Each time you activate a layer; the channels associated with the layer automatically come into play. That means that if you make any edits in the Layers palette, they are reflected in the Channels palette, and vice versa. Knowing this can be very helpful when you make editing decisions.

The Channels palette can hold a maximum of 56 channels, including spot and alpha channels. *Spot channels* are used to overprint specially mixed inks and varnishes. *Alpha channels* are used to store selections and data that can be used by filters, such as Lighting Effects, or commands, such as Apply Image. In contrast to using default color channels, you can move alpha channels up and down the stack, though their order has no effect on the image. On the other hand, the order of the spot channels is important; spot channels overprint in the same order as they appear in the Channels palette.

Creating Alpha Channels

Alpha channels are very important in the scheme of things. They are used to hold selections and masks. You can also use alpha channels to create intricate selections by using painting tools, editing tools, or filters and, by the same token, to modify existing selections and resave them. By painting with black-and-white and shades thereof, you can also create some very interesting bevels and contours if you then use the Lighting Effects filter and select the alpha channel as the source for the texture channel (see Chapter 18). Before the advent of Layer Styles, this was the way they were created. Some people still swear by them—although others swear *at* them from the sanctuary of the Layer Style dialog box!

Alpha channels resemble the default color channels in more ways than they differ from them. They differ only in that they cannot be interchanged with the default color channels and are always addendums to the default channels; otherwise, they hold the information in the same way as the default color channels: as grayscale images (Figure 3-5).

FIGURE 3-5: **Showing the Channels palette containing the default color channels, a spot channel, and an alpha channel.**

To create an alpha channel, choose New Channel from the Channels palette menu or click the Create New Channel button.

Creating Spot Channels

When you need to print a specific color that cannot be printed by using process inks, such as a corporate logo, you can use spot channels to create additional plates that are then used to overprint the process colors. Spot colors can also be used to create a two- or three-color job, which may work out cheaper than using four colors. You can create up to 52 spot channels, but unless you have an unlimited printing budget, you're unlikely to use more than one or two at the most.

To create a spot channel, take the following steps:

1. Load the elements to which you want to apply the spot color as a selection. For example, if it's type, Ctrl-click (Windows), ⌘-click (Mac OS) on the type layer's thumbnail.

2. Choose New Spot Channel from the Channels palette menu.

3. In the New Spot Channel dialog box (Figure 3-6), click the color box and specify a spot color from the Color Libraries in the Color Picker. Note: You can also specify the Solidity in the New Spot Channel dialog box, but the setting will affect only the preview and not the separations. However, the setting is applied when the file is output to a composite printer, such as a deskjet.

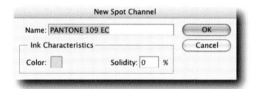

FIGURE 3-6: **The New Spot Channel dialog box.**

4. Click the OK button.

5. Save the file in the DCS 2.0 format or as a PDF.

You don't have to load the elements as a selection before you create the spot channel. If you like, you can do it after the channel has been "filled" with the spot color.

You can also create spot channels from existing alpha channels. To do so, select the alpha channel and then choose Channel Options from the palette menu. In the Channel Options dialog box, select Spot Color and then either enter the spot color's name, if you know it, or choose it from the Color Libraries in the Color Picker by clicking the color box.

Saving Selections

If you have spent considerable time creating a selection, you owe it to yourself to save it. You never know when the gremlins are going to huff and puff and crash Photoshop to the ground! Just make sure that the selection is active, of course, and then choose Save Selection from the Select menu or click the "Save selection as channel" icon at the bottom of the palette (Figure 3-7).

FIGURE 3-7: **Saving a selection in the Channels palette for future use.**

Saving a selection is a painless procedure that can help you avoid wrist ache and cussing further down the line when you have to recreate the selection and the clock is racing toward the inevitable deadline. It really is a good idea to get into the habit of saving selections that take longer than a few seconds to make.

Combining Selections

The Channels palette is also the place to combine selections manually. You can combine any active selection with one saved as an alpha channel. To do so, take the following steps:

1. Save your selections in alpha channels by clicking the "Save selection as channel" button in the Channels palette (Figure 3-7).

2. Ctrl-click (Windows), ⌘-click (Mac OS) on one of the alpha channels to load selection.

3. Use the following modifier keys while you click the second alpha channel:

   ▪ To add, press the Shift key.

   ▪ To subtract, press Alt (Windows), Opt (Mac OS).

   ▪ To intersect, press both of the modifier keys.

At Step 2, you can also use the Select ➔ Load Selection command and then make your choices in the Load Selection dialog box. The dialog box also gives you the choice of loading a second selection from another open document.

Saving selections as alpha channels gives you more flexibility than having to make decisions as you create the selections. Furthermore, you can tweak and twine them all you want.

Splitting and Merging Channels

The Channels palette lets you split your image into a multichannel image (not to be confused with converting to a Multichannel mode) and recompile it by merging the channels. You can also merge grayscale images into single-color mode images, provided that they have the same pixel dimensions and color depth. Splitting and combining channels has rare uses. If your need warrants it, take the following actions:

- To split channels, choose Split Channels from the palette menu. This will result in separate documents in Grayscale mode being created from each channel.

- To merge channels, open the grayscale images that you want to combine; then choose Merge Channels from the palette menu. You will be prompted for a color mode and then asked to assign one image to each channel.

Color

The Color palette provides an alternative way of choosing foreground and background colors to the Color Picker (Figure 3-8). In contrast to the Color Picker, it comes with an assigned keyboard shortcut (F6) that you can use to access it quickly. If you prefer a different shortcut, you can change it in the Keyboard Shortcuts dialog box (Edit → Keyboard Shortcuts).

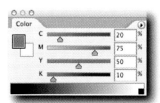

FIGURE 3-8: **The Color Palette showing CMYK color sliders and a Grayscale color ramp.**

The palette supports up to six color models: RGB, HSB, CMYK, Lab, Web, and Grayscale. Depending on your need, you can choose a suitable color model from the palette menu.

Cycling through the Available Spectrums

You can define the foreground or background color not only by using the sliders but also by sampling from the spectrum displayed in the color ramp at the bottom of the palette (Figure 3-8). You can change the model that the spectrum is based on from the palette menu or by pressing the Shift key while clicking anywhere in the spectrum. Although the latter method is quicker, you may need to keep an eye on the Info palette to see which model is being presented as the spectrum displays one color model while the color ramps below the sliders display in another color model. To define the background color, press Alt (Windows), Opt (Mac OS) as you click in the ramp.

Dynamic Color Sliders

The color ramps above the sliders in the Color palette update automatically to reflect the values added by the other sliders. If you prefer the ramps to read only in the component color, you can deselect the option Dynamic Color Sliders in the General screen of the Preferences dialog box (it's on by default).

Curves

The Curves command is probably the most versatile command for correcting tones and colors in an image. Although the Levels command has some similarities, the Curves command lets you make nonlinear adjustments in a way that Levels cannot, nor was designed to do. Because the Curves command is a little bit harder to master than the Levels command, most people shy away from it, which is a shame because they miss out on the fine control that they could exercise over their images when they make adjustments.

This section introduces you gently to some of the not-so-obvious ways of working in the Curves dialog box, and with any luck, you will lose some of your fear and explore its potential to help you fine-tune your images.

Working in the Curves Dialog Box

The Curves and Levels commands can both be used to adjust the tonal range of an image. However, in contrast to the Levels command, which allows adjustments to be made only to the shadow, highlight, and gamma, the Curves command lets you adjust any value along the tonal curve, while keeping 15 values constant (Figure 3-9).

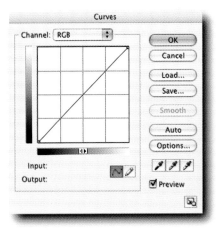

FIGURE 3-9: The default view of the Curves dialog box, showing values in levels and a large grid.

When you open the dialog box, you will see a straight diagonal line representing the current distribution of tonal values. By adding anchor points to this tonal curve, you can alter the tonal values represented. The curve can be moved up to increase the tonal values or down to decrease the tonal values. Similarly, the points can be moved horizontally to increase and decrease the contrast.

Customizing the Dialog Box

You may like to take advantage of three different views that the dialog box offers.

- You can view the grid behind the curve in 10% or 25% views (Figure 3-10). To toggle between the two views, press Alt (Windows), Opt (Mac OS) as you click in the grid.

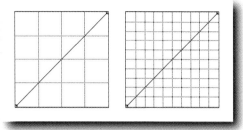

FIGURE 3-10: **Section view of the Curves dialog box. Left—The default 25% grid view. Right—A 10% grid view, selected by Alt-clicking (Windows), Opt-clicking (Mac OS) in the grid.**

- Enlarge the whole window by clicking the two-view icon at the lower-right corner of the dialog box. The button acts as a toggle between regular and large size.

- If you have a prepress background and you are used to working in percentages instead of levels, you can click anywhere on the horizontal gradient bar and read the Input/Output values in percentages.

NOTE When you click the gradient bar to alter the display to read in percentages, the 0, 0 shadow and 255, 255 highlight points are flipped, so that the 0, 0% highlight point is at the bottom left and the 100, 100% shadow point is at the upper right.

Awakening the Input and Output Text Fields

When you enter the Curves dialog box, you may notice that you cannot enter Input and Output values into the text fields (Figure 3-11). That's because neither of the end points on a new curve is selected. So, how do you input values? Well, you could either move the curve or click the points at the end of the curve, or you could—and this option is much more elegant because it doesn't disturb the curve—press the Ctrl key as you then press Tab. The action selects the shadow anchor point and allow you to enter values in the Output and the Input text fields.

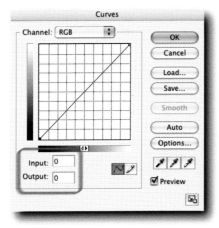

FIGURE 3-11: **You can press Ctrl+Tab to awaken the Input/Output text fields in the Curves dialog box.**

Placing Anchor Points without Modifying the Curve

When you add anchor points to a curve, it's very easy to disturb it and thereby change the input and output values. To get around this obstacle, move the mouse pointer outside the dialog box, hold down Ctrl (Windows), ⌘ (Mac OS), and then click the point in the image that you would like to adjust. Photoshop will place a corresponding anchor point on the composite curve based on the sample point (Figure 3-12).

NOTE If the image is in CMYK mode, this method of placing anchor points has no effect on the composite curve, though you can place them on the curves for the individual channels. If the image is in Lab mode, the anchor point is placed on the Lightness channel.

To place corresponding anchor points on the curves for the individual channels, press Ctrl+Shift (Windows), ⌘+Shift (Mac OS) as you click in the image. This keyboard shortcut places anchor points only on the individual channel curves and not the composite channel.

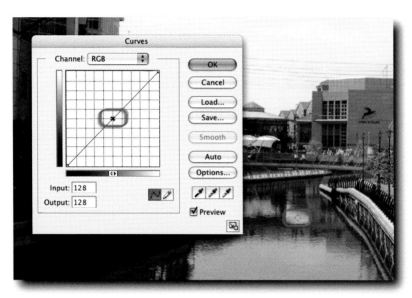

FIGURE 3-12: You can place an anchor point on the curve by Ctrl-clicking (Windows), ⌘-clicking (Mac OS) in the image.

Cycling through the Anchor Points on a Curve (Mac OS)

After you have placed a number of anchor points on a curve, clicking to select one can easily alter the Input/Output values, as noted previously. To avoid this situation, hold down the Ctrl key and then press Tab to cycle upward. Hold down Ctrl+Shift to cycle downward. The direction is reversed if you have reversed the gradient bars in order to read the Input/Output values in percentages rather than levels.

Moving Anchor Points without Using the Mouse

There is a very neat method for modifying the curve in tiny increments. After you start using it, you'll soon make it the de facto way of modifying a curve. To use this method: Ctrl+Tab to select the anchor point that you want to move up, down, left, or right and then use the Up, Down, Left, Right Arrow keys. It's much neater and more precise than using the mouse. You can also click in the Input or Output text field and then use the Up and Down Arrow keys to increase the values in single values or in multiples of 10 by pressing Shift while using the Up or Down Arrow keys.

Selecting Anchor Points

If you need to move a segment of a curve, you can select multiple anchor points by Shift-clicking each one. By the same token, you can also Shift-click an anchor point to deselect it.

If you simply want to deselect the currently selected anchor point, press Ctrl+D (Windows), ⌘+D (Mac OS), or click in the grid to deselect all anchor points.

Deleting Anchor Points

Placing anchor points on a curve couldn't be easier. Just click the curve and it's done. Deleting anchor points, however, is a little bit less intuitive (unless you are familiar with deleting Color Samplers). To delete an anchor point, you must click it and then drag it off the grid. Unfortunately, the contextual menu with a delete item or the trusty old scissors aren't available this time.

However, there are a couple of dignified and graceful methods for clearing an anchor point: Select it by Ctrl+Tabbing and then pressing the Backspace (Windows), Delete (Mac OS) key. Alternatively, Ctrl-click (Windows), ⌘-click (Mac OS) the anchor point.

Creating Freeform Curves with the Arbitrary Map Tool

You can use the Pencil tool to create some unique filter effects by drawing arbitrary maps with it (Figure 3-13). After drawing a map, use the Smooth button to iron out the abrupt transitions and sharp corners on the curve. If you press Shift while drawing with the Pencil tool, you can click and create straight lines.

TIP You can also use the Pencil tool to quickly add anchor points to the curve. To do so, select the Pencil tool, click one of the end points, press Shift and then click the other end point (watch the Input/Output values to make sure that you click levels 0–255). Click the curve icon (next to the Pencil tool) and you should have seven anchor points added to the curve, ready to go.

Using the Eyedroppers

The Set Black Point and Set White Point Eyedropper tools (Figure 3-14) let you assign target tonal and color values and then use those values to adjust shadows and highlights when you click in the image. It's a two-step process. To set the target values, double-click the eyedroppers and then enter a value in the Color Picker when it opens. For example:

1. Double-click the Set Black Point Eyedropper.

2. In the HSB (Hue, Saturation, Brightness) section of the Color Picker, enter a value of 5 in the B text box, and click the OK button (this will correspond to a maximum 95% dot on press).

3. Double-click the Set White Point Eyedropper, enter a value of 95 in the B text box, and click OK (this will correspond to a minimum 5% dot on press).

4. Move the cursor into the image window and Right-click (Windows), Ctrl-click (Mac OS) and select 3 × 3 Average from the pop-up menu.

5. While the Set Highlight tool is still selected, find a highlight in your image (watch the Info palette for readouts) and drag the Eyedropper over it. The highlights will take on the target value you set in Step 3.

6. Repeat Step 5 for shadows—obviously, first selecting the Set Black Point Eyedropper tool.

FIGURE 3-13: Left—Original. Right—Special effect created using the freeform Pencil tool to draw arbitrary curves in the composite, red, green, and blue channels and then applying the Smooth button. Below—Details from the Curves dialog box showing the arbitrary maps.

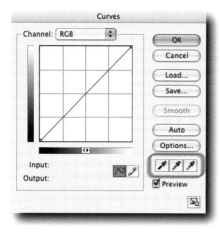

FIGURE 3-14: The Curves dialog box with the Eyedropper tools highlighted.

The Eyedropper tools function exactly the same in Levels, with the added advantage of your having the capability to preview your image in threshold mode, which makes it easier to find the highlight and shadow end points.

The Set Gray Point tool, available only in color images, does not affect the tonal values, as does the middle, gamma slider in the Levels dialog box. What it does instead is to affect the color components and to bring them into line so that a colorcast can be diminished or eliminated altogether. To affect a colorcast, find an element that you think should be a neutral color and then click it with the Eyedropper.

Undoing Curve Moves

While in the Curves dialog box, you can undo the last move by pressing Ctrl+Z (Windows), ⌘+Z (Mac OS). If you need to undo more moves, just hold down Alt (Windows), Opt (Mac OS) and then click the Cancel button when it changes to the Reset button.

Histogram

The Histogram palette is used to visually evaluate an image in a scientific way. You can do this in two ways, by looking at the graph or the statistical data. The graph represents the number of pixels contained in your image and their intensity at any one of the levels. The levels are plotted along the horizontal axis and the number of pixels at any given level on the vertical axis (Figure 3-15).

Statistical data is also provided to help you assess the image. Additionally, you can view histograms for individual channels, including alpha and spot channels, view luminosity values, or see how the color is distributed throughout your image. Furthermore, adjustments made to the image are monitored and the histogram updated dynamically.

Evaluating Images

You can form a quick judgment of the integrity of the data in your image by looking at the histogram. To help you form that judgment, look for the following hints when you read the histogram:

- A histogram made up of smooth contours and data distributed evenly across the full 256 levels means that you have a good scan or capture from a digital camera (Figure 3-15).

- A histogram that is weighted toward one side, to the left or right, almost certainly means that the full 256 levels are not being used (Figure 3-16).

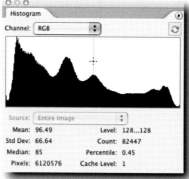

FIGURE 3-15: A histogram showing a properly exposed image with good shadow and highlight detail and full use of the 256 levels. It also shows that at level 128 there are 82,447 pixels with the same intensity value.

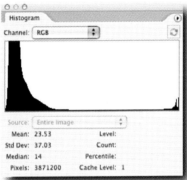

FIGURE 3-16: **A histogram showing an underexposed image; not all the levels are being utilized.**

- A histogram made up of peaks and troughs (Figure 3-17) is not necessarily a sign of a bad scan or capture; it could be just a reflection of the image content.
- A histogram containing gaps (Figure 3-18) means that no pixels are present at those levels because either your scanner or your camera didn't capture them to begin with or they were eliminated in Photoshop when edits, transforms, or adjustments were applied.

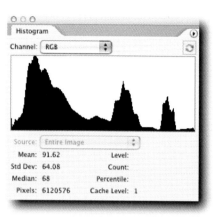

FIGURE 3-17: **A histogram showing a properly exposed image but unusual image detail.**

You can also back that histogram up with statistical data; to see statistical data, hover the pointer over the histogram or click with the mouse anywhere in the histogram. Furthermore, you can view data from a range of values by clicking in the histogram and then dragging. Here's a quick breakdown of the statistical information:

- **Mean**—The average brightness value of the total pixels in the image or in a selection.

- **Level**—The numeric level underneath the pointer; levels are graphed horizontally from 0–255.

- **Std Dev (Standard deviation)**—The variance between the highest and lowest intensity values.

- **Count**—The total number of pixels corresponding to the numeric level underneath the pointer.

- **Median**—The middle brightness value of all the pixels in the image, or in a selection.

- **Percentile**—The total number of pixels at or below the numeric level underneath the pointer, that is, darker than the pixel underneath the pointer.

- **Pixels**—The total number of pixels in the image, or selection, used to calculate the histogram.

- **Cache**—The level of the cache (between 1 and 8) that the histogram is based upon. Level 1 represents the histogram based on actual pixels.

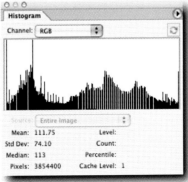

FIGURE 3-18: A histogram showing missing levels or clipped colors.

Viewing Histograms

You can view a histogram for any one of the channels in your image, including alpha and spot channels, or a composite of all the modal color channels. By default, the histogram is based on the entire image, but you can view a segment by making a selection. Here is a list of the different views and how to access them:

- To view an Expanded or Compact palette, choose an option from the palette menu.
- To view all channels, choose All Channels View from the palette menu.

- To view channels in color, choose Show Channels in Color from the palette menu.

- To view channels in color and compact mode, view in Expanded mode, select Colors from the Channels pop-up, and then select Compact View from the palette menu.

- To view individual channels in Expanded View, choose an option from the pop-up menu for Channel (the pop-up is available only in Expanded View).

- To view statistics, choose an option from the palette menu (by default, statistics are displayed in the Expanded View and All Channels View).

- To view a histogram based on the current layer, choose an option from the pop-up menu for Source.

When the histogram is based on cached data instead of the document's current state, a yellow warning triangle appears (the cache level is specified in the Preferences ➜ Memory & Image Cache). You have a number of options at your disposal for displaying a histogram based on the document's current state. You can:

- Double-click anywhere on the histogram.

- Click the cached data-warning icon (Figure 3-19).

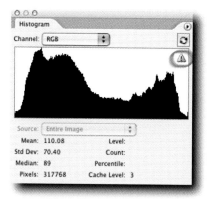

FIGURE 3-19: **Cached data warning icon.**

- In expanded view, click the "Uncached Refresh" button at the top of the palette (Figure 3-20).

- Choose Uncached Refresh from the Histogram palette menu.

When viewing histograms, keep in mind that a bad histogram, that is, one that looks like a comb, doesn't necessarily mean that you have a bad image. Chances are it will print just fine if the missing "teeth" aren't wide enough to cover several missing levels. If the gaps are too wide—say, bridging three or four levels—then posterization will occur.

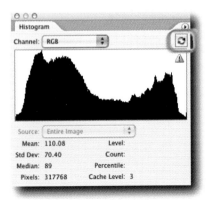

FIGURE 3-20: Uncached Refresh data warning icon.

TIP Some people go to great length to hide the missing levels after doing excessive edits. Although that may fool some people when you submit your image, it will do your reputation no good when that image is printed or manipulated further. To minimize the risk of posterization, you can work in 16-Bits/Channel mode for as long as you possibly can and then convert down to 8-Bits/Channel for output or submission.

History

As you apply changes to your document, the histories feature creates snapshots and stores them in RAM or on your hard disk that you have assigned as the scratch disk. Each history state is given a name to correspond with the command applied to the document. When the maximum number of history states has been reached, as specified in Preferences ➜ General, in order to make room for the next history state any references to the first history state is erased from the History palette, as well as from memory. However, these snapshots, or history states, are only temporary. When you close the document or quit Photoshop, all history states are erased from memory.

You might ask, what is the point of keeping snapshots of your work in progress? Well, as long as the document is open, its history states can be accessed from the History palette and used as an aid to editing. For example, when you select a history state, the document reverts to that state—not only visually but also with respect to all other properties, such as layers and channels and visibility; these are restored.

You can make use of any one of the available history states to paint from by electing it as the source for the History Brush tool. To give another brief example, you can run the Smart Sharpen filter (Filters ➜ Sharpen ➜ Smart Sharpen) on a layer containing a portrait, select the History Brush tool, elect the previous state—thus undoing the effect of Smart Sharpen—and paint selectively over the eyes, nose, and lips from the Smart Sharpen state. This way, only the areas you paint will take on the sharpening, thus avoiding the sharpening of the skin or hair. You also have control over the opacity of the brush strokes, the blend mode, and, if you employ a pen and tablet, pressure sensitivity.

To make the most of the history feature, here are a few hacks relating to the History palette.

Creating a New Snapshot Automatically

When you open a document, you can force Photoshop to create a snapshot of the current state of the document automatically. This can be a good thing because it will let you revert to the open state should you accidentally perform a save. If you do not create a snapshot, the open history step will be deleted after the maximum number of histories, as specified in Preferences ➜ General, has been exceeded.

To create a new snapshot automatically, choose History Options from the History palette menu (Window ➜ History) and then make sure that Automatically Create First Snapshot is selected (Figure 3-21).

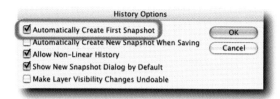

FIGURE 3-21: **Creating a new snapshot automatically in the History Options dialog box.**

Allowing Nonlinear History

By default, new history states are added from the top down: oldest history states at the top and newest at the bottom. If you select a history state, all states that follow are dimmed and then deleted when you apply an edit. The new history state is then appended below the currently selected state. This method allows new histories to be added linearly.

However, there is a downside to working in a linear history mode: When you delete a state, all states that follow will also be deleted. If you prefer to hedge your bets and keep all the history states, you can force Photoshop to work in a nonlinear history mode. In this mode, when you select a history state and apply edits to the image, the new state will be added to the bottom of the list and the states that follow the targeted state won't be deleted. To set nonlinear history mode, choose History Options from the palette menu and then select Allow Non-Linear History (Figure 3-22).

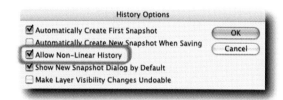

FIGURE 3-22: **Specifying nonlinear histories in the History Options dialog box.**

TIP When working in linear history mode, you can use the Undo command to undo the last change and restore the eliminated states.

Showing New Snapshot Dialog Box Automatically

When you create a new snapshot, if you simply click the "Create new snapshot" icon at the bottom of the palette (Figure 3-23), you are not presented with any options. There are two ways to see the New Snapshot options.

- One, press Alt (Windows), Opt (Mac OS) as you click the Create New Snapshot icon.

- Two, let Photoshop show it automatically each time you click the Create New Snapshot icon. To do so, choose History Options from the palette menu and then select Show New Snapshot Dialog by Default (Figure 3-24).

FIGURE 3-23: **The Create New Snapshot icon located at the bottom of the History palette.**

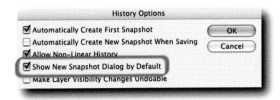

FIGURE 3-24: **You can tell Photoshop to show the History Options dialog box automatically each time you create a new history snapshot.**

Making Layer Visibility Changes Undoable

By default, if you turn layer visibility on/off, it's not recorded as a history step, which means that you cannot undo the step. Now, you have the option to include layer visibility in the history steps. To turn on the option, choose History Options from the palette menu and then select Make Layer Visibility Changes Undoable (Figure 3-25).

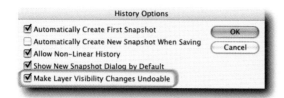

FIGURE 3-25: **You can make layer visibility changes undoable in the History Options dialog box.**

CAUTION   Make sure that you actually want this undo history step enough to sacrifice other history steps. When this option is enabled, it will overwrite a history step each time you toggle the visibility of a layer off and each time you turn it back on.

Purging Histories

Depending on the size of your documents, histories can easily consume a large part of your resources. If you find yourself running low or even on empty, you can:

- Delete all but the topmost history state by choosing Clear History from the palette menu.

- Delete all but the topmost history state by holding down Ctrl (Windows), ⌘ (Mac OS) and clicking the trash icon.

- Delete single histories by selecting and then clicking the trash icon; hold down Alt (Windows), Opt (Mac OS) if you do not want to verify the command.

- Delete single histories by selecting and then dragging to the trash.

- If you don't fancy a trip to the History palette, you can choose Edit → Purge → Histories.

NOTE   If you use the Edit → Purge → Histories command, you cannot undo it, as you can with the Clear History command in the History palette. What happens to the states that follow the one you have just deleted is dependent on the mode you have selected for histories in History Options—linear, the default, or nonlinear. See "Allowing Non-Linear History," earlier in the chapter.

Info

The Info palette displays color values of the pixels beneath the pointer and, depending on which tool is currently active, measurements for tools. For example, it can provide instant feedback for color and tonal values, pointer coordinates, width and height of transforms and selections, measurements made with the Measure tool, color sampler readouts, document status information, and tool hints (Figure 3-26)—all useful information that you can gainfully employ when you make adjustments, transforms, and edits.

FIGURE 3-26: **The Info palette, showing before and after color readings, document info, and tool hints.**

The color values seen under the pointer can be displayed for the current color mode and one other mode. Being able to display values in a second color mode can be very useful when, for example, you are working in RGB mode but need to see the corresponding CMYK or Web-safe color values in order to target your adjustments. If the CMYK colors are out of the gamut of the selected color space in Color Settings, a warning in the form of an exclamation mark is displayed next to the values so that you can make adjustments accordingly. However, the warnings should not be taken as gospel but interpreted and tempered by experience.

When color or tonal adjustments are applied to the image, such as Curves or Levels adjustments, the palette displays the before and after values. This again, as with seeing the values in a second color mode, can be very useful in helping you to form editing decisions based on numbers rather than a visual assessment. To view the before and after values, move the pointer into the image while the adjustment dialog box is open.

CAUTION   If you change the units of measure in the Info palette for tracking the pointer coordinates, for example, from pixels to percentages, be aware that the settings for the rulers (Preferences ➡ Units & Rulers ➡ Units ➡ Rulers) are also altered.

How the Info palette displays the information can be changed in two ways: You can click on the Eyedropper icons and select an item from the pop-up menu (Figure 3-27), or select Palette Options from the palette menu and then make your choices in the Info Palette Options dialog box (Figure 3-28). You can specify in the dialog box whether you would like to see document status information; this is in addition to the information displayed in the status bar; also useful, if you are a beginner, are dynamic tool hints.

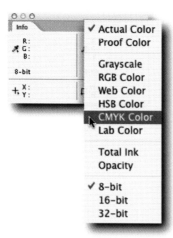

FIGURE 3-27: You can change the Info palette display by clicking the eye-dropper icons.

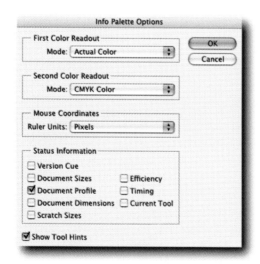

FIGURE 3-28: The Info Palette Options dialog box.

Layers

The Layers palette is where all the action takes place. From it, you can control the position and the appearance of all the data in your image. It would not be an exaggeration to say the Layers palette is at the heart of any image editing (Figure 3-29).

Apart from giving you control over layers, the palette also gives you access to Layer Styles and layer Blending Options. Layer Styles are simply effects, such as drop shadows, bevels, glows, and so forth, applied to a layer. Blending Options is a feature that lets you apply advanced blends to layers, as opposed to the simple blends that you can apply from within the Layers palette (more on layers and blending modes in Chapter 6, and layer styles in Chapter 7).

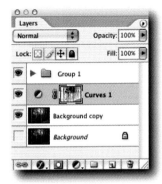

FIGURE 3-29: **The Layers palette, at the heart of Photoshop.**

Locking and Unlocking Layers

The four lock icons at the top of the layer stack allow you to partially or wholly lock the layer content (Figure 3-29). Locking content can be useful, for example, when you want to paint but do not want the paint to intrude into the transparent area, or want to paint but not move the content accidentally.

From left to right, the icons allow the following controls:

- **Lock Transparent Pixels**—Clicking the icon locks the transparent areas on the layer— useful for filling and painting without affecting the transparent pixels on the layer.

- **Lock Image Pixels**—Clicking the icon prevents filling and painting. You can still move, crop, and slice the content, but changing the color values is not allowed.

- **Lock Position**—This is essentially the opposite of Lock Image Pixels. While the icon is in the down position, you may change the values of the pixels but not move them on the grid.

- **Lock All**—Just as its name implies, clicking this icon locks the transparent areas and prevents editing and moving of all pixels on the layer. Basically, about the only thing it will permit is slicing and cropping.

Take note, the icons act as toggles; click a second time to unlock. When Lock Image Pixels is selected, Lock Transparent Pixels is not available. This may seem paradoxical until you realize that the transparent areas also contain pixels (see the Tip that follows). If all the icons are grayed out, the options are not available for the current layer.

TIP To paint transparent pixels without affecting the opaque pixels, choose the Behind blend mode in the options bar for the Brush tool.

Adding Color to Layer Tiles

Sometimes you can create so many layers that it can be difficult to find one particular one when you are quickly scrolling the tiles up and down. Although this may not be the case very often when you manipulate images, it soon becomes the norm when you design interfaces that contain, for example, buttons with text overlay and each button having a normal, over, and down state. For this kind of work, organizing the layers into groups is essential. However, you can speed up your workflow by colorizing layers and thereby making it easier to find them in the palette. To do so, Right-click (Windows), Ctrl-click (Mac OS) on the visibility icon and select a preset color from the pop-up menu (Figure 3-30).

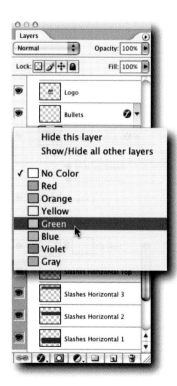

FIGURE 3-30: **Assigning a color to a layer for easier identification.**

Specifying Palette Thumbnails, Icons, and Masks

You now have the choice of viewing dynamically changing thumbnails or old-style thumbnails for layers, composite thumbnails for layer groups, and generic icons for adjustment layers. To specify your preference, open the Layers Palette Options dialog box from the Layers palette menu and then make your choice (Figure 3-31). Here's what happens when you select an option:

- If you select **Layer Bounds** under Thumbnail Contents, the thumbnail will grow dynamically as you move content out of the document bounds.

- If you select **Entire Document**, the thumbnail will show the content within the document bounds.

- If you select **Show Group Thumbnails**, a thumbnail made from a composite of the layers in a group will be displayed; otherwise, a generic group icon will be used to identify the group.

By default, a reveal-all mask is added each time you create an adjustment layer, ready for you to work on should you need it. If you prefer not to have the mask added automatically, you can deselect Use Default Masks on Adjustments in the Layers Palette Options dialog box.

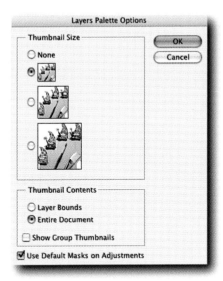

FIGURE 3-31: You can specify in the Layer Palette Options dialog box how you want to see thumbnails, icons, and masks for adjustment layers by default.

Levels

When people first start to use Photoshop and want to lighten or darken an image manually, most people gravitate toward the Levels command. Nothing wrong with that; the design of the Levels dialog box is simple and elegant, and you don't need to stock up with a supply of "Whoops!" before going to work in it . . . or so you thought! It's only when you hack the Levels dialog box that you realize the damage that you have been doing unknowingly to your images by moving those seductive sliders first this way and then that way.

The dialog box is divided into four broad sections. At the top, you have the means to change the Input levels. In the middle, you have a histogram for charting the number of levels (0 to 255, left to right) and the pixels contained at each level (bottom to top). At the bottom, you have the means to change the Output levels. To the right are the various buttons for loading saved settings, saving the settings, applying auto commands, and setting the options for the auto command; additionally, there are three eyedropper tools for setting the black, gray, and white points, respectively (Figure 3-32). The next part of the chapter looks at each section in more detail.

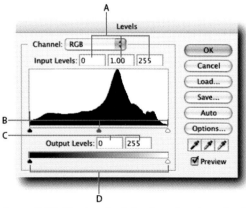

FIGURE 3-32: The Levels dialog box showing a healthy histogram. A—Input Levels text fields; corresponding to the three Input sliders (B). B—Input Levels sliders: Black Point (Shadows), Gamma (Midtones), and White Point (Highlights), respectively. C—Output Levels text fields; corresponding to the two Output Levels sliders (D). D—Output Levels sliders.

Input Controls

The Input Levels controls let you change the tonal range of the image without affecting the color balance. However, if severe moves are made to the sliders because data is clipped and thrown away, posterization may occur and the image may print with visible banding. You can change the values for the black, gamma, and white sliders by moving the sliders or inputting the values into the corresponding text boxes.

97

Black Input Levels

When you move the black Input Levels slider to the right, you are telling Photoshop to make the level where the slider comes to rest the new black point and to *clip* all the levels *below* that point. For example, if you move the black Input Levels slider to level 10, any pixels below level 10 will be clipped and level 10 will become the new level 0. The other levels, 10–255, will expand to fill the entire range of 0–255 levels. The color balance is not affected because the corresponding pixels are adjusted proportionately (Figure 3-33).

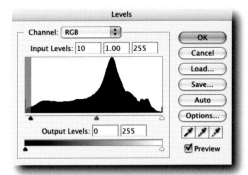

FIGURE 3-33: **In the figure, the black Input Levels slider has been moved to level 10; consequently, any pixels within the red overlay range will be clipped and level 10 will become the new level 0 after you click the OK button.**

White Input Levels

When you move the white Input Levels slider to the left, you are telling Photoshop to make the level where the slider comes to rest the new white point and to *clip* all the levels *above* the point. For example, if you move the white Input slider to level 245, any pixels above level 245 will be clipped, and level 245 will become the new level 255. The other levels, 0–245, will expand to fill the entire range of 0–255 levels (Figure 3-34).

Gamma Input

When you move the Gamma Input slider (the middle Input slider) to the left, you are telling Photoshop to set the value where the slider comes to rest as the new midtone gray (50% gray or level 128). For example, if you move the Gamma Input slider to the left, the image will become lighter, the shadows will stretch and the highlights compress. The image will become lighter because you have told Photoshop to make darker pixels the new level 128. When you move the Gamma Input slider, the highlight and shadow end points are not affected. The moves don't seem intuitive because you half expect the opposite to happen: moving the slider toward the shadows will make the image go darker, and vice versa. Fortunately or unfortunately, depending on your point of view, the sliders provide a truer picture of what is happening behind the scenes. Furthermore, the Gamma slider reads in a Gamma scale from 0.10 to 9.99, where 1.00 = midtone gray, unlike the other sliders that read in incremental levels from 0–255.

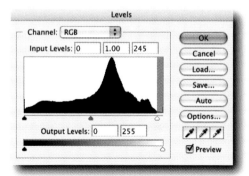

FIGURE 3-34: In the figure, the white Input Levels slider has been moved to level 245; consequently, any pixels within the red overlay range will be clipped and level 245 will become the new level 255 after you click the OK button.

Output Controls

The Output Levels sliders are mainly used to set the maximum shadow and minimum highlight dots of an image before it's output to print. For example, if your image contains important information at either end of the range from 0–255 levels and you know the press cannot produce the full range of levels, you can compress the data into a smaller range that the press can handle (see Chapter 16 for more information on outputting to print). In contrast to the Input Levels sliders, which clip levels, these controls compress the levels into a printable range. The following sections describe, in a nutshell, how the sliders work.

Black Output Levels

When you move the *black* Output Levels slider to the right, you are telling Photoshop to make all the pixels where the slider comes to rest the new black end point and to shunt all the levels toward white by applying compression. For example, if you move the black Levels Input slider to level 10, any pixels that were at level 0 will move to level 10, and at level 1 to level 11, and so forth.

White Output Levels

When you move the *white* Output Levels slider to the left, you are telling Photoshop to make all the pixels where the slider comes to rest the new white end point and to shunt all the levels toward black by applying compression. For example, if you move the white Levels Input slider to level 245, any pixels that were at level 255 will move to level 245, and at level 254 to level 244, and so forth.

Clipping Display

The Levels dialog box has one very useful, rather hidden feature for identifying the darkest and lightest areas in an image, thus making it easier to set the black and white end points. When you hold down Alt (Windows), Opt (Mac OS) and move the Input Levels sliders, a high-contrast image is displayed, which makes it easier to identify the darkest and lightest part of the image (Figure 3-35).

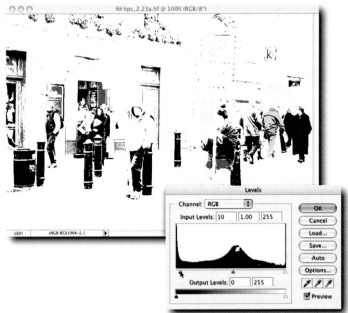

FIGURE 3-35: Top—Image being viewed in normal mode. Bottom—Same image viewed in Threshold mode in order to identify shadow data.

Here's how it works: When you move the *black* Input Levels slider to the right, the darkest parts of the image are made visible first and, as you move the slider up the scale, the lighter parts of the image become progressively visible until only the very lightest remain visible. The reverse happens when you move the *white* Input Levels slider to the left.

You can also use Threshold mode to find the threshold levels in individual channels. To do so, simply select the channel from the Channels pop-up menu in the Levels dialog box and then proceed as previously described.

NOTE The Threshold mode is not available to images in CMYK, Lab, Indexed Color, or Bitmap mode.

Navigator

When you magnify your image's view by a percentage higher than 100%, you can use the Navigator palette to show the hidden areas of the image. There are three ways you can do this: One, use the buttons at the bottom of the palette; two, use the Hand tool inside the view box (it's visible only if the magnification is higher than 100%) to drag the hidden areas into view; three, click the area you wish to center in the image window.

Although denigrated by many, the Navigator palette is actually quite useful when you work at large magnifications and your document view fills either the whole screen or almost the entire screen. With its aid, you can locate the section of the image that you wish to work on very easily. If you like, you can enlarge the palette by dragging from the lower-right corner. To return the palette to the default size, click the radio button in the title bar marked with the plus sign.

Furthermore, just in case the view border in the Navigator proxy window clashes with image content, you can change it to a color of your choice. To do so, choose Palette Options from the palette menu and then either select a preset color from the pop-up menu or click the color box and select a color in the Color Picker (Figure 3-36).

FIGURE 3-36: **The Palette Options dialog box for the Navigator palette.**

Swatches

When you are working with a strict color scheme on a project, the Swatches palette is indispensable. The palette allows you to create, save, and store colors that are particular to your project and share the saved libraries with fellow workers (Figure 3-37). Even if you work alone, you can use the palette to store frequently used colors and save yourself the trouble of having to define them repeatedly in the Color Picker or Color palette.

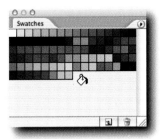

FIGURE 3-37: **A new swatch being added to a custom library in the Swatches palette.**

You can create a swatch from the foreground or the background color, as defined in the Toolbox (the color can be sampled with the Eyedropper tool or selected in the Color Picker). Having defined a color, you have no fewer than four ways of saving it as a swatch:

- Click the swatch icon at the bottom of the Swatches palette; to name the swatch, hold down Alt (Windows), Opt (Mac OS) and type the name in the Color Swatch Name dialog box (Figure 3-38).

- Choose New Swatch from the palette menu and type a name in the Color Swatch Name dialog box.

- Hover over an empty part of the palette and click when the pointer icon turns to a bucket.

- Right-click (Windows), Ctrl-click (Mac OS) in the empty part of the palette and then type a name in the Color Swatch Name dialog box.

To save the current collection of swatches, select Save Swatches from the palette menu. Be sure to save the set in the ~\Adobe Photoshop CS2\Presets\Color Swatches folder so that you can load it from the palette menu.

NOTE You can exchange swatches between the applications in the Creative Suite. To do so, select Save Swatches for Exchange from the palette menu.

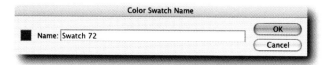

FIGURE 3-38: **The Color Swatch Name dialog box.**

Deleting a swatch in the swatches palette is slightly unintuitive because you cannot select a swatch in the conventional sense. You have two options: click and then drag to the trash icon or hold down Alt (Windows), Opt (Mac OS) and click when the pointer turns to a scissors.

TIP If you need to organize the swatches, you are better off doing it in the Preset Manager than in the Swatches palette. You can access the Preset Manager from the palette menu or from the Edit menu.

Tool Presets

The tool options that appear on the Option bar when you select a tool can be saved in a preset and stored in the Tool Presets palette for easy access. This can save you hours of work over the course of a few lengthy editing sessions. Furthermore, you can exchange tool presets with colleagues and load them from the palette menu or the Preset Manager.

Defining a New Tool Preset

Defining a new tool preset is straightforward: Select a tool and define its settings on the options bar. Next, click the Create New Tool Preset icon at the bottom of the Tool Presets palette (Figure 3-39) or choose New Tool Preset from the palette menu or by clicking the tool's icon in the options bar and selecting New Tool Preset from the pop-up palette menu. In the New Tool Preset dialog box, enter a memorable name and select the options presented (they differ according to the tool). Click the OK button.

If the preset is important to you and you intend to use it repeatedly, make sure that you save it. To save a preset, enter the Preset Manager (Edit ➜ Preset Manager), choose Tools from the pop-up menu, select one of the presets, and then click Save Set.

CAUTION Using custom tool presets can catch you off guard because the settings remain in force until you select another custom preset or reset the tool. For example, if you just used a brush preset that had the blend mode set to Overlay and you then selected the Brush tool, it will still have the blend mode set to Overlay! To revert to the default tool setting, Right-click (Windows), Ctrl-click (Mac OS) the tool icon in the options bar (the first icon from the left) and select Reset Tool.

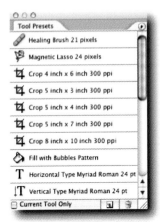

FIGURE 3-39: **The Tool Presets palette,
showing presets for an assortment of tools.**

Sorting Saved Tool Presets

By default, the Tool Presets palette, which includes the pop-up version, shows all the tool presets. This can make it difficult to quickly select, say, a preset Rectangular Marquee tool from the crowd. Fear not! At the bottom of the palettes is an option to show presets for only the currently selected tool (Figure 3-40). Appropriately enough, it's called Current Tool Only. If you have an aversion to pressing buttons, you can choose Show Current Tool Presets from the palette menu.

FIGURE 3-40: **The Tool Presets palette,
showing presets for only the current tool.**

Summary

As you have seen from this chapter, Photoshop uses palettes to store tools, tool options, presets, and just about everything else needed to adjust, edit, transform, optimize, and embellish an image.

During the course of any editing session, you will find yourself working in the Layers palette as a general rule and the other palettes on a fairly, regular basis. With the hacks you have learned about customizing and handling palettes, you should be able to find your way around the work area a lot more easily, and also find yourself saving time and working with less frustration.

Hacking the work area is an integral part of mastering Photoshop. Think of it as a musician learning boring scales and arpeggios in order to build a base for a sound technique. Once learned, you can more easily learn the intricate harmonies that underline everything from a popular song to a sonata and even a symphony.

In the next chapter, you will learn how to hack Bridge, the new standalone file browser, and that will be the last chapter focusing on hacking the work area.

chapter 4

Browsing with Bridge

With the explosion of digital capture in recent times, Adobe introduced the File Browser as a means of finding, managing, and previewing files before opening them in Photoshop. One of its main downfalls was its tendency to hog Photoshop processes when it needed to cache file information. With the introduction of Bridge, the next generation in file browsing, the umbilical cord between Photoshop and the File Browser has been cut, and the file browser is now, to all intents and purposes, an independent, freewheeling sibling.

The name Bridge may seem odd for a browser until you realize that it is designed to serve all the applications in the Creative Suite. If you have only Photoshop, then Bridge has a few features missing, such as global color management, Bridge Center, Version Cue file management options, and some automate settings; apart from these missing features, it acts as a bridge between Photoshop and Camera Raw and functions as a full-blooded, standalone file browser.

Viewing from Bridge

To make the viewing experience both practical and enjoyable, Bridge offers several options for displaying the browser window. One, you can rearrange the panels and save the new configuration as a workspace. Two, you can open a total number of 14 windows, view a different location in each one, and assign a different workspace to each one. To open a new window, choose File ➜ New Window or Ctrl+N (Windows), ⌘+N (Mac OS). Three, you can view the window in compact or ultra-compact mode. The next sections look at them in more detail.

Launching Bridge

You can launch Bridge automatically when you launch Photoshop, from within Photoshop after it's up and running, or independently of Photoshop, just as with any other application. To launch Bridge automatically with Photoshop, open the Photoshop Preferences dialog box and select Automatically Launch Bridge from the General screen. To launch Bridge from within Photoshop, you can use the now familiar File Browser icon on the options bar, or the command File ➜ Browse. You can also use the shortcut Ctrl+Opt+O (Windows), ⌘+Opt+O (Mac OS).

Viewing Full, Compact, or Ultra-Compact Mode

Although selecting the different viewing modes is intuitive, you can easily lose your footing if you don't know how the modes interact with each other. With that little forewarning in mind, take a look at the different options in detail and see how to switch between the viewing modes.

- **Full Mode**—By default, Bridge opens in full view mode. This is probably the mode you will use most. However, you may want to try the two other display modes ; both have their uses. They are Compact mode and Ultra-Compact mode.

- **Compact Mode**—This mode displays the toolbar and content while hiding the panels. To switch to Compact mode, click the icon in the upper-right corner of the toolbar (Figure 4-1) or press Ctrl+Enter (Windows), ⌘+Return (Mac OS).

FIGURE 4-1: **Detail from the Bridge toolbar in Full mode.**

- **Ultra-Compact Mode**—This mode displays the toolbar while hiding the content and the panels.

When you're in Compact mode, you can switch to Ultra-Compact mode by clicking the Switch to Ultra-Compact icon in the toolbar (Figure 4-2) or return to Full mode by pressing Ctrl+Enter (Windows), ⌘+Return (Mac OS).

FIGURE 4-2: **Detail from Bridge toolbar in Compact mode.**

The Switch to Ultra-Compact mode icon is added after you are in Compact mode; this icon isn't available in Full mode. A button for pop-up menus is also added, similar to palette menus. This contains the menu item Compact Window Always on Top, which cannot be accessed from any-where else. If you don't want the Compact mode window to always stay on top of other windows, deselect the item.

When you're in Ultra-Compact mode, you can switch to Compact mode by clicking the appro-priate icon on the toolbar (Figure 4-3). Alternatively, you have the choice of returning to Full mode by either clicking the appropriate icon or pressing the keyboard shortcut Ctrl+Enter (Windows), ⌘+Return (Mac OS). Whichever mode you jump from to full mode, when next you use the keyboard shortcut, the view will return to that mode. For example, if you jump from Compact mode, you will return to Compact mode, but if you jump back from Ultra-Compact mode, you will return to Ultra-Compact mode. This feature can lead to confusion unless you are aware of the different view modes and their interaction on each other.

Switch to
Full Mode

Switch to Compact Mode

FIGURE 4-3: **Detail from the Bridge toolbar in Ultra-Compact mode.**

NOTE If you have Creative Suite, you cannot switch to Compact or Ultra-Compact modes while you are in the Bridge Center.

Customizing Thumbnail Views

The background color for the thumbnails is set to equal amounts of RGB = 186. You can change it to any value between RGB 0–255. To do so, choose Edit ➜ Preferences (Windows), Bridge ➜ Preferences (Mac OS) and then move the slider under Thumbnails in the General pane.

Unfortunately, the only way to return to the default values requires you to either delete the Preferences file or use a utility that can measure screen values and then apply a bit of guesswork while you measure the color and tweak the slider. If you don't have a utility, you can use the Eyedropper tool in Photoshop to measure the thumbnails background color by clicking in an open document and then *dragging* it to the thumbnails background. Next, hover the pointer over the foreground color box in the Toolbox and read the values in the Info palette.

TIP Mac OS comes with the DigitalColor Meter, which can be found in the Utilities folder. If you are PC based, you may want to try Eyedropper from www.inetia.com. You can also find freely available utilities listed on www.versiontracker.com.

In the same Preferences ➜ General pane, you can select what metadata information, apart from the filename, you want to view underneath the thumbnail. You can choose up to three lines. To do so, simply tick the Show box and then select an item from the pop-up menu.

TIP To hide/show metadata information below the thumbnails, you can use the keyboard shortcut Ctrl+T (Windows), ⌘+T (Mac OS).

In addition to the options in the Preferences dialog box for viewing thumbnails, more controls are available in the status bar (Figure 4-4). You can use the slider to increase and decrease the size of the thumbnails. Choose between thumbnails, details, or filmstrip view. You can change the orientation of filmstrip view by clicking the button at the bottom of the preview pane. Of course, you can also choose these views from the View menu.

FIGURE 4-4: **Detail from the status bar, showing controls for viewing thumbnails. A—Resize Thumbnails. B—Thumbnails View. C—Filmstrip View. D—Details View. E—Versions and Alternates View.**

NOTE Versions and Alternates are available but work only if you have Version Cue installed as part of the Creative Suite.

Customizing and Saving Bridge Views

Just as you can customize and save your workspace in Photoshop, so can you in Bridge. Although the application ships with preset workspaces, you may still want to tweak them, save them with new names, or invent your own workspace configurations.

One popular workspace that you may want to try shows the largest possible previews and gives quick access to all the panes. It's more difficult to describe how to set it up than it is to actually do (Figure 4-5). Here are the steps:

1. Choose Window ➜ Workspace ➜ Reset to Default Workspace.

2. Drag the upright divider to the right until one row of thumbnails shows as a filmstrip.

3. Drag the Metadata panel by the tab and drop it into the slot next to the Folders tab.

4. Drag the Keywords panel by the tab and drop it into the slot next to the Metadata tab.

5. Drag the Preview panel by the tab and drop it into the slot next to the Keyword tab.

FIGURE 4-5: **Custom Bridge view, showing large preview and all the panel tabs.**

You should now have five tabs lined up next to each other. By clicking any one of them, you can view the contents in large view. Enlarge the Bridge view to fill the screen and you should be able to view an almost full screen preview. You may have to drag the upright divider to the right as you enlarge the window in order to view a single row of thumbnails. When you are satisfied with the layout, save it as a workspace from the Window ➜ Workspace submenu. Assign a keyboard shortcut if you want to switch in and out of this view.

TIP To toggle between large preview and Lightbox view, click the Show/Hide Panels button in the bottom left of the status bar.

Slideshow Mode

You can view a folder of images or selected images as a slide show. This can be handy when you want to automatically cycle through large previews of the files in a folder. Unfortunately, you cannot save the slide show, so its usage is limited.

To start the slide show, make sure that a folder is selected or that images that you want to include in the slideshow are selected. Next, choose View ➜ Slideshow or Ctrl+L (Windows), ⌘+L (Mac OS). When the slide show starts, instructions on how to control the slide show are displayed. You can hide them by pressing H and, likewise, reveal them by pressing H again.

- To start and pause, press Spacebar.

- To decrease duration, press Shift+S.

- To increase duration, press S.

- To turn looping on/off, press L.

- To exit, press Esc or double-click anywhere.

- To view manually, use the Left and Right Arrow keys.

By default, the slideshow starts with the file selected in the contents panel. If you want it to start with the first file in a list, make sure that it's selected or that no files are selected. To deselect all files, choose Edit → Deselect All, or Ctrl+Shift+A (Windows), ⌘+Shift+A (Mac OS).

Managing Files with Bridge

Bridge is designed from the ground up to help you manage files and to preview their content. Furthermore, you can apply Camera Raw settings to raw files without opening Photoshop and batch process files, though the latter does require Photoshop. You can do extensive searches for files. The searches are not just confined to the contents pane; they can cover all mounted drives. The searches can be saved as collections for future reference.

If need be, you can open more than one browser window. Doing so can be helpful or confusing, depending on how you make use of the feature. If multiple windows don't appeal to you, you can switch among the different workspaces by using the keyboard shortcuts assigned to each workspace.

Applying Camera Raw Settings

Bridge has several options for applying Camera Raw settings to files. You can apply settings that have previously been saved as a setting or have already been applied to other raw files. Having the options on hand can be very useful when you need to apply the same setting to multiple files without opening the files. Simply select the files, apply the settings and, straightaway, you can be in a position to view decent previews and slide shows and to create Web Photo Galleries without any further work on the files. If need be, you can undo the work and apply the default Camera Raw settings, and even clear the file of all associated settings.

To apply the same settings to multiple files, select the files in Bridge and then choose an item from the Edit → apply Camera Raw Settings submenu. Alternatively, right-click (Windows), Ctrl-click (Mac OS) and choose an item from the contextual menu (see Chapter 14 for more information on how to save settings).

One other way of applying Camera Raw settings is by copying the settings from one file and then applying them to single or multiple files. It's a straightforward copy-and-paste procedure. The only difference is in the keyboard shortcut. You have to add a modifier key to the normal copy/paste shortcut, like so:

- To copy, select the file or files and then Ctrl+Alt+C (Windows), ⌘+Opt+C (Mac OS).

- To paste, select the file or files and then Ctrl+Alt+V (Windows), ⌘+Opt+V (Mac OS).

When you paste, you are given the option of which settings you would like to apply. Select from the pop-up panel and click OK (Figure 4-6).

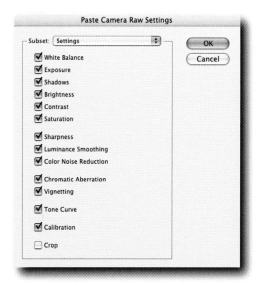

FIGURE 4-6: **The Paste Camera Raw Settings dialog box.**

Opening Files from Bridge

You can open files from Bridge into any of the supported applications or applications associated with the file. You have a number of methods at your disposal for opening the file, apart from the most common File ➡ Open command. Here's a quick rundown of the most useful methods (assuming that the raw files you are attempting to open are associated with Camera Raw and not another raw file converter). You can change file associations from the File Type Associations pane in Preferences.

- Select a file or files and press Enter (Windows), Return (Mac OS). Adding Alt (Windows), Opt (Mac OS) to the shortcut will close the Bridge window.

- In the content area or Preview panel, double-click a file.

- Select a file and then choose File ➜ Open With. Next, select the name of the application from the submenu with which to open the file.

- Drag and drop the file into the working area of an application, for example, a JPEG into a Word document or into a browser window.

- Drag a file from the content area and drop it onto the application icon.

- To edit the Camera Raw settings for a raw file, choose File ➜ Open with Camera Raw.

To help you open the most often accessed files or folders, you can make them into favorite items. You can do this in one of three ways:

- Select the file or folder and then choose File ➜ Add to Favorites.

- Right-click (Windows), Ctrl-click (Mac OS) and choose Add to Favorites from the contextual menu.

- Drag the file or folder into the Favorites panel.

To remove items from the Favorites panel, Right-click (Windows), Ctrl-click (Mac OS) and choose Remove from Favorites.

All in all, a number of ways for opening files are at your disposal. Choose the one that suits your workflow.

Opening Raw Files in Bridge or Photoshop

Although Camera Raw does the actual processing of raw files, you can "edit" the Camera Raw settings under the auspices of Bridge or Photoshop. For some workflows, editing in Bridge is preferable, whereas for others you may want to edit in Photoshop. The choices at your disposal are as follows:

- To edit Camera Raw settings in Photoshop, select a file and then choose File ➜ Open, or Ctrl+O (Windows), ⌘+O (Mac OS).

- To edit Camera Raw settings in Photoshop and close the Bridge window, select a file and then use Ctrl+Alt+O (Windows), ⌘+Opt+O (Mac OS), or Ctrl+Alt+Enter (Windows), ⌘+Opt+Return (Mac OS).

- To edit Camera Raw settings in Bridge, select a file and then choose File ➜ Open in Camera Raw, Ctrl+R (Windows), ⌘+R (Mac OS), or double-click the file.

- To edit Camera Raw settings in Photoshop by double-clicking a file, choose Edit ➜ Preferences (Windows), Bridge ➜ Preferences (Mac OS) and then, in the Advanced pane, deselect Double-click edits Camera Raw settings in Bridge. Click OK to apply changes.

- To open files in Photoshop and bypass the Camera Raw dialog box, select file(s) and then Ctrl+Shift+double-click (Windows), ⌘+Shift+double-click (Mac OS).

NOTE When you bypass the Camera Raw dialog box, either the stored settings associated with the raw file are automatically applied, or, if no settings are associated, the default Camera Raw settings are applied. You can also select file(s) and then Shift+Enter (Windows), Shift+Return (Mac OS)

Nonraw files will open, of course, in the application that they are associated with; for example, selecting a PSD file and then pressing Enter (Windows), Return (Mac OS) opens the file in Photoshop. Adding Alt (Windows), Opt (Mac OS) to the shortcut closes the Bridge window and opens the file.

Rating and Labeling Files for Easier Identification

If you shoot a large number of exposures, you will find the means of rating and filtering files indispensable. The method is akin to Chinagraphing contacts in the bad old, good old days of film. You can assign from 0–5 stars. To rate, use the following methods:

- Select files and then click one of the dots just below the thumbnail (Figure 4-7). If you do not see any dots, increase the thumbnail size by using the slider in the status bar. The rating ramps from left to right.

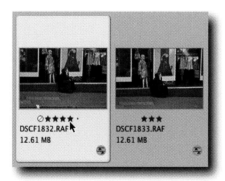

FIGURE 4-7: **Clicking the dots below the thumbnails is just one way of Rating files.**

- After selecting files, choose a rating from the Label menu.
- To increase rating, press Ctrl+Period (Windows), ⌘+Period (Mac OS).
- To decrease rating, press Ctrl+Comma (Windows), ⌘+Comma (Mac OS).
- To apply ratings in slide show mode, press Period to increase or Comma to decrease.

NOTE The rating information is stored in XMP metadata. If the file format does not support XMP metadata, the rating information gets stored in the central cache and does not travel with the file.

After you have rated files, you can view them according to rank by selecting View → Sort → By Rating. You can also filter files according to a rating. To filter, click the Filtering icon in the tool-bar and select a rating: one star, two stars, three stars, and so forth.

If rating doesn't appeal to you or you want to rank files by applying custom text, you can use color labels. To apply a label, select a file or files, right-click (Windows), Ctrl-click (Mac OS), and choose a color from the Label submenu. To peel the label off, as it were, choose No Label from the same submenu.

If you find it hard to remember the labeling by colors alone, you can add custom text to the labels. To do so, open Preferences and then select Labels from the items on offer. The labels will appear in the pane on the right. Type your preferred label in the text field (Figure 4-8) and click the OK button to apply changes.

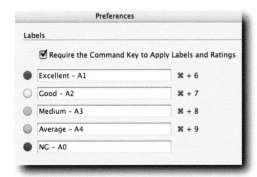

FIGURE 4-8: **Applying custom labels in the Preferences dialog box.**

Just as you can filter rated files, so can you filter labeled files. To filter, click the Filtering icon in the toolbar and select a rating or label.

Having rated and/or labeled the files, you can then filter them and view only the ones that you wish to see. Having the ability to view by rating or labeling makes sorting files easy. For example, you can mark the unusable ones, create a subfolder for them, make sure that the Folders panel is in view, select them all, and then drag them into that folder or delete them if you are absolutely sure that they are beyond redemption.

To view labeled files only, choose an item from the Label menu or click the Unfiltered icon in the toolbar and choose from the pop-up menu. The files in the contents panel will reflect your choice and the icon name will change to Filtered. To return to unfiltered view, choose Show All Items from the same menu or press Ctrl+Alt+A (Windows), ⌘+Opt+A (Mac OS). You can also use keyboard shortcuts to filter files. You will find them listed next to the menu items.

TIP When you select files, you can use the usual keyboard shortcuts to select all, Ctrl+A (Windows), ⌘+A (Mac OS). However, if you want to deselect, don't use the same combo you use in Photoshop to deselect selections; you will end up duplicating all the selected files. Instead, use Ctrl+Shift+A (Windows), ⌘+Shift+A (Mac OS). You can use the usual Shift-click method to select multiple files or noncontiguous selections with Ctrl (Windows), ⌘ (Mac OS).

Finding Files and Saving Searches

You can use Bridge to find files on your hard drive by using the Find dialog box (Figure 4-9), Edit ➜ Find. The dialog box has options for adding criteria and allows you to enter basic Boolean logic, and asterisks (*) for wild cards.

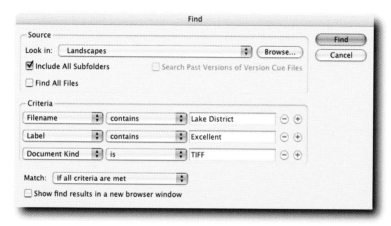

FIGURE 4-9: **The Find dialog box, showing three criteria being used to find files in a chosen folder and subfolders.**

When a search has been completed, you can save it as a Collection by clicking the Save As Selection button, located at the top-right corner of the Find Results window, just below the toolbar. To see your saved collections, select Collections in the Favorites panel and then double-click a collection to view its contents. You can also select Collections from the Look In menu in the toolbar.

When you come to save your search as a Collection, you can select Start Search From Current Folder so that when you are in the Collection and you elect to use Edit Collection, the new search will be confined to the current folder. Don't feel pressured into making the decision, though. The same option is available in the Find dialog box when and if you do decide to edit the collection.

117

By default, the search results are shown in a new browser window. Unless you know that the results will be displayed in a new browser window, it can be quite disconcerting to see all your folders disappear. If you wish to see the results in the current browser window, make sure that Show Find Results in a New Browser Window is not ticked in the Find dialog box (Figure 4-9).

Creating and Applying Keywords to Files

You can use the Keywords panel (View → Keywords Panel) to create keywords and to organize keywords into sets (Figure 4-10). Keywords can be applied to single or multiple files and used to find files on your hard drive. When the files with a shared keyword are found, they are displayed as a group, making it easy to identify them and to copy or sort into different folders.

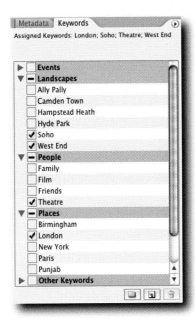

FIGURE 4-10: **The Keywords panel.**

To create a new keyword or set, click the appropriate icon in the bottom of the Keywords panel (Figure 4-10). If a set is selected beforehand, keywords are created in the selected set.

To apply keywords, select a file and then click the checkbox next to a set or single keyword. To remove keywords, select a file and then deselect the appropriate set or keyword. You can apply keywords and sets to multiple files by selecting them and then checking a set or keyword.

You can also add keywords via the Info Palette's Description pane. To open the Info dialog box, select a file and choose File ➜ File Info or press Ctrl+Alt+Shift+I (Windows), ⌘+Opt+Shift+I (Mac OS). In the dialog box, enter the words manually or paste them from a text editor and click the OK button. The added keywords appear in italics under Other Keywords in the Keywords panel in Bridge. To make the keywords persistent, right-click (Windows), Ctrl-click (Mac OS) and then select Persistent from the contextual menu or drag them into a set.

Appending and Replacing Metadata

Metadata is now being used extensively to add nonimage data to files, and such data can be anything from copyright, author, color space, or keywords to comments relating to workflow or even a history of the steps taken to create a file. The information can be used to track or find files locally, or over a network.

The metadata can be stored in the file if the format supports it; otherwise, it can be stored in an XMP sidecar file, as is the case with raw files (DNG raw files being the exception). You can view metadata in the Metadata panel for any file by selecting it in the Bridge window. Furthermore, the fields shown in the Metadata panel can be selected in Preferences ➜ Metadata.

NOTE If you select more than one file, only metadata that is common to the selected files is shown.

You have three ways of working with metadata in Bridge. You can use the Metadata panel (View ➜ Metadata Panel), the Keywords panel (View ➜ Keywords Panel), or the File Info dialog box (File ➜ File Info). All three let you enter new metadata; the Metadata and File Info panels also let you append or replace existing metadata.

To append or replace metadata, you must first create a template. You can do so in the File Info panel by entering text and then choosing Save Metadata Template from the dialog box menu (to access the menu, click the round button at the top right of the dialog box). After a template is saved, you can append or replace the existing metadata from the Metadata panel menu, the Advanced screen of the File Info dialog box, or the Tools menu.

You can append and replace metadata from single or multiple files. Simply select the file(s) in the Bridge window and then use any one of the preceding means to access the append/replace commands.

NOTE You cannot edit the metadata for File Properties or Camera Data (EXIF) in the Metadata or File Info panel. EXIF stands for Exchangeable Image File Format.

Batch Renaming Files

When you shoot digitally, the files usually have sequential names for easier sorting but not necessarily for easier identification. You can overwrite the generic names with more creative and identifiable names by group or batch, making the task of renaming hundreds of files a breeze. For example, say that you want to rename all the files in a folder so that the filenames all begin with the date of the shoot followed by the project name and then sequential numbers, and you want to preserve the original extension and the filename in XMP metadata. All this can be done in one neat dialog box (Figure 4-11). To do so, just take the following steps:

1. Select a folder in the Folders panel (if you do not select files, all the files in the folder will be renamed).

2. Choose Tools ➜ Batch Rename, or Ctrl+Shift+R (Windows), ⌘+Shift+R (Mac OS) to call up the Batch Rename dialog box.

3. Choose an option in the Destination Folder section (Rename in Same Folder is the default option).

4. Choose Text from the pop-up menu in the New Filenames section and enter the date (in the example, the sequence YYMMDD is used).

5. Add another element by clicking the plus button.

6. Choose Text again and type your project name.

7. Add another element by clicking the plus button.

8. Choose Sequence Number and Three Digits from the third pop-up menu.

9. If you are copying to another folder, select Preserve Current Filename in XMP Metadata in the Options section (the option provides good insurance for tracking the original files).

10. When you are happy with the new name, as displayed in the Preview section, click the Rename button.

Depending on the option you selected in Step 3, the files will be renamed in the same folder, moved, or copied to another folder.

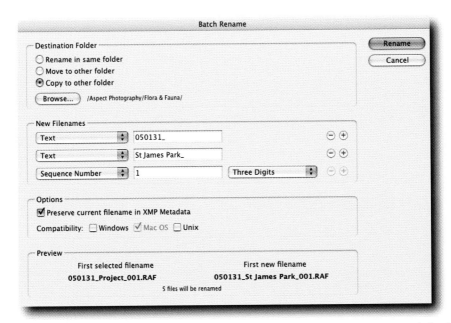

FIGURE 4-11: **Renaming and copying files to another folder using the Batch Rename dialog box.**

Viewing Quicker Previews from a CD

When you archive raw files to a CD or DVD, if you are using a centralized cache, instead of distributed, the cache you created for thumbnails and previews when you first viewed the files will not be copied to the CD. This fact results in the cache's having to be created all over again when you view the files from the CD. Likewise, if you have elected not to save the XMP metadata generated by Camera Raw as sidecar files, it, too, has to be regenerated. It all adds up to slower previews from CDs.

Consider taking the following steps to ensure speedier previews:

1. Choose Preferences ➡ Advanced ➡ Use Distributed Cache Files When Possible. This will put the caches in the folders that you are viewing, making it easier to transfer them to the CD or DVD. However, it will also put caches in every folder you view, including your desktop. That's something to be aware of before you select this option.

2. If you prefer to use a centralized cache, possibly for the preceding reason, choose Tools ➡ Cache ➡ Export Cache; doing so creates a copy of the cache in the current folder, which you can copy to the CD or DVD.

3. Elect to save XMP metadata as sidecar files in the Camera Raw Preferences dialog box so that they always travel with the raw files that they are describing. If you have elected to store Camera Raw settings in a central database because you prefer not to see sidecar files in your folders, select the raw files (maximum is 24 at a time), open them in Camera Raw, and then choose Export Settings from the Camera Raw menu. That will export the settings, which you can then copy with the raw files.

Finally, when you burn the CD, make sure that Adobe Bridge Cache.bct, Adobe Bridge Cache.bc, and sidecar (.xmp) files are all present in the same relationship to the files as on the hard disk. The sidecar and cache files are not visible by default. To see them, choose View ➡ Show Hidden Files.

Deleting the Preferences File

If Bridge starts to act unexpectedly, try deleting the Preferences file to see whether doing so cures the erratic behavior. The easiest way to go about it is to press Ctrl+Alt+Shift (Windows), ⌘+Opt+Shift (Mac OS) immediately after you launch Bridge. When the Reset Settings dialog box appears, choose Reset Preferences.

If thumbnails or previews start to play up in any way, it's best to purge the cache for the folder that's being viewed. In severe cases, you may have to try all these options. Ouch!

Summary

Though a standalone application in its own right, Bridge is an integral part of Photoshop and Camera Raw. By its close integration and viewing capabilities, it transforms the old ways of working nonvisually from a system file browser and makes the experience much more enjoyable.

If you take a little time to learn Bridge's viewing modes, file-sifting capabilities, and automating functions, you'll receive the dividends when you work on projects that require you to work with speed and precision, whether on a team or alone.

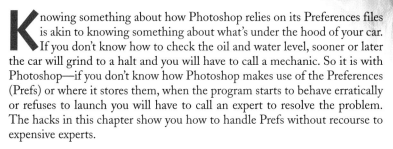

chapter **5**

Hacking Preferences and Documents

K nowing something about how Photoshop relies on its Preferences files is akin to knowing something about what's under the hood of your car. If you don't know how to check the oil and water level, sooner or later the car will grind to a halt and you will have to call a mechanic. So it is with Photoshop—if you don't know how Photoshop makes use of the Preferences (Prefs) or where it stores them, when the program starts to behave erratically or refuses to launch you will have to call an expert to resolve the problem. The hacks in this chapter show you how to handle Prefs without recourse to expensive experts.

In contrast to Prefs, which tend to lurk behind the scenes, documents are in front of you practically all the time. You are constantly creating, opening, manipulating, and saving documents. It's the staple diet of any Photoshop work. Overall, you can get by without delving too deeply into their backgrounds. However, if you want to increase your productivity and streamline your workflow, the hacks on documents in this chapter can help you.

Hacking Prefs

Photoshop, ImageReady, and Bridge all use preference files to store application settings. For example, the Adobe Photoshop CS2 Prefs file contains all the options for general display; history logs; file saving; cursor; transparency and gamut; units and rulers; guides, grids, and slices; plug-ins and scratch disks; and memory allocation. The file lives in the Adobe Photoshop CS2 Settings folder, along with a host of other files that keep track of your Preferences and settings, such as Color Settings, New Doc Sizes, and so forth. Settings for Adobe Camera Raw, Save for Web, and paths are kept separately in the Registry by Windows, whereas the Mac OS keeps them in the Preferences folder, located in the user's Library folder.

Restoring Prefs

When you are satisfied with your customizing of Photoshop, it's a good idea to save the Adobe Photoshop CS2 Settings folder. You can find the folder in the following location for Windows and Mac OS, respectively:

```
C:\Documents and Settings\Administrator or UserName\Adobe\Photoshop\
9.0\Adobe Photoshop CS2 Settings
```

```
Macintosh HD\Users\UserName\Library\Preferences\Adobe Photoshop CS2
Settings
```

To understand the rationale behind the decision to save the settings folder, you have to know how Photoshop makes use of the files and that, occasionally, you have to delete them. Each time Photoshop closes in an orderly fashion, it updates the settings files that need updating, saving any modifications that you may have made; for example, you may have added new actions or made changes to the color settings, in which case the files relating to the Actions palette and Color Settings are updated. If Photoshop quits unexpectedly, any customized settings made since Photoshop was last closed are lost. However, occasionally, even if you quit in an orderly fashion, Photoshop may start to behave erratically. If that happens to you, you have two choices: either you can delete the settings files and let Photoshop create default settings files or you can replace the files with the saved files, hence the need to save the settings folder.

To delete Prefs, take the following steps: Immediately after launching Photoshop or ImageReady, hold down Ctrl+Alt+Shift (Windows), ⌘+Opt+Shift (Mac OS). You will be presented with a dialog box (Figure 5-1); make your choice and click the OK button.

FIGURE 5-1: **The dialog box that appears when you use the modifier keys to launch Photoshop to replace the currents Prefs with factory default settings.**

If the problem disappears, you can then replace the default Prefs with the saved files and reset any Preferences that were changed since you saved the Adobe Photoshop CS2 Settings folder. If the problem returns, as it can sometimes, revert to the default settings, customize them again and then resave the settings folder.

Changing Scratch Disks and Plug-Ins at Launch Time

To select an alternative scratch disk, press Ctrl+Alt (Windows), ⌘+Opt (Mac OS) immediately after launching Photoshop.

If you have plug-ins installed in more than one folder, you can select an additional plug-ins folder by pressing Ctrl+Shift (Windows), ⌘+Shift (Mac OS) immediately after launching Photoshop.

Specifying Update Prefs

If Bridge and Photoshop irritate you when they periodically check for the latest updates, chances are you have not clicked on the Preferences button in the Adobe Updater dialog box when it has finished checking. To do so, choose Help ➜ Updates in either application and then, after the Adobe Updater has finished checking for new updates, click the Preferences button. Doing so opens the Adobe Updater Preferences dialog box (Figure 5-2). In the dialog box, you specify how you want to check for and where to download any available updates for Photoshop, Bridge, Help Center, and Stock Photos.

FIGURE 5-2: **The Adobe Updater Preferences dialog box lets you control how and when it checks for updates, where it downloads the files to, and how it deals with the installation.**

Installing Plug-Ins into a Safe Folder

Installing plug-ins into the default plug-ins folder in the Adobe Photoshop CS2 folder is quick and painless. Just point the installer to it and sit back. However, saving a little time when installing can cost a lot more time down the line. For example, when you need to reinstall Photoshop, it's easy to accidentally delete the plug-ins folder even though you had every intention of keeping it (especially on Mac OS, where dragging application folders to the Trash is a common practice). When you come to upgrade Photoshop to the next version, you may find that you have to reinstall some if not all the plug-ins because you cannot just copy them into the new version. If you do, some of them are sure to require a reinstall, owing to the name change of the top-level folder. It all adds up to a loss of time.

To avoid reinstalls and save time, you can take advantage of a little known Photoshop functionality. If you drop a shortcut (Windows) or alias (Mac OS) into any of the folders within the application folder, Photoshop can see the path and find the folder at the end of it. Therefore, by installing the plug-ins once into a designated folder away from the main Photoshop folder, creating a shortcut/alias to it, and then dropping it into the plug-ins folder, you can do away with the need to reinstall and reduce the chance of accidentally deleting the folder. You can even create shortcuts/aliases from the individual plug-ins and drop those into the plug-ins folder one at a time. That way, you can control how many plug-ins load into memory each time you launch Photoshop. Furthermore, if you don't fancy making shortcuts/aliases, you can simply choose the designated folder in Preferences ➜ Plug-Ins & Scratch Disks as the Additional Plug-Ins Folder and have Photoshop find it automatically at launch time.

Hacking Documents

Documents are what you encounter every time you open Photoshop, so it's only fitting to know as much about their mode of behavior as possible. The following hacks should help you overcome some of the problems encountered on a regular basis when creating new documents or working with open documents.

Specifying Default Resolution for New Preset Documents

When you create a new preset for a custom document size in the File ➜ New dialog box, Photoshop uses the resolution values set in the Units & Rulers screen in the Preferences dialog box. The default resolution is 300 ppi for print and 72 ppi for screen. These settings affect all presets that you select from the Preset pop-up menu in the New dialog box. If you find yourself constantly changing the resolution, you can customize the settings. To take advantage of this opportunity, open the Preference dialog box to the Units & Rulers screen and then in the New Document Preset Resolutions section, specify a resolution for Print and/or Screen. For example, if the current setting of 300 ppi is too high or too low for your desktop printer, change it to 240 or 360 ppi, or whatever. This will change the resolution of *all* your presets for documents destined for print, such as Letter, A4, and so forth. It won't affect the document presets destined for the screen, such as 640 × 480, NTSC DV 720 × 480, HDV 1280 × 720, or D4, unless, of course, you change the default 72 ppi.

Specifying Document Width in Columns

When you need to create a new document or resize an existing one to fit within the columns in a page layout program, such as InDesign or QuarkXPress, you can do it on a case-by-case basis in Photoshop. The New document, Image Size, and Canvas Size dialog boxes all support columns as a unit of measurement. This feature can prove very useful when you're creating documents for publications that use columns as their general width measurement and you need to fit images to a given column width. To set the column size, open Preferences and then in the

Units & Rulers screen, under Column Size, enter new values for Width and Gutter (the space between the columns).

Matching New Document to Existing Document

If you have a document open in Photoshop and you need to create another document with the same dimensions and color mode, you have a couple of ways of automating the process. One, choose File ➜ New and then, from the Window menu, select the opened document whose dimensions and color mode you want to match. Two, create the new document and then from the Preset pop-up menu in the New document dialog box, select the document that you want to match.

It should be noted that although the color mode of the new document is matched to the opened document, the color space is not; instead, the current working color space is assigned to the new document. To assign another color space, click the Advanced button in the dialog box and then choose a profile from the Color Profile pop-up menu. You might be tempted to choose a profile for a printer or a scanner. Resist the temptation and select a working space profile, such as Adobe RGB (1998), ColorMatch RGB, ProPhoto RGB, sRGB, and so forth. The working spaces are linearized and suitable for editing, whereas the other color spaces are more suited to converting to as a final step or for soft proofing.

Finding the Center of a Document

How many times have you needed to find the center of a document and had to resort to the calculator to find it? Here are three ways, and none requires any math:

■ Make sure that the Rulers are showing and then click Select ➜ All followed by Edit ➜ Free Transform, bring in a horizontal and a vertical guide (click a Ruler and drag into the document) so that they cross in the center, and then press Escape. The center of your document will be where the two guides cross (Figure 5-3).

■ Although there's nothing wrong with the preceding method, the following is slightly quicker if the current layer is filled completely. First, make sure that the Rulers are showing and that View ➜ Snap is turned on. Next, *slowly* drag in a horizontal guide to the center and then a vertical guide, letting go when you feel them snap to the center of the document. Where the two guides cross will be the center of your document.

You can include the preceding steps in an action, assign a keyboard function key, and find the center of any document, regardless of its dimensions, at the press of a key. Just make sure that before you start recording, or even during the recording, the unit of measure for the Rulers is set to read in *percentages* and not fixed units, such as pixels. To change the units, right-click (Windows), Ctrl-click (Mac OS) on a Ruler and choose Percentages from the contextual menu.

■ This third method doesn't require the rulers to be visible: Choose View ➜ New Guide. In the New Guide dialog box, select the Horizontal radio button, enter **50%** in the Position text field, and then click OK. Enter the dialog box a second time, select the Vertical radio button, enter 50% in the Position text field, and click the OK button. As with the previous method, you can record the steps as an action and assign a function key for quick access.

FIGURE 5-3: One method for finding the center of a document involves Selecting All, invoking the Free Transform command, bringing in vertical and horizontal guides, and then dismissing the transform.

Duplicating Documents in ImageReady on the Fly

In ImageReady, you can either duplicate an open document from the Image menu or, if you prefer something slightly faster, hold down Alt (Windows), Opt (Mac OS) and then drag the Show Original Image tab or the Show Optimized Image tab in the document window. When you see an outline of the window, release the tab to have ImageReady create a perfect duplication of the document (Figure 5-4).

Comparing Documents for Differences

Sometimes you need to compare two files that might look identical when opened but that you suspect differ in some minor detail. You can do this in Photoshop without having to rely on visual feedback. To do so, take the following steps:

1. Open the two files that you want to compare.

2. Select the Move tool.

FIGURE 5-4: Duplicating a document in ImageReady by dragging a tab.

3. Working in the document windows, drag the contents of one file into the other by pressing Shift (holding down the Shift key will ensure that the content of the two files "pin registers"). For best results, the two documents need to have the same pixel dimensions.

4. Change the blend mode of the top layer (the one you just dragged) to Difference.

5. Merge the two layers either by using the shortcut keys of Ctrl+E (Windows), ⌘+E (Mac OS) or choosing Merge Visible or Flatten from the Layers palette menu.

6. Close the original.

At this stage, you can simply hover the mouse cursor over the image and see whether the color readings change in the Info palette. However, to be absolutely sure, you can let Photoshop do the work by choosing Image ➜ Adjustments ➜ Equalize. If the two images are exactly the same, Photoshop will warn that it cannot equalize because the image contains only one brightness value. If there is a difference, it will be accentuated and you should be able to see it (Figure 5-5).

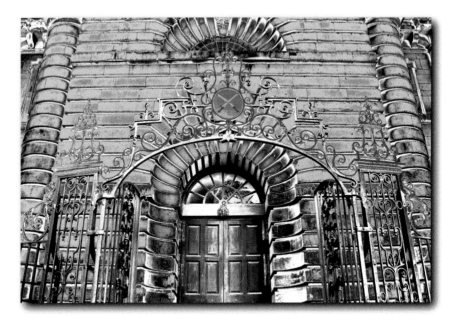

FIGURE 5-5: **Comparing two documents for dissimilarity by using the Difference layer mode followed by the Equalize command.**

Opening a Composite Version of a Layered Document

Sometimes it can be useful to open a composite version of a layered document—especially if it contains hundreds of layers and may take eons to open and you need only to do some quick retouching or editing that doesn't require layers. To do so, hold down Alt+Shift (Windows), Opt+Shift (Mac OS) while clicking the Open button in the Open dialog box (the button and dialog box might be named differently depending on your platform). You can also hold down the same modifier keys and double-click a thumbnail in Bridge or select File ➜ Open.

One small caveat: The file must have been saved with a composite layer or Photoshop can show you only the following warning in four different languages: "This layered Photoshop file was not saved with a composite image." If you change your mind and decide to open the layered file, just click the Cancel button.

Adding Canvas Size

The Canvas Size command, located in the Image menu, enables you to increase or decrease the document dimensions in any one of eight configurations, as well as equally on all four sides. To increase size, enter new units in the Width and Height text fields. To decrease size, add the minus sign before the figure.

If your current canvas size is an odd size, for example, 12496 × 1689 pixels, and you want to increase/decrease the size by a known number of pixels, select the Relative checkbox and then add the figure in the text appropriate field. Sometimes this action can be faster than searching for a calculator or trying to do the math in your head.

Adding Text and Audio Annotations

When you work in a collaborative environment and need to hand off complex files, you can protect your back by adding text notes or audio annotations (Figure 5-6). In the same vein, you can include information to remind yourself while working on a document that may take days or even weeks to edit.

FIGURE 5-6: **A nonprintable note added as a reminder that the file has been targeted for newsprint.**

The notes are nonprintable and can be placed anywhere on the canvas or the document window: right in the middle to make people take note (pun intended) or in one corner of the canvas so that it's unobtrusive. You can collapse the note window by clicking the Close button on the grab bar and expand it again by double-clicking on the note icon. The notes can be read and annotations heard in Photoshop and Acrobat.

To add an annotation, select the Notes tool from the Toolbox, click in the document window, and then select options as required:

1. Enter an author name or other text. The text will appear in the title bar of the notes window.

2. Choose a font size from the pop-up menu.

3. Select a color for the title bar; this will also be used for the note and audio annotation icon.

4. Click in the note window and type your message; you can compose your message in a text editor if it's long, perform a spell check, and then paste it.

To add an audio annotation:

1. Make sure that a suitable microphone is plugged into the audio-in port of your computer and that it's working.

2. Select the Audio Annotation tool, click in the document window, and then select options as required (see preceding list).

3. Click in the document window and then select Start in the Audio Annotations dialog box. When you have finished, click the Stop button.

Notes and Audio Annotations may also be imported from a PDF or FDF (Form Data Format) file. To load, choose File ➔ Import ➔ Annotations and then click the Load button.

NOTE Although resizing an image does not affect annotation icons or the note windows, other than to reposition them relatively, cropping an image moves any annotations outside the canvas area.

Saving Files

You would think that saving files would be dead easy: Select Save and click OK. If only it were that simple. There are a few gotchas that can, well, get you. The following hacks show you how to avoid some of them, as well as how to include, exclude, and, should you need to, prevent unauthorized access to your files.

Failsafe Way of Including a Background Layer

Background layers are essential in some workflows because not all applications can read a Photoshop layered file. However, they will read a PSD file provided that it has the image on the Background layer or that Maximize PSD File Compatibility is turned on in Preferences (it will increase the file size and take longer to save, and that can be a big minus). Programs that cannot read features, such as adjustment layers, effects, and so forth, will ignore them and use only the composite version. If you are flattening files, it's a good idea to fall into a workflow that minimizes the chances of your making mistakes. For example, you can create an action that duplicates documents and then flattens the duplicate for output, thus ensuring that the master layered files are kept out of harm's way.

You can also make any layer into a Background layer from the Layer ➜ New submenu. If your data is spread over lots of layers, stamp them all into a new layer and then convert that layer into a Background layer. To stamp all visible layers into one layer, Ctrl+Alt+Shift+E (Windows), ⌘+Opt+Shift+E (Mac OS).

Saving in Large Document Format

If the file you are working on grows beyond 4GB (the maximum file size supported by the TIFF and PSD formats) and you want to save all the Photoshop features, such as adjustment layers, vector data, and so forth, you can save your document in the large document PSB file format. PSB supports documents up to 300,000 pixels in both directions. The one downside of saving in this format is that you can open it only in Photoshop CS or Photoshop CS2. To save in PSB format, select the Enable Large Document Format (.psb) option in the File Handling screen in Preferences.

Password Protecting Files

Do you need to send a file to a client but don't want the client to make changes to it or print it? Save the file as a PDF and then, in the Save Adobe PDF dialog box, limit the permissions. To do so, choose File ➜ Save As and then from the Save Type As (Windows), Format (Mac OS) dialog box, choose Photoshop PDF. In the Save Adobe PDF dialog box, select Security from the options and then select the options for Security and Permissions. You can require the recipient to use a password to open the document, print it, make changes to it, copy it, or extract data from it.

Appending File Extensions Automatically

Are you a Windows user? Do you constantly receive Macintosh-originated files that have either an incorrect file extension or no extension appended to the filename? Have a word with the senders and point out to them the options for automatically appending extensions. They can be found in Preferences ➜ File Handling. The three available options are Never, Always, and Ask When Saving. Chances are they have the Never option selected because extensions are not needed by the Mac OS in the same way as they are by Windows.

Saving Previews

The default settings for image previews in the File Handling screen of Preferences always create an icon and a thumbnail and then embed them in your file (Figure 5-7). This is so that utilities such as Explorer (Windows) and Finder (Mac OS) can show an icon-sized preview and a thumbnail-size preview to help you locate the right files on your hard drive.

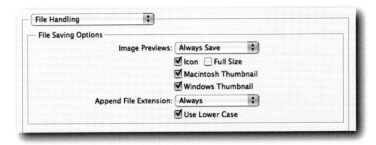

FIGURE 5-7: **In the File Handling section of Preferences, you can choose how you want to save previews with your file.**

You can change the Preferences to include a full-sized preview along with the icon and the thumbnail. This option adds a compressed JPEG that can be used by third-party image browsers, such as ACDSee, IrfanView (Windows), iView MediaPro (Mac OS), and so forth. Because it has the same dimensions as the image, it can add considerably to the file size, and you may wish to leave this option off unless you see the benefits in your third-party application.

You can also choose not to include an icon or a thumbnail if you so wish by setting the Image Previews option to Never Save, or Ask When Saving. When you choose the latter option, you are given the choice in Windows to embed a thumbnail and on Mac OS an icon and or a thumbnail.

Reverting an Accidentally Saved Document

If you have accidentally pressed Ctrl+S (Windows), ⌘+S (Mac OS) when you meant to do a Select All, or meant to press another key combo, don't despair or throw your keyboard across the room. All is not lost. To undo any consequential damage:

- Select a previous history state in the history palette, do a save, and then select the last history state to get back to where you were before the accidental save—this is one good reason for selecting Allow Non-Linear History in the History palette options.

- Select the first snapshot to revert to the open document state, do a save, and then select the last history state. This recourse is available only if you have selected Automatically Create First Snapshot from the History palette options (see later in this section).

Unfortunately, if you applied any color management settings when you opened the file and then saved it, there is no way of reverting to the state it was in before you opened it. For instance, if you assigned a profile or converted it to your working color space, selecting a history state or snapshot won't revert the file back to the original state. After you have saved, accidentally or in order to revert to the original, the file on disk will be overwritten and include the changes made to the color in the Missing Profile or Embedded Profile Mismatch dialog box. This is because Photoshop bases the first snapshot on the opened document state and not the state of the file on disk.

Although the Automatically Create First Snapshot option eats into your Photoshop RAM allocation, especially if the document happens to be a large document, in 16-Bits/Channel mode, or both, it's a good tradeoff if you can spare the RAM or put up with Photoshop writing to scratch disk earlier than it would otherwise. As pointed out previously, a first snapshot can pull you out of the mire when you have to revert to the opening state at any time during an editing session, or when you have to revert elements to the opening state by using the History Brush tool (you can do the latter as long as you haven't rotated or resized the document since it was opened).

To turn the Automatically Create First Snapshot option on/off, select History Options from the History palette menu and then choose Automatically Create First Snapshot from the pop-up dialog box. Click OK.

Removing Camera (EXIF) Metadata

Digitally captured images include camera EXIF data that applications and plug-ins can use to process and correct images, such as autocorrecting distortion or vignetting. However, having made use of the data, you will have occasions when you do not want to impart this data to a client. That's when you discover Photoshop refusing point-blank to edit the metadata categories for Camera Data 1 and Camera Data 2 or to exclude the categories when you come to save the file. Together, the categories can include the make of camera and model, date/time when you made the capture, shutter speed, aperture value, ISO speed rating, focal length, lens type, and other data that you may consider too sensitive to divulge.

Although Photoshop may not let you edit the EXIF data, you can strip it from the file altogether. You can do this by using Save for Web, but the problem is that you are limited to saving the image as a JPEG or PNG-24 and will need to open it and save it again if you wish to send it in another format. Furthermore, depending on your resources and the size of the document, large documents may take too long to preview when you enter the dialog box.

Another method involves a little workaround and goes like this:

1. Open the document containing the camera EXIF data.

2. In the File Info dialog box, save any info other than the EXIF data: Select the Advanced option and then click the Save button at the base of the dialog box.

3. Create a new document and make sure that it has the same dimensions as the document on which you are working. To do that, go to File ➜ New and then, from the Preset pop-up menu, select the working document. If the two documents are in different color spaces, click the Advanced button and then choose a color profile from the pop-up menu.

4. Select the Move tool, hold down the Shift key, click in the working document's window, and drag and drop into the new document's window. (If the working document is composed of multiple layers, you will either have to select or link the layers first or flatten the file—and if you flatten the file, make sure that you do not save it!)

5. In the File Info dialog box, load the information that you saved earlier as an .xmp file.

6. Save the new document.

Should you need to exclude the EXIF data from a number of files, the preceding steps can be included in an action and used in a Batch action. Rather than use the drag-and-drop method, use Select All and then copy and paste into the new document. If the data is spread over several layers, use the Copy Merged command. You can add a step to purge the clipboard if the files are large and RAM is limited.

Summary

Knowing something about Prefs and Photoshop's reliance on them will definitely help you get out of sticky situations without having to wait for expensive answers on the end of telephone lines. Being able to replace the Photoshop CS2 Settings folder with a saved version can also save time when the program starts to behave erratically. Don't wait to save it until you have a need for it.

Knowing some of the peculiarities of creating, viewing, and saving documents, such as appending file extensions automatically, password protecting, adding annotations, and so forth, can all aid in small and large ways to streamline a workflow. The hacks included in this chapter should go a considerable way toward helping you save time, effort, and wasted energy.

chapter **6**

Working with Layers

Photoshop uses layers to construct and deconstruct a composition in much the same way as old-style animators used to do. Whereas they drew elements onto clear acetate sheets and then aligned the sheets in registers to form a composite, Photoshop places elements on their own layers and then forms a composite preview of the elements on the fly.

Because you are effectively painting and drawing on "clear sheets" when you work in Photoshop, you can see through the nonpainted parts of the layers, and not only to the layer below but all the way to the background. It makes for a very versatile method of working on complex images that require minor or major adjustments, and one that permits an almost literally infinite number of changes and still permits access to the original content.

If you want to work effectively in Photoshop, it pays to learn as much about layers as you can possibly stomach. It's no exaggeration to say that layers are the foundation on which image editing is based. Therefore, the more knowledge you have at your fingertips, the more inclined you will be to think laterally and find ingenious ways to adjust and manipulate images. Think of it this way: The more comfortable you feel about working on an image without thinking twice about the technical aspects, the easier you will find the whole process of creating, manipulating, and editing images.

in this chapter

- ○ Creating new layers
- ○ Managing layers
- ○ Editing layers
- ○ Blending layers
- ○ Importing and exporting layers

Creating Layers

By default, new documents always contain a single Background layer, as do newly acquired scans and digital captures. However, you can easily create additional layers when the document is open in Photoshop. RAM and disk size permitting, you can create up to a maximum of 8,000 layers, enough to satisfy the needs of the most ardent layers fan.

With the option of creating so many layers, Photoshop provides a means of organizing them into neat sets. You can do that by creating a group and then herding the layers into the group (manually or automatically). If you need to compact the layers still further, you can nestle the groups within new groups, up to five levels deep, in fact.

Above or Below Current Layer

When you create a new layer, it's always created above the currently active layer or layer group. That makes perfect sense after you understand how the stacking order affects the appearance of a composition: Opaque pixels on a layer hide pixels on the layers below. However, at times you need to do the senseless thing and create a layer below the active layer. So, how do you set about creating a new layer below the currently active layer? Most people create the new layer above the active layer, or group, and then drag it to the position they want it to adopt in the stack in the first place. There is, as always, a neater and more elegant way and this one does it in one step. When you click the New Layer button in the Layers palette, press Ctrl (Windows), ⌘ (Mac OS). That's it! The new layer will be created below the currently active layer. If the currently active layer is the Background layer, you must first convert it to a normal layer because layers cannot exist below the Background layer (see next segment).

Background Layer from a Normal Layer

A Background layer differs in as much as it does not support transparency. This can be a good thing and, at times, a bad thing. Regardless, there are times when you need to create a background layer from a normal layer. Rather than go through hoops, simply select the layer and then choose Layer ➔ New ➔ Background from Layer, or double-click the layer and then click the OK button in the New Layer dialog box. The layer can be anywhere in the stack. It does not necessarily have to be at the bottom of the stack.

Single Layer from Multiple Layers

When image content is spread over several layers, at times you need to have it on one layer, without flattening the image (see note below) and losing all the advantages of working on separate layers. For example, you might want to apply a filter, such as Smart Sharpen, or you might want to amalgamate several shapes or types of layers into one and apply a Layer Style. Then again, having applied a style, you might want to rasterize the effects and merge them into a copy of the layer they were applied to. In the past, you had to create a new layer and then merge the visible content into it. Not anymore; you can now do it in one step.

To merge visible layers into a new layer, make sure that the layers whose content you want to merge are the only ones that are visible (click the eyeball icon to turn off visibility). Select the layer above which you would like Photoshop to create the merged layer and then press Ctrl+Alt+Shift+E (Windows), ⌘+Opt+Shift+E (Mac OS).

NOTE Flattening an image merges all visible layers into a Background layer. The process also discards hidden layers and fills transparent areas with white. To flatten layers, choose Flatten Image from the Layers menu or the Layers palette menu. It can help to view the image at 100% magnification when the command is applied; otherwise, the preview may appear to change.

NOTE If no layers are selected, and this is possible now, the merged layer will be created at the top of the stack. If you have a large number of layers, that's where you should look for it.

Adjustment Layers

One feature that Photoshop supports that the old-style animators would have given their right arm for (actually not that big a sacrifice when you realize that most artists are left-handed anyway!) is adjustment sheets, or adjustment layers to use Photoshop terminology.

Adjustment layers behave just as normal layers do: You can turn off their visibility, alter their opacity, create a clipping mask, or change their blend mode. However, the biggest advantage to using adjustment layers, as opposed to the commands in the Image → Adjustments submenu, comes from their capacity to store settings and apply them only once, as and when required. Before their advent, people went through any number of hoops to edit layers and retain the original data.

Adjustment layers work by applying changes to a layer, or layers, without altering the values of the pixels in the layers they are affecting. Instead, any changes you apply via an adjustment layer are stored and their effect displayed as a preview. When you are ready, you can merge the adjustment layers with the underlying layers and, at that stage, the stored values are applied to the normal underlying layers and their pixel values altered to match the preview. Adjustment layers are applied automatically to the image when you flatten it, save it in a format that doesn't support layers, or send it to your desktop printer.

By default, when you click the Create New Fill or Adjustment button in the Layers palette, new Adjustment layers are created above the active layer and affect all layers below them in the stack. That's all well and fine if you want to affect every layer below the active layer, but suppose you don't. You have a choice. You can choose not to use the button and instead choose from the Layer → New Adjustment Layer submenu, or you can hold down Alt (Windows), Opt (Mac OS) before you click the Create New Fill or Adjustment button. Both methods will bring up the New Layer dialog box (Figure 6-1). When the dialog box is open, select Use Previous Layer to Create Clipping Mask. Doing so ensures that the settings in the Adjustment layer affect only the layer that was active and not any layers below it in the stack.

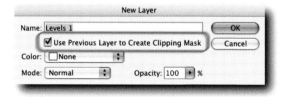

FIGURE 6-1: **New Layer dialog box with the option Use Previous Layer to Create Clipping Mask selected.**

139

Groups from Multiple Layers

The old layer sets have gone . . . well, not really; they have transmogrified into groups. Layer sets, in case you weren't aware, were used to organize layers. Now when you have too many layers cluttering up the Layers palette or you want to move a cluster of layers up and down the stack together, you can group them. Here are a few things you should know about grouping layers.

- **To group layers**—Select the layers and then choose New Group from Layers from the Layers palette menu. Enter a name in the New Group from Layers dialog box (Figure 6-2) or do it later in the Layers palette by double-clicking the default name. You can give the group a color to identify it visually and change the blend mode, if necessary (of course, you can do both later on in the Layers palette as well). Alternatively, if you don't want to see the dialog box, Ctrl+G (Windows), ⌘+G (Mac OS).

- **To delete group and contents**—Select the group, hold down Alt (Windows), Opt (Mac OS), and choose Delete Group from the palette. Alternatively, select the group and then Alt-click (Windows), Opt-click (Mac OS) on the Trash icon, or drag the group to it.

- **To ungroup only**—Select the group, hold down Ctrl+Alt (Windows), ⌘+Opt (Mac OS), and then select Delete Group from the palette menu. Alternatively, select the group and then Ctrl+Alt-click (Windows), ⌘+Opt-click (Mac OS) on the Trash icon, or drag the group to it. Doing so deletes the grouping without affecting the content.

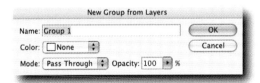

FIGURE 6-2: **The New Group from Layers dialog box.**

Smart Objects

A *Smart Object* is simply a container for holding a composite version of a raster or vector file. When the Smart Object is modified in the originating application and saved, Photoshop updates the embedded composite in line with the modifications. For example, you can create a composite version of an Illustrator vector file as a Smart Object and have it update automatically each time you make changes to the file in Illustrator.

You can create a Smart Object by *placing* a file or by converting an existing layer. When you place a file in a document, it's automatically converted to a Smart Object for you, and the layer thumbnail changes to indicate that the layer now contains a Smart Object (Figure 6-3). Similarly, when you convert an existing layer to a Smart Object, though the only visible indication is the change in the thumbnail, the content is wrapped inside a container, ready for you to open and apply edits.

FIGURE 6-3: **The Layers palette, showing a normal layer and a thumbnail icon indicating a Smart Object.**

NOTE   Because a file or a layer is being embedded in the document, the file size can increase proportionally, so it's something that you need to be aware of.

Smart Objects can be created and modified as follows:

- To create a Smart Object from a layer, select the layer and then choose Layer ➜ Smart Objects ➜ Group into New Smart Object, or choose the same command from the palette menu.

- To create a Smart Object for a placed file, first choose File ➜ Place. Next, locate the file, resize the composite data, and press Enter (Windows), Return (Mac OS).

- To replace a Smart Object, first select the layer containing a Smart Object. Next, choose Layer ➜ Smart Objects ➜ Replace Content and then locate the file on your hard drive.

- To edit the layer containing a Smart Object, first, double-click its thumbnail, edit the Smart Object when it opens as a document, and then save it. Next, select the parent document to apply the changes.

If you intend to transform a layer but you are not sure whether it will be transformed again, create a Smart Object; then, you can resize it as many times as you like without fear of losing quality, provided that you do not resize beyond its original pixel dimensions. This way of working requires thinking ahead but can bring enormous benefits when, for example, you're showing soft proofs to a client whose mind might not be made up yet, or you are creating composites and want the freedom to change your mind.

TIP When you edit a Smart Object created from a layer by double-clicking it, the child document that opens has its own history states, independent of those of the parent document. You can take advantage of this feature to revert the Smart Object while keeping any edits that you may have made to the parent document since the Smart Object was created.

NOTE You might have noticed that when you try to edit a layer containing a Smart Object, a number of commands are not available. The commands are available only for the Smart Object. They also become available for editing the layer after the layer is rasterized. However, then the layer will lose its connection with the Smart Object and be effectively demoted back to a normal layer. To take advantage of the added functionality provided by a Smart Object, always double-click the thumbnail and then apply the commands to the Smart Object. Should you need to rasterize the layer, you can do so by selecting the layer containing the Smart Object and then choosing Layer → Smart Objects → Convert to Layer; alternatively, Right-click (Windows), Ctrl-click (Mac OS) on the layer tile and choose Rasterize Layer from the contextual menu.

Layer Comps

When you need to show different versions of a work in progress to your clients, you could create multiple versions and then view them as a slide show from Bridge. However, trying to keep track of all the different versions, incorporating the client's comments, and creating modified files and then another slide show can become tiresome and lead to errors. A much better option is to create Layer Comps. You can quickly cycle through them and keep comments in the file by using Annotations. What's more, the Layer Comps are saved with the master file so that you can update them or view them at your convenience. If your client can't come to you, you can export the Layer Comps as a slide show by saving it as a PDF presentation or as a Web Photo Gallery.

To create a Layer Comp, peg the view that you would like to capture as a composition. In the Layer Comps palette (Window → Layer Comps), click the Create New Layer Comp button in the bottom of the palette. When the New Layer Comp dialog box appears (Figure 6-4), select the options that you want to include:

- **Visibility**—Refers to layer visibility.

- **Position**—Refers to the position of the layer in the document.

- **Appearance (Layer Style)**—Refers to any applied layer style and its blend mode.

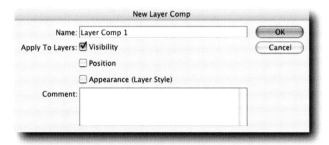

FIGURE 6-4: The New Layer Comp dialog box.

Enter any comments in the Comment text box and click the OK button. Repeat for different compositions.

To create a PDF presentation, choose File ➜ Scripts ➜ Layer Comps to PDF. Click the Browse button in the Layer Comps to PDF dialog box and choose a location to save the PDF. Check the boxes as required and then click Run to create the PDF presentation (Figure 6-5).

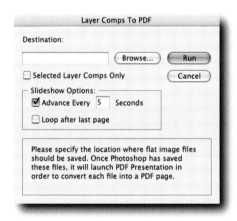

FIGURE 6-5: The Layer Comps to PDF dialog box.

To create a Web Photo Gallery, choose File ➜ Scripts ➜ Layer Comps to WPG and select from the options presented (see Chapter 18).

While you're working on the document, if a caution icon appears next to the Layer Comp name, it means that a Layer Comp cannot be updated because you have deleted merged a layer, converted it to a background, or converted to another color mode.

Managing Layers

In an ideal world, Photoshop would read your mind and do all the mundane work behind the scenes so that you could concentrate on creating masterpieces. Unfortunately, we live in an imperfect world and sometimes have no option but to perform the mundane tasks ourselves; such as selecting layers, moving them, or protecting the content from being accidentally altered. The Layers palette contains some buttons and commands to help you manage layers, but, unfortunately, it can't read your mind—yet. However, you can employ keyboard shortcuts to add a bit of spice to the humdrum routines. The next sections discuss the various options on offer for managing layers.

Showing/Hiding Multiple Layers

As you work on a multilayered document, you will want to turn off the visibility of some layers to see how a layer or layers interact or to create variations of the composition you are working on. For example, you might have a button with layer effects applied on one layer and three text layers with different names for each button state, such as normal, over, and down. By turning off layer effects and text layers in various combinations, you can view the different states and save each one by using slices or Layer Comps, without having to duplicate layers.

Toggling the visibility for single layers is obvious and straightforward; simply click the eye icon next to the layer thumbnail. However, what is not so obvious is that you also toggle the visibility of multiple layers by holding down Alt (Windows), Opt (Mac OS) and then clicking the same visibility icon. This feature can be very helpful in many situations.

When you have grouped layers and the groups are nestled, you can hide the actual tiles by clicking the triangles to the left of the folder icon. That again is obvious and straightforward, but what is not so obvious is if you hold down Alt (Windows), Opt (Mac OS) and click the triangle at the top of a group, all the nestled groups will close. In contrast, holding down Ctrl+Alt (Windows), ⌘+Opt (Mac OS) will close the top-level group and all the layers in the nestled groups.

If you have created a clipping group and wish to see just the layers in the group, Alt-click (Windows), Opt-click (Mac OS) on the layer that is being clipped (that is, the top layer in the group).

Renaming Layers

Although text layers are named automatically and you have the option of naming new layers, you still face occasions when you need to rename a layer or layer group. You have two ways of renaming a layer or a group. One, double-click the name itself and enter new text. Two, hold down Alt (Windows), Opt (Mac OS) and double-click the layer tile. This will bring up the Layer Properties dialog box and allow you to rename and to assign a color (see next section) in one go (Figure 6-6).

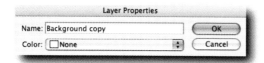

FIGURE 6-6: You can rename and assign a color to a
layer in the Layer Properties dialog box.

Adding Color to Layer Tiles

Sometimes you can create so many layers that it can be difficult to spot the one you are after
while quickly scrolling the tiles up and down. Although this might not be the case very often
when you manipulate images, it soon becomes the norm when you work on documents containing 40–50 layers. When you are faced with that many layers, organizing them into groups is
essential. However, you can speed up your workflow by colorizing layers and thereby making it
easier to find them in the Layers palette when you scroll up and down.

To colorize a layer or group, Right-click (Windows), Ctrl-click (Mac OS) on the visibility icon
and select a preset color from the pop-up menu (Figure 6-7).

FIGURE 6-7: Assigning a color to a
layer for easier identification.

145

Unlocking a Background Layer

The Background layer is a lion among layers. It just will not let you manipulate it in the same way that you can manipulate normal layers. Before you can apply transforms, you must unlock it. Similarly, to apply filters, tools, and commands that require the layers to support transparency, you have to sneak up on it and convert it to a normal layer; that is, one that supports transparency. Fortunately, unlike taming a lion, unlocking and converting a Background layer to a normal layer does not require the same Herculean effort.

To unlock a layer, choose Layer ➔ New ➔ Layer from Background, or simply double-click its thumbnail in the Layers palette (you can double-click a clear section of the tile as well) and either type a name in the New Layer dialog box when it appears or press Enter (Windows), Return (Mac OS). If you do not care to give the layer a name, hold down Alt (Windows), Opt (Mac OS) as you double-click to bypass the dialog box.

Protecting Layer Content

Having worked on a layer or group extensively, you might want to protect the content partially or wholly from being painted or edited. You can do this in three ways:

- To lock a single layer, click the appropriate icons just above the layer stack in the Layers palette
- Choose Layer ➔ Lock All Layers in Group (Figure 6-8)
- Choose Lock All Layers in Group from the palette menu

FIGURE 6-8: **Lock All Layers in Group dialog box.**

TIP If you want to unlock multiple layers, select them and then choose Lock Layers from the Layer menu or the Layers palette menu. Although the icons in the Layers palette will not lock/unlock multiple selected layers, the menu commands will.

Selecting Layers and Groups

With the last few upgrades, Photoshop has become more and more of an object-oriented program. The most recent leap affects layers. It used to be well nigh impossible to select multiple layers and then work on them or manage them in the Layers palette. This impediment has now been removed.

You can select multiple layers by using the normal selection methods. For example, you can Ctrl-click (Windows), ⌘-click (Mac OS) to make noncontiguous selections or to take layers out of a selection. You can Shift-click to make contiguous selections and then use Ctrl (Windows), ⌘ (Mac OS) to take layers out of the selection.

Furthermore, you can select all the layers, including groups, by choosing Select ➜ All Layers or Ctrl+Alt+A (Windows), ⌘+Opt+A (Mac OS). Having selected all, you can then deselect some layers using Ctrl (Windows), ⌘ (Mac OS). Sometimes, this method can prove quicker for selecting multiple noncontiguous layers.

Unfortunately, Photoshop has no default keyboard shortcut for deselecting all layers, but you can always assign one in Edit ➜ Keyboard Shortcuts if you select layers often. You could try Ctrl+Alt+Shift (Windows), ⌘+Opt+Shift (Mac OS). It sits neatly with the previously mentioned shortcut for selecting layers and, therefore, should be easy to remember. You can also deselect all layers by clicking an empty space beneath the layer stack in the Layers palette.

You can also select individual layers using keyboard shortcuts. (See Table 6-1.) This can be very useful if you are using keyboard shortcuts to do other work on layers. It means that you do not have to alternate between the mouse, or pen and pad, and the keyboard.

Table 6-1: Keyboard Shortcuts for Selecting Individual Layers

To	Press (Windows)	Press (Mac OS)
Select the layer above the currently active layer	Alt+]	Opt+]
Select the layer below the currently active layer	Alt+[	Opt+[
Select the topmost layer	Alt+Period	Opt+Period
Select the bottommost layer	Alt+Comma	Opt+Comma
Consecutively select layers above the currently active layer	Alt+Shift+]	Opt+Shift+]
Consecutively select layers below the currently active layer	Alt+Shift+[	Opt+Shift+[
Select all layers above the currently active layer	Alt+Shift+Period	Opt+Shift+Period
Select all layers below the currently active layer	Alt+Shift+Comma	Opt+Shift+Comma

The first two shortcuts in Table 6-1 also allow you to cycle through the stack.

Selecting Layers Automatically

The Move tool has had an Auto Select Layer option going back a number of releases. When elected, it does what it says on the package: It enables the Move tool to automatically select the layer, provided that the pixels under the pointer have more than 50% opacity. However, it's a much underused option and possibly rightly so because it can land you in deep water by moving content that you didn't mean to move—especially if you happen to be working in full screen mode when you might not discover the erroneous move well into the editing session. Ouch!

Here are three alternatives that are safer to use and almost as quick, though they require you to learn keyboard shortcuts. The first alternative is to select the Move tool (M), hold down Ctrl (Windows), ⌘ (Mac OS), and then click a 50% opaque pixel. The second alternative is to Right-click (Windows), Ctrl-click (Mac OS) the content and choose the layer from the contextual menu. The third alternative doesn't require you to select the Move tool or make a choice from the contextual menu but requires you to hold down more keys: Ctrl+Alt+Right-click (Windows), ⌘+Opt+Ctrl-click (Mac OS).

What happens in fact when you use the last alternative is that the contextual menu is still being used, but because you have hidden it by holding down Alt (Windows), Opt (Mac OS) and said OK to the first named layer on the menu (usually the one under the pointer) by clicking, it feels like an alternative method. Whatever happens under the hood, it still is probably the most versatile method because you don't have to select the Move tool or make a choice in the contextual menu.

Moving Layers Up and Down the Stack

Moving layers up and down the stack is a common requirement when you're editing images. However, moving them in tandem in the past required that you put them into sets, or groups as they are now called, before you could move them together. Now all that's required is to select the layers, move them up or down the stack with the pointer, and drop them below or above a layer.

To move the layer above the currently selected layer, you can press Ctrl+] (Windows), ⌘+] (Mac OS). To move the layer below the currently active layer, press Ctrl+[(Windows), ⌘+[(Mac OS). To move a layer to the top or the bottom of a stack, add the Shift key to the preceding key combination. Of course, these keyboard shortcuts do not allow you to move a layer below the Background layer.

Linking Layers and Groups

Linking layers allows you to apply commands simultaneously to more than one layer or group. After they're linked, you can move, align and distribute, and transform (though not warp) layer content as if it were a single object.

Although the effect is similar to selecting multiple layers, which you couldn't do prior to this version of Photoshop, the effect differs in as much as the links remain in force even when the layers have been deselected.

You gain other benefits from linking layers and sets. When you select one of the linked layers, all the layers in the chain are automatically selected, whereas with selecting you have to reselect each layer again. Having linked layers makes it easy to reselect the same set of layers repeatedly by just selecting one layer. You can also create sets of linked layers. For example, link layers one, three, five and create another linked set from two, four, six, and so forth. Unfortunately, just in case you try to search for such indications, you'll find no visual clues to tell you that a layer belongs in set *x* or *y*.

You can link layers in one of several ways after you have selected two or more layers. You can:

- Click the "Link layers" icon in the bottom of the Layers palette.
- Choose Link Layers from the Layer menu.
- Choose Link Layers from the palette menu.
- Right-click (Windows), Ctrl-click (Mac OS) on one of the selected layer tiles and choose from the contextual menu.
- Ctrl+Right-click (Windows), ⌘+Ctrl-click (Mac OS) on the image content and choose Link Layers from the contextual menu.

You can select all linked layers in a set to work on them collectively. Doing so also makes it easy to unlink all the linked layers in a set in one go, as opposed to scrolling the layers, selecting the linked layers one by one, and then unlinking them.

NOTE Selecting all linked layers does not mean all linked layers, just the layers linked to the active layer. So, if you have two or three sets of linked layers, you have to invoke the command two or three times.

To select all linked layers, select one in the chain and then choose one of the following methods.

- Choose Select Linked Layers from the Layer menu.
- Choose Select Linked Layers from the palette menu.
- Right-click (Windows), Ctrl-click (Mac OS) on the layer tile and then choose Select Linked Layers.
- Right-click (Windows), Ctrl-click (Mac OS) in the image window and choose Select Linked Layers from the contextual menu.

Unlinking Single Layers

To take a layer out of a linked set, select it and then click the Link Layers icon at the bottom of the Layers palette. You can also break the links temporarily between a layer and the set by Shift-clicking the link icon on the layer tile, not the one at the bottom of the Layers palette. The icon will change to include a red cross to indicate that the link is temporarily disabled. Click again to enable the link.

Editing Layers

Having the ability to compose an image on separate layers, or to break down an existing image into component parts and put each part on its own separate layer, provides endless alternatives for editing the various elements that make up the image. It makes editing each element separately possible (unless, of course, you specifically want to do otherwise) and, when you're satisfied with the result, to merge the various elements seamlessly into a single layer for output. The following section looks at the means at your disposal for editing layers and some of the methods and techniques used to make the process more palatable.

Aligning and Distributing Layer Content

Making collages, images bound for the Web or for multimedia output, can often require you to align or distribute content that has been spread over different layers. You can use the clunky method of creating guides and grids and then employing the Move tool to place the content, or use more graceful, easier and, overall, more accurate methods. One such method involves the Move tool and its options (Figure 6-9); the other involves commands available from the Layer ➜ Align and Distribute submenus.

A B C D E F G H I J K L

FIGURE 6-9: The align and distribute buttons on the options bar. The options are from left to right:
A—Align top edges. B—Align vertical centers.
C—Align bottom edges. D—Align left edges.
E—Align horizontal centers. F—Align right edges.
G—Distribute top edges. H—Distribute vertical centers.
I—Distribute bottom edges. J—Distribute left edges.
K—Distribute horizontal centers. L—Distribute right edges.

Before you can use either method, you need to link the layers that you want to either align or distribute, or select them in the Layers palette. Note that to distribute content, you must select a minimum of three layers. After the layers have been linked or selected, the commands become available to you. Then it's just a question of deciding whether you want to use the commands from the Layer menu or the options for the Move tool, and how you want to align or distribute the content, for example, by their centers or their left top, right, or bottom edges.

Aligning or distributing content to the image canvas bounds requires one further step. You must first select the canvas. This you can do by choosing Select ➜ All or Ctrl+A (Windows), ⌘+A (Mac OS). When the canvas is selected, you can use the commands in the Layer ➜ Align Layers to Selection or Distribute submenu or select the Move tool and use the buttons on the options bar to make your choice.

To align content to specific areas in an image, first, make a rectangular selection by using the Rectangular Marquee tool (M). Next, select the layers; you can select a single layer if the content is not being distributed. Then, use the commands in the Layer ➜ Align Layers to Selection or Distribute submenu or select the Move tool and use one of the align or distribute buttons on the options bar.

If you want to distribute the layers content unevenly or specify the number of pixels between the edges, you can do so by opening the image in ImageReady and then taking the following steps:

1. Select the Move tool.

2. Select the layers you want to distribute (you must select a minimum of three layers).

3. Enter a value in the text box, located to the right of the Distribution buttons in the options bar (Figure 6-10). The value you enter will determine the number of pixels that will separate the content edges.

4. Click the Distribute Layer Vertical Space or Distribute Layer Horizontal Space button to complete the distribution process.

FIGURE 6-10: **The Align and Distribute options in ImageReady. They differ from the options available in Photoshop.**

CAUTION Files in CMYK mode are not supported by ImageReady.

Rasterizing Layers

When layers are composed of vector data, such as shapes, fill content, type, vector mask, or Smart Objects, the data needs to be rasterized before the layers will accept painting or filtering. When layers are rasterized, the vector data is converted to pixels and each pixel's location described on a raster. The conversion permits tools and filters that require pixels to function.

To rasterize a layer, select the layer. Next, choose an item from the Layer ➜ Rasterize submenu. Alternatively, Right-click (Windows), Ctrl-click (Mac OS) the layer tile and select the appropriate item from the contextual menu.

There are three downsides to rasterizing vector data. One, the file size is increased because not only must each pixel's location be described using bits but so must its color values. Two, images composed of pixels are resolution dependent and can suffer from loss of quality when they are output to a larger-than-optimal resolution. Three, the operation cannot be reversed without recourse to expensive third-party plug-ins.

TIP Before rasterizing a layer, consider creating a duplicate that you can fall back on should the need arise.

Changing Fill and Opacity

The fill and opacity of the layer content determines not only appearance but also how the layers blend with each other. Furthermore, they determine how the layer effects interact with the layer content. Although you can control the opacity with the Opacity slider (located at the top of the Layers palette) or from the Layer Styles dialog box, the fill levels can be controlled with the Fill command. When you lower the fill level, any effects (Layer Styles) are unaffected. If you have ever tried to apply a Layer Style to a blank, new layer and given up because it did not "stick," try filling the layer first, applying the Layer Style, and then reducing the fill level (Figure 6-11).

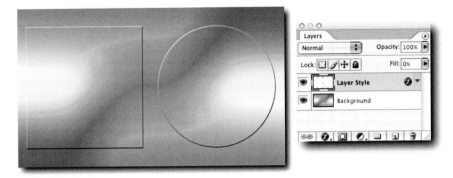

FIGURE 6-11: **A Layer Style applied to a filled layer and then the fill level reduced to zero.**

Copying and Pasting All Visible Layers

You would think that copying and pasting would be straightforward, and so it is. However, when you try to invoke the Copy command, it's usually grayed out. That's because Photoshop needs to know what you wish to copy and for you to tell it by making a selection. Furthermore, only the content on the currently selected layer is copied. To copy the data in all the visible layers, take the following steps:

1. Choose Select ➔ All.

2. Select Edit ➔ Copy Merged to copy the data.

3. Select Edit ➔ Paste to place the data where you want it.

Alternatively:

1. Click Ctrl+A (Windows), ⌘+A (Mac OS) to select all.

2. Click Ctrl+Shift+C (Windows), ⌘+Shift+C (Mac OS) to copy merged.

3. Click Ctrl+V (Windows), ⌘+V (Mac OS) to paste data.

NOTE You cannot copy multiple selected layers, nor can you copy a layer that has a Smart Object embedded.

When you're copying single or multiple layers to another document, dragging is preferred because it doesn't consume resources in same way that copying does. If you do copy large amounts of data, use the Purge command in the Edit menu to expunge the data from the Clipboard.

Merging Layers

Layers consume resources, just as surely as a glutton consumes sweetmeats. The more layers you create, the more your resources will be consumed and, depending on the size of the file, this can amount to a substantial loss. If you find that you need to conserve file size, RAM, or scratch disk space, you can merge the layers that you are sure you will not need as standalone layers in the future. Here are some "dos and don'ts" for merging layers.

- You can merge two adjacent layers by selecting the top layer and then choosing Merge Down from the Layer or palette menu, or Ctrl+E (Windows), ⌘+E (Mac OS). The selected layer merges with the layer immediately below it. Furthermore, you can Right-click (Windows), Ctrl-click (Mac OS) the layer tile and then select Merge Down from the contextual menu.

- To merge visible layers, choose Merge Visible from the Layer or palette menu, or Ctrl+Shift+E (Windows), ⌘+Shift+E (Mac OS).

- To merge to a new layer and leave original layers untouched, hold down Alt (Windows), Opt (Mac OS) and then choose Merge Visible from the Layer or palette menu, or press Ctrl+Alt+Shift+E (Windows), ⌘+Opt+Shift+E (Mac OS). Doing so creates a new layer and stamps the content from the visible layers into it.

- You cannot use adjustment, fill, shape, and type layers as the target layers.

- You can merge adjustment and fill layers, but you cannot merge two layers containing type or shapes, at least not without rasterizing them first.

CAUTION After you have merged layers, you cannot unmerge them without going back in history, which may invalidate changes you have made since the merge. If you're at all unsure, create a duplicate document (Image → Duplicate) and save it as insurance. You can drag the original layers back into the working document if need be.

Blending Layers

You can affect the appearance of your image by changing the opacity of the layers or by blending one or more layers. By default, layers have the Normal blend mode assigned to them, whereas groups have Pass Through. These modes tell the layers not to affect the layers below. In contrast, the other layer blending modes alter the pixel values of the underlying layers according to predefined algorithms. In total, not counting Normal and Pass Through, there are 22 blend modes, each capable of creating a different affect when applied.

You can blend layer content in one of several ways:

- In the Layers palette, choose a mode from the Blend Mode pop-up menu.

- Choose the same modes from the General Blending section of the Layer ➜ Layer Style ➜ Blending Options dialog box.

- Use the Blend If commands from the Layer ➜ Layer Style ➜ Blending Options dialog box.

- Use the Image ➜ Apply Image command.

Although the layer Blend Mode and the General Blend options in the Layer Style dialog box do the same job, the Blend If sliders and the Apply Image command do not (see the upcoming sections "Using Apply Image Command" and "Using Blend If").

The layer Blend Mode pop-up is probably the most accessible and most often used, possibly because of its prominence and ease of use. However, it's worth exploring the other options available to you for their power, if not ease of use.

Cycling through the Layer Blend Modes

When you need to see the effect of a layer blend mode, you can click the Blend Mode pop-up at the top of the Layers palette and choose from the menu. Alternatively, you can use a keyboard shortcut to quickly cycle through all the available blend modes and settle on the one that gives you the effect you are after.

To use the keyboard shortcut, make sure that a painting tool is not selected (pressing M for marquee tool is usually quick and safe). Next, hold down the Shift key and then press the Plus key to go down the list or the Minus key to go up the list. You can also go straight to a blend mode using specific keyboard shortcuts (see Table 6-2).

Table 6-2: Keyboard Shortcuts for Layer Blend Modes

Blend Mode	Keyboard Shortcut (Windows)	Keyboard Shortcut (Mac OS)
Normal	Alt+Shift+N	Opt+Shift+N
Dissolve	Alt+Shift+I	Opt+Shift+I

Blend Mode	Keyboard Shortcut (Windows)	Keyboard Shortcut (Mac OS)
Darken	Alt+Shift+K	Opt+Shift+K
Multiply	Alt+Shift+M	Opt+Shift+M
Color Burn	Alt+Shift+B	Opt+Shift+B
Linear Burn	Alt+Shift+A	Opt+Shift+A
Lighten	Alt+Shift+G	Opt+Shift+G
Screen	Alt+Shift+S	Opt+Shift+S
Color Dodge	Alt+Shift+D	Opt+Shift+D
Linear Dodge	Alt+Shift+W	Opt+Shift+W
Overlay	Alt+Shift+O	Opt+Shift+O
Softlight	Alt+Shift+F	Opt+Shift+F
Hardlight	Alt+Shift+H	Opt+Shift+H
Vivid Light	Alt+Shift+V	Opt+Shift+V
Pin Light	Alt+Shift+Z	Opt+Shift+Z
Linear Light	Alt+Shift+J	Opt+Shift+J
Hard Mix	Alt+Shift+L	Opt+Shift+L
Difference	Alt+Shift+E	Opt+Shift+E
Exclusion	Alt+Shift+X	Opt+Shift+X
Hue	Alt+Shift+U	Opt+Shift+U
Saturation	Alt+Shift+T	Opt+Shift+T
Color	Alt+Shift+C	Opt+Shift+C
Luminosity	Alt+Shift+Y	Opt+Shift+Y
Pass Through (Groups)	Alt+Shift+P	Opt+Shift+P

Using the Apply Image Command

A considerable number of Photoshop users shy away from the Apply Image command because they fail to see its usage. It's actually a very powerful command (Figure 6-12) for applying blends between two documents. You can use it to blend not only layers but also channels between the source document and the target document. Furthermore, you can apply the blending through a channel, selection, or mask; the channel can be a color channel or an alpha channel.

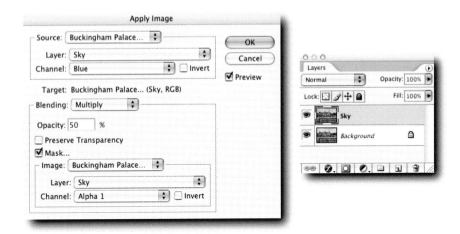

FIGURE 6-12: The Apply Image dialog box being used to blend a layer into itself using an alpha channel to mask areas.

To use Apply Image, open the two documents that you want to blend. Make sure that they both have the same pixel dimensions (Image ➜ Image Size) and then take the following steps:

1. Select the document that you want as the target (the blending will be applied to this document).

2. Choose Image ➜ Apply Image.

3. In the Apply Image dialog box, select the source file from the Source pop-up menu.

4. Next, select a layer and channel from the Layer and Channel pop-ups.

5. In the Blending section, select a blend mode from the pop-up and specify an opacity level, or leave it at 100%.

At this stage, you can click OK and exit or continue if you want to apply the blend through a mask.

1. Check the Mask box.

2. Select the document that you want to use as the source for the mask from the Image pop-up.

3. Choose a layer as the source for the mask from the Layer pop-up, or leave it on Merged.

4. Choose a channel or alpha channel from the Channel pop-up, or leave it on Gray for default composite channel. If you selected an alpha channel, you can invert the mask by checking the Invert box. You are not restricted to inverting only the alpha channel; you can invert the single channels or the composite channels.

5. Click the OK button to apply the blend.

NOTE If you're using another image as the source, the pixel dimensions of the source and the target images must match. If the color modes of the source and target images differ, you can blend single channels but not the composite channels. For example, if you like the detail on the black plate of a CMYK file, you can blend the Black channel from the CMYK (source) image into the composite of the RGB (target) image, or the L channel from a document in Lab mode.

Using Blend If

When you blend layers or groups using the Blend Mode pop-up in the Layers palette, all the data from the default channels is blended. You can specify the level of opacity for the top layer, but that's about the only control you can exercise.

Suppose that you need not only to specify which layers and channels to blend but also to limit the blending to shadows, midtones, or highlights. The Blend If feature is made for just such a supposition. It works on an "If true, then do" basis. You specify the criteria that have to be met; the feature applies the blends if your criteria are met. For example, if you want to blend only the blue pixels between two layers and restrict the blending between levels 50–150, you can do so. You can also take the harsh edge off the transitional areas by partially blending pixels with specific values. In fact, Blend If is a great feature for blending pixels without having to create masks in order to restrict the blending.

Now, take a deeper look at the feature, starting with a simple blend that knocks out a block of color. Admittedly, you can accomplish more or less the same with the Magic Wand or the Background Eraser, but Blend If gives you the option both of bringing back the deleted color because it was only masked and also of creating a smooth, transitional edge between the masked color and the visible content.

Before calling the Blend If dialog box, select the layer to be blended. Next, choose Layer ➜ Layer Style ➜ Blending Options, or click the Add a Layer Style button in the Layers palette and then choose Blending Options. When the dialog box opens, you will see two gradient ramps in the bottom part of the dialog box, the Blend If section—the top one named This Layer, which refers to the active layer and the bottom one named Underlying Layer, which refers to not only the layer immediately below the active layer but also any visible layers below it.

Just below the gradient ramps are sliders that control the brightness range of the blended pixels on a scale from 0 (black) to 255 (white). For the white background in Figure 6-13 to be masked, the white slider for This Layer was moved inward to level 240. This action masked all the levels from 240–255 but also created a sharp cutoff at level 240. For a smooth transition, or blend, to be created, the slider was split by Alt-clicking (Windows), Opt-clicking (Mac OS) and the innermost half dragged to level 230. This action effectively created a 10-level transparency ramp from level 240 to 230 that allowed the pixels to blend smoothly.

FIGURE 6-13: **Left—Before Blend If applied. Right—After Blend If applied. The white slider for This Layer was moved to level 240, split, and the inner half moved to level 230 to create a smooth transition.**

One upside of using Blend If is that it behaves a little bit like Layer Styles in as much as you can modify the settings or undo them altogether at any time. To do so, simply call up the dialog box again and make any changes. The mask used to make the blend will be altered or deleted and the layer returned to normality.

CAUTION When you apply Blend If to a layer, you will not see a visible indication to set the layer apart. This lack can lead to confusion. To save frustration at a later date, either color it or add Blend If to the layer name as a reminder.

When you blend data from the layers below the active layer, the feature behaves slightly differently and can lead to confusion or simply a quick exit! It's worth taking a little time to learn how the This Layer and Underlying Layer sliders act on the active layer. Here's how they differ in their approaches.

When you use the sliders for This Layer, data is clipped in the active layer to reveal data below (Figure 6-14). When you use the sliders for the Underlying Layer, the data *punches* through the active layer. For example, to blend all detail from level 0–50 and to create a smooth zone between levels 40–50, move the black slider inward and stop when you see the figure above the gradient ramp read level 50. Next, Alt-click (Windows), Opt-click (Mac OS) the slider to split it and move the left half to the left until the figure above the gradient ramp reads 40/50.

NOTE The sliders for the Underlying Layer affect all underlying layers and not just the one immediately below the active layer.

NOTE To blend all channels, leave the pop-up menu above the sliders set to Gray (the default) or click it and select a channel (see also "Excluding Channels when Blending," which follows this Note). Furthermore, you can choose a blend mode and opacity in the General Blending section or select it in the Layers palette.

FIGURE 6-14: Left—Original image. Middle—This Layer clipped to levels 50 and 205. Right—Detail from the Blending Options dialog box, showing data from underlying layer with levels 0–50 punching through the upper layer and levels 40–50 blending smoothly.

Excluding Channels when Blending

When you use the Blending Options dialog box to blend layers or groups, by default all the channels that go to make up the image are blended. However, you can restrict the blending to one or more of the channels. To give one example of the option's usage, you could increase the shadow density in a CMYK file without affecting the color balance by taking the following steps:

1. Dupe a layer.

2. Apply a curve.

3. Double-click the layer thumbnail to open the Blending Options dialog box.

4. Deselect C, M, Y in Advanced Blending.

5. Hold down Alt (Windows), Opt (Mac OS) and drag the This Layer slider to the left to restrict the blend (holding down the key splits the slider).

6. Move the right part of the slider to the left so that pixels blend smoothly without a harsh transitional edge.

Blending Options can be put to good use when you need to create montages, composite objects over a background or even into a background, remove backgrounds, and the like. The more you use it, the more uses you can find for it.

Importing and Exporting

Importing and exporting files are an integral part of the image editing process. Sooner or later, you need to either export layers to files or to import layers from another document. Fear not; it's a straightforward process and one that does not require much *savoir faire* (though a smattering of French helps!).

Importing Layers from Another Document

Nothing could be more straightforward than importing a layer from another document. You do need to be aware of a few characteristics of the process, but generally speaking, it's just a question of having the two documents open (the target and the source) and then dragging the layers from the source to the target. Just be aware of the following:

- You can drag the source layers from the document window or from the Layers palette. The latter is probably more elegant and less prone to errors.

- When you drop the layers into the target document's window, hold down the Shift key in order to center the incoming content, otherwise, it will be placed wherever you happen to drop it. If the two documents have the same dimensions, the content will appear to pin register.

- You can import more than one layer or group. No need to link them, as in the olden days; just select the layers or groups and then drag and drop

NOTE Importing multiple files as layers requires scripting because there is no hard-wired command. You can write your own or download one written by Trevor Morris of GFX. The script not only imports multiple files as layers but also names the layers using the filenames. See `http://user.fundy.net/morris/photoshop28.shtml`.

Exporting Layers as Separate Files

Just as there is no hard-wired command to import files as layers, the converse is also true: There is no hard-wired command to export layers as separate files. Fortunately, the solution is similar but closer to home. Photoshop ships with a readymade script.

To invoke the command, choose File ➜ Scripts Export Layers to Files. In the dialog box (Figure 6-15), you can specify a location and a filename prefix. You can also select options for each file format, such as compression, quality, ICC profile embedding, and bit depth.

You can save files in the following formats: PSD, TIFF, PDF, JPEG, BMP, and TARGA. Unfortunately, you cannot save in the Macromedia Flash (SWF) file format. To do that, you need to open the document in ImageReady: File ➜ Edit in ImageReady or Ctrl+Shift+M (Windows), ⌘+Shift+M (Mac OS). The File ➜ Export ➜ Layers as Files command in ImageReady is hard wired and has many more options. Because ImageReady is primarily designed to save images for the screen, you cannot save as TIFF, PDF, or BMP. However, you can save in all the Web-supported formats. You can also elect which layers you want to export, something you cannot do with the script in Photoshop. Furthermore, you can specify a file format for each layer by selecting it from the Layer pop-up menu and then choosing a setting in the File Formats section of the dialog box. You can specify filenaming conventions by clicking the Set button in the File Options section of the dialog box; also, when saving in the SWF format, you can set options for appearance, dynamic text, and bitmap options.

FIGURE 6-15: **The Export Layers To Files dialog box.**

Summary

Mastering the complexities of working with layers is a surefire guarantee of taming Photoshop and making it go some way toward doing your bidding. With the insights into creating, managing, and editing layers revealed in this chapter, you should have the foundation on which to build a solid workflow for constructing your dream compositions, while retaining the ability to change your mind at a future date.

chapter 7

Creating and Applying Layer Styles

Layer styles are simply compilations of effects—such as drop shadow, stroke, bevel and emboss—that you can apply to layer content when you want to change its appearance.

In the old days, before effects were introduced, you had to use alpha channels, filters, or a combination of both, or you had to resort to third-party plug-ins to change a layer's appearance. Nowadays, all you need to do is select a box to apply a drop shadow, an inner glow, an outer glow, or a bevel and emboss, to name just a few of the popular effects. Having applied the effects, you can then save them collectively as a style and apply them again at the click of a mouse button, saving time, effort, and energy in the process.

After being applied to a layer, a style adjusts automatically to fit layer content when the layer is transformed. For example, you can create a type layer, apply a layer style, transform the type or warp it into any shape, and the effects in the layer style automatically adjust to fit the new shape.

You can create, view, and apply layer styles from three places: the Layer Style dialog box, the Style palette, and the pop-up Style Picker, available from the options bar when you select Shape Layers for a pen or shape tool. This chapter discusses how you can make the most of them to create, save, apply, and organize styles.

in this chapter

- ◉ Creating, saving, and organizing styles
- ◉ Applying styles
- ◉ Converting styles into layers
- ◉ Moving, scaling, and repositioning styles

Creating, Saving, and Organizing Styles

The Layer Styles dialog box is the place to create new custom styles. By combining the various effects available in the dialog box or changing their settings, you can create styles that mimic wood, metal, chrome, ruby, glistening water droplets, or fragile glass buttons; in fact, the list is limitless. The available effects include Drop Shadow, Inner Shadow, Outer and Inner Glow, Bevel and Emboss, Satin, Color, Gradient and Pattern Overlay, and Stroke (see Figure 7-1).

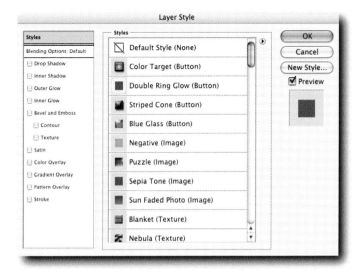

FIGURE 7-1: **The Layer Style dialog box in Large Detail mode (modes may be selected from the dialog box's pop-up menu). You can click any effect name in the left pane to see its options.**

To create a new Layer Style, take the following steps:

1. Start with a new document (File ➔ New). In the New dialog box, choose White for Background Contents.

2. Create a new layer by clicking the Create a New Layer icon in the Layers palette.

3. Make a selection in the middle of the layer with the rectangular or the elliptical marquee tool and fill it with 50% gray (choose Edit ➔ Fill ➔ Contents ➔ 50% Gray). Deselect the selection (choose Select ➔ Deselect).

4. Double-click the layer thumbnail to launch the Layer Style dialog box or click the Add a Layer Style icon (second from left) in the Layers palette and choose Blending Options from the pop-up menu. You can also choose Layer ➔ Layer Style ➔ Blending Options; right-click (Windows), Ctrl-click (Mac OS) a layer tile and choose Blending Options from the contextual menu.

5. In the Layer Style dialog box (Figure 7-1), click an effect name in the left side of the dialog box that you want to include in the new style (the box next to it will be checked for you and the options for the effect displayed in the right side of the dialog box).

6. Accept the default settings or modify them (you should see instant feedback in the document window, provided that the Preview option is checked). To familiarize yourself with the options, apply them one at a time. Just be aware, Color Overlay hides Gradient Overlay, which in turn hides Pattern Overlay.

7. When you are happy with the effect, select another and modify that one. When you are happy with the style created by combining the effects, click the New Style button and follow the instructions to save it. The style is saved and added to the current styles library (click Styles at the top left of the dialog box to see the current library).

8. Click the OK button to exit the dialog box.

You can also save an effect as a preset style without recourse to the Layer Style dialog box: After an effect, or effects, has been applied to a layer, select the layer and then click in an empty area of the Style palette (Window ➜ Styles). Name the style when the New Style dialog box opens and click the OK button; alternatively, click the Create New Style button in the Styles palette.

TIP If you create styles for future use, remember to save the current set in case Photoshop quits unexpectedly. You can save styles by choosing Save Styles from the Style palette or Layer Style dialog box menu. By default, the styles are saved in the Presets ➜ Layer Styles folder inside the application folder; Photoshop can see the contents in the Presets subfolders and creates lists from each file in the appropriate menus when it is launched. It's always a good idea to save the Presets folder to another hard drive or removable media, in case you accidentally delete your custom presets when you have to reinstall Photoshop or format your disk.

Should you need to, you can delete individual styles in the previously mentioned palettes and dialog boxes by dragging them to the Trash icon or by pressing Alt (Windows), Opt (Mac OS) while clicking the style when the pointer icon turns to a scissors. With the exception of the Styles palette, where selecting a thumbnail applies a style, you can also select a style thumbnail and then choose Delete Style from the palette menu or click the Delete button in the Preset Manager. If those weren't enough ways to delete a style, you can also right-click (Windows), Ctrl-click (Mac OS) a style and choose Delete from the contextual menu.

Photoshop ships with a number of style libraries, which you can load from the Style palette menu, the Style Picker menu, the Layer Style menu, or the Preset Manager (Edit ➜ Preset Manager) dialog box menu.

NOTE If you want to reorganize the styles in the libraries, you must use the Preset Manager.

Applying, Clearing, and Converting Styles

Layer styles are inexorably linked to layers and layer content. If the layer contains only transparent pixels, you can apply a style, but it becomes visible only after the layer is painted on, or filled with a color. There are two exceptions to be aware of: You cannot apply a layer style to an adjustment layer or layer groups.

Although a style is applied to a layer, technically speaking it is applied only when you flatten a document or output it in a file format that does not support layers and styles. Until such time, the style affects only the appearance, not the pixels in the layer. This means that you can change the effects' settings as many times as you like without fear of damaging the content. The only caveats are that you cannot blend layer styles or apply filters (see "Converting Styles into Layers," later in the chapter).

When it comes to actually applying a style to a layer, probably the easiest and quickest method is to have the Style palette open, select a layer, or layers, and then click a style thumbnail in the palette. You can also drag a style thumbnail to the layer or drop it in the document window; in which case the style is applied to the active layer. However, if more than one layer is selected, it is applied only to the topmost layer in the selection.

You can also apply a style when you use the pen and shape tools in Fill mode. To do so, after selecting a tool, click the Shape Layers icon in the options bar and then click the Style icon to call up the Style pop-up palette and select a style (Figure 7-2).

FIGURE 7-2: **The options bar with the "Shape layers" and Style picker icons highlighted.**

NOTE If you need to create a path or shape without applying a style and the Default Style (None) is not available in the Style pop-up palette, choose No Style from the palette's menu or right-click (Windows), Ctrl-click (Mac OS) the tool's icon in the options bar and then choose Reset Tool.

TIP By default, if you add a style on top of an existing style, the current style is replaced. If you want to add to the existing style, press the Shift key as you click before you drag and drop.

Applying to Another Layer Quickly

After you have applied a style to a layer, you can, of course, copy and paste it to another layer or layers. To do so, take the following steps:

1. Right-click (Windows), Ctrl-click (Mac OS) the effects icon (shaped like an *f*) in the Layers palette.

2. Select Copy Layer Style from the contextual menu and then paste onto the target layer.

Alternatively, hold down Alt (Windows), Opt (Mac OS) and drag the effects icon from the source layer onto the target layer.

If you just wish to copy an effect to another layer, take the following steps:

1. Click the downward-pointing triangle on the source layer to unfurl the style.

2. Press Alt (Windows), Opt (Mac OS).

3. Click the effect's icon on the source layer that you wish to copy, drag to the target layer, and let go.

When you drop the icon, Photoshop copies the corresponding effect to the target layer (Figure 7-3).

If you wish to *move* a style or a single effect, just drag the effects icon to the target layer.

FIGURE 7-3: Copying an applied style
to another layer by dragging.

Applying Same Style to Multiple Layers

If you want to apply the same layer style to multiple layers, you have two options. Number one, have the Style palette open, select all the layers you want to apply the style to, and then click the style thumbnail in the palette; number two, if the style is already applied to a single layer, copy and paste it by taking the following steps:

1. Select the source layer in the Layers palette.

2. Right-click (Windows), Ctrl-click (Mac OS) the *f* icon of the source layer and choose Copy Layer Style, or choose Layer ➜ Layer Style ➜ Copy Layer Style.

3. Select all the target layers.

4. Right-click (Windows), Ctrl-click (Mac OS) one of the target layers and then choose Paste Layer Style, or choose Layer ➜ Layer Style ➜ Paste Layer Style.

Of course, if the style has been previously saved, you can select the layers and simply click the style thumbnail in the Styles palette and the style will be applied to all the selected layers.

Applying a Rollover Style

If you need to design rollover buttons for a Web site, you may be tempted to use the Rollover Buttons or the Web Rollover Styles in Photoshop (available from the Style palette and Layer Styles dialog box menus). Unfortunately, Photoshop is not equipped to show the two or three states needed for a true rollover; nor can it output the necessary JavaScript to make the rollover function in a browser. Fortunately, ImageReady is tailor made for creating rollovers.

When you load the rollover styles in ImageReady (Figure 7-4), the correct states are automatically created in the Web Content palette and the layer is converted to a Layer Based Slice for you. When you save the optimized file, the different states are saved as separate images and the correct JavaScript generated in the HTML file.

FIGURE 7-4: **The rollover style thumbnails in ImageReady are distinguished from the others by a black triangle in the upper-left corner.**

Clearing and Hiding Styles

After you have applied a style, if you need to clear the effects, there's no need to go into the Layer Style dialog box and deselect each style. Simply right-click (Windows), Ctrl-click (Mac OS) the layer tile (not the thumbnail) and then choose Clear Layer Style from the contextual menu, or with the layer selected, choose Layer ➜ Layer Style ➜ Clear Layer Style. Alternatively, click the *f*-shaped effects icon and drag to the Trash. There's very little difference between using the contextual menu and dragging to the Trash, but knowing both can enable you to choose the quicker method in your given situation. Sometimes it's quicker to use the Trash; at other times— for example, when it's too far from the layer tile—the contextual method can be quicker.

Although applying a style to multiple layers is relatively easy, clearing styles from multiple layers is not so easy, because there is no command or button to clear styles from multiple selected layers (MSL). As always, there is a way, even if it is not as intuitive as applying styles. What you need to do is select the layers and then click the Default Style (None) thumbnail in the Styles palette; it's the first style in the palette and has a red line drawn diagonally through it. If you cannot see it, you will have to choose Reset Styles from the palette menu and either append the default styles or replace the existing styles.

If you want to hide applied effects temporarily, you can do it in two easy steps:

1. Unfurl the style by clicking the down-pointing triangle next to the *f* icon on the layer tile.

2. Click the eyeball icon next to Effects to turn off all effects applied to that layer, or one next to the named effect to turn off individually.

You can also turn off all applied effects in the document. To do so, right-click (Windows), Ctrl-click (Mac OS) the *f* icon and then choose Hide All Effects from the contextual menu; alternatively, choose Layer → Layer Style → Hide All Effects. The commands are toggles, which means that you can show the hidden effects at any time by choosing Show All Effects from the same menus.

Converting Styles into Layers

Because of the nature of layer effects, they do not accept adjustments, filtering or blending. However, you can convert the effects to normal layers, and then they happily accept all the modifications accepted by a normal layer.

To create layers from an applied style, choose Layer → Layer Style → Create Layers; alternatively, right-click (Windows), Ctrl-click (Mac OS) the *f* icon in the Layers palette and then choose Create Layers from the contextual menu.

When the new layers are created, they are clipped to the base layer that you applied the style to in order to keep the appearance of the style. You can work on them as they are or release them from the clipping mask by Alt-clicking (Windows), Opt-clicking (Mac OS) the dividing line between the layers.

You can also convert a single effect to a layer. To do so, unfurl the style by clicking the down-pointing triangle next to the *f* icon; then, turn off the visibility for the layers that you do not want to turn into layers. Right-click (Windows), Ctrl-click (Mac OS) the unfurled effects and choose Create Layer from the contextual menu. The visible effect is turned into a layer and clipped to the base layer.

Applying and Creating Custom Contours

The effects available in the Layer Style dialog box can all be modified by using the options provided. One of those options is a contour map. *Contours* control the shape of the Drop Shadow, Inner Shadow, Outer Glow, Inner Glow, Bevel and Emboss, and Satin effects over a specified range. They do this by allowing you to define how the shadow fades for a Drop Shadow effect; to create rings of transparency for a solid color Outer and Inner Glow; to vary the repetition of the gradient color and the opacity for gradient-filled glows; and to sculpt the bumps, ridges, and valleys that define the emboss for Bevel and Emboss.

You can assign contour maps to an effect from a predefined list or define your own custom contours. To see the subtle changes produced by assigning a different contour, create a simple object filled with 50% gray, apply an effect to it in the Layer Style dialog box, such as a drop shadow, and then cycle through the predefined contours one by one. To select a different contour, click the down-pointing triangle on the Contour icon (Figure 7-5) to call the Contour Picker.

To define your own custom contour, take the following steps:

1. In the Layer Style dialog box, select any one of the effects that uses contours.

2. Click anywhere on the Contour icon to call the Contour Editor, but not the down-pointing triangle, which calls the Contour Picker (Figure 7-5).

3. Modify the curve in the Contour Editor pop-up dialog box (Figure 7-5). Check the Corner box if you want your curve to have a sharp segment.

4. Click the New button (not the Save button), give the contour a memorable name, and then click the OK button.

5. Click the Save button in the Contour Editor if you want to save the contour by itself, or click the OK button to exit.

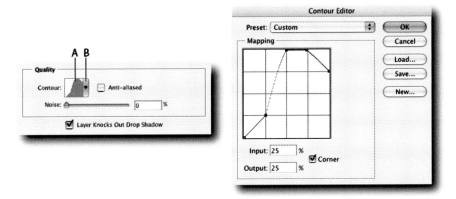

FIGURE 7-5: Detail from the Drop Shadow options in the Layer Style dialog box and the Custom Contour Editor dialog box. A—Click to access custom contour pop-up. B—Click to choose a predefined contour.

If you want to save the new contour as part of the current set, in the Layer Style dialog box, click the down-pointing triangle of the icon for the Contour Picker and choose Save Contours from the pop-up Contour Picker's menu.

When you relaunch Photoshop, the saved contour, or set, can be loaded from the Contour Picker menu, provided that you saved it in the default location: ~\Adobe Photoshop CS2\Presets\Countours.

NOTE The contours in the Contour Picker cannot be rearranged within the Contour Picker itself. To rearrange contours, use the Preset Manager (Edit → Preset Manager).

Defining Default Global Light for All Documents

The effects Drop Shadow, Inner Shadow, and Bevel and Emboss all share a global lighting angle to give the appearance of light emanating from the same source. The default angle for all layers is 120 degrees and the Altitude for Bevel and Emboss is 30 degrees. You can change the angle on a case-by-case basis for each layer or define a new custom angle for all documents.

To change the angle for the current layer without affecting other layers, simply deselect Use Global Light in the effects options and then alter the angle.

To define a new default angle for all documents, take the following steps:

1. Close all documents.

2. Choose Layer → Layer Style → Global Angle.

3. In the Global Light dialog box (Figure 7-6), define a new Angle for Global Light and, if need be, for Altitude.

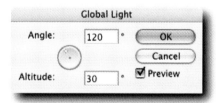

FIGURE 7-6: **Global Light angle and altitude dialog box.**

If you find yourself constantly setting the angle to, say, 135 degrees, you can save some time by defining a new default just once.

Moving and Repositioning Effects

By default, gradients and patterns used in a layer effect have their origin point linked to the document. However, should you need to, you can change it by moving the mouse pointer into the document window and dragging the gradient or pattern to a new position (Figure 7-7).

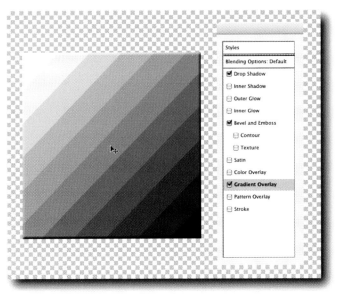

FIGURE 7-7: **You can realign the Gradient Overlay effect by dragging the mouse pointer in the document window.**

Furthermore, the effects are usually linked to the object's bounding box. This ensures that the applied gradient or pattern moves with the object when it is repositioned. Normally, that is something you would want to happen automatically; however, should you need to move the object independently of the gradient or pattern, you can override the behavior by taking the following steps in the Layer Style dialog box:

- To unleash Gradient Overlay, select the effect and then deselect the Align with Layer option.

- To unleash Texture and Pattern Overlay, select the effect and then deselect the Link with Layer option.

The object can then be moved while the effect remains rooted in its origin.

Scaling Layer Styles

The default settings for each effect in the Layer Style dialog box are designed to look good for the current size of the object. However, you might have noticed that when you transform the object, the effects do not scale in tandem with the object. To correct this problem, you can use the Scale Effects command in the Layer ➜ Layer Style submenu and resize the effects visually, which can be a bit hit or miss, or you can scale them correspondingly by using the following workaround:

1. Transform the object using Edit ➜ Free Transform, or Ctrl+T (Windows), ⌘+T (Mac OS).

2. Enter a percentage figure in the Width and Height text fields on the options bar, or enter once and click the link icon between the two text fields. If you're transforming manually by using the handles on the bounding box, make a note of the percentage figure in the options bar (ignore any fractions).

3. Choose Layer ➜ Layer Style ➜ Scale Effects. In the Scale Layer Effects dialog box (Figure 7-8), enter the figure you noted in step 2.

4. Click the OK button to apply the setting.

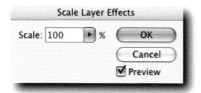

FIGURE 7-8: **The Scale Layer Effects dialog box.**

When you resize an image, as opposed to a layer, the layer styles should scale automatically. If you find that they are not doing so, choose Image ➜ Image Size and make sure the Scale Layer Effects option is checked.

Summary

Whereas the Layer Styles dialog box takes the drudgery out of creating effects, style libraries enable users to save time by making it possible to share the styles. What's more, because of their relatively small size, they are easy to exchange over the Internet.

Furthermore, the styles can be easily modified and resaved as a fresh style. In fact, modifying layer styles that ship with Photoshop and saving them with a different name is a good way to learn how to create your own.

Numerous sites on the Internet offer free and commercial styles. Two good sites at which to begin your search are Adobe Studio Exchange (http://share.studio.adobe.com; a one-time registration is required) and Graphics Software, hosted by Sue Chastain (http://graphicssoft.about.com).

chapter 8

Hacking Layer Masks

L ayer masks are incredibly useful devices for hiding underlying content without affecting the values of the pixels that make up the content. They behave like clear acetate sheets that you position over layers and paint on to hide the content underneath; you can reveal the content again by "scraping" off the paint. When you are happy with the shape of the mask, you can apply it to the layers below, at which stage the pixels are irrevocably altered (barring History steps). Furthermore, masks can be duplicated, their transparency varied and, as long as the file format supports layers and masks, saved with the image.

Essentially, Photoshop supports two types of masks: grayscale and vector (Figure 8-1). They can be further classified as layer masks, used to hide content; alpha masks, used to store selections; and temporary masks, used to create or modify existing selections. This chapter is devoted to layer masks, which are used principally for hiding content. Selection masks are covered in Chapter 9.

Grayscale masks are composed of grayscale images, stored as alpha channels and revealed in the Channels palette when the layer they are applied is selected. As can grayscale images, grayscale masks can be modified with painting tools and edited by using commands and filters. Grayscale masks are ideal for blending content because of their support for transparency and anti-aliasing, two aspects most responsible for creating seamless blends. However, they are resolution dependent and can suffer if an image is not output at its optimal size.

in this chapter

- ○ Creating and applying layer masks
- ○ Viewing layer masks
- ○ Editing and modifying masks

FIGURE 8-1: A grayscale mask (left) contrasted to a vector mask (right).

Vector masks are composed of mathematically defined lines and curves, more commonly referred to as paths. Vector masks store their data in the Paths palette and are revealed when the layer they are applied to is selected. They can be modified using the pen or shape tools or the transform commands. The hard-edged quality of the paths makes it possible to composite images with absolute precision. Furthermore, they are not restricted to image resolution, as are grayscale masks, and can print to the resolution of the imagesetter (a device used to make plates for offset printing).

Temporary masks are stored temporarily in the Channels palette while you create a new selection or modify an existing selection. They are called Quick Masks (see Chapter 9). After you exit Quick Mask mode, only the temporary selection exists. Because of the interchangeability of masks and selections, you can modify a layer mask by converting it to a selection, modify the selection in Quick Mask mode, and then fill the mask to take on the contours of the modified selection.

Creating, Viewing, and Applying Masks

Grayscale masks can be created in the Layers palette and added to a layer or group. The exception to the rule is a Background layer, which does not include transparency. By default, masks are added automatically to new adjustment layers. However, you can turn off the option in the Layers palette menu, but there is very little or no advantage in doing so.

Masks can be created from existing image data or from an existing path. For example, you can create a selection and then load the content in the selection to define a grayscale mask; likewise, create a path and then use it to define a vector mask.

Masks can be *applied* to a layer so that the underlying content in the layer is permanently altered, or they can be deleted without affecting the layer content. Existing masks can also be applied to another layer or multiple layers.

These are just a few things you can do with masks; the following sections look at each one in more detail.

Grayscale Masks

When you create a grayscale mask, you have two options at your disposal: You can either create a mask that hides the layer content (ready for you to reveal underlying content) or one that reveals all (ready for you to hide underlying content). Both have their uses in the scheme of things.

Masks work on the principle that where the mask is black, it hides content directly underneath; where the mask is white, it reveals content directly underneath; where the mask is a shade of black and white, it partially hides the content directly underneath. Put another way: *black* conceals content, as the night does; *white* reveals content, as the daylight does; *gray* partially conceals content, as does a foggy day.

To add a mask to the active layer that does not hide the layer content, choose Layer ➜ Layer Mask ➜ Reveal All, or click the Add layer mask icon, located at the bottom of the Layers palette (Figure 8-2).

FIGURE 8-2: **Detail from the Layers palette.**
A—Link layers. B—Add a layer style.
C—Add layer mask. D—Create new fill or
adjustment layer. E—Create a new group.
F—Create a new layer. G—Delete layer.

NOTE You cannot create a mask for a Background layer; you must convert it to a normal layer first by double-clicking it.

When you create a mask, the foreground and background colors change to white and black, respectively. Before you can paint on the mask, you need to switch the colors around by pressing X (white on white doesn't show too well!). Next, select the Brush tool and an appropriate brush tip and then paint on the mask to hide the layer content; paint with white to reveal again (press X to switch colors). When painting on masks, it helps to turn off the brush dynamics by choosing Clear Brush Controls from the Brushes palette menu, or by checking them off one by one.

NOTE Sometimes, knowing whether you are working on a mask or the layer content can be difficult. You can tell by observing the thumbnails in the Layers palette: The active thumbnail always has a border around it.

To create a mask that hides the layer content initially, choose Layer ➜ Layer Mask ➜ Hide All, or hold down Alt (Windows), Opt (Mac OS) and then click the Add Layer Mask icon (Figure 8-2), located at the bottom of the Layers palette.

You can also create a Reveal All or Hide All mask based on an active selection. Follow the preceding steps after making sure that a selection is active. Rather than choose Reveal All or Hide All from the Layer Mask submenu, choose Reveal Selection or Hide Selection.

TIP If you would like the mask to have a soft edge, feather the selection. You can do that by choosing Select→ Feather or pressing Ctrl+Alt+D (Windows), ⌘+Opt+D (Mac OS) and then entering a value in the Feather Selection dialog box. Alternatively, use the Gaussian Blur filter on the mask after it has been created.

To delete a mask, drag it to the Trash icon in the Layers palette or choose Layer→ Layer Mask→ Delete. You can also right-click (Windows), Ctrl-click (Mac OS) the mask thumbnail and choose Delete Layer Mask from the contextual menu. You are then asked to apply or delete the mask. If you choose the former, the layer content is changed permanently in line with the mask. If you choose the latter, it is discarded without affecting the layer.

Vector Masks

If you are creating a design that contains elements with clear, defined outlines and you need to hide parts of it, instead of adding a grayscale mask, try adding a vector mask. Vector masks are infinitely editable and do not increase file size in the way that grayscale masks do. You can also use them in conjunction with a grayscale mask to create a soft- and hard-edged mask. Vector masks can also be converted to a grayscale mask if required.

To add a vector mask to the active layer that does not hide layer content initially, choose Layer→ Vector Mask→ Reveal All, or hold down Ctrl (Windows), ⌘ (Mac OS) and then click the Add Layer Mask icon (Figure 8-2), located at the bottom of the Layers palette.

If you followed the preceding steps, you might have noticed that nothing much has changed. That's because you need to create a path to define the clipping border. To do so, select a pen or shape tool and draw a path; make sure that the tool's option is set to drawing paths (the default when you create a vector mask) and not shapes; to set the option, click the second icon from the left on the options bar, not counting the tool icon (Figure 8-3).

FIGURE 8-3: Options bar. A—Paths. B—Custom Shape tool.
C—Custom Shape pop-up palette.

To add a vector mask that hides the layer content initially, choose Layer→ Vector Mask→ Hide All, or hold down Ctrl+Alt (Windows), ⌘+Opt (Mac OS) and then click the Add Layer Mask icon, located at the bottom of the Layers palette.

You have yet another way of adding a vector mask, and it's similar to create a grayscale mask from an active selection. To do so, create a path and then choose Layer→ Vector Mask→ Current Path, or Ctrl-click (Windows), ⌘-click (Mac OS) the Add Layer Mask icon, at which point the data is clipped to the path and a vector mask thumbnail added to the layer.

TIP You can base a vector mask on custom shapes by setting the option for the pen or shape tool to draw paths in the options bar, selecting the Custom Shape Tool icon, and then selecting a custom shape from the Shape pop-up palette (Figure 8-3).

To delete a vector mask, drag the thumbnail to the Trash icon in the Layers or the Paths palette; alternatively, right-click (Windows), Ctrl-click (Mac OS) the thumbnail and choose Delete Vector Mask (Layers palette) or Delete Path (Paths palette) from the contextual menu.

If you find that a vector mask is not giving you the control you need and a grayscale mask is required, or if you want to combine it with a grayscale mask (a layer accepts a grayscale and a vector mask at the same time), rather than start again, convert the vector mask to a grayscale mask. To do so, right-click (Windows), Control-click (Mac OS) the mask thumbnail and then choose Rasterize Vector Mask. If a grayscale mask exists, the vector mask is rasterized and combined; otherwise, it is converted to a grayscale mask.

Luminosity-Based Masks

Masks based on the brightness values of an image are very useful for tonal corrections. They can limit the corrections to the highlights or the shadows. Furthermore, they can be created from the brightness values belonging to the composite channel or an individual channel. To give one example of their use, you can limit a Curves adjustment to just the highlights by taking the following steps:

1. Ctrl-click (Windows), ⌘-click (Mac OS) on the composite channel to load the luminosity mask, or Ctrl+Alt+Tilde (Windows), ⌘+Opt+Tilde (Mac OS). The Tilde key is the one marked with a "~" sign. To be precise, you are using the grave accent "`" key, but tilde is commonly used to refer to the key.

2. Choose Layer → New Adjustment Layer → Curves, or click the Create New Fill or Adjustment icon in the Layers palette and then choose Curves. Photoshop creates an adjustment layer and an accompanying mask thumbnail and includes a grayscale image of the composite channel in the mask.

3. In the Curves dialog box, adjust the curve and click the OK button to exit.

When you make any adjustments in the Curves dialog box, the changes made to the highlights show in accordance with the density of the mask, but the changes applied to the shadows are masked.

To affect the shadows, press Ctrl+Shift+I (Windows), ⌘+Shift+I (Mac OS) after step 1 to invert the mask, or you can click the mask thumbnail at any time and invoke the preceding shortcut.

After becoming aware of this technique, you can quite easily find other uses for it. For example, you can use it to confine the effect of layer blends, Hue/Saturation adjustments, global sharpening, colorized layers, or sepia-like effects.

Clipping Masks from Layer Transparency

The concept of creating clipping masks from layer transparency sounds like something straight out of a science journal. In fact, it's nothing more than the transparency of the bottommost layer in a group being used to mask the content of the upper layers. Layer clipping masks are used, for example, whenever you need to place an image inside text or the outline of image content; most notably in posters advertising films or exotic holiday places. You can clip as many layers as you like to create the effect you are after. However, they must be successive layers in the layer stack.

To create a clipping mask from layer transparency, make sure that the layer you want to use as the mask source is positioned below the layer whose content you want to mask (Figure 8-4). Choose Layer ➔ Create Clipping Mask, or Ctrl+Alt+G (Windows), ⌘+Opt+G (Mac OS). You can also hold down Alt (Windows), Opt (Mac OS) and click the line separating the two layers (Figure 8-4). When the mask is created, the thumbnail of the upper layer is offset to the right and a downward-pointing triangle is added to differentiate the layer.

FIGURE 8-4: A clipping mask being applied, showing a base layer (Background) and a layer containing the transparency (Logo) used to clip the content of the layer above it (Insert).

To release the clipping mask, choose Layer ➔ Release Clipping Mask, or Ctrl+Alt+G (Windows), ⌘+Opt+G (Mac OS). You can also hold down Alt (Windows), Opt (Mac OS) and click the line separating the two layers. In case the shortcuts sound familiar, they are the same for a creating clipping mask.

By default, the blend mode of the bottommost layer in a clipping group applies to the clipped layers. However, you can override the default behavior and preserve the blend mode of the clipped layer(s). To do so, choose Layer ➔ Layer Styles ➔ Blending Options, or double-click an empty section of the layer tile to call the Layer Style dialog box and then, under Advanced Blending, deselect Blend Clipped Layers as Group and click the OK button. This way, the original blending appearance of the layers is preserved.

Viewing Layer Masks

Layer masks can be turned off temporarily, or disabled, by pressing the Shift key while clicking the mask thumbnail. When you click, Photoshop adds a red cross to the thumbnail to show that the mask is temporarily disabled. The shortcut is a toggle, meaning that you can use it to enable a disabled mask. Alternatively, right-click (Windows), Ctrl-click (Mac OS) the mask thumbnail and choose Disable Layer Mask from the contextual menu. To enable a disabled mask this way, call up the contextual menu again and choose Enable Layer Mask.

Viewing in the Document Window

When you create a mask using brushstrokes, it's easy to miss areas. The mask can look fine until you print an A3 and hold it up to the light! To avoid embarrassing calls from clients, you can scrutinize any mask at close quarters by viewing it in the document window. To do so, Alt-click (Windows), Opt-click (Mac OS) on the mask thumbnail. When it is displayed in the document window, you can magnify the preview and scroll to see whether you have missed any areas. Paint over the cracks in the window as you would normally and then Alt-click (Windows), Opt-click (Mac OS) the mask thumbnail again to preview the image.

One downside to viewing and working on a mask in the document window is that it does not show the underlying image. To overcome this impediment, you can view the alpha channel that contains the mask and work on it as if you were in Quick Mask mode. To do so, Alt+Shift-click (Windows), Opt+Shift-click (Mac OS) the mask thumbnail. Do whatever work needs to be done and then use the same shortcut to return to normal view.

TIP If the color overlay clashes with image content when you work on a mask's alpha channel or you want to view the overlay at a different opacity level than the default 50%, double-click the mask thumbnail and customize the color in the Layer Mask Display Options dialog box (Figure 8-5). Click the color box to specify a new color or enter a preferred value in the text box to specify a new opacity level.

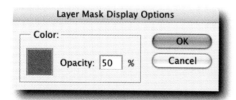

FIGURE 8-5: **You can specify an overlay color and opacity level in the Layer Mask Display Options dialog box.**

NOTE Both the color overlay and the opacity settings affect how the mask is displayed and not the underlying layer content.

Applying Existing Masks to Other Layers

Sometimes you need to add an existing mask to another layer. You cannot do it in the conventional way by copying and pasting. That is, you *can* do it that way, but it involves extra steps (see the following steps). The quicker method is to use the drag-and-drop method. To do so, hold down Alt (Windows), Opt (Mac OS) and then drag the source mask thumbnail to the target layer. When you have it over the target layer, let go, at which point Photoshop adds a copy of the mask to the target layer. If the target layer already contains a mask, you are given the chance to replace it (Figure 8-6).

FIGURE 8-6: Applying a layer mask to another layer by dragging and dropping.

TIP Should you need to reverse the mask at the same time as apply it, add the Shift key to the preceding keyboard shortcut.

If you want to use copy and paste, take the following steps:

1. Ctrl-click (Windows), ⌘-click (Mac OS) the source layer mask thumbnail to view it in the document window.
2. Ctrl+A (Windows), ⌘+A (Mac OS) to select all and then Ctrl+C (Windows), ⌘+C (Mac OS) to copy the mask onto the Clipboard.
3. Click the target layer mask thumbnail to view the mask in the document window.
4. Ctrl+V (Windows), ⌘+V (Mac OS) to paste the Clipboard contents into the document window.
5. Alt-click (Windows), Opt-click (Mac OS) the target layer mask thumbnail to return to document view.

Although adding a copy of a mask to another layer is relatively easy, adding it to multiple layers in one go is just not possible, though that might change in future versions. However, you can get around the present limitation by applying it to a group! To do so, select the target layers and create a group by choosing Layer ➔ New ➔ Group from Layers, or Ctrl+G (Windows), ⌘+G (Mac OS). Hold down Alt (Windows), Opt (Mac OS) and drag the mask thumbnail to the target group.

Editing and Modifying Masks

Grayscale masks, being grayscale images, can be edited and modified by using the same commands, filters, and painting tools that you use to edit grayscale images. Vector masks, being mathematical shapes, require a different treatment and can be edited by using the pen and shape tools.

For grayscale masks, the Edit ➜ Transform and Image ➜ Adjustments commands are probably the most useful in this regard. Among the Adjustments commands, the Brightness/Contrast and Levels commands are good workhorses.

Although you can apply most filters to a grayscale mask for special effects, the Blur ➜ Gaussian Blur, Sharpen ➜ Unsharp Mask, Stylize ➜ Median, and Other ➜ Maximum, Minimum filters are very useful for modifying.

Among the tools, the Brush tool is the most consistently used, but you can employ the other tools that use a brush tip, such as Dodge and Burn, and even the Clone Stamp tool.

TIP You can always tell whether you are editing layer content or a layer mask by observing the thumbnails in the Layers palette. Not only do they redraw as you edit one or the other, but the active thumbnail always has a border around it.

Using Painting Tools

The power of masks lies in their ability to hide layer content nondestructively and in your ability to edit them ad infinitum. The painting tools, such as the Paint Brush, Dodge, Burn, Gradient, and the Fill command, can all help in the editing process. To edit a Hide All grayscale mask (that is, one filled with black; see earlier in the chapter on how to create masks) with the Paint Brush tool, take the following steps:

1. Select a Brush tool in the Toolbox.

2. Open the Brushes palette (Window ➜ Brushes, or click the palette icon in the options bar).

3. Select a brush tip; the size depends on the size of the file.

4. Make sure that all the dynamics are turned off (you can do that from the palette menu by selecting Clear Brush Controls or deselecting them one by one) and start painting.

If you make a mistake, reverse the foreground and background colors (press X) and paint over your previous brush strokes. You can change the tip size temporarily by pressing the square bracket keys. Press [to decrease, press] to increase; add the Shift key to soften and harden the brush tip, respectively.

If you use a pen and art pad, you can set the options for the brush to use pen. To do so, take the following steps:

1. Select the Brush tool in the Toolbox.

2. Open the Brushes palette (Window ➜ Brushes, or click the palette icon in the options bar).

3. Click Shape Dynamics to display its options.

4. Choose Pen Pressure for Size, Angle, and Roundness jitter from the pop-ups (Figure 8-7).

5. To control the Opacity and Flow jitter, click Other Dynamics and choose Pen Pressure from the pop-ups.

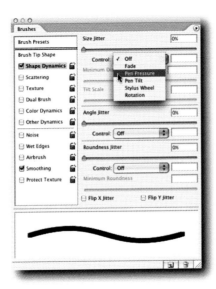

FIGURE 8-7: **Selecting pen pressure for a pen and art pad in the Brushes palette.**

To avoid having to redefine custom brushes, save the brush as a tool preset by clicking the Brush tool icon on the options bar and then clicking the Create New Tool Preset icon, just below the button for palette menu, or choose New Tool Preset from the palette menu.

Contracting and Spreading Masks

In addition to the painting tools and commands that you can employ to edit masks, you can use a couple of very useful filters to contract and spread masks. Both can be found in the Filter ➜ Other submenu. To contract, use Minimum; to spread, use Maximum.

Briefly, this is how they work: The Minimum filter works by contracting the white areas inward while spreading the black areas of color. The Radius value in the filter dialog box controls the amount of contraction. The Maximum filter works in the opposite way to that of the Minimum:

It spreads the white areas of color while contracting the black areas inward. One way to remember the functions of the two filters is to think of their names as describing the effect they have on the white fill. Minimum minimizes white; Maximum maximizes white.

Changing the Opacity

When you paint on a mask, you can alter the opacity of the strokes by using pen pressure or by specifying the opacity level for the Brush tool in the options bar. However, after a mask has been created, you have no obvious way to lower its opacity or, rather, it becomes obvious only after you remember that a grayscale mask is composed of a grayscale image. After you remember that little fact, it requires only a small leap to link a change in opacity with the Levels command: more precisely, the use of the bottom two Output Levels sliders (Figure 8-8). To make the mask more opaque (black), move the white slider to the left. To make the mask more transparent (white), move the black slider to the right.

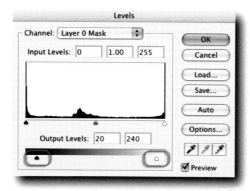

FIGURE 8-8: You can use the Output sliders in the Levels dialog box to alter the opacity of a grayscale layer mask.

Via Alpha Channel or Selection

Layer masks and selections have one thing in common: They both store their information as grayscale images in alpha channels. This commonality makes it easy to create a layer mask from a selection or a selection from a layer mask. It also opens up the possibility of modifying a grayscale layer mask by working directly on the alpha channel or, alternatively, loading the mask as a selection, altering the selection with selection tools or selection transform commands (or both), and refilling with black or white.

To work on the alpha channel, Alt+Shift-click (Windows), Opt+Shift-click (Mac OS) the layer mask thumbnail. You should see the masked areas take on a rubylith color and the foreground and background colors reset to default, ready for you to paint with black (to expand mask) and white (to contract mask). You can also add a selection and fill with black or white. Use the same shortcut to go back to the composite channel view.

To load the mask as a selection, Ctrl-click (Windows), ⌘-click (Mac OS) the layer mask thumbnail. Modify the selection (Select→Transform Selection). Fill the modified selection with black or white and then deselect (Select→Deselect).

CROSS-REFERENCE See Chapter 9 for more information on working with selections.

Modifying Vector Masks

Needless to say, none of the aforementioned techniques for modifying grayscale layer masks can be applied to a layer vector mask unless you rasterize the mask first. To modify a vector mask, click the mask thumbnail to select the work path; alternatively, if the layer is active, you can click the work path in the Paths palette (Window→Paths). When the work path is selected, use any of the pen tools or the Direct Selection tool (A) to modify the path; if a pen tool is selected, you can select the Direct Selection tool temporarily by holding down Ctrl (Windows), ⌘ (Mac OS).

CROSS-REFERENCE See Chapter 10 for more information on drawing and painting.

Transforming Masks

By default, masks are linked to the underlying layer content. When you move or transform the layer content, the mask moves and transforms in tandem. However, should you need to move or transform the mask by itself, the link can be broken easily.

To unlink a layer mask, click the link between the layer and the mask thumbnails (Figure 8-9). To restore the link, click the link icon again. After being unlinked, the mask can be transformed or repositioned independently of the layer content by using the transform commands in the Edit→Transform submenu. You can also use keyboard shortcuts: Ctrl+T (Windows), ⌘+T (Mac OS) to invoke Free Transform and then use modifier keys on the bounding box handles.

FIGURE 8-9: **Clicking the highlighted link icon in the Layers palette unlinks a layer mask from the layer content.**

Importing Elements and Preserving Layer Mask

When you import a layer into an existing document, Photoshop always creates a new layer and puts the contents into it. This can be a hindrance if what you want to do is insert the content into an existing layer and preserve the mask that's been applied to it. Time for a workaround:

1. Have the two document windows display side by side.

2. Select the layer into which you want to import the content.

3. Click the target document's window to display its layers in the Layers palette.

4. To center the content in the target document, drag the source layer tile into the target document window. To place it approximately, select the layer and then use the Move tool (M) to click in the source window and drag and drop into the target window.

5. The incoming layer should now be sitting above the target layer. Reposition the content with the Move tool so that it sits exactly where you want it, because after the next step you won't be able to move it.

TIP You can create a safety net by generating a snapshot in the History palette and return to this state if required, provided the document hasn't been closed.

6. Press Ctrl+E (Windows), ⌘+E (Mac OS) and choose Preserve from the pop-up dialog box.

Photoshop merges the layer and preserves the mask. Unless you have a pressing need to import the data into an existing layer, it's always a good idea not to merge layers and to keep them separate for as long as possible for the flexibility separate layers can provide.

Summary

Layer masks are incredibly useful because they allow you to blend layers without affecting the underlying content. Furthermore, because they are composed of grayscale images or vector paths, they are infinitely editable. You can use layer masks wisely or unwisely without fear because you know they won't damage the underlying content.

If keeping the file size to a minimum or not having enough resources is a problem, consider using vector masks; in many cases, they will do the same job as a grayscale mask but without the overheads.

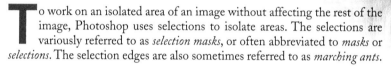

chapter 9

Hacking Selection Masks

To work on an isolated area of an image without affecting the rest of the image, Photoshop uses selections to isolate areas. The selections are variously referred to as *selection masks*, or often abbreviated to *masks* or *selections*. The selection edges are also sometimes referred to as *marching ants*.

When an area is selected, you can move the selection, or the content encompassed by the selection, around the image. You can even move the selection or the content to another open document. You can hide a selection from view, disable it altogether, or invert it so that the masked areas become exposed to editing and the unmasked areas become impervious to editing.

Creating and Saving Selection Masks

Selections can be created in a number of ways. They can be created from the ground up using the selection marquee or lasso tools, or with painting tools by entering Quick Mask mode, or they can be based on the luminosity or the color data in the image. They can also be created from existing paths and path components. In ImageReady, you can create selections from slices.

To prevent an oval- or irregular-shaped selection from viewing and printing with a stair-stepping effect, you can create selections with feathering or anti-aliasing so that they lack hard edges, and select content gradually inward and outward from the selection boundary. The feathering can be specified before the selection is created or after the event; however, the anti-aliasing has to be specified before an oval or irregular selection is created.

Selections can be contiguous or non-contiguous. You can add to or subtract from existing selections and draw freehand or in straight lines and even horizontal or vertical lines. After a selection is created, you can hide it temporarily so that you can see the image that you are working on without being distracted by the animated selection outlines.

Selections are temporary by default but can be stored as grayscale images in alpha channels, loaded from the alpha channel at any time, or exported to another open document.

NOTE Remember, not all file formats support alpha channels; the most popular file formats, PSD, PDF, TIFF, BMP, Targa, and Pixar do, but another very popular format, JPEG, does not.

Creating Circles and Squares Using Marquee Tools

You can create rectangular and elliptical selections easily in Photoshop by using the Rectangular Marquee or the Elliptical Marquee tools (M), respectively. However, odd as the omission might seem, Photoshop does not include dedicated selection tools for creating round, square, or round-cornered selections. The absence of such tools often throws off novice users. Therefore, the following hack is just for you if you happen to belong to such a group.

You have two ways of making a round or square selection. You can use the selection tools or the shape tools. Using the selection tools, take the following steps:

1. Select the Elliptical or the Rectangular Marquee tool from the Toolbox.

2. Press the Shift key. This action constrains the marquee to a circle or a square, depending on the active tool.

3. Click in the document window and drag to form a round or square marquee, respectively.

For the second method, using the shape tools, take the following steps:

1. Select the Rectangle or the Ellipse Shape tool (U).

2. Select the Paths option for the tool from the options bar (it's the second icon from the left, barring the tool icon).

3. Press the Shift key. Doing so constrains the path to a circle or square, depending on the active tool.

4. Click in the document window and drag to form a round or square path, respectively.

5. Hold down Ctrl (Windows), ⌘ (Mac OS) and press Enter (Windows), Return (Mac OS) to create a selection from the path, or choose Make Selection from the Paths palette menu and have access to extra options.

At first sight, it can seem labor intensive to create a selection from a path. However, with a little practice, you can go through the steps without thinking.

TIP To create rectangular or square selections with rounded corners in Photoshop, use the Rectangle Shape tool to draw a path and then create a selection from it (see step 5 in the preceding numbered list).

Color-Based Masks

The ability to make selections based on a particular color or hue can be very useful at times. For example, maybe you need to adjust or change the color of someone's red shirt or blue jeans. You can do this by using the Magic Wand tool, but Photoshop includes a command that gives you more control over what is selected and what is not, as well as the ability to select highlights, midtones, shadows, and out-of-gamut colors. The command can be found in the Select menu and goes by the name Color Range (Figure 9-1).

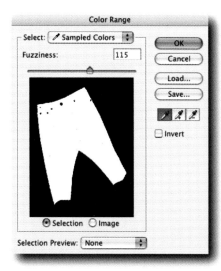

FIGURE 9-1: Use the Color Range command to select colors, highlights, midtones, shadows, and out-of-gamut colors.

The Fuzziness setting in Color Range works in a slightly different way from how the Tolerance setting for the Magic Wand tool determines which pixels should be added to the selection. Whereas Tolerance determines the range of fully selected pixels, Fuzziness also determines the range of partially selected pixels. In other words, you can create more subtle masks with the Color Range command than you can with the Magic Wand tool, which is very good at selecting broad ranges of color.

When you enter the Color Range dialog box, a selection is made for you based on the foreground color. If you would rather start with a blank slate, press Alt (Windows), Opt (Mac OS) before you select the command. You can also limit the selection to a specific area by making a selection before you enter the Color Range dialog box.

In the dialog box, you can add or subtract from the selection by using the eyedropper tools. The sample tool is selected by default, and you can drag it in the document window to define the selection range. Rather than switch tools by clicking the icons, you can press Shift to add and Alt (Windows), Opt (Mac OS) to subtract from the selection range.

You can also use the eyedropper tools in the proxy window by selecting the Image button, next to the Selection button. The proxy window always shows a 100% magnification, and this can be useful if the complete image isn't in view in the document window (though you can still use the options under the View menu and the related shortcuts to change the document magnification). Furthermore, you can choose from four types of previews, not including None, from the Selection Preview pop-up at the bottom of the dialog box.

In addition to using the eyedropper tools to define a selection range, you can choose from preset colors in the Select pop-up menu at the top of the dialog box. Note that The Out of Gamut range is based on the CMYK working space defined in Edit ➜ Color Settings. When you leave the dialog box, the selection is applied for you.

TIP To toggle between the Image and Selection previews, press Ctrl (Windows), ⌘ (Mac OS).

Luminosity-Based Masks

Selections based on the luminosity values contained in an image can be created from the composite or default color channels. They can be used to protect a range of levels from highlight to shadow when you apply adjustments and, with a bit of work, clamped to mask changes to extreme highlights, shadows, or midtones when you use them in adjustment layer masks.

You can base the mask on the composite channel by pressing Ctrl+Alt+Tilde (Windows), ⌘+Opt+Tilde (Mac OS), or on the individual channels, including the composite, by Ctrl-clicking (Windows), ⌘-clicking (Mac OS).

You can also convert a duplicate to Grayscale mode and use its single channel to load the selection, or to Lab mode and use the L channel, or to CMYK mode and use the K channel (each produces a slightly different mask).

After the selection is loaded, you can import it into the parent document. To do so, choose a selection tool, click in the selected area (the icon should change to a white arrow with an accompanying rectangular selection outline when you are over the selected area), and then drag the selection into the parent document. Hold down the Shift key when the mask is over the target window to center the selection.

Having loaded the selection, you can use the adjustment commands, such as Curves or Hue/Saturation, directly on a layer or create an adjustment layer and have the mask applied automatically.

By default, the highlights are selected and the shadows masked. You can easily inverse the selection by choosing Select ➜ Inverse, or Ctrl+Shift+I (Windows), ⌘+Shift+I (Mac OS).

To clamp or restrict the luminosity mask, save it as an alpha channel and then apply a curve that basically clips the highlight, midtone, or shadow values Likewise, if the luminosity mask was loaded in an adjustment layer mask, target the mask and then use Curves to restrict the adjustment's influence on the layer content (Figure 9-2).

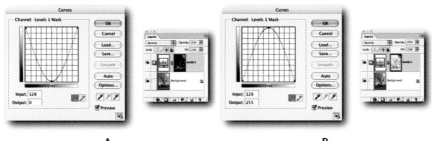

A   B

FIGURE 9-2: A luminosity mask loaded in a layer mask and then a curve used to restrict the mask to (A) midtones, (B) highlights, and shadows.

Channel-Based Masks

When you're creating a selection, channels are often good candidates for the basis of a mask, and in some images, one might yield a mask without much work. For example, you might have an image of a red building against a blue sky. By finding the channel that contains the strongest contrast between the red and blue, you can create a copy of the channel, increase the contrast and "discover" a mask (Figure 9-3). To view individual channels, click each one in turn in the Channels palette. It helps to view them as grayscale when evaluating channel content. If you are seeing them in color, choose Preferences → Display & Cursors and deselect the option Color Channels in Color. When you find a likely candidate for a mask, create a copy by dragging it to the Create New Channel button, located next to the Trash in the Channels palette.

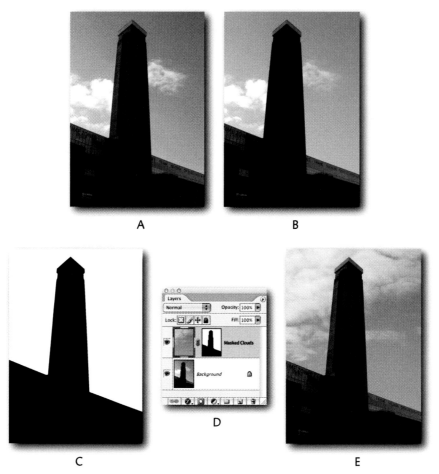

FIGURE 9-3: A—An image of the Tate Modern Gallery (London) that could benefit from having the burned out clouds replaced. B—A copy of the blue channel used as the basis for a mask. C—Levels used to crush shadows, expand highlights, and then stray levels painted with white and black to perfect the mask. D—Mask applied to a clouds layer. E—Final image minus burned-out clouds.

The copied channel might need a little bit of work to perfect the mask, which you can do easily with the Brush tool by painting with black or white (see "Using Painting Tools and Filters," later in the chapter). When you are happy with the mask, Ctrl-click (Windows), ⌘-click (Mac OS) to load it as a selection.

In addition to the Brush tool, you can use the Dodge and Burn tools on the channel to lighten or to darken detail around the mask's edges. To do so, select the corresponding range on the options bar (Shadows, Midtones, or Highlights) and then apply to remove unwanted detail. This way, you can preserve the mask edge while sending unwanted detail on either side of the edge to black or to white. This technique is particularly useful when you're creating masks with irregular edges, such as hair.

TIP You can use keyboard shortcuts to switch between the ranges for the Dodge and Burn tools. Shadows: Alt+Shift+S (Windows), Opt+Shift+S (Mac OS); Midtones: Alt+Shift+M (Windows), Opt+Shift+M (Mac OS); Highlights: Alt+Shift+H (Windows), Opt+Shift+H (Mac OS). You can also temporarily switch between the tools by holding down Alt (Windows), Opt (Mac OS).

Defining a Selection from an Exact Center Point

When you use the marquee tools to define a selection, the starting point is always the top-left corner of a rectangular selection or, in the case of an elliptical selection, an imaginary rectangular box. This can be problematic if what you want to do is to center the selection on an exact center point. For example, having drawn a circular object, you might want the selection to center on the epicenter of the object in order to adjust it. The workaround is to define the epicenter of the object, or of the first selection if you intend to overlap two selections, by using guides and then draw outward from the epicenter.

To find the epicenter of an existing object, take the following steps:

1. Activate the layer for the object.

2. Press Ctrl+T (Windows), ⌘+T (Mac OS) to activate the object's bounding box. Alternatively, select the Move tool (M) and select Show Transform Controls on the options bar.

3. Make sure that rulers are showing (View ➡ Rulers) and then drag from the ruler to create a guide and let it snap to the fulcrum icon; do the same from both rulers. You should now have a cross over the epicenter of the object.

4. Press Esc if you used the transform command in step 2.

5. Having defined the epicenter, choose a selection tool (it helps to have Other Cursors in Preferences ➡ Display and Cursors set to Precise for the next step).

6. Hover over the cross formed by the guides and position the pointer on the epicenter; use the change in color of the tool icon to guide you to the epicenter.

7. Hold down Alt (Windows), Opt (Mac OS) and draw outward.

You don't need to press Alt (Windows), Opt (Mac OS) before you start to define the marquee; you can do it at anytime during the operation, as long as you have not lifted the pointer off the document.

Defining an Aspect Ratio for a Selection

The Rectangular and the Elliptical Marquee tools have some options that are often overlooked. You can preset their width and height to a fixed size or define a width-to-height ratio. For example, if you want to create a marquee that's three times as wide as it is high, click the Style pop-up menu in the options bar (Figure 9-4), select Fixed Aspect Ratio, and then enter **3** in the Width text field and **1** in the Height text field. Now, when you drag with the marquee tool, your selection will be three times as wide as it is high.

FIGURE 9-4: **Choosing a style for the Rectangular Marquee tool from the options bar.**

If you need to crop an image by a given number of pixels using the Crop command, as opposed to the Crop tool, you can define the marquee from the same Style pop-up menu. Just select Fixed Size and then enter the pixel dimensions. You can set the width and height in any of the supported units (pixels, inches, cm, mm, points, picas, and percent).

When you enter values in text fields on the options bar, you can right-click (Windows), Ctrl-click (Mac OS) in the box and choose from the supported units in the pop-up menu. Furthermore, you are not restricted to whole numbers but can use fractions. For example, you can choose an aspect ratio for 1.85 to 1.

If you use a particular fixed size or aspect ratio repeatedly, save it as a tool preset by clicking the tool icon on the options bar and then choosing New Tool Preset from the pop-up Tool Preset Picker menu; give it a memorable name for easier identification.

Irregular Selections

One way to create irregular selections is by using the lasso tools. The other way, less intuitive but more exciting, is to use filters. Although you cannot define a selection with a filter, you can modify it (Figure 9-5). Try the following:

1. Create a new document.

2. Create a selection with the Rectangular Marquee tool.

3. Choose Select → Modify → Border and enter a value that looks good for the marquee size.

4. Press Q to enter Quick Mask Mode.

5. Choose Filter ➔ Distort ➔ Wave and play with the settings.

6. Exit the Wave dialog box and then press Q to exit Quick Mask mode.

7. Create a new layer and fill the selection with a color.

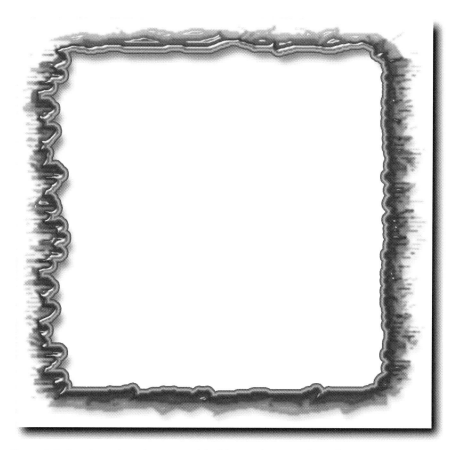

FIGURE 9-5: **A rectangular selection modified by invoking Quick Mask mode, stacking filter effects in the Filter Gallery dialog box, and then applying a style.**

Try other filters on differently shaped selections. Also, try reapplying the filters or stacking filter effects using a combination of filters. You can do that in the Filter Gallery dialog box (Filter ➜ Filter Gallery) by clicking the New Effect Layer icon, located at the bottom of the window, and then applying another filter.

Selection from a Work Path

Using paths to create selections opens a number of options. Should you need to make a selection with rounded corners, you can use the Ellipse Shape tool to define a path and then load it as a selection. You can also use the Pen tool to create a very precise path and then load that as a selection. Furthermore, you can load path components as selections.

To create a selection from a work path, take the following step:

1. Draw a path with the pen or shape tools (if it's a complex path, remember to save it from the Paths palette menu).

2. Hold down Ctrl (Windows) and press Enter, or hold down ⌘ and press Return (Mac OS). You can also click the Load Path as a Selection button in the Paths palette (located third from left).

To create a selection from a path component, select it with the Path Selection tool (A) and then click the Load Path as a Selection button in the Paths palette. The keyboard shortcut to load a path as a selection will not work in this case because it will load the entire path.

TIP   The converse to creating a selection from a path is also possible. To create a path from a selection, select Create Work Path from the Paths palette menu and enter a tolerance value between 0.5 and 10. The lower the value, the more accurately the path will follow the selection edges.

Feathered Selections

When you use a selection to make compilations of images, extract elements from their background, apply edits, or make tonal adjustments, *feathering* can help to blend the object being worked upon into the background by creating a soft edge around the selection edge. The soft edge is not unlike the anti-aliasing applied to elliptical and irregular selections. However, it differs in one respect. It extends inward and outward from the selection edge, whereas anti-aliasing creates a soft transitional zone only on the inside of the selection edge (Figure 9-6).

You can apply feathering before you create the selection by specifying it in the options bar or after the event by choosing Select ➜ Feather, or Ctrl+Alt+D (Windows), ⌘+Opt+D (Mac OS).

One popular use of feathering involves the use of an elliptical, feathered selection to create a vignette (Figure 9-7). The following steps will create a vignette and add a new background and watermarks around the vignette.

1. Make sure that the image is on a normal layer and not a Background layer.

2. Select the Elliptical Marquee tool and enter a value in the Feather text box. The figure that you enter will, of course, depend on the pixel dimensions of the image and size of the soft edge you desire.

3. Make the selection and then choose Select → Inverse. Doing so masks the areas that you want to conserve and exposes the peripheral areas.

4. Press Backspace (Windows), Delete (Mac OS) to delete the peripheral areas.

5. Add a new layer below the image layer and fill it with a solid color of your choice.

6. Finally, to add strokes around the vignette, create a new layer above the image layer and apply strokes to rectangular or elliptical selections.

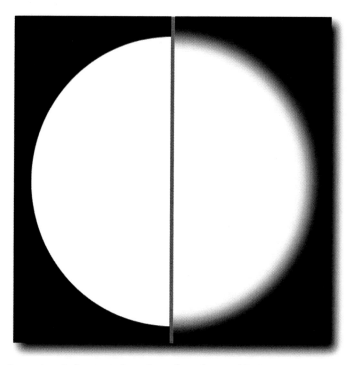

FIGURE 9-6: Left—Anti-aliased circular selection filled with black.
Right—Selection feathered by 6 pixels and then filled with white.

Feathering, though essential, can be notoriously difficult to see, making it difficult to judge which parts of the image will be affected or, indeed, how much feathering you should apply in the first place. This is because the marquee shows only the parts of the mask that are 50% or more opaque. To have a more precise idea of how the feathering tapers off, take the following steps:

1. Create a selection and apply feathering (see preceding paragraphs).

2. Press Q to enter into Quick Mask mode.

You should be able to see how the selection tapers off. If you still cannot see it too well, double-click the Quick Mask icon below the color boxes in the Toolbox and then change the opacity to 100%.

Photoshop includes one other method for applying feathering. The end result differs slightly from the feathering applied via the Select menu or the options for the marquee tools. To take advantage of it, after creating the selection, enter Quick Mask mode and then apply Filter ➜ Blur ➜ Gaussian Blur. You can also apply the other blur filters to vary the effect or to create special effects. For example, if you are making compilations, rather than settle for just a soft edge, try a Shape Blur (Figure 9-8).

FIGURE 9-7: A vignette created by applying an elliptical selection to an image on a normal layer.

FIGURE 9-8: **A Shape Blur applied to an object and then a Layer Style added for good measure.**

Saving a Selection with a File

Regardless of the method you use to create a selection, they are temporary affairs and can disappear altogether if Photoshop quits for some reason or you have a system freeze and have to shut down. To avoid having to recreate a selection that you have spent hours creating, you can convert it to an alpha channel and save it in the file. You then have the option of loading the selection at any time. Alpha channels do add to file size, but the tradeoff is more than worth it for the time that can be saved not having to recreate the selection down the line.

To save a selection, take the following steps:

1. With the selection active, choose Select ➡ Save Selection, or click the Save Selection as Channel button in the bottom of the Channels palette (second from left).

2. If you intend to save more than one selection, give the alpha channel a name. You can do it by double-clicking the default name or pressing Alt (Windows), Opt (Mac OS) before you click the Save Selection as Channel button and then entering a name in the New Channel dialog box.

3. Save the file—especially if the selection took you more than a few seconds to make!

As mentioned earlier in the chapter, not all file formats support alpha channels. However, the most popular formats, such as PSD, PDF, TIFF, BMP, PICT, Targa, and Pixar do support alpha channels.

Modifying Selections

Very rarely is a new selection perfect. Invariably, you have to do some work on it before you can use it. Fortunately, after you have stored the selection in an alpha channel, you can modify it in a number of ways. You can use painting tools, transform commands, or filters to modify the alpha channel and then load it as a selection mask.

Using Painting Tools and Filters

Because selection masks are composed of grayscale images, you can use only black and white paint, or shades of the two, to modify a mask. When you activate an alpha channel containing a selection that you wish to modify, the foreground and background colors are automatically set to *white* and *black*, respectively. However, when you enter Quick Mask mode (Q), the foreground and background colors are set to *black* and *white*, respectively.

Painting with black in the alpha channel expands the masked areas and contracts the selected areas; painting with white has the opposite effect: masked areas contract and selected areas expand. If you paint with a shade of gray, areas become partially masked or partially selected, depending on the intensity of the gray. You can paint with a shade of gray by varying the opacity for the Brush tool from the options bar, or by using the numeric keyboard: Tap 1 to 10 to alter in 10% increments, for example; tap 2 to change the opacity to 20%; or tap a figure between 1 and 100.

There is one other way to paint with shades of gray without having to change the foreground color. If you have a pen and tablet, you can open the Brushes palette and enable Pen Pressure in the options for Other Dynamics. Now when you paint, you can control the shades by simply applying more or less pressure.

When it comes to modifying active selections, the Quick Mask mode is particularly good for running filters on the selection. When the mode has been invoked, you can use filters to contract, expand, soften, harden, or transform selection edges. For example, you can use the blur filters to soften edges (as noted previously), the Maximum and Minimum (Filter ➜ Other) to expand and contract selected areas, respectively, and the distort or artistic filters to create fanciful selections. Try the various filters to see which ones work and which don't (Figure 9-9). Not all filters can be applied in Quick Mask mode.

Here's another use for Quick Mask mode and filter combo. It's almost impossible to create smooth selections with the Lasso tool. If you need to smooth the jagged edges before you can use a selection, you have two options. One, choose Select ➜ Modify ➜ Smooth and enter a numeric value in the Smooth dialog box or, two, enter Quick Mask mode and apply Filter ➜ Noise ➜ Median. Both will produce similar results, but with the latter method, you will have visual feedback.

FIGURE 9-9: A frame created by (1) applying a border to a selection, (2) entering Quick Mask mode, (3) applying the Fresco filter, (4) creating a new layer and filling with a color, and (5) applying a layer style.

Warp Command

The new Warp command warps not only filled objects, type, and shapes but also selections. Using a combination of preset and custom warps, you can create almost any shape you can imagine. To warp a selection, take the following steps:

1. With a selection active, choose Select ➜ Transform Selection or right-click (Windows), Ctrl-click (Mac OS) the selection and then choose Transform Selection from the contextual menu.

2. Next, click the warp icon in the options bar to invoke the Warp command (Figure 9-10).

FIGURE 9-10: **The options bar showing options for the transform command: A—Warp Style pop-up menu. B—Change The Warp Orientation (available after a warp style is selected). C—Switch Between Free Transform and Warp Modes.**

3. To effect a distortion, drag one of the four corner handles, one of the eight individual control points, or click in the mesh and then drag (Figure 9-11).

4. When you are happy with the distortion, click the commit icon in the options bar or press Enter (Windows), Return (Mac OS).

To move the selection bounding box, hold down Ctrl (Windows), ⌘ (Mac OS), click in the bounding box, and drag.

As does the Type tool, the Warp command has preset warps that can be accessed from the Warp Style pop-up menu in the options bar after the command is invoked (Figure 9-10). Furthermore, after you select a style, two other options become available to you. One, you can enter precise numeric values in the bend and distort text boxes; two, you can change the orientation by clicking the Change Warp Orientation button next to the Warp Style pop-up menu (refer to Figure 9-10).

NOTE You cannot enter numeric values if you have chosen None or Custom from the Warp Style pop-up menu.

Preventing Rounded Corners when Expanding

When you expand a rectangular selection and stroke it by more than a pixel, you might have noticed that the stroke acquires rounded corners (Figure 9-12). This is not caused by a setting that you might have overlooked; it's just the way the feature works. To prevent this unwanted side effect, you can employ one of the following three workarounds:

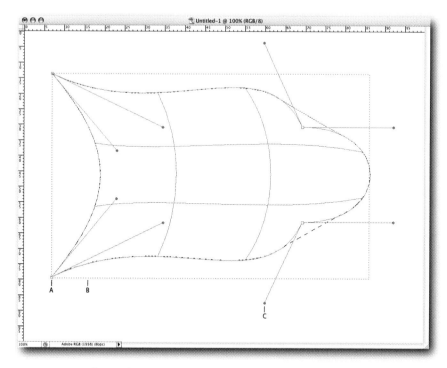

FIGURE 9-11: A selection being warped by using the Edit ➜ Transform Selection ➜ Warp command; A—Corner handle. B—Original selection bounding box. C—Control point.

1. Stroke inside the selection but be prepared to lose some of your image content.

2. Expand the selection in one-pixel increments and then stroke inside. To do so, choose Select ➜ Modify ➜ Expand. If you need to modify by a large amount, create an action and run it on the selection as many times as necessary (see Chapter 15).

3. With the selection active, enter Quick Mask mode. Choose Filter ➜ Other ➜ Maximum and enter the number of pixels by which you want to expand the selection. Exit Quick Mask mode and then stroke inside without fear of rounded corners.

205

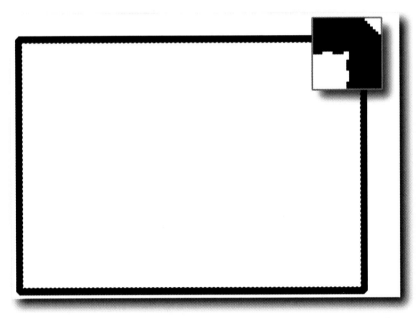

FIGURE 9-12: **Rectangular selection produces rounded corners when stroked on the outside.**

Selection Mask Quick Hacks

The following hacks cover some of the methods most commonly used for creating selection masks. They are presented here in one place for your consumption. Feast on them from time to time when you feel hungry.

- **Switching Lasso Tool Modes.** When you use the Lasso tool to draw freehand selections, press Alt (Windows), Opt (Mac OS) to draw in straight lines. To revert to freehand, raise the tool modifier key *after* a click.

- **Switching Polygonal Lasso Tool Modes.** When you use the Polygonal Lasso tool to draw straight lines, press Alt (Windows), Opt (Mac OS) to draw freehand. To revert to straight lines, raise the tool modifier key *after* a click.

- **Changing Sample Size for Magnetic Lasso Tool.** When you use the Magnetic Lasso tool, use a large width for smooth areas and a small width for detailed areas. You can change the width of the sample area by using the square bracket keys or clicking the pen icon in the options bar if you use a pen and tablet.

- **Moving Selections.** To move a selection marquee while drawing, hold down the Spacebar and drag to a new position.

- **Moving Selection Content.** To move a selection marquee and the enclosed content, select the Move tool and then click and drag or use the arrow keys. You can access the Move tool temporarily by holding down Ctrl (Windows), ⌘ (Mac OS), except when the active tools are the Hand, Pen, shape, path selection, or slice tools.

- **Moving and Duplicating Selection Content.** To move a selection marquee and duplicate the content at the same time, select the Move tool, hold down Alt (Windows), Opt (Mac OS), and then drag or use arrow keys. Alternatively, hold down Ctrl+Alt (Windows), Opt (Mac OS) and then drag.

- **Hiding the Marching Ants.** Press H to hide marching ants (marquee boarder). Press once more to reveal. What is hidden or not hidden by the keyboard shortcut can be specified in View ➜ Show ➜ Show Extras Options.

- **Positioning Active Selection Precisely.** You can reposition an active selection mask by selecting a marquee or lasso tool, placing the tool pointer in the selection, and then dragging the selection to a new position. If you need to position it precisely and you know the coordinates of where you want to reposition it, choose Select ➜ Transform Selection, or select the command from the contextual menu and then enter the coordinates in the options bar. You can also use the arrow keys to nudge the selection, regardless of whether it's being transformed.

- **Selecting Similar Colors.** To select colors next to similar colors with the Magic Wand tool, create a Levels or Curves adjustment layer, increase the contrast, make the selection, and then delete the adjustment layer.

- **Resizing Marquees Proportionally.** To create a marquee half the size of your document, regardless of the size, select Fixed Size in the options bar and then, in the Height and Width fields, enter 100% in one and 50% in the other. Try other combinations; for example, enter 50% in both fields.

- **Modifying Selections.** To modify a selection, choose Select ➜ Modify; then, from the submenu, choose Border, Smooth, Expand or Contract and enter a value in pixels in the pop-up dialog box.

- **Adding, Subtracting, and Intersecting Selections.** You can add to, subtract from, or intersect with a selection while creating it or after the event. To do so, press Shift to add; Alt (Windows), Opt (Mac OS) to subtract; Alt+Shift (Windows), Opt+Shift (Mac OS) to intersect. You can also specify an option for the selection tool in the options bar before you use it by clicking one of the buttons. The options are, from left to right, New Selection, Add to Selection, Subtract from Selection, and Intersect with Selection.

- **Rotating Selections.** When you need to rotate a selection, you have two choices.

  - Choose Select ➜ Transform Selection and then drag the pointer outside the bounding box.

  - If you need more control, after choosing Transform Selection, insert the curser in the Set Rotation text field on the options bar (third from the right and marked with a protractor icon) and then ride the Up and Down Arrow keys.

- **Inversing Selections.** To select unselected areas and deselect selected areas, choose Select ➜ Inverse or press Ctrl+Shift+I (Windows), ⌘+Shift+I (Mac OS). Press again to revert.

- **Growing Selections.** Having used the Magic Wand tool to select a range of colors, you can add to the range by holding down Shift and clicking another sample area. However, sometimes that can yield unexpected results. Instead, use the Grow command in the Select menu to add adjacent pixels that fall within the tolerance set for the Magic Wand tool. For example, if you set Tolerance to 10 and click a pixel with a value of 120, Photoshop selects all pixels that have values between 110 and 130.

- **Adding Similar Colors.** To add noncontiguous pixels with a similar color value to a selection, choose Select ➜ Similar. As with the Grow command, Photoshop uses the tolerance set for the Magic Wand tool to determine which pixels to add to the selection.

- **Loading Selections from Open Documents.** To load a selection from another open document, you can either drag and drop between source and target document windows or save the selection as an alpha channel from the Channels palette and then choose Select ➜ Load Selection. In the Load Selection dialog box, choose the source document and the alpha channel from the pop-up menus. This method has the added advantage of giving you the option of adding, subtracting, or intersecting the incoming selection with any active selection in the target document.

- **Resurrecting Selections.** When creating selections, you can easily click in the document window with the selection tool and obliterate the selection, or so it would appear. The selection is still lurking somewhere and requires only the right command to bring it back. Provided that you haven't made another selection, choose Select ➜ Reselect, or Ctrl+Shift+D (Windows), ⌘+Shift+D (Mac OS) and, *voilà*, instant resurrection.

- **Transforming Selections.** To adjust a selection after it has been drawn, right-click (Windows), Ctrl-click (Mac OS) in the selection and choose Transform Selection. To scale, skew, distort, and change perspective, hold down the Ctrl, Alt (Windows), ⌘, Opt (Mac OS), or Shift keys singularly or in combos and then move handles; you can also scale in one direction by dragging a corner handle or rotate by dragging outside the bounding box (the companion Web site for this book, at www.wiley.com/go/ extremetech, has information about keyboard shortcuts available).

Summary

Regardless of whether you call them selections, selection masks, or just masks, being able to isolate an area of an image to work on is an essential part of image editing. With the techniques, hints, and tips included in this chapter, you should be well armed for creating selection masks that fit the bill for almost any image-editing assignment.

When you have the various techniques under your belt, try to use them in a unconventional way and thereby discover new shortcuts, workarounds, and techniques. For example, sometimes it's easier to use the Magic Wand tool to select the areas that you want to mask rather than select and then inverse the mask, so that the masked areas become the selected areas, which is what you wanted in the first place.

chapter 10

Drawing and Painting

I n Photoshop, you draw with *paths* and paint with *strokes*. You can draw from the ground up and create realistic-looking objects, everything from a nut and bolt to a guitar or a limousine. You can color black and white line art, create charcoal sketches, or paint in an oil or watercolor style from the ground up. In fact, you are limited only by your ability and your imagination to use Photoshop's various vector and painting tools.

This will show you how to use the drawing tools and related commands productively and, in the process, liberate your mind so that you are free to imagine ingenious ways of using them to draw and to paint.

Drawing Paths

The Pen tool holds terrors for many people and that, unfortunately, deprives them of a very useful tool for creating precise paths that can be turned into shapes, selections, and masks. There is only one way to lose the fear and gain confidence: Practice using the tool for 10–15 minutes a day. With a little perseverance, you should be able to produce useable paths within a week, if not the first day.

Briefly, paths are made up of mathematically defined straight lines, curves, corner points, and cusps. Each end of a straight line, also called a *segment*, ends in an anchor point, and each end of a curve ends in a cusp. When a curved segment is selected, the anchor points display direction lines that end in direction points. Moving the direction points changes the curve's tangent (Figure 10-1).

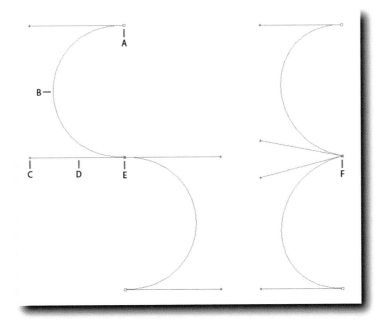

Figure 10-1: A—Anchor point. B—Curve. C—Direction point. D—Direction line. E—Cusp or Smooth point. F—Corner point.

Curves can end in a smooth point or a corner point. Smooth points are used to conjoin two curves whose arc forms a circular path or traverse in obverse directions; the letters C and S, respectively, are good examples. Corner points are used to conjoin two curves whose arcs form an obtuse angle; the letter B is a good example (Figure 10-1). Smooth points can be converted into corner points, and vice versa, using the Convert Point tool (hidden under the Pen tool).

Paths can be open ended or closed. For example, a circular path is a closed path whereas a straight line is open at either end (Figure 10-2).

To get a feel for drawing paths, start by drawing straight lines. To do so, select the Pen tool (P), make sure that its option is set to Paths in the options bar (hover over the buttons and hold the pointer still to see their functions), click once, lift and move the pointer to another location, and click again. You have just drawn an open-ended path segment. To close a path, click the first anchor point. This is very similar to closing a selection.

If you make a mistake, you can delete the last anchor point by using Undo, or delete any anchor point by using the very appropriately named Delete Anchor Point tool.

When you draw a new segment, Photoshop creates a work path in the Paths palette behind the scenes and, as long as the work path is active, all new segments are added to it and become one path. To avoid confusion while practicing, save the work path by double-clicking it. This way, when you draw a new path, Photoshop will create a new work path if none is active. You can activate each work path one at a time to see your progression.

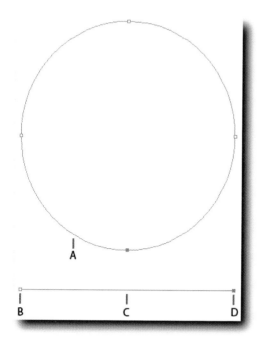

A

B   C   D

FIGURE 10-2: A—Closed path. B—Unselected anchor point. C—Open-ended path. D—Selected anchor point.

Next, try something more ambitious, such as a curve. Try drawing an S-shaped path, either a standing-up S or one lying on its side. To draw a standing-up S shape (refer to Figure 10-1), take the following steps:

1. Select the Pen tool and make sure that its options are set to draw paths, not shape layers, by clicking the second icon in the options bar.

2. Drag out a vertical guide from a Ruler (R).

3. Click the guide about a quarter of the way down and drag to the left in a straight line.

4. Click the guide halfway down and drag in a straight line to the right. When you see an even arc, stop.

5. Click the guide three quarters of the way down and drag in a straight line to the left. Stop when you see an even arc.

You have just drawn an open-ended, obverse arc containing two end points and a smooth anchor point in the middle, or, in layman's language, an S-shaped path. To manipulate the path, press Ctrl (Windows), ⌘ (Mac OS) to temporarily access the Direct Selection tool; then, drag on the direction points. Click the anchor points to access both direction lines.

You can move the direction lines independently of each other by pressing Alt (Windows), Opt (Mac OS) and then dragging the direction points. This effectively changes the smooth point to a corner point. When you now drag on the direction points, the direction lines should move independently of each other and influence only the arc below or above the anchor point.

To draw a path that requires corner points, after drawing a curve, press Alt (Windows), Opt (Mac OS) to temporarily access the Corner Point tool and click the anchor point (refer to Figure 10-1). Then continue drawing the path.

TIP One of the best ways to practice creating paths is by tracing the alphabet. For example, create a new document, view at 100% magnification, select the Type tool, choose a chunky font without serifs, such as Impact, type the letter A, resize until it fills the document window, and then trace with the Pen tool. Next, do the same to the letter B, and so forth. In no time at all, you will wonder why you were ever afraid of the Pen tool.

Here are a few pointers to bear in mind when drawing paths. They might just make that learning curve a little less steep.

- **Previewing Path Segments.** The Pen tool has an option that lets you preview a path segment before you put down the next anchor point. It can be a help or a hindrance, depending on your ability to previsualize. To enable it, click the downward pointing triangle next to the Custom Shape button on the options bar and select Rubber Band.

- **Automatically Adding/Deleting Anchor Points.** By enabling Auto Add/Delete on the options bar when you're drawing paths with the Pen tool, you can save yourself some time. When the option is enabled, you can add anchor points without having to select the Add/Delete Anchor Point pen tools. Simply hover over an *active* path segment and then click to add an anchor point, or hover over an anchor point and then click to delete it (the tool icon changes as you hover over path segments and anchor points). You can temporarily disable the option at any time by pressing Shift.

- **Picking Up a Path from where You Left Off.** If you accidentally close a path before you've finished, when you click again you will start a new path. To pick up where you left off or to add a segment to a saved path, click in the last drawn anchor point and then continue drawing (Figure 10-3). The new segment will be conjoined to the old.

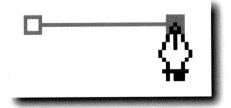

FIGURE 10-3: Picking up a path by clicking inside an anchor point.

Creating a Path from a Selection

Should you need to turn a selection into a work path, perhaps to create a vector mask, a clipping path, or just to store it as a path to save on file size, you can do it by clicking the Make Work Path from Selection button in the Paths palette (Figure 10-4).

FIGURE 10-4: **Detail from the Paths palette with the Make Work Path from Selection button highlighted.**

If the selection is a simple rectangle or oval, you will have a faithful path to work with. However, if it is irregular, you might have to smooth it or use the tolerance setting for all new paths created from selections. To access the setting, choose Make Work Path from the Paths palette menu, or Alt-click (Windows), Opt-click (Mac OS) the Make Work Path from Selection button. Enter a value between 0.5 and 10 pixels in the Make Work Path dialog box and click the OK button. Lower values produce more faithful work paths; higher values produce less faithful work paths.

Converting Individual Path Components to a Selection

If you try to convert a path to a selection, Photoshop includes all path components in the selection by default. However, what if you need to convert only some of the path components to a selection? In that case, take the following steps:

1. Shift-click with the Path Selection tool the component paths that you do want to turn into selections.

2. Press Ctrl+X (Windows), ⌘+X (Mac OS) to cut the selected component paths and to transfer them onto the Clipboard.

3. In the Paths palette, deactivate the current Work Path tile by clicking anywhere in an empty area or pressing Esc.

4. Press Ctrl+V (Windows), ⌘+V (Mac OS) to paste the component paths as a new work path.

5. Hold down Ctrl (Windows), ⌘ (Mac OS) and press Enter (Windows), Return (Mac OS) to load the work path as a selection.

That's all there is to it! Because work paths act independently of each other, you can separate any number of path components this way and then edit them or turn them into selections.

Avoiding Disappearing Paths

When you draw a work path, it can disappear altogether if you deselect it and then draw another work path. This can prove painful if you spent half an hour drawing a complex path! To avoid the problem disappearing paths, you must save the work path. To do so, choose Save Path from the palette menu or, alternatively, double-click the Work Path tile and when the Work Path dialog box pops up, accept the default name or give it a memorable name if you intend to export it or create several paths.

Creating Clipping Paths

Clipping paths are often used in layout programs to clip parts of an image so that unwanted parts do not print. However, if you have drawn a path and tried to define it as a clipping path, you might have noticed that the Clipping Path option is grayed out. That's because the path needs to be saved before it can be defined as a clipping path. To save a clipping path, take the following steps:

1. Double-click the Work Path tile.

2. Name the path in the Save Path pop-up dialog box and then click the OK button.

3. Choose Clipping Path from the Paths palette menu. The path should be selected for you in the Clipping Path dialog box. Leave the Flatness text field blank (see the paragraph that follows) and click the OK button.

When you save a clipping path, the flatness value that you enter in the Clipping Path dialog box controls how faithfully the clipping path's curve will be reproduced by the RIP (Raster Image Processor). If you enter a lower flatness value, it translates into a more accurate curve because a greater number of straight lines are used to draw the curve; a higher flatness value translates into a less faithful curve because fewer straight lines are used to draw the curve.

Generally speaking, flatness values from 8 to 10 are recommended for high-resolution printing (1200 to 2400 dpi) and values from 1 to 3 for low-resolution printing (300 to 600 dpi). If you are not sure what value to enter, leave the field blank and let the printer use a default value.

TIP If you can't distinguish between the object and the background when you draw a clipping path (for example, a tire on a car that happens to be in deep shadow), use a Curves or Levels adjustment layer to adjust the image, make the path, and then delete the adjustment layer.

Creating Compound Clipping Paths

A compound clipping path is made up of two or more subpaths used to mask each other. For example, if you need to enclose an image in a doughnut-like shape, you can draw two circular paths to clip the image inside and outside the O shape. The shape doesn't have to be circular; it can be any shape, as long as the paths are not open (Figure 10-5).

FIGURE 10-5: A compound clipping path used to create a vector layer mask.

To create a compound clipping path, assuming that you want your image to appear inside a doughnut-shaped ring, take the following steps:

1. Select the Ellipse tool (one of the hidden shape tools).

2. In the options bar, select the Paths icon (second from left) and the Exclude Overlapping Path Areas icon (last of the four inline icons).

3. Create a cross with guides to mark the center of the doughnut.

4. Press Alt+Shift (Windows), Opt+Shift (Mac OS), click the cross, and draw an inner circle.

5. Press Alt+Shift (Windows), Opt+Shift (Mac OS), click the cross, and draw an outer circle.

6. Save the work path by double-clicking the Work Path tile in the Paths palette and then name it for good measure.

7. Choose Clipping Path from the Paths palette menu and select the path that you just named. Leave the Flatness value text field blank.

It doesn't matter whether you draw the inner circle or the outer circle first; as long as the Exclude Overlapping Path Areas option is active when you draw the path, it ends up as a compound clipping path.

You can double-check whether a work path is a compound path by choosing a pen or shape tool, pressing Ctrl (Windows), ⌘ (Mac OS), drawing a marquee around the subpaths, and then seeing which icon highlights on the options bar. The Exclude Overlapping Path Areas icon (the last options icon) should highlight if the work path is a proper compound path. If the icon does not highlight, click it to convert the selected work path to a compound path.

Previewing How Closely Your Clipping Paths Fit

If you are making lots of clipping paths, or even the occasional one, and need to see how tightly they will clip the edges when turned into a selection, use the following hack to see any gaps:

1. With the path active, hold down Ctrl (Windows), ⌘ (Mac OS) and press Enter (Windows), Return (Mac OS). This action loads the path as a selection.

2. Choose Select ➜ Inverse or press Ctrl+Shift+I (Windows), ⌘+Shift+I (Mac OS) to inverse the selection.

3. Press Q to enter Quick Mask mode.

4. If you see any gaps between the path and the image you are trying to clip, click the work path to activate it and then modify it with the pen and Direct Selection tools.

5. Press Q again to exit quick Mask Mode and then choose Select ➜ Deselect or Ctrl+D (Windows), ⌘+D (Mac OS) to deselect the selection.

Repeat the steps as many times as necessary until the path hugs the image as closely as possible (Figure 10-6).

FIGURE 10-6: A clipping path viewed in Quick Mask mode with the color overlay set to black and 100% opacity for the selected areas.

Moving, Transforming, and Stroking Paths

Having drawn a path, it's only natural that you should want to or need to work on it. Photoshop offers the usual aids for moving, transforming, aligning, distributing, and stroking. Some of the commands, such as stroke and move, are dedicated, but others, such as transform used to affect fills, double up when a path is active. This feature can be confusing at first, but when you are aware that the menu items change according to mode, it should not pose a problem.

Moving Paths

After a path has been drawn, you may move it around the document or even to another document. Furthermore, paths can be duplicated (Figure 10-7) or exported to an Illustrator file from the File ➜ Export submenu. To move a path, use the following methods:

- Select the Path Selection tool (A), click the path, or inside it, and then drag to a new position.

- Use the Direct Selection tool (A) to draw a marquee around the path, click it, and then drag to a new position.

- If the Direct Selection tool is already active, press Ctrl (Windows), ⌘ (Mac OS), place the pointer inside the path or on it, click, and then drag to a new position.

FIGURE 10-7: **You can duplicate a path by holding down Ctrl+Alt (Windows), ⌘+Opt (Mac OS) and dragging to a new position while a pen or shape tool is active.**

NOTE Activating the Path Selection tool this way is sticky. If you want to continue editing the path, you must go to the Toolbox and select the Direct Selection tool again or Ctrl-click (Windows), ⌘-click (Mac OS) the path once more.

- If the Pen tool is active, to access one of the selection tools temporarily, press Ctrl (Windows), ⌘ (Mac OS). Just remember to draw a marquee with the tool to select the whole path; otherwise, only the segment you click is affected.

Moving a Path in Tandem with Layer Content

Moving a path is relatively easy using either the Path Selection or the Direct Selection tool and then dragging it to a new position (see previous section). However, if you've created a path to fit layer content and then want to move both the content and the path while keeping them in register, it requires a little extra effort:

1. Select the path with the Path Selection tool.

2. In the Layers palette, make the layer with the content active by clicking its tile.

3. Ctrl-click (Windows), ⌘-click (Mac OS) the Add Layer Mask button, located third from left at the bottom of the Layers palette. Doing so adds a vector mask.

4. Shift-click the vector mask to hide it. Click the layer thumbnail and move the content.

When you move the layer content, the path moves in tandem. If you want to save the path in the new position, make sure that the layer is still selected (necessary to reveal the mask) and then drag the LayerName Vector Mask tile in the Paths palette to the Create New Path button. Save the new work path by double-clicking it.

Combining Path Components

You can combine existing subpaths to form a single path and thereby create new and interesting paths. You can also add, subtract, exclude, or overlap an existing path with new subpaths.

To combine two subpaths, select the Path Selection tool, marquee the subpaths or Shift-click them, and then select Combine from the options bar.

To add subtract, exclude, or overlap, select the subpaths and then select an option from the options bar, or select it before you draw the second subpath. To fill the combined subpaths, make sure that the path is active and then choose Layer ➔ New ➔ Solid Color (Figure 10-8).

FIGURE 10-8: **Two subpaths combined, filled with solid color and then a layer style added.**

You can see simple path combinations straight away, but combinations that add, subtract, exclude, or overlap become apparent only when you fill a path. It can help to visualize how the components will interact when combined if you have the thumbnail options for the Paths palette set to medium or large; you can access Palette Options from the palette menu.

Aligning and Distributing Paths

When it comes to aligning filled objects manually, using Smart Guides is a great help (View ➜ Show ➜ Smart Guides). However, Smart Guides has no affect on paths. Fortunately, if you need to align or distribute two or more path components on a single work path, you can do it automatically. To do so, take the following steps:

1. Click the work path in the Paths palette to activate the component paths.

2. Select the Path Selection tool and then marquee the component paths, or Shift-click them.

3. Select an alignment option from the options bar.

The component paths will align automatically for you according to the selected option. To distribute, make sure that you have three or more component paths selected and then at step 3 select a distribution option from the options bar.

Transforming Clipping Paths to Fit Resized Layer

Have you ever spent hours creating a clipping path and then got the call to transform the layer content? Faced with repetitious work, do you try to talk your client out of resizing the object or, worse still, try to talk yourself out of it, or do you dig deeper into your resources and try to come up with a solution? No need to dig too deeply; the solution lies very much at the surface. To transform layer content and the clipping path, take the following steps:

1. With the selection active, choose Edit ➜ Free Transform, or Ctrl+T (Windows), ⌘+T (Mac OS).

2. Transform the content by normal means: dragging the bounding box handles or entering values in the text fields on the options bar.

3. Choose Select ➜ Deselect or press Ctrl+D (Windows), ⌘+D (Mac OS) to deselect the selection.

4. Activate the work path by clicking its tile in the Paths palette.

5. Choose Edit ➜ Transform Path ➜ Again, or press Ctrl+Shift+T (Windows), ⌘+Shift+T (Mac OS).

The transformed path should scale by the same amount as the first transform and fit as snugly as it did before it was transformed. One satisfied client and that old enemy, boredom, thwarted before it could take a foothold.

NOTE Fortunately, there is no need for a workaround if the client asks for the entire image to be resized. When you use the Image Size command, paths are automatically scaled to fit.

Stroking Paths

Did you know that you can stroke a path with no fewer than 16 tools? That's an awful lot of scope for creativity. You can use any one of the following tools: Pencil, Brush, Eraser, Background Eraser, Clone Stamp, Pattern Stamp, Healing Brush, History Brush, Art History Brush, Smudge, Blur, Sharpen, Dodge, Burn, Sponge, and Color Replacement.

To stroke an existing path using any one of the preceding tools, take the following steps:

1. Specify the settings of the tool you wish to use to stroke (that is, Brush, Blur, Clone Stamp tool, and so forth).

2. Activate the path by clicking the path tile in the Paths palette.

3. From the Paths palette menu, select Stroke Path and choose the tool in the pop-up dialog box. Note that you can also call up the Stroke Path dialog box by holding down Alt (Windows), Opt (Mac OS) and then clicking the Stroke Path with Brush button in the Paths palette (Figure 10-9).

223

FIGURE 10-9: Detail from the Paths palette with the Stroke Path with Brush button highlighted.

When you click the OK button, the path will be stroked with the foreground color—unless, of course, you decide to use the Eraser tool!

TIP Here's a quick-and-dirty way to stroke a path: While the work path is active, press B (for Brush). Next, select a brush shape and foreground color and then press Enter (Windows), Return (Mac OS).

Stroking Paths with Gradients or Images

Although there are 16 tools to choose from when stroking a path, the Gradient tool is not among the list. Here's a little workaround that allows you to stroke with the Gradient tool:

1. Create your gradient on a new, blank layer.

2. Create a new, blank layer below it and name it.

3. Draw the path to be stroked.

4. Select the Brush tool and a suitable tool tip.

5. Make sure that the path is still active by clicking its tile in the Paths palette and then, from the Paths palette menu, choose Stroke Path.

6. Select Brush tool from the Stroke Path pop-up dialog box and click the OK button.

7. Hold down Alt (Windows), Opt (Mac OS) and click the line dividing the two layer tiles, or make sure that the gradient layer is still selected and then press Ctrl+Alt (Windows), ⌘+Opt (Mac OS). This step clips the gradient layer to the stroke in the layer below it (Figure 10-10).

You can just as easily stroke with an image as you can with a gradient. The principle is the same.

TIP Paths can be stroked not only with a history state but also with a pattern. Furthermore, you can fill paths with Solid Color, Pattern, or History. To fill, choose Edit→ Fill and then select History from the pop-up menu, or choose Fill Path from the Paths palette menu and then select History from the pop-up menu in the Fill Path dialog box; holding down Alt (Windows), Opt (Mac OS) and clicking the "Fill with foreground color" icon, first from left, in the Paths palette also gives you access to the same dialog box.

FIGURE 10-10: **A path effectively stroked with a gradient and then a layer style applied.**

Creating and Editing Shapes

Shapes are essentially composed of a clipping path filled with solid color. You can create a shape out of a layer filled with color, or you can create the path first and then fill it with color. For example, you could fill a layer with a gradient, create a path, and then choose Layer → Vector Mask → Current Path, or you could create a path, choose Layer → New Fill Layer, and then from the submenu choose Solid Color, Gradient, or Pattern.

If you have invested time learning to draw and modify paths, creating and modifying shapes should not present a problem for you. The following quick hacks should highlight some of the connections and refresh the old memory, and even add to it.

- **Drawing from the Center Outward.** Press Alt (Windows), Opt (Mac OS) as you draw with any of the shape tools, barring the Line tool.

- **Drawing Proportional Shapes.** Press Shift as you draw with any of the shape tools, barring the Line tool. You can also specify options for each shape tool by clicking the downward-pointing triangle next to the Custom Shape tool icon. The options allow you to draw a fixed size or proportional marquees repeatedly, and to draw arrowheads with the Line tool.

- **Repositioning while Drawing.** Press the Spacebar and drag to new position.

- **Drawing Diagonal Lines.** Press Shift to constrain the Line tool to 45° angles.

- **Base Shapes on Fonts.** You can create some interesting shapes from fonts; for example, from Wingdings, Dingbats, and Symbol fonts. After the shapes are created, you can use all the editing tools, transforms, and Layer Styles to create something original. To do so, select the type layer and then choose Layer ➜ Type ➜ Convert to Shape, or right-click (Windows), Ctrl-click (Mac OS) the type layer and choose Convert to Shape from the contextual menu.

- **Creating Pixels with Shape Tools.** Though this method is not as versatile as rasterizing a shape layer, you can create a shape that contains pixels from the onset. To do so, select Fill Pixels from the options bar *before* you draw a shape. It's the third options button from the left.

- **Hiding Shape Outlines.** If you find it difficult to see what you are doing to a shape layer, for example, when applying an effect, you can hide the shape outlines. To do so, click the shape tile in the Paths palette or press Ctrl+H (Windows), ⌘+H (Mac OS). For the shortcut to work, you must have Target Path selected in View ➜ Show ➜ Show Extras Options. Alternatively, press Ctrl+Shift+H (Windows), ⌘+Shift+H (Mac OS).

- **Aligning and Distributing Shapes.** You can align and distribute shapes in the same way that you can paths. The difference being, you must select the shape layers as opposed to a work path. After the layers are selected, select the Move tool and then select an option to align or distribute on the options bar.

NOTE You must select three or more layers to distribute.

Combining Existing Shape Layers

Each time you create a shape, Photoshop places it on its own layer. However, you can combine shapes if required, but not in the conventional way of combining pixel-based layers—at least, not without rasterizing the two layers first. To do so, take the following steps:

1. In the Layers palette, click the vector mask of the source shape layer that you want to combine.

2. Choose Edit ➜ Copy, or Ctrl+C (Windows), ⌘+C (Mac OS). If you want to delete the source shape layer, select the path with the Path Selection tool and then cut the path by pressing Ctrl+X (Windows), ⌘+X (Mac OS).

3. Select the vector mask of the target shape layer.

4. Choose Edit ➜ Paste, or Ctrl+V (Windows), ⌘+V (Mac OS).

Photoshop combines the two shapes and applies any effects that might be present in the target layer.

Applying Gradients to Shape Layers

When you create a shape using the pen or shape tools, by default the clipping path is filled with a solid color. However, suppose that you want to fill it with a gradient? You have three choices, and, no, the Gradient tool is not one of them, because it cannot be used on a shape layer without first rasterizing the layer.

- You can apply a gradient layer effect after you have created a shape filled with color.

- You can create a layer style that uses just a gradient and then select it as a style in the options bar for whichever tool you are using to draw the shape.

- You can create the shape as a path and then fill a new layer with a gradient and have it clipped to the shape of the path.

To add a layer effect, take the following steps:

1. Double-click the layer tile to call up the Layer Style dialog box.

2. Click Gradient Overlay.

3. Click the downward-pointing triangle by the side of the gradient preview pop-up and select a gradient from the Gradient chooser.

4. Click the OK button to exit the dialog box and to apply the effect.

To save a layer style so that you can select it in the options bar before you draw a shape, take the following steps:

1. Choose a gradient in the Layer Style dialog box as previously described.

2. Save it as a new Layer Style by clicking the New Style button. Alternatively, rather than choose from preset gradients, click the gradient bar, create a new gradient in the Gradient Editor when it pops up, and then save it as a new style.

When you exit the dialog box, the style will be available to the pen and shape tools from the options bar. Select it before you draw a shape. You can also select it at any time after you have drawn the shape, as long as the vector mask is selected.

To create the shape as a path and then fill the layer with a gradient, take the following steps:

1. Use the pen or shape tools to create a closed path by choosing the Paths option for the tool from the options bar.

2. Choose Layer ➡ New Fill Layer ➡ Gradient.

3. In the New Layer dialog box, name the layer for good measure and click the OK button.

4. In the Gradient Fill dialog box (Figure 10-11), click the downward-pointing triangle by the gradient preview pop-up and choose a suitable gradient.

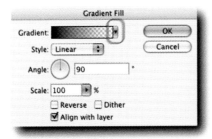

FIGURE 10-11: **The Gradient Fill dialog box. Click the highlighted arrow to access the Gradient chooser.**

5. Select a Style, Angle, Scale, Reverse, or Dither option (the Dither option reduces banding by applying dithering to the gradient) as required and then click the OK button to exit.

The layer is clipped to the shape of the path and a new gradient filled shape layer is created for you. The keen-eyed might have noticed that at step 2 you can choose to fill the path with a solid color or a pattern. It's something to store for future use when thinking creatively.

Drawing Arrow Heads and Tails

There is no dedicated tool in Photoshop for drawing arrows. However, the Line tool has options to add arrowheads at either end of a line (Figure 10-12). To create an arrow, take the following steps:

1. Select the Line tool from the Toolbox (one of the "hidden" shape tools).

2. On the options bar, select the Shape Layers icon (the first icon of the three in line).

3. Click the Geometry Options icon (located by the Custom Shape Tool icon; looks like a downward-pointing triangle).

4. In the Arrowheads pop-up, enter settings for the Arrowheads: Start, End, Width, Length, Concavity.

NOTE These settings cannot be applied retroactively.

5. Enter a suitable line weight in the Weight text box. You can right-click (Windows), Ctrl-click (Mac OS) in the text box to choose a different unit from the contextual menu to the one specified for rulers in Preferences.

6. Choose a style by clicking the Style icon or a color by clicking the color box.

7. Click in the document window and drag to draw your arrow.

That's it! If you didn't apply a layer style in step 6, you can apply it or change the color and position retroactively, as you can with any shape layer.

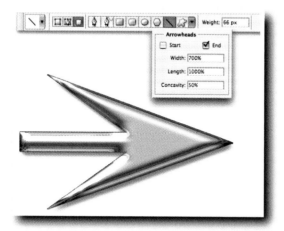

FIGURE 10-12: The Line tool used to draw arrowheads.

Painting

The various painting tools in Photoshop allow you to apply color as an artist would apply color to a canvas or wet media. Chief among the painting tools is the Brush tool, followed closely by the Gradient tool and the Fill command. Other tools, such as the Eraser, Blur, and Smudge tools are used to modify existing color.

To untap the power of the painting engine, it pays to spend some time in the Brushes palette and learn how the different dynamic settings affect the brush strokes. For example, you not only can customize each brush tip extensively but also set the color dynamics, brush shape dynamics, texture, and the way the paint is scattered. The combination of the customizable tool tips and brush dynamics alone makes the Brush tool incredibly powerful. To add to the explosive mixture, you can set controls for fade, pen pressure, and stylus wheel. Furthermore, the options bar also contains options that you can include in the preset, chief among them being the blending mode option.

Brush Shape Dynamics

Although there is no substitute for "playing" in the Brushes palette (Window ➜ Brushes, or click the palette icon in the options bar), the following figures (Figures 10-13 through 10-18) and brief, technobabble-free explanations should help you to understand how the settings affect a brush preset. The stroke on the left of the figures was applied using a No Style brush and those on the right using a style. Click the item name, for example, Shape Dynamics, in the left side of the Brushes palette to access its settings.

FIGURE 10-13: Shape Dynamics determines the randomness of the brush footprints. You can specify to what extent the brush footprints will change size, diameter, roundness, and angle.

FIGURE 10-14: Scattering takes into account the axis of the stroke and then scatters the brush footprints to either side. You can also increase the footprint count and vary the count's randomness.

FIGURE 10-15: Texture enables you to add a texture to the footprints and to control its depth and the randomness of the depth. With a texture selected, the stroke appears as though it is painted on the chosen texture.

FIGURE 10-16: Dual Brush enables you to paint with two brush tips. Having set the options for the first brush tip, select Dual Brush, choose a second brush tip, and then set its options independently of the first.

FIGURE 10-17: Color Dynamics varies the randomness of the foreground and background color used in the footprint to create a stroke. In this example, the spacing for the tip shape was increased to 100% to amplify the effect.

FIGURE 10-18: Other Dynamics determine how paint changes over the course of a stroke. You can control the randomness of the opacity and of the flow.

In addition to the settings illustrated in Figures 10-13 through 10-18, you also have the following options at your disposal:

- **Noise** adds additional randomness to brush footprints. Soft footprints can be beneficial, especially when you enable this setting.

- **Wet Edges** adds color along the edges of a brush stroke while leaving the rest semi-transparent, useful for creating watercolor effects.

- **Airbrush** simulates traditional airbrush used by artists to build up color gradually while retaining a soft edge. The effect is similar to spray painting.

- **Smoothing** evens out the brush footprints, thereby producing smoother curved brush strokes.

- **Protect Texture** substitutes the texture in the current preset in all saved presets, useful for ensuring consistency when using several presets to paint an area that must have the same look and feel. For example, if the strokes from different presets must have a canvas texture, change the texture for the current preset to canvas and then select Protect Texture. The texture specified in the saved presets will be overridden and replaced by the canvas texture.

Creating Brush Tip Shapes

You are not limited to using the brushes that ship with Photoshop. You can download brushes from the Internet (start with Adobe Studio Exchange: `http://share.studio.adobe .com/`) or create your own. To create a custom brush is simple. To do so, take the following steps:

1. Select part of an image by using the Rectangular Marquee tool (set Feather to 0 px).

2. Next, choose Edit ➜ Define Brush.

3. Name the brush and click OK.

That's it! It's that simple. You can, of course, create custom brushes using an irregular selection and feathering, or even define a brush using type as the basis.

NOTE The brushes will be saved with gray values only, which rules out using the brush tip shapes to stamp RGB image elements.

Avoiding Jaggy-Edged Brush Strokes

When you create strokes using large, hard brushes with a footprint of over 25 pixels, you might have noticed that your strokes have a serrated, jagged edge. The effect is not so noticeable on strokes created with soft brushes because they tend to hide the effect.

The reason the strokes can look serrated or jagged is that the brush footprints do not overlap to form a smooth, continuous edge. The remedy is to reduce the brush spacing from the 25% default to 15%, or lower.

The brush stroke preview window in the Brushes palette provides dynamic feedback that you can use to foresee whether your chosen brush tip will produce a "scalloped" stroke when you're using the 25% default spacing (Figure 10-19).

FIGURE 10-19: **A scalloped stroke (top) and nonscalloped stroke (bottom) created by reducing the brush spacing from the default 25% to 10%.**

Painting Dotted Straight Lines

Whereas painting straight lines is fairly straightforward in Photoshop, the way to paint a dotted line is not at all obvious. You can do it in Photoshop, but first you need to customize a brush. To do so, take the following steps:

1. Select the Brush tool and choose a hard-edged brush from the Brushes palette (Window ➜ Brushes or click the palette icon in the options bar).

2. Click Brush Tip Shape at the head of the left column and move the Set Brush Spacing slider (Figure 10-20) toward the right to increase the spacing.

3. Make sure that there are no ticks in the left column of the Brushes palette if you want to draw a plain, straight, dotted line. If you want to create shapes other than dots, play with the Diameter, Angle, Roundness, or Hardness settings.

4. Set your foreground color to a color of your choice.

5. Hold down the Shift key, click to define the start point of the line, and then click again to define the end of the line.

Save your custom brush as a Preset Tool and then use it from the Tools palette each time you need it. To save the current brush as a preset tool, take the following steps:

1. Click the brush icon on the options bar.

2. Click the New Tool Preset icon in the popup palette.

3. Name the brush and click the OK button.

If you have the Preset Tools palette open, you can also save a custom tool from the palette menu.

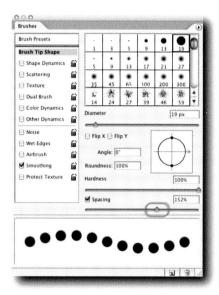

FIGURE 10-20: **The Brushes palette. Spacing increased to 152% to define a custom brush tip for painting dotted lines.**

Painting Quick Hacks

The following list of quick hacks can help you optimize your painting tasks:

- **Selecting a Brush Tip on the Fly.** While the Brush or Pencil tool is active, right-click (Windows), Ctrl-click (Mac OS) in the document window and select a tip from the pop-up Brushes palette. To dismiss the palette, start painting, click anywhere in the canvas, press Esc or Enter (Windows), Return (Mac OS); the Enter key on the numeric keypad can also be used.

- **Applying Airbrush Strokes.** The Airbrush tool can be accessed from the options bar after you select any one of the following tools: Brush, History Brush, Clone Stamp, Pattern Stamp, Eraser (brush mode), Sponge, Dodge, or Burn.

- **Modifying Brush Tips on the Fly.** You can change the size of the brush tip temporarily by using the square bracket keys. Press the left bracket key to reduce the diameter and the right bracket key to increase it. Similarly, you can alter the hardness by holding down Shift while you press the square bracket keys: Shift+[softens a brush tip, whereas Shift+] hardens it.

- **Turning Off Brush Dynamics.** The Brush tool's dynamics can more often than not get in the way when you are painting on a mask. To turn them off, choose Clear Brush Controls from the Brushes palette menu. To restore dynamics, click Brush Presets in the Brushes palette and then click the current preset.

- **Filling by Using Keyboard Shortcuts.** It's much quicker to fill by using keyboard shortcuts than by calling the Fill command if all you want to do is fill with either the foreground or the background color. To fill with foreground color, hold down Alt (Windows), Opt (Mac OS) and then press Backspace (Windows), Delete (Mac OS). To fill with background color, hold down Ctrl (Windows), ⌘ (Mac OS) and then press Backspace (Windows), Delete (Mac OS).

- **Filling Opaque or Transparent Areas.** By default, when you use the Fill command (Edit ➜ Fill), either the selected areas are filled or, if a selection is not active, the layer is filled, regardless of whether it contains transparent areas or not. If you need to protect the transparent areas, rather than make a selection, select Preserve Transparency in the Fill dialog box or if using keyboard shortcuts, hold down Alt+Shift (Windows), Opt+Shift (Mac OS) and then press Backspace (Windows), Delete (Mac OS) to fill with the foreground color. To fill with the background color, hold down Ctrl+Shift (Windows), ⌘+Shift (Mac OS) and then press Backspace (Windows), Delete (Mac OS).

- **Selecting a Color on the Fly.** If you are using a paint tool and you need to select another foreground color, hold down Alt (Windows), Opt (Mac OS) to access the Eyedropper tool temporarily.

- **Setting Foreground and Background Colors to Known Values.** If you have a color that you constantly use, you can save it as a swatch. However, if your Swatches palette is overflowing, you might find it easier to set it up as an action and assign a function key so that it's available as a foreground or background color at the press of a key. To do so, start recording an action, assign a function key, and set the foreground or background color as required.

Summary

With the inclusion of the vector tools, Photoshop took a giant leap toward Illustrator; with the inclusion of the updated painting engine, Photoshop took a giant leap toward Painter. Although the vector and painting capabilities are not nearly as powerful as those found in the dedicated programs, with a little bit of perseverance and lateral thinking you can create results that are every bit as professional and innovative as those created in the dedicated programs.

chapter 11

Editing, Transforming, and Retouching Images

T he terms *editing* and *transforming* can cover a wide range of manipulations applied to an image. However, that can often lead to confusion when imparting or searching for methods and techniques for manipulating images. To avoid confusion, the term *editing* is used here in the traditional sense of moving material around or deleting superfluous material. The term *transforming* is restricted to changing an object's length, width and height, and perspective within the image and not its general appearance.

Cropping, Rotating, and Positioning Layer Content

You would think that surely there couldn't possibly be that much to cropping, rotating, or positioning layer content. In some respects, you would be right. However, as always, Photoshop holds a few pleasant surprises when you start looking behind the deceptively simple façade and the tools and commands. For example, the Crop tool has hidden modes that become apparent only after you define a crop. Furthermore, the tool not only lets you crop excess data but also hide data. The next sections cover the various options available for cropping, rotating, and positioning layer content in more detail and start by looking at the different modes the Crop tool has to offer.

Crop Tool Modes

The Crop tool in Photoshop is a combined crop, perspective correction, image size, and canvas size tool. There are slight variations in the way the tool works in Photoshop and in ImageReady.

Although some options are patently obvious when you select the Crop tool, others are revealed only when you actually define a crop. For example, when you draw a crop marquee, you can shade the area that will be discarded or hidden. The shaded area is called the *crop shield*; you can toggle it off and on by pressing the forward slash key while a crop is active. You can also define its color and opacity from the options bar after a marquee has been drawn. The next sections take a closer look at the four modes available with the Crop tool.

Crop Mode

In this mode, the excess image area is discarded without affecting the image area within the crop marquee. To crop an image, leave all the text fields in the options bar empty, draw a crop marquee, and commit the crop by pressing Enter (Windows), Return (Mac OS), or by clicking the Commit Current Crop Operation button on the options bar (it looks like a tick mark).

After you commit a crop, all data outside the crop marquee is deleted. However, you can hide the cropped data rather than discard it, if you think you might need it. You can reveal it again at any time by choosing Image ➜ Reveal All or by using the Move tool. The option is not available if you are cropping an image that resides only on a Background layer.

Perspective Mode

In this mode, keystoning can be corrected and the image cropped and rotated at the same time. *Keystoning* occurs when a photo is taken with a camera lens looking upward rather than straight on. To correct keystoning, take the following steps:

1. Select the Crop tool and draw a crop marquee around your document.

2. Select Perspective on the options bar (the option is available only after a crop marquee has been drawn).

3. Next, hold down the Shift key and drag the vertical marquee crop lines from the middle or the corner handles until they align with visible converging lines (Figure 11-1). Holding down the Shift key is not essential, but it does prevent accidental vertical distortion, unless, of course, it's something you desire.

4. Keeping their angle, drag the marquee crop lines outward until the bottom corner boxes reach the edge of the image (if you go over the edge, Photoshop will add background pixels or transparency, depending on the layer fill); you will probably need to experiment a little until you get the hang of it.

5. Double-click in the crop marquee to commit the crop, or press Enter (Windows), Return (Mac OS).

After the crop has been committed, you may find that the image looks a little squat. To correct it, increase the Canvas size if you think it needs it and then use the Free Transform command to stretch it vertically; press Ctrl+T (Windows), ⌘+T (Mac OS) to activate the Free Transform command. The command is not available if your image is on a Background layer. To use the command on a Background layer, double-click the layer to change it to a layer normal with transparency. Flatten the document after the image has been transformed.

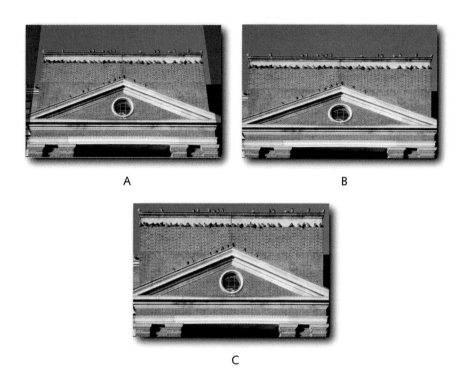

A   B

C

FIGURE 11-1: A—The crop marquee has been adjusted to identify the angle of the keystoning effect. B—Committing the crop resulted in a squat image. C—The Free Transform command was used to stretch the image vertically to counteract the squat effect.

Image Size Mode

When values are added in the Width, Height, and Resolution text fields, the Crop tool combines some of the features of the Image Size dialog box. To change the size of an image, enter the target values in the Width, Height, and Resolution text fields on the options bar, draw the crop marquee, and commit the crop.

Canvas Size Mode

When a crop is larger than the document dimensions, the Crop tool can do the work of the Canvas Size dialog box (Image ➜ Canvas Size). To add an even number of pixels to all four sides of a document (see Figure 11-2), take the following steps:

1. Check that the options View ➜ Snap and View ➜ Snap To ➜ Document Bounds are selected.

2. Resize your window so that the displayed image has a good border all around it (if your image is on a Background layer, change the Background color in the Toolbox to the desired color for the extra canvas size about to be added).

3. Select the Crop tool and ensure that the text fields are clear on the options bar (if need be, click the Clear button).

4. Draw a crop marquee and let it snap to the document bounds.

5. Hold down Alt+Shift (Windows), Opt+Shift (Mac OS) and drag outward by one of the corner handles.

6. Double-click in the crop marquee to commit the crop, or press Enter (Windows), Return (Mac OS).

FIGURE 11-2: The Crop tool used to increase canvas size evenly around all four sides of the image.

Holding down the modifier keys adds an even number of pixels around all four sides. If you want to add pixels unevenly, just drag one side of the marquee and commit.

Defining the Crop from the Center of a Document

Sometimes you need to shave off equal amounts of excess content around the four sides of your image. You could do it by using the Measure tool to set guides, draw a marquee with the Crop tool or the Rectangular Marquee tool, make sure it snaps to the guides, and then crop. Problem is, that makes it difficult to judge visually how much content needs to be cropped. What you can do instead is use the technique outlined previously for adding canvas size.

1. Check that the options View ➔ Snap and View ➔ Snap To ➔ Document Bounds are selected.

2. Select the Crop tool and ensure that the text fields are clear on the options bar (if need be, click the Clear button).

3. Draw a crop marquee and let it snap to the document bounds.

4. Hold down Alt+Shift (Windows), Opt+Shift (Mac OS) and transform the crop by one of the four corner points (Figure 11-3).

5. Double-click in the crop marquee to commit the crop, or press Enter (Windows), Return (Mac OS).

If you find that the crop marquee is not transforming evenly around the axis, make sure that the option Perspective is not selected.

TIP When drawing a crop marquee, you are not restricted to defining a crop from the point where you first click with the mouse. You can define any point as the center of your crop (this is true of all marquees that can be constrained). To do so, select the Crop tool, hold down Alt (Windows), Opt (Mac OS), click the canvas, and then define your crop marquee. You can press Alt (Windows), Opt (Mac OS) at any time after you have started to define the crop, as long as you do it before you have lifted the pointer off the canvas.

Preventing the Crop Tool from Snapping to the Edge

When the image is displayed at a low magnification, it can be difficult to crop close to the edge if you have View ➔ Snap enabled. You can disable Snap temporarily while using the Crop tool by clicking the crop marquee border and then holding down Ctrl (Windows), ⌘ (Mac OS) as you reposition the border.

Alternatively, go to View ➔ Snap To and deselect Document Bounds or use the shortcut key combination of Ctrl+Shift+Colon (Windows), ⌘+Shift+Colon (Mac OS) to toggle all the snapping options off.

FIGURE 11-3: Crop equal amounts around the borders of a document with the Crop tool by drawing the marquee from the center.

Using the Rectangular Marquee and Trim to Crop

In some situations, the Rectangular Marquee tool can prove more useful when you're cropping. For example, after a crop marquee is drawn, you cannot resize it precisely, whereas you can resize a selection marquee very precisely by transforming the selection (Select → Transform Selection). When a transform is active, use the text fields on the options bar to plug values or click in them and then use the Up and Down Arrow keys (located by the numeric keypad). Commit the transform by double-clicking in the marquee or pressing Enter (Windows), Return (Mac OS); then, choose Image → Crop.

If you made a selection with the Rectangular Marquee tool but find that when you use the Image → Crop command your image won't crop to the edge of the visible selection, make sure that the selection is not feathered. Enter a zero value in the options bar for the Feather option and try again.

The Trim command can prove extremely useful when you want to remove a block of color that surrounds your image. For example, if you take a screenshot against a white background, you can trim the excess in one fell swoop rather than spend time trying to marquee the content that you want to preserve. Include the command in an action, and you can save yourself considerable time over the course of trimming just 10–20 screenshots. To use the command, choose Image → Trim and in the dialog box specify the target pixels. You can choose between transparent pixels or colored pixels located at any one of the four corners of the image or all four (Figure 11-4).

Cropping and Straightening Photos Automatically

If you do a lot of scanning and find that your images are crooked when brought into Photoshop, you can automatically straighten the image and simultaneously delete the excess background around the image. To use the feature, after bringing the image into Photoshop, choose File → Automate → Crop and Straighten Photos. Your scanned image will be straightened, excess space trimmed, and a copy produced, ready for you to save to disk, leaving the original untouched (Figure 11-5).

The feature is really designed to produce single documents from multiple photos that have been scanned in one pass, but it can be employed to straighten single scans just as successfully.

FIGURE 11-4: **The Trim command can be used to crop an image based on color or transparency.**

NOTE For the feature to work properly, the photos must have a contrasting edge to the background and the background must be noise free. Bear in mind that whenever an image is rotated, unless it's rotated by 90 degrees exactly, the image will be interpolated and some quality loss might occur. So, try to avoid using the feature altogether if you can by scanning the photos one at a time and making sure that the photos are straight to begin with.

FIGURE 11-5: A photo straightened and cropped using the auto Crop and Straighten Photos command.

Straightening Crooked Images

The Measure tool is a fantastic tool for measuring distances between two points in a document. You can measure a distance in any of the units set for Rulers in Preferences → Units & Rulers → Units. If you are not sure of the current units of measure, just double-click a ruler to bring up the Units & Rulers preferences screen.

To use the tool, click and drag out a line in any direction and then read its length and angle in the Info palette or the options bar. Hold down the Shift key to constrain the measure lines to 45, 90, 135, 180, -135, -90, and -45 degrees.

The tool has a couple of "hidden" features that are not displayed on the options bar when you select it. These include the ability to rotate image data arbitrarily and to measure angles the way a protractor does. Both of the features can be used with great success to straighten crooked images or to rotate objects with great precision.

To invoke the protractor mode to measure angles, take the following steps:

1. Select the Measure tool (hidden under the Eyedropper tool in the Toolbox).

2. Draw a measure line by clicking and dragging with the tool; the line can be at any angle.

3. Hold down Alt (Windows), Opt (Mac OS), hover over the either end point and, when the icon acquires a protractor and a plus sign, click and draw another measure line at an angle to the first (Figure 11-6). You can also double-click the end point to invoke the protractor mode.

4. Read the measurements either on the options bar or in the Info palette.

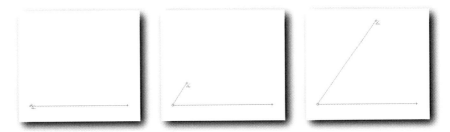

FIGURE 11-6: **Switching the Measure tool from measure lines to protractor mode.**

When you're working with the Measure tool, here are a few pointers to keep in mind:

- To change the angle of the measure lines, click an end point and then drag.
- To extend an existing measure line, drag outward from either end point.
- To reposition a measure line, or the protractor, click it and then drag to a new position.
- To draw an absolute straight measure line, hold down the Shift key as you draw.
- To clear a measure line, or a protractor, click the Clear button on the options bar, or drag it out of the document window with the pointer.

When you use the Measure tool to straighten a composite image, it requires a slightly different treatment to straightening objects on a layer. Take a look at the steps required to straighten a composite image first and then objects on a layer.

1. Select the Measure tool.

2. Find a straight line in your image, one that you want to be perpendicular. Draw a measure line beside it by clicking and dragging with the tool.

3. Choose Image → Rotate Canvas → Arbitrary.

4. You will see the angle by which the canvas needs to be rotated displayed in the angle text box (Figure 11-7). Click the OK button to apply the measurement; the image will upright itself.

FIGURE 11-7: Straightening a crooked photo with the Measure tool and the Image → Rotate Canvas → Arbitrary command.

If you want to use the preceding method to rotate an object arbitrarily on a layer, first, it's not at all obvious which command you should use (for example, Rotate Canvas ➔ Arbitrary obviously won't do because it rotates the whole canvas). Second, after you have found the right command and invoked it (it's actually Edit ➔ Transform ➔ Rotate), the object rotates counter to expectations. That is to say, if you want it to rotate clockwise, it rotates counterclockwise, and vice versa. To overcome the contrary behavior, you need to use the Measure tool in protractor mode, or enter a negative value in the Set Rotation text field, after the command has been invoked.

To rotate an object arbitrarily using the Measure tool in protractor mode, take the following steps:

1. Select the Measure tool and draw a horizontal measure line; hold down the Shift key to constrain it to a straight line.

2. Hold down Alt (Windows), Opt (Mac OS) and draw out a protractor edge from the start of the horizontal line so that it hugs a diagonal line that you want to be perpendicular (Figure 11-8).

3. Choose Edit ➔ Transform ➔ Rotate (if the command is not available, make sure that you are working on a normal layer and not a Background layer).

4. Accept the transform by pressing Enter (Windows), Return (Mac OS).

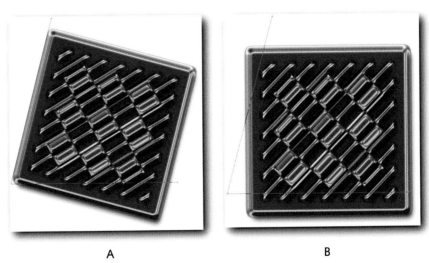

A   B

FIGURE 11-8: A—The Measure tool in protractor mode ready to rotate an object. B—The object rotated by selecting Edit ➔ Transform ➔ Rotate.

The content will be rotated by the number of degrees described by the protractor. Remember—apart from 90-degree transforms, all rotations result in the content's being interpolated, using the Image Interpolation algorithm set in Preferences to resample the data.

Rotating Layer Content Incrementally

If you need to rotate layer content very precisely, you might be tempted to step outside the transform bounding box and then drag the pointer clockwise or counter clockwise. Although this method is fine for quick-and-dirty rotations, it's not very reliable for precise rotations. Instead, use the following method, which allows for rotations in increments of a tenth of a degree:

1. Choose Edit ➔ Transform ➔ Rotate, or press Ctrl+T (Windows), ⌘+T (Mac OS) to select the Free Transform command.

2. Click in the Set Rotation text field on the options bar and then use the Up and Down Arrow keys to rotate the layer content incrementally.

If changing values in increments of a tenth of a degree is too small for you, hold down the Shift key while using the Up and Down Arrow keys to increase or decrease the values in 1-degree increments.

You can also apply this technique to repositioning objects horizontally and vertically by clicking in the *x*, *y* text fields and then using the Up and Down Arrow keys.

Matching the Rotation of Two Scans

Ever had to scan a map or a poster in two passes because it wouldn't fit on your flatbed and then tried to blend the two scans seamlessly into one image? Trying to align the two scans can prove to be hit or miss and even time consuming. There are various ways of solving this problem in Photoshop. Probably the easiest way is to, one, make sure that the two scans receive the same exposure; two, ensure that there is some overlap of the image content; three, combine the two into one document; then, change the blend mode of the top layer to Difference so that you can see the *difference* between the two layers (Figure 11-9). The exact steps for carrying out this method are as follows:

1. Open one of the scans in Photoshop and then double-click its Background layer to convert it to a normal layer.

2. Enlarge the document canvas (Image ➔ Canvas Size) either horizontally or vertically, depending on the orientation of the image, so that you have sufficient headroom to accommodate both scans; the document window should now be divided into two, one half containing the image and the other transparency.

3. Open the second scan and then drag its layer and drop into the window of the previously opened and enlarged document.

4. Close the second document. There's no need to have it open anymore. It has served its purpose.

5. Use the Move tool to position the top layer approximately so that the two images overlap but otherwise appear, more or less, as one continuous image.

6. In the Layers palette, change the blend mode of the top layer from Normal to Difference; at which point the layer content will turn black where it matches the content of the layer below it and where it does not, it will display in inverted colors.

7. Choose Edit ➜ Free Transform, or press Ctrl+T (Windows), ⌘+T (Mac OS).

8. Click in the Set Rotation text field on the options bar (third from right) and then use the Up and Down Arrow keys to rotate the layer until the overlap area turns to maximum black.

9. Accept the transform by pressing Enter (Window), Return (Mac OS).

10. Change the blend mode from Difference back to Normal.

11. Create a layer mask on the top layer and then use a soft-edged brush to paint over any of the overlap area that may be obscuring the layer below; you can also apply a gradient to the mask to blend the seam gradually (see Chapter 8 on how to create layer masks).

To make a more precise match between the two layers, you might have to alter the x (horizontal), y (vertical) coordinates, but basically, you want to make as much of the image black as possible by rotating or repositioning the layer content. When you are satisfied with the registration, accept the transform (to minimize loss of quality, perform only one transform).

FIGURE 11-9: **The result of comparing two layers in Difference mode. The matched content is displayed in black and the unmatched content in an inverted color. The Layers palette shows the top layer set to Difference mode.**

Aligning and Distributing Content on Multiple Layers

You can use the Align and Distribute commands or the Move tool to arrange objects and to allocate the space between the objects. The objects can be aligned according to their top, bottom, left, or right edges or their vertical and horizontal centers. Likewise, the space between the objects can be allocated according to the same parameters (Figure 11-10).

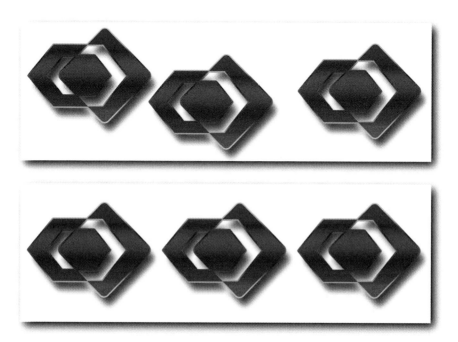

FIGURE 11-10: **In this example, the commands Align Horizontal Centers and then Distribute Horizontal Centers were used to align and distribute objects on three separate layers.**

To align objects, select two or more layers and then choose an item from the Layer ➜ Align submenu or select the Move tool and then select the appropriate align button. The objects align according to their edges or centers. For example, if you select Align Top Edges, all the objects on the selected layers move and align to the edge of the object that has the topmost edge.

To distribute objects evenly, select three or more layers and then choose an item from the Layer ➜ Distribute submenu, or select the Move tool and then select the appropriate distribute button (located to the right of the align buttons on the options bar). The objects distribute according their edges or centers. For example, if you select Distribute Top Edges, all the objects on the selected layers move and distribute in line with the edge of the object that has the topmost edge.

251

The case is slightly different if you want to align or distribute objects relative to the object on the active layer. You must first select the layers, choose Layer ➜ Link Layers, or click the link button in the Layers palette. Next, select the layer containing the object you wish to align to or use as the basis for the distribution.

NOTE The Distribute Linked command becomes available only when the following conditions are met: (a) when three or more layers are selected or linked, (b) when the layers do not have their positions locked, (c) the Background layer is not included among the selected or linked layers

Centering Layer Content

When you want to center objects in Photoshop, the steps required are very similar for aligning objects to the canvas center or to its edges. The secret step they both require is for you to select the whole canvas before the menu item Align to Selection appears on the Layer menu. To center objects, take the following steps:

1. Select the layer containing the object that you want to center or align.

2. Choose Select ➜ All, or Ctrl+A (Windows), ⌘+A (Mac OS).

3. Choose Layer ➜ Align to Selection ➜ Horizontal Centers and then select Vertical Centers.

That will center the object on the layer. You can also use the Move tool to align objects by using the Align Vertical Centers and Align Horizontal Centers buttons on the options bar. However, the same secret step has to be taken: You must select the whole canvas before you can access the buttons.

Revealing and Deleting Hidden Data

In the course of editing, data might move off the canvas intentionally or unintentionally. For example, when you transform a layer, some of the visible image content might disappear beyond the document bounds. The overspilled image content is not lost but remains hidden beyond the document bounds (Figure 11-11). To give another example, when you use the Crop tool in Hide mode, as opposed to the normal Crop mode, the cropped or shielded image content is made invisible by redefining the document bounds.

FIGURE 11-11: **The bounding box indicates that the layer being transformed contains hidden data.**

There are plusses and minuses to hiding data. The obvious plus is that you can move it back into the visible image area at any time or reveal it by extending the document bounds. The not-so-obvious minus is that hidden data adds to the file size.

You can reveal the hidden data by choosing Image ➜ Reveal All. Unfortunately, the command is not a toggle, so you have no way to reverse the revelation after you have performed another command—well, not without a little workaround. If you think you will need to get back to the document bounds before you invoked the command, use guides to mark the document bounds. You can then use the Crop tool to draw a marquee that snaps to the guides, choose Hide from the options bar, and commit the crop.

If you are certain that you will not use the hidden data and you do want to reduce the file size, use the Rectangular Marquee tool to select the visible image area and then choose Image ➜ Crop.

Extracting Image Content from Backgrounds

Every day, content is extracted from its background on thousands of workstations around the globe so that it can be imposed over a different background. Therefore, it should come as no surprise to learn that Photoshop contains no fewer than three eraser tools and one filter to help you carry out this mundane but necessary task. They are, in ascending order of sophistication, the basic Eraser tool, the Magic Eraser tool, the Background Eraser tool, and the Extract filter. The next sections look at all four in detail.

The Eraser Tool

The Eraser tool has three modes: Block, Pencil, and Brush. In Block mode, the only control you have is to erase to history or to alter the size of the block by changing the magnification of the document.

- To erase, select the tool and then drag in the document. If the layer is a normal layer, pixels are erased to transparency; if you drag on a Background layer or a layer with locked transparency, pixels are painted with the background color.

- To erase to history, select Erase to History on the options bar and then choose a history state as the source in the History palette. You can also switch between normal Block mode and Erase to History by holding down Alt (Windows), Opt (Mac OS).

- To increase the block size, zoom out; to decrease it, zoom in.

- To change from Block to either Pencil or Brush mode, right-click (Windows), Ctrl-click (Mac OS) and select a mode from the contextual menu.

In Pencil mode, you can use any one of the available brush presets, control the opacity of the strokes, and Erase to History. However, the brush tips cannot be softened, nor can the strokes be anti-aliased to provide smooth edges. In Brush mode, you have access to all the following options: Opacity, Flow (the latter controls how quickly or slowly the paint is applied), Airbrush, and Erase to History.

The Magic Eraser Tool

The Magic Eraser tool works in a similar fashion to the Magic Wand tool. The difference is that rather than create a selection based on the sampled color, it erases the pixels to transparency. Furthermore, unlike the Eraser tool, if you use the Magic Eraser on a Background layer, rather than paint it with the background color, it converts it to a normal layer and then erases the pixels to transparency.

The settings on the options bar let you modify the tool's behavior. They include:

- **Tolerance**—Higher settings erase more shades of the sampled color. For example, if you have a low setting and you click a red color, all instances of that red go to transparency. If you increase the settings, for example, from 32 to 64, any shades leaning toward orange on one side and purple on the other are also deleted.

- **Anti-alias**—Ensures a smooth edge for the area that you have extracted.

- **Contiguous**—Forces the tool to erase only adjacent pixels that fall within the tolerance value.

- **Sample All Layers**—Uses data from merged layers to determine what data to erase.

- **Opacity**—Controls the level to which the erased pixels are opaque or transparent.

The Background Eraser Tool

The Background Eraser tool offers more options for controlling what is erased and what is not than the Eraser and Magic Eraser tools. The tool works by erasing the sampled color under the brush tip. It also protects any color that matches the foreground color set in the Toolbox.

- **Sampling Continuous, Once, or Background Swatch**—In Continuous sampling mode, the tool samples the color under the brush tip constantly as you drag. In Sample Once mode, the sample is taken only once when you click. In Background Swatch sampling mode, whatever color is set as the background color in the Toolbox is erased under the brush tip. To change the background color quickly, press X to switch the foreground and background color boxes, hold down Alt (Windows), Opt (Mac OS), sample, and then press X again to switch the color boxes back to default.

- **Limit: Contiguous, Discontiguous or Find Edges**—When the Limits option is set to Contiguous or Discontiguous, the erasure affects only pixels that fall within the Tolerance setting and are either adjacent to each other or disconnected, respectively. The Find Edges option ensures that the integrity of the edge detail is better protected while the sampled color is being erased from continuous areas.

- **Tolerance**—Lower settings ensure that only the sampled color is erased, whereas higher settings erase more shades of the sampled color.

- **Protect Foreground Color**—When this setting is selected, whatever color is set in the foreground color box in the Toolbox is protected from erasure. You can alter this color at any stage by holding down Alt (Windows), Opt (Mac OS) and clicking in the document.

The Extract Filter

For extracting content that contains fine, wispy detail, such as glass or hair, the Extract filter is the ideal tool of all the extract tools in Photoshop. Using it requires a little more care, but by doing multiple extractions, you can achieve results that can surpass even some of the expensive plug-ins on the market (Figure 11-12).

FIGURE 11-12: **The Extract filter in action.**

To extract content:

1. Copy the layer: Layer ➜ New ➜ Layer via Copy, or Ctrl+J (Windows), ⌘+J (Mac OS). It's always a good idea to work on a copy because the filter will erase pixels to transparency.

2. Choose Filter ➜ Extract, or Ctrl+Alt+X (Windows), ⌘+Opt+X (Mac OS).

3. In the dialog box, draw an outline with the default Highlighter tool (B) around the area you want to extract. Make sure that the highlight straddles the background and the outline of the object you wish to extract.

4. Next, select the Bucket tool (G) and click inside the highlighted border to fill it (clicking a filled area again with the Fill tool removes the fill).

5. Click the Preview button to see the extraction and then use the Cleanup tool (C) or the Edge Touchup tool (T) to refine the extraction's outline.

6. Click the OK button to commit the extraction and exit the dialog box.

If you are still unhappy with the extraction, use the History brush or the other extraction tools to do any refining. For example, use the Background Eraser tool to remove any stray color around the fringes of the extracted object by using the tool's options to protect foreground color while extracting background color (if need be, refer to the previous section in this chapter, "The Background Eraser Tool").

Although some of the options in the Extract dialog box, such as Show and Brush Size, are obvious, others are not so obvious and have an extra kick that you can use to improve the extraction.

- **Smart Highlighting**—This option changes the brush tip's behavior from that of a freewheeler to one that follows a well-defined edge closely. If it strays when it sees two well-defined edges, decrease the brush size so that the sampling area is reduced.

- **Channel**—Before entering the Extract dialog box, you can define an edge by creating a selection outline, creating an alpha channel, stroking the selection, applying a slight Gaussian Blur to the stroke, and, finally, inverting the alpha channel so that the stroke sits on a white background. When you select the alpha channel from the Channel pop-up, the edge highlights automatically.

- **Force Foreground**—This option is particularly useful for extracting wispy objects that have no clear interior, such as a dragonfly with its transparent wings or a glass half filled with liquid. You may need to use it several times and then combine the extractions to get good results. For example, select the highlights on the first pass, midtones on the next, and so forth.

- **Preview**—After you have seen a preview, you can toggle between it and the original view from the Preview section of the dialog box by choosing Original from the Show pop-up menu.

Transforming Images

Transforming changes an object's physical appearance by modifying its length, width, or height. You can transform entire images, individual layers, grouped layers, linked layers, and selected segments.

The transform functions in Photoshop include scaling, rotating, skewing, distorting, modifying perspective, warping, and flipping. You can find the transform commands in the Transform sub-menu under the Edit menu.

Resizing and Resampling Images

People frequently get confused concerning what constitutes image size and document size. Briefly, *image size* is determined by factors such as the number of pixels, the color mode, bits per channel, embedded profiles, and the type and amount of compression applied. *Document size* is determined by how the pixels are resolved per inch/cm when output to a printer. For example, a document containing 1200 × 1200 pixels and one that has its resolution set to 300 pixels/inch will create a print that's 4 × 4 inches: 1200 pixels divided by 300 pixels/inch equals 4 inches.

Although the Image Size dialog box is laid out very logically, it still perplexes many people (Figure 11-13). If you look carefully, you will see that it's divided into two halves by etched lines. The top half is devoted to Pixel Dimensions and the bottom half to Document Size. Perhaps if Document Size were called Print Size, there would be less confusion (the term *Document Size* is used elsewhere to indicate file size, and open files are usually referred to as documents). Nevertheless, the Resolution setting refers to print size only and should not be confused with the size of the document when displayed on-screen. That's because on-screen resolution is determined by your video card and your monitor's screen size, whereas the resolution of the print is determined by the Resolution setting in Image Size.

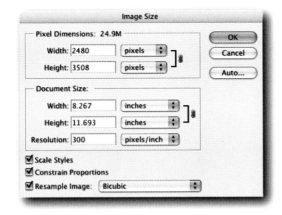

FIGURE 11-13: **The Image Size dialog box. If you observe the etch lines, you can see the dialog box delineated between Pixel Dimensions (top) and Document Size (bottom).**

- **With Resample selected**—Changing the pixel dimensions changes Document Size, and vice versa, but not the Resolution. Changing the Resolution changes the Pixel Dimensions but not the Document Size.

- **With Resample deselected**—Changing Width/Height changes the Resolution (as one drops, the other rises) and the Pixel Dimensions are unaffected.

TIP The default Resample Image algorithm that you see in the Image Size dialog box can be set in the Preferences dialog box. It's a good idea to keep an eye on it because, although all transforms make use of it, the default is not suitable for all transforms. For example, transforms applied to photos benefit if Bicubic Smoother is used when resized upward but Bicubic Sharper if resized downward.

Correcting Perspective

Although you can use the Crop tool in Perspective mode to correct keystoning, it usually distorts the image, so then *that* needs to be corrected. Here's another method that takes some of the guesswork out of applying the second transform:

1. Make sure that your image is not on a Background layer. If it is, double-click it to change it into a normal layer.

2. Drag in some vertical guides from the Ruler (R) so that you have something with which to align the verticals in your image.

3. Select the Move tool and then press Ctrl+T (Windows), ⌘+T (Mac OS) to invoke the Free Transform command.

4. When you see the bounding box, hold down Ctrl+Shift (Windows), ⌘+Shift (Mac OS) and drag one of the top corner handles outward until a vertical aligns with a guide (Figure 11-14). Do the same to the other corner if the keystoning is severe.

5. To apply the icing on the cake, while the transform is still active, click the link button between the width and height fields on the options bar. This action forces the height to constrain to the same distortion percentage as that applied to the width.

6. Commit the transform by pressing Enter (Windows), Return (Mac OS).

A

B

FIGURE 11-14: A—Original with heavy keystoning. B—Free Transform used to correct keystoning.

Using the preceding method, you won't have to guess just how much you need to stretch the image height-wise to restore the original proportions.

Warping Layer Content Using Nodal Points

Before Photoshop CS2, if you wanted to warp an image, you had only two choices: You could use the Shear filter or buy a plug-in. Now you have a third choice: You can use the Warp command to distort a selection, path, or pixel-based layers. When invoked, the command gives you access to four nodal points and eight direction points. Furthermore, when you use preset warp shapes, which you can select from a pop-up menu on the options bar, you can change the warp orientation and the degree of warp as well as the vertical and horizontal distortion.

To warp an object:

1. Make sure that the object is not on a Background layer.

2. Choose Edit ➜ Transform ➜ Warp, or Ctrl+T (Windows), ⌘+T (Mac OS) and then click the Warp icon on the options bar (fourth from right).

3. Drag the corner points or the direction points or click in the mesh and then drag.

4. Alternatively, choose a predefined shape from the pop-up menu on the options bar and then use the Bend, Horizontal, or Vertical distortion text boxes to redefine the shape (Figure 11-15).

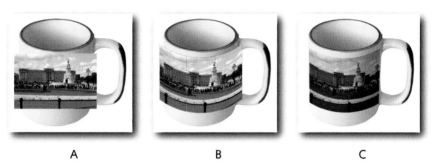

A   B   C

FIGURE 11-15: A—The image to be warped and the target. B—Custom Arch shape used to warp the image and then a negative figure used in the Bend text box to arch it downward. C—Blend mode set to Multiply and a Hue/Saturation adjustment layer used to color the layer.

To show or hide the warp mesh and control points, choose View ➜ Extras.

Correcting Distortion Caused by a Taking Lens

If you receive files that exhibit common flaws caused by cheap lenses, or even expensive lenses that were used on a sensor for which they weren't specifically designed or were used at an extreme angle that results in keystoning, you can use the Lens Correction filter (Filter ➜ Distortion ➜ Lens Correction) to counteract the distortions. The filter can correct the most common flaws: barrel, pincushion, chromatic aberration, vignetting, and vertical and horizontal perspective.

The Remove Distortion slider in the dialog box corrects for barrel distortion when moved to the left and pincushion distortion when moved to the right. *Barrel distortion* is most noticeable on images taken with retrofocus wide-angle lenses; the result is a bulging out of the straight lines, resulting in a barrel-like effect. *Pincushion distortion* is caused by a telephoto lens that has a negative rear group of elements. The effect is usually more pronounced at the tele end of a zoom lens, which might also exhibit barrel distortion at the wide end (see Figure 11-16 for an example of an exaggerated pincushion distortion).

FIGURE 11-16: **Left—Exaggerated barrel distortion. Right—Exaggerated pincushion distortion.**

Another lens flaw commonly encountered is chromatic aberration (Figure 11-17). *Chromatic aberration* is the result of a combination of factors caused by the light's registering incorrectly on a digital sensor (it's also present in film-originated photography but is not so apparent).

The effect is most pronounced when wide-angle lenses are used, and is noticeable on high-contrast edges, such as foliage or buildings shot against the sky or a steel chair against a dark background.

Previously, there were no commands for correcting chromatic aberration within Photoshop; you could do this only within Camera Raw. However, now you can correct chromatic aberration not only on your raw files but also if you output JPEGs directly from your digital camera.

The filter has two sliders for correcting chromatic aberration. One slider corrects red/cyan color fringing and the other blue/yellow color fringing.

FIGURE 11-17: Exaggerated chromatic aberration (left), most noticeable around the outline of the dragon and the plinth, and corrected version (right).

To correct color fringing, take the following steps:

1. Choose Filter ➜ Distortion ➜ Lens Correction.

2. Zoom into the image by using the Zoom tool from the toolbox in the dialog box, or use the usual keyboard shortcuts for changing the magnification.

3. Move the Fix Red/Cyan Fringe slider to adjust the red channel relative to the green channel. This reduces or fixes any red/cyan color fringing.

4. Move the Fix Blue/Yellow Fringe slider to adjust the blue channel relative to the green channel. This reduces or fixes any blue/yellow color fringing.

5. Click the OK button to apply settings and exit.

If the grid gets in the way, turn it off by deselecting the Show Grid option at the bottom of the dialog box.

Vignetting is caused by a number of factors that result in light falloff toward the edges of a photograph, manifesting as unacceptable dark corners. It might be caused by a lens aperture being used wide open, an incorrectly set matte box, or a lens hood. Though it's always best to avoid vignetting in the field, if confronted with an image that cannot be reshot, the Vignetting sliders of the Lens Correction filter can be used to minimize the falloff or even cure it in most cases (Figure 11-18).

FIGURE 11-18: **Exaggerated vignetting effect (left), noticeable around the perimeter of the image, and corrected version (right).**

If the lens type, focal length, and f-stop used to take the photo are included in the Camera Data (Exif), you can use the filter's Set Lens Default button to save any values in the Settings section of the panel. Next time you use the lens, you can apply the values by selecting Lens Default from the Settings pop-up menu. However, all three fields need to be present before the button becomes active. If the button is grayed, information in one or more of the Camera Data fields is missing. If your image lacks one of the required fields, you can still use the panel's menu to save any custom settings, including the Transform settings, which the Set Lens Default button does not save. To access the Lens Correction panel menu, click the right-pointing triangle by the Settings pop-up menu and select Save Settings.

Retouching Images

Retouching an image can involve anything from simple everyday humdrum retouching, such as filling in dust spots and scratch marks and covering pimples, to complex and convoluted retouching, such as fixing rips and tears, extracting unwanted elements that detract from a scene, or adding or substituting new elements from other related or totally unrelated scenes. Although the former may not raise an eyebrow, the latter has sparked many a debate about the ethics of altering the original scene in any form or shape whatsoever. Some guidelines go as far as specifying to what extent an image's contrast can be changed! So, although the following hacks are unlikely to lead to sparkling ethical or philosophical debates, they will help you get through the tedium of everyday humdrum retouching.

Filling in Dust Spots and Scratch Marks

Regardless of how carefully you clean your scanner and your prints, some dust spots nearly always manage to escape the net. The following hack removes dust spots and small scratch marks without doing undue damage to the detail.

1. Duplicate the image layer.

2. Next, apply Filter ➜ Noise ➜ Dust & Scratches.

3. Set Threshold to 0 and then increase the Radius until you see the dust spots begin to disappear. You can make a judgment call by watching the document window or the proxy window. To compare a before and after preview, deselect the Preview checkbox to see a before display in the document window or, if using the proxy window, click in it and hold down the mouse button.

4. Increase the Threshold until you see the dust spots reappear and then decrease it steadily until there is a fine balance between the loss of fine detail and the dust and scratches.

5. Change the blend mode of this layer from Normal to Darken if the spots are white or to Lighten if they are black.

To refine the filter application further, play with the opacity or the Advanced Blending options to specify which pixels from the filtered layer affect the unfiltered layer below it. Learning to use the Blending Options feature (Layer ➜ Layer Style ➜ Blending Options) will enable you to do a lot of tasks that otherwise would require making complex selections! You might also, of course, apply a layer mask to the filtered layer and then mask any fine details that were lost, such as highlights, eyelashes, and so on.

There is one other way to use Dust & Scratches that's worth a mention here, though using a layer mask as described previously makes it rather redundant and not so versatile. After applying the filter, undo its effect (Edit ➜ Step Backward). Next, in the History palette, click in the left column of the Dust & Scratches history state to set it as the source, select the History Brush tool, choose an appropriate brush tip, and then paint over the dust and scratches.

NOTE The Dust & Scratches filter is not really designed for best results as a global filter, although you can use it that way. Where possible, after duplicating the layer, use a feathered selection to isolate the affected area before invoking the filter; also, a small addition of noise or healing might be required after filtering but before deselecting.

In addition to the Dust & Scratches filter, you can also use the new Spot Healing Brush tool for minor healing, or its big brother the Healing Brush tool for serious healing. It's useful to know as many options and methods as possible because not all images require the same treatment.

The Spot Healing Brush Tool

To use the Spot Healing Brush tool (J), choose a brush tip slightly larger than the spot or scratch you want to heal and then lightly drag across it. That's about all there is to it!

In contrast to using the Healing Brush tool, you don't need to define a source; the tool samples automatically from around the brush tip. For that reason, you might need to increase or decrease the brush tip occasionally; otherwise, the healing may not match its immediate surroundings.

If the healing isn't to your satisfaction, you can try another blending mode from the options bar; for example, try switching between Normal and Replace blend modes (or one of the other modes). Replace tries to preserves noise, film grain, and texture at the edge of the healing strokes. Try also switching to a different source sampling type. There are two types to choose from: Proximity Match and Create Texture. The former is the default; the latter tries to create a texture from the pixels within the sampling area.

The Healing Brush Tool

For healing large areas, the Healing Brush tool is preferable to the Spot Healing Brush tool. To use the tool, choose a brush tip slightly larger than the area you want to heal. Hold down Alt (Windows), Opt (Mac OS) and click to define a sample point from an area that has similar texture. Click or drag over the area to be healed. If the area being healed is small, the healing should take place almost instantaneously when you lift the mouse button. However, if you dragged across a large area and the file you are working on is huge or your resources are low, it might take time for the healing to take place. It's usually a good idea to heal in small strokes; that way, you can easily undo just the last stroke (see also the Tip on healing later in this section).

- **Blend Modes**—As with the Spot Healing Brush tool, if the healing isn't to your satisfaction, you can try another blending mode; for example, try switching between Normal and Replace blend modes (or one of the other modes). Replace tries to preserve noise, film grain, and texture at the edge of the healing strokes.

- **Source**—There are two sources to choose from: Sampled or Pattern. Sampled uses the texture, lighting, transparency, and shading from the sample point to heal the target healing area. Pattern uses a pattern, which you can select from the pop-up Pattern Picker by clicking the icon next to the option, to blend into the target healing area.

- **Aligned**—Selecting this option sets the sampled source point so that it constantly realigns with the current position of the brush tip each time you click. When this option is not selected, the sampling is taken from the same source point each time you click.

- **Sample All Layers**—This option, as the name implies, samples data from not just the current layer but also all layers, including the layers above the active layer.

- **Using Stylus Pressure**—If you are using a stylus and tablet, you can vary the size of the stroke by applying pressure to the stylus. To enable the option, click the Brush icon in the options bar and from the pop-up palette choose Pen Pressure from the Size pop-up menu. You can also choose Stylus Wheel to base the deviation on the position of the pen thumbwheel. Furthermore, you can call up the pop-up palette at any time by right-clicking (Windows), ⌘-clicking (Mac OS) in document window. These stylus options are available for both the Spot Healing Brush and the Healing Brush tool.

TIP When healing, you are not confined to healing on the current layer. You can create a new layer and have the healed data placed for you on a new layer. This approach can give more options, such as blending modes, opacity control, and the option of turning off the layer visibility.

To avoid smudges and smears when healing close to the edge of the document bounds or high-contrast areas, make a selection around the area being healed and exclude the darker edges or change the brush tip to an ellipse and rotate it so that it avoids the dark edges. Smudges and smears occur when the tool tries to sample from outside the healing area in order to blend the sampled data. Creating a selection or changing the shape of the brush tip avoids sampling from the darker areas around the healing area.

Reducing Color and Luminosity Noise

Noise can be quantified as unwanted luminosity or color data, also known as chrominance signal-to-noise ratio. Noise is mostly apparent in images taken with consumer cameras, but prosumer cameras are also prone to it. It can appear as random patterns of color, most noticeable in light areas, such as skies, and dark areas, such as shadows.

Noise is a byproduct of a number of factors. It can be attributed to heat generated by sensors, the proximity of photosites (small sensors crammed with too many photosites), images taken with a high ISO setting, or long exposures. Typically, the green channel tends to exhibit less noise than the red or the blue, the latter being the noisiest of the three.

Photoshop has a new filter for counteracting noise: Reduce Noise. It does a good job of removing noise and JPEG artifacts while preserving edge detail. It has two modes: Basic and Advanced. In Basic mode, noise reduction is applied to all channels. When it's set to Advanced mode, you can apply per channel noise reduction.

To use Reduce Noise, take the following steps:

1. To see which channel has the most noise, click the separate channels one at a time in the Channels palette. Most likely, it will be the blue channel. Select the composite channel to return to composite view.

2. Choose Filter ➜ Noise ➜ Reduce Noise.

3. Accept the default settings or move the sliders until you strike a balance between noise reduction and detail loss (Figure 11-19). The Preserve Details slider removes the most luminance noise when set to 0% and the least when set to 100%. The Reduce Color Noise slider removes random color noise as expected: Higher percentage values remove more noise. The dialog box has a good-sized proxy window, which you can click to see a before and after view. As with most filters, you can also toggle the view in the document window by clicking the Preview checkbox.

4. Click the Advanced radio button and then review the noise in the separate channels by selecting a channel from the Channel pop-up menu.

5. Move the Strength slider to specify a noise reduction in the chosen channel (click in the B&W proxy window to see a before and after view).

6. If you think you will return to the same settings in future sessions, you can save the settings by clicking the button next to the Settings pop-up menu. Give the settings a memorable name in the pop-up dialog box and click the OK button to return to the Remove Noise dialog box.

7. Click the OK button to exit.

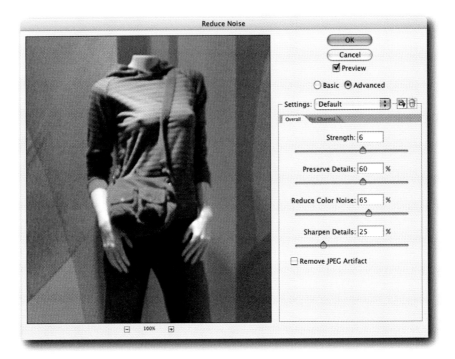

FIGURE 11-19: **The Reduce Noise filter.**

Bearing the following pointers in mind when using Reduce Noise can help:

- If you're processing files in Camera Raw, turn off Color Noise Reduction and Sharpness under the Detail tab.

- Try not to overdo the noise reduction. In some circumstances, high settings used in Camera Raw could result in blotchy channels that might not separate as expected.

- Apply any adjustments that might increase noise, such as Curves moves or Shadow/Highlight, before applying Reduce Noise.

- Inspect the channels before you enter Reduce Noise. Use the channel controls available in Advanced mode if your image has greater noise in one channel (usually the blue channel).

- Apply minimum sharpening in Reduce Noise; use Smart Sharpen or Unsharp Mask to apply sharpening.

Dodging and Burning Nondestructively

In the old days of wet darkrooms, printers routinely employed a technique called Dodging and Burning to change the exposure locally when printing. They did this by blocking the light from the enlarger that fell on the paper (dodging) with their hands or implements and, conversely, allowing the unblocked areas to receive more light (burning). This technique worked well in most cases, but if you didn't get the exposure right, you had to start all over.

Photoshop has had the Dodge and Burn tools for a number of iterations, and they are very powerful tools in their own right. However, similar to wet darkroom printing, if you don't get it right, histories not withstanding, you will have to start all over. Rather than use the Dodge and Burn tools, here's another method that you may want to try that can increase your options.

1. Create a new layer above your image layer and give it a memorable name; for this exercise, call it Dodge & Burn.

2. Choose Edit ➔ Fill.

3. In the Fill dialog box, choose Use: 50% Gray from the Contents pop-up menu and click the OK button.

4. Change the Dodge & Burn layer's blend mode from Normal to Overlay.

5. Press D to set the foreground and background colors to their default setting.

6. Select the Brush tool and a suitable brush tip and paint on the layer as if you were painting on a mask.

Painting with *black* is similar to applying the Burn tool, whereas painting with *white* is similar to applying the Dodge tool. If you make a mistake, change the foreground color to 50% gray (in the Color Picker, enter the following percentages: **H0, S0, B50**) and paint over your strokes to undo the effect. Press X to switch foreground and background colors, which will have the effect of switching between the Dodge & Burn tools.

You can vary the strength of the effect in a number of ways by changing the options for the Brush tool.

- Apply pen pressure to the strokes.

- Change the opacity level.

- Select the Airbrush option.

- Change the blend mode, for example, to Lighten or Darken, to gain finer control over which tones are affected (remember to change the foreground color, because some modes treat black as neutral whereas others treat white as neutral).

Finally, you are not confined to painting with only black and white; you can choose a shade of black or white to fine-tune the effect of the brush strokes.

Smoothing Skin Tones and Wrinkles

Although imperfect skin and wrinkles are a part of life, photographers and retouchers are routinely asked to confine them to the X dimension. Fortunately for busy professionals, Photoshop makes the task easy.

To smooth skin, take the following steps:

1. Make a selection of the skin areas by using the selection tools or Select ➜ Color Range command.

2. Copy the selected area onto a new layer: Ctrl+J (Windows), ⌘+J (Mac OS).

3. Apply the Dust & Scratches filter or the Median filter (both can be found in the Filter ➜ Noise submenu). The value will depend on the pixel dimensions but apply a high enough setting to smooth any defects and blemishes.

4. Hold down Alt (Windows), Opt (Mac OS) and then click the Add Layer Mask button in the Layers palette. This action applies a Hide All layer mask.

5. Select the Brush tool and an appropriately sized soft brush tip and then paint on the defects and blemishes. The filtered layer should unmask and, in the process, smooth the defects and blemishes.

   To prevent banding in the filtered content, especially in skin areas approaching maximum white, add the following steps:

6. Create a new layer above the filtered layer and fill it with 50% Gray. Choose Edit ➜ Fill and then, in the Fill dialog box, select Use: 50% Gray from the Contents pop-up menu. Click the OK button to exit.

7. Set the layer blend mode to Overlay and apply the Noise ➜ Add Noise filter. This adds noise but tapers it off gradually toward the shadows and highlights.

Although it's possible to smooth out wrinkles with the preceding method with a little application, the Healing Brush and the Patch tools can do a far better job. The Patch tool is fine for small healing jobs, but if your subject exhibits an overabundance of wrinkles, the Healing Brush tool is the correct tool to use.

To use the Healing Brush tool to smooth wrinkles and aging lines, take the following steps:

1. In the Layers palette, duplicate the image layer: Ctrl+J (Windows), ⌘+J (Mac OS).

2. Select the Healing Brush tool and a soft brush tip slightly larger than the wrinkle lines (make sure that it encompasses the highlights that usually accompany the dark lines). Turn off brush dynamics by selecting Clear Brush Controls from the Brushes palette menu.

3. On the options bar, set Mode to Normal, Source to Sampled, and deselect Aligned.

4. Alt-click (Windows), Opt-click (Mac OS) in a similar tonal area to the wrinkle you are trying to remove to define a sample point. Drag the tool across the wrinkle. Repeat the action until all the wrinkles have been removed.

NOTE As you paint, the stroke shows you a preview of the sampled content; if it's wildly off, undo and resample from an area with a similar texture and tone.

When you have removed all the wrinkles, you might find that the person looks as if he or she has had extreme plastic surgery and appears "Hollywood-ish" and quite unnatural (Figure 11-20). To counteract the unnatural look, reduce the opacity of the healed layer to taste. Because you were working on a duplicate layer, it should blend quite naturally with the original layer below it.

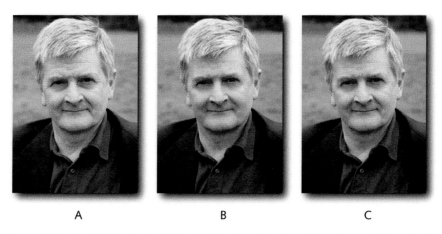

A   B   C

FIGURE 11-20: A—Original portrait. B—Healing Brush tool used to reduce wrinkles. C—Healing reduced by 40%.

Correcting Unwanted Highlights on Faces

The Shadow/Highlight adjustments command is a great feature for rescuing burned out highlights and blocked shadows. However, it works globally and cannot always do as good a job as some of the other tools. For example, the portrait in Figure 11-21 received an unplanned kick from a low-angle three-quarter backlight. Otherwise, the portrait is good and worth rescuing. Using Shadow/Highlight brings out some unflattering detail, but painting over the burned out cheek solves the problem in one go and does away with the need to mask a global move.

FIGURE 11-21: Left—The light has caught the cheek at an unflattering angle and resulted in burned-out detail. Right—Using the Healing Brush tool on a layer set to Darken mode and painting the burned-out areas has added detail where there was none or very little.

1. Create a new layer above the image layer and change its blend mode from Normal to Darken.

2. Select the Healing Brush tool and an appropriate soft brush tip. Make sure that the blend mode is set to Normal, Source to Sampled, offset to Aligned, and sampling to Sample All Layers.

3. Alt-click (Windows), Opt-click (Mac OS) a suitable skin area to set the sampling point.

4. Paint over the burned-out areas. Depending on the size of the area being repaired, you might need to define different sample points. Reduce or enlarge brush tip as needed by using the square bracket keys: press [to reduce or] to enlarge.

If you need to remove a dark blemish, such as a mole or a tattoo, create another layer and then change its blend mode to Lighten. Of course, you don't need to heal on a separate layer, but doing so does give you more flexibility. For example, you can turn the layer visibility off/on, lower its opacity, erase the healing in part or completely, and start all over again.

Sharpening

Somewhere along the capture chain, images lose their acutance or, put another way, the edges lose their contrast and so the image appears soft and mushy. When you use one of Photoshop's sharpening filters, the acutance is exaggerated, giving the illusion of increased sharpness.

The technique used by Photoshop to sharpen images is similar to a technique used in wet-darkroom printing in which a duplicate, lower-contrast positive is made of the negative, the two films are sandwiched slightly out of phase to "mask out" the unsharp tonal transitions, and a print is made. Hence the name of the most commonly used filter to sharpen images, Unsharp Mask (USM), which confuses many people. Photoshop creates the unsharp negative in the background and uses it to find the edges and then fattens the edge by creating light and dark pixels on either side of it.

Photoshop includes no fewer than five sharpening filters: Sharpen, Sharpen More, Sharpen Edges, Smart Sharpen, and Unsharp Mask. The first three work automatically and have limited application. The next two sections look at the other two in detail.

Using Unsharp Mask

The Unsharp Mask (USM) filter has been used to sharpen images for many years and probably will continue to be used for some time to come because of its inclusion in actions, available freely and commercially, used on a daily basis.

On the face of it, the filter looks deceptively easy to use, but in practice it trips up many a traveler. Briefly, the Amount slider controls the strength of the halo, the Radius the width, and the Threshold the intensity. The key to understanding its interface lies not in just the effect each control has on the image but also the order in which they are used.

When you enter the dialog box, it's usually a good idea to find the appropriate width of the halo first by setting Amount to 400–500% and Threshold to 0%. Having found the optimum radius setting, decrease the Amount and then increase the Threshold incrementally to decrease the intensity of the halo. You would think that increasing an intensity value would increase the intensity, but in the case of Threshold, the opposite is true.

Rather than apply sharpening to the original layer, apply it to a copy. This way, you can increase your options to modify the effect. For example, you can reduce the opacity and lessen the effect, change the layer blend mode to Luminosity and ensure that the color is unaffected, or reduce the halos by using the Blend If controls found in the Layer Style dialog box (Layer ➜ Layer Style ➜ Blending Options). To do so, move the white slider for This Layer inward to limit a white halo or the black slider to limit the black halo. You can Alt-click (Windows), Opt-click (Mac OS) to split the sliders; when you slide them apart, the blend transitions less harshly (see Chapter 6 for more information on blending layers).

The filter works on only one layer at a time; if your content is spread over several layers, stamp the layers into a new layer. The quickest way to do that is by pressing Ctrl+Alt+Shift+E (Windows), ⌘+Opt+Shift+E (Mac OS).

To use the Unsharp Mask filter, take the following steps:

1. Make sure that the layer you want to sharpen is active and the display magnification is set to 100% (View ➜ Actual Pixels) if outputting to a monitor, or 50% or 25% if outputting to an offset printer. You do this because some of the illusion of sharpness can be reduced when an image is halftoned; viewing at a lower magnification can help you judge the end effect (do not view at fractional magnifications, such as 66.67%, 33.33%, and so forth, because the anti-aliasing applied by Photoshop at fractional magnifications can cloud your judgment).

2. Select Filter ➜ Sharpen ➜ Unsharp Mask.

3. Drag the Amount slider to 500%, the Radius slider to 0%, and Threshold to 0%.

4. Drag the Radius slider to the right or click in the text field and then use the Up and Down Arrow keys to increase/decrease the radius incrementally. There is no formula that works for all images; use your judgment to find the best value.

5. Reduce the value of the Amount slider (you may have to juggle Radius and Amount to find the best setting).

6. Increase the Threshold value incrementally if the image contains large areas of color that you do not want to sharpen, such as skin or sky. Avoid setting values too high, because doing so will result in reduced sharpening.

7. Click the OK button to exit.

While the dialog box is open, you can click in the proxy window to see a before and after view. You also have the luxury of judging the sharpness by referring to the document window, which provides a live preview and can be toggled off/on with the Preview button. If your resources are low or you are sharpening particularly large files, you might wish to deselect the live Preview to speed the process and use the option only after you have established the settings.

Images containing fine, fractal detail, such as leaves and grass, require a lower Radius setting. This is because the edges tend to be very narrow in such images. The reverse is true of images containing broad washes of color and fewer or wider edges, such as cars and faces, which might also benefit from a higher Threshold setting to exclude noise, grain, and skin blemishes from being sharpened.

Figure 11-22 shows the various phases of the sharpening process.

A

B

C

D

FIGURE 11-22: The Unsharp Mask filter dialog showing the various phases of the sharpening process. The color chips at the top indicate the halo width and intensity. A—All values set to their lowest. B—The Amount value set to 500%, in order to better judge the next step. C—The Radius value increased incrementally. D—The Threshold value increased to show its effect: the skin has been softened but so has the hair.

Using Smart Sharpen

If you are accustomed to using the Unsharp Mask filter, the new Smart Sharpen filter will fit right into your workflow and will probably replace the Unsharp Mask in no time at all. Whereas Unsharp Mask has very few controls, Smart Sharpen has controls for reducing halos as well as removing motion blur, Gaussian blur, and lens blur. Furthermore, it has the option to save the current settings and apply them in a future sharpening session.

To use Smart Sharpen, take the following steps:

1. If the image contains noise, use the Reduce Noise filter to decrease it as much as possible. View the image at 100% magnification (View ➜ Actual Pixels) so that you are not viewing cached data (see the section about the Unsharp Mask filter earlier in the chapter for viewing tips).

2. Choose Filter ➜ Sharpen ➜ Smart Sharpen (Figure 11-23).

3. Set the Radius by dragging the slider or entering a value in the text field. The Radius defines the width of the halo around the edge.

4. Set the Amount by dragging the slider or entering a value in the text field. The Amount defines the intensity of the halo around the edge.

5. Choose an item from the Remove pop-up menu. You can choose between Gaussian Blur, Lens Blur, and Motion Blue algorithms. Gaussian Blur is faster, Lens Blur takes up more CPU time but produces a better result in most cases because it has better edge detection and a more subtle application, and Motion Blur tries to eradicate blur caused by subject or camera movement. If you select Motion Blur, enter an angle in the text field for the blur direction or click the clock face.

6. Select More Accurate to perform multiple iterations of the filter (not recommended on noisy images).

7. If you see unsightly halos, select the Advanced radio button and then click either the Shadow or the Highlight tab, depending on which halos you want to reduce.

8. Specify a Tonal Width to tell Smart Sharpen which tones that make up the halo you wish to affect. Smaller values restrict the fade to the darkest or lightest parts that make up the halo. Likewise, specify a Radius value to set the scale of the correction.

9. Specify a value for Fade Amount; this is similar to the Amount slider under the Sharpen tab except that it fades the effect rather than increases it.

10. Click the OK button to exit or the Save button by the Settings pop-up menu before you exit. After a custom setting has been saved, you can select it from the pop-up menu in the current or future editing sessions.

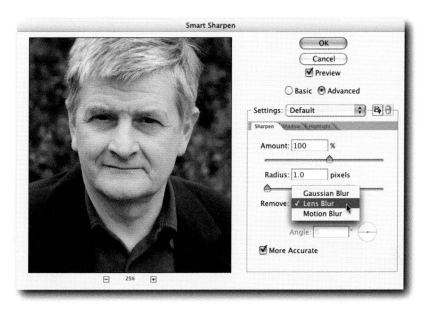

FIGURE 11-23: **Choosing Lens Blur in the Smart Sharpen dialog box; opened in Advanced view.**

If you are used to Unsharp Mask, you might find that you can achieve better results using smaller Amount and Radius settings.

TIP Because the sharpening process increases contrast, you should use it before setting the shadow and highlight end points when optimizing images for output to an offset printer.

A Flexible Method for Sharpening Images

When you are sharpening an image, the sharpening filters apply the illusion of sharpening globally unless limited by a selection. The effect is also destructive in as much as it has to be applied to a layer and cannot be modified (you can undo it as long as the history states are still present in the History palette, but you cannot modify it after the Fade command following the sharpen state has been superseded by the use of another command). You can employ two other methods to limit the effect, and they both provide much more control and flexibility than applying the filter through a selection.

The first method involves applying one of the sharpening filters, setting the sharpen history state as the source in the Histories palette, and then using the History Brush tool to paint from the future. The method is quite well known and used widely. To employ it, take the following steps:

1. Create a new layer above the image layer (you don't have to, but it gives more options for controlling the sharpening) and give it a memorable name, such as Sharpen. To create a new layer, click the Create New Layer button at the bottom of the Layers palette or press Ctrl+Alt+Shift+N (Windows), ⌘+Opt+Shift+N (Mac OS).

2. Select the image layer and apply any one of the sharpening filters from the Filters ➜ Sharpen submenu (see the sections "Using Unsharp Mask" and "Using Smart Sharpen," earlier in the chapter).

3. From the History palette menu, choose New Snapshot and select Merged Layers from the pop-up menu, or hold down Alt (Windows), Opt (Mac OS) and then click the Create New Snapshot button in the History palette.

4. Step back in history by selecting the previous state in the History palette or pressing Ctrl+Alt+Z (Windows), ⌘+Opt+Z (Mac OS). The Sharpen layer should become active because of the move.

5. In the History palette, click in the column to the left of the snapshot you created in step 2. When you click, a History Brush icon should appear in the column. This will set it as the source for the History Brush tool.

6. Select the History Brush tool and a suitable soft brush tip. Turn off the brush tool's dynamics by choosing Clear Brush Controls from the Brushes palette submenu.

7. Paint the areas where you would like the sharpness to be applied. For example, if it's a portrait, paint the eyes, lips, nose, ears, and so forth and avoid the forehead, cheeks, neck, and so forth. Make sure that you are painting on the Sharpen layer at all times, the one you created in the first step, and not the image layer.

Finally, set the opacity of the Sharpen layer to taste. The preceding steps may seem convoluted at first but with practice can easily become second nature.

The second method employs a duplicate layer and a layer mask. To employ it, take the following steps:

1. Duplicate the layer that you want to sharpen. If your content is spread over several layers, stamp them into a new layer. The quickest way to do that is by pressing Ctrl+Alt+Shift+E (Windows), ⌘+Opt+Shift+E (Mac OS).

2. Apply any one of the sharpening filters from the Filters ➜ Sharpen submenu (see the sections "Using Unsharp Mask" and "Using Smart Sharpen," earlier in the chapter).

3. Apply a Hide All layer mask by holding down Alt (Windows), Opt (Mac OS) and clicking the Add Layer Mask button in the Layers palette.

4. Select a soft brush and make sure that its dynamics are turned off by choosing Clear Brush Controls from the Brushes palette menu.

5. Make sure that the foreground and background colors are set to white and black, respectively.

6. Paint out/in the area(s) you want to hide/show: to hide, paint with black; to reveal, paint with white. You can ride the X key to switch between the foreground and background colors (Figure 11-24).

FIGURE 11-24: Left—The image layer duplicated and sharpened. The hair and background appear oversharpened. Right—A layer mask added to the sharpened layer and the hair and background masked so that the original shows through from the layer below.

279

By using the preceding methods, you will also gain access to layer opacity and the layer blend modes. Furthermore, advanced layer Blend If options (Layer ➜ Layer Style ➜ Blending Options) can be used to control the halos created by the filter and, of course, you still have your original layers to fall back onto should you need to repurpose the file.

An Alternative Method for Sharpening Images

One alternative to using the filters in the Sharpen submenu is to use the High Pass filter. The filter works by increasing contrast on the edges of the image and leaves large, flat areas unaffected. The filter has only one setting: Radius. To apply the filter, take the following steps:

1. Duplicate the layer that you want to sharpen and give it a descriptive name, such as High Pass.

2. Set the magnification to 100% for screen output or to 50–25% if outputting to an offset printer.

3. Choose Filter ➜ Other ➜ High Pass.

4. Apply a low Radius setting if the image contains a large number of edges, such as a scene containing foliage, or a larger value if the image contains fewer edges, such as a portrait. Your duplicate layer should turn a mushy gray, but you should be able to discern the edges through it (Figure 11-25). Decrease the Radius if grain or noise starts to materialize in broader areas of color.

5. Click the OK button to apply the setting and to exit the dialog box.

6. Back in the Layers palette, change the blend mode of the High Pass layer from Normal to Overlay. Soft Light and Hard Light can also be used; each produces a slightly different result.

To refine the filter effect, decrease the opacity of the filtered layer, or use the Blend If sliders to localize the effect (Layer ➜ Layer Style ➜ Blending Options).

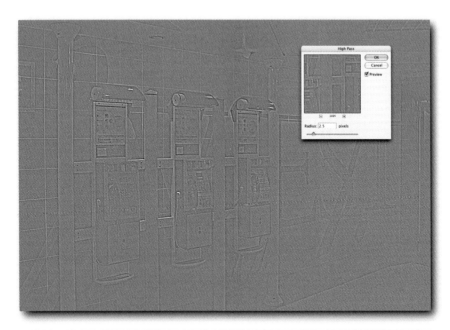

FIGURE 11-25: Using the High Pass filter to sharpen a noisy image and the result.

Summary

That was editing, transforming, and retouching images. The hacks showed you how to accomplish simple, everyday tasks that form the backbone of most Photoshop work. They are by no means exhaustive (retouching could easily have taken a whole chapter, if not the book!) but should be enough to form a good, solid foundation of techniques on which you can build at your own leisure.

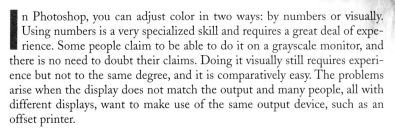

chapter 12

Adjusting and Correcting Colors

I n Photoshop, you can adjust color in two ways: by numbers or visually. Using numbers is a very specialized skill and requires a great deal of experience. Some people claim to be able to do it on a grayscale monitor, and there is no need to doubt their claims. Doing it visually still requires experience but not to the same degree, and it is comparatively easy. The problems arise when the display does not match the output and many people, all with different displays, want to make use of the same output device, such as an offset printer.

In the past, people overcame the problem by using a closed-loop system. Basically, the monitors were calibrated to match the print. However, the system soon broke down when digital photography and printing began to take off. Before long, anyone who wanted to use a print shop was required to use that shop's proprietary system. Unfortunately, that meant that you had to repurpose a file each time it was printed by another print shop, and you had to adjust your monitor to suit each print shop. In stepped color management. Adobe introduced it in Photoshop 5.0 and refined it in Photoshop 6.0. It introduced the idea of a synthetic working space for editing files and tagging the file with the working space profile. When a file was opened, provided that the conditions of the output monitor were known and a profile was created describing those conditions, Photoshop could open it in the same working space and replicate the appearance by doing a conversion on the fly between the working space profile and the monitor profile. This is the system now widely adopted by most people, as well as print shops and printers. It underpins all color correction and color adjustments made in Photoshop.

Using Profiles

The color management system (CMS) used by Photoshop requires ICC profiles as an engine requires fuel. That's to say, they are pretty important. So, what exactly is a profile? Profiles describe synthetic color spaces, such as Adobe RGB (1998), sRGB, and ColorMatch RGB, and the conditions and the color gamut of the output devices, such as monitors and printers. Whenever Photoshop outputs a file, it does a conversion on the fly between the two spaces, thus ensuring a close match.

For example, each time a file is opened, Photoshop looks at any profiles embedded in the file to determine the tagged working space. It knows the color space you are working in from your color settings, compares the two color spaces, and then gives you various options on how to proceed, depending on how you have dictated the Color Management Policies in Color Settings. These options range from viewing the file in the embedded profile's color space to assigning other color spaces for viewing purposes to converting the numbers, the ones and zeros that make up the file, to another color space or to not color managing and instead viewing the file in your monitor's color space.

Needless to say, a CMS is only as good as the profile it uses. For that reason, it's imperative to calibrate your monitor periodically (monitors drift, CRT models more so than LCD models). If your viewing conditions change—for example, the lighting changes from daylight to artificial at night—you should have profiles for both conditions and change them accordingly. You can use software, such as Adobe Gamma Utility on the PC (located in the Control Panel) or the Display Calibrator on the Macintosh (located in `System Preferences\Displays\Color`), to characterize your monitor and to create a monitor profile that Photoshop can utilize.

NOTE Ideally, the viewing conditions should stay consistent with the conditions under which a profile is created, but in reality most people don't have that luxury. The two-profile solution is a compromise at best. If you can afford it, block out any daylight and install professional light sources that can mimic daylight, such as SoLux: `www.solux.net`.

For best results, you can use a combination of commercially available hardware, which calibrates your monitor to a standard white point, and software, which then creates a profile in much the same way as Adobe Gamma Utility and Display Calibrator. The hardware can be a colorimeter or the more expensive spectrophotometer. Separate software can also be used to create profiles that require a wider range of white points and advanced gamma control to match a range of monitors. Four of the most successful and popular companies that manufacture and sell hardware and software are, not in any hierarchical order, basICColor, ColorVision, GretagMacbeth, and Monaco (see the book's companion Web site at `www.wiley.com/go/extremetech` for some useful Web sites to visit).

NOTE Before the release of Photoshop CS2, you could not turn off color management. If you elected not to color manage a file, Photoshop would display the file in your working space. Now when you elect the same option, Photoshop displays the file in the monitor's color space. This is not an option to be used lightly, because it will force you to work in a proprietary working space, and the whole point of a CMS is not to be forced into editing in a proprietary, closed-loop color space.

Color Settings and Working Space

As often happens in computing, language is bent and modified almost on a daily basis, giving rise to possible confusion. In Photoshop terminology, two very similar phrases are used to describe entirely unrelated practices. One is called the *working space* and the other the *workspace*. The first refers to color spaces used to view, manipulate, and output images. The second refers to the way the interface is customized, specifically, palette locations, menu colors and visibility, and keyboard shortcut sets (all of which can be set and then saved as a workspace).

When you first install Photoshop, you are given the opportunity to modify the Color Settings. It's quite possible you were either in a hurry to try Photoshop or your eyes glazed over at the very thought of color management. Unfortunately, if you want to do any kind of tonal or color correction in Photoshop, choosing the right working space and policies is essential, so the following sections help you painlessly choose a working space and color policies.

Accessing Color Settings

Color Settings is accessed from the Edit menu (Figure 12-1) or Ctrl+Shift+K (Windows), ⌘+Shift+K (Mac OS). The dialog box is divided into five logical parts: Working Spaces, Color Management Policies, Conversion Options, Advanced Controls, and Description. The settings in each part can be customized and the four parts saved as one custom setting and then selected from the Settings pop-up menu at the top of the dialog box.

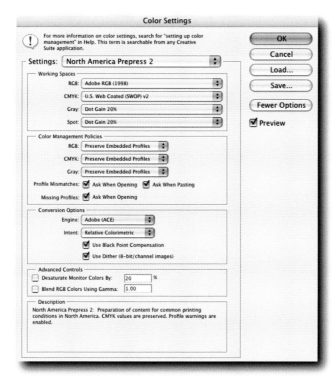

FIGURE 12-1: **The Color Settings dialog box, showing all the available options.**

The default dialog box includes North American factory settings, a smaller choice of working spaces, and advanced settings hidden from view. Selecting the More Options button gives access to the worldwide settings and to all the working space profiles available on your system; it also reveals the advanced settings.

Choosing a Working Space

Working spaces are defined by choosing a profile from the RGB, CMYK, or Gray pop-up menus.

The two most popular RGB working spaces are Adobe RGB (1998), for images destined for print and archiving, and sRGB, for output to the Internet, also favored by digital print shops. ColorMatch RGB is favored by some print houses for its smaller color gamut. Apple RGB is a legacy color space and should not be chosen simply because you are using a Macintosh; choose it if you're opening many legacy files that have no profile embedded. ProPhoto RGB has the widest color gamut and is recommended for preserving as much of the color gamut in the master file as possible. However, it's best suited to files in 16-Bit/Channel mode, because performing large adjustments to files in 8-Bit/Channel mode may lead to posterization. The choices also include Monitor Color, which you should avoid unless you have a very good reason for choosing it and understand its implications.

The CMYK working spaces are standard color spaces and good starting points. Choose one that closely matches the printing conditions, that is, if printing in the United States on a sheetfed printer on coated stock, choose U.S. Sheetfed Coated v2. For the best match, ask your printer to send you a profile of its proofer.

The Gray working space lets you specify a dot gain percentage for printing or a gamma level for viewing images in Grayscale mode. When More Options is selected, you can specify a custom dot gain or a custom gamma and save and load settings and profiles.

When choosing a dot gain percentage, choose one that suits your paper type and ink combination (coated paper absorbs and spreads less ink and therefore requires a smaller dot compensation, whereas uncoated paper, such as newsprint, absorbs and spreads more ink and therefore requires a higher dot percentage compensation). You can determine the dot gain either through trial and error or by printing patches, measuring them with an instrument, and then entering the values in the Custom Dot Gain dialog box (accessed from the Gray pop-up menu). If a service bureau or commercial printer tells you that the dot gain is somewhere between the available 10, 15, 20, 25, or 30%—for example, 12%—open the dialog box and enter **62%** in the 50% text field (Figure 12-2). Dot gain is usually measured from the 50% tint, or patch, hence the addition to the 50% text field.

For images destined for the screen, choose a gamma setting of 1.8 or 2.2. The latter is favored by the PC and increasingly by the Macintosh. You can, if you wish, also choose a custom gamma setting by opening the Custom Gamma dialog box (accessed from the Gray pop-up menu). You can enter a value between 0.75 and 3.0 (Figure 12-3). The settings can be saved from the pop-up menu as a profile and used elsewhere in Photoshop, for example, in Proof Setup, or by color savvy programs, or passed on to colleagues in a work chain. Profiles may also be loaded from the pop-up menu.

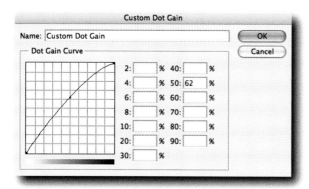

FIGURE 12-2: The Custom Dot Gain dialog box lets you specify custom settings for grayscale images destined for output to an offset printer.

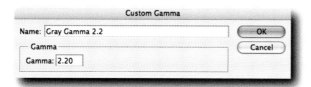

FIGURE 12-3: The Custom Gamma dialog box lets you specify a gamma setting between 0.75 and 3.0.

The Spot working space settings let you choose a dot gain for spot channels and duotones from a pop-up menu, save values, similar to Gray working space, or specify a custom value.

Setting Color Management Policies

Color Management Policies are simply a set of rules for opening files with and without embedded profiles. Unless you have a pressing need to choose otherwise, select Preserve Embedded Profiles for RGB, CMYK, and Gray. For Profile Mismatches, deselect Ask When Opening and select Ask When Pasting. You can leave the first option on if you want to be warned of a profile mismatch, but because Photoshop can honor the embedded profile and display a document in the embedded profile's color space, it can save one step. You just need to be vigilant and keep an eye on the document profile, which you can view in the status bar (located at the bottom of the document window), or the Info palette.

Setting Conversion Options

Conversion Options allow you to choose defaults for converting between color spaces.

- **Engine** allows you to choose a Color Management Module (CMM) used to map the color gamuts between the color spaces. Adobe (ACE) is highly recommended (ACE stands for Adobe Color Engine). Stay with it unless you have pressing needs to choose otherwise.

287

- **Intent** allows you to choose between the different rendering intents. Choose Relative Colorimetric (recommended overall) or Perceptual. The former clips out-of-gamut colors but does not alter the in gamut colors; the latter preserves the relationships between the in gamut colors, avoids clipping, but may desaturate some colors. These options affect conversions if you have elected a color policy that converts a file upon opening or choose to convert a file in the Print dialog box before outputting to a local printer. They also set the defaults in the Convert to Profile dialog box, though the settings can be overridden in the dialog box.

- **Use Black Point Compensation** allows the black point of the source and the target profiles to be taken into consideration when a document is converted. It's best to keep this option selected; otherwise, the conversion might result in washed-out or blocked shadows.

- **Use Dither (8-bit/channel images)** allows for automatic dithering of colors when you're converting between color spaces that might otherwise cause banding where colors are clipped. To avoid increased file size and make compression less effective, deselect it. If you think a file can benefit by adding dither, you can use the Convert to Profile command and select the option on a case-by-case basis.

Using Advanced Controls

Advanced Controls allow you to view out-of-gamut colors and to override default RGB blending.

- **Desaturate Monitor Colors By** allows you to differentiate between colors that would otherwise appear as a single color because they were out of the monitor's color gamut. The option should be used with care because it can result in mismatched colors between the display and the print output.

- **Blend RGB Colors Using Gamma** allows you to specify a gamma that's different to the working space gamma. When the option is selected, Photoshop blends RGB colors using the specified gamma, rather than blend independently in CIE XYZ color space (a device-independent color space based on human perception and developed in 1931 by the Commission Internationale de l'Eclairage, or CIE). This can result in better blending where colors transition sharply but will also display differently in applications that support layers but not this option.

Description

The Description area of the dialog box is reserved for displaying any information that may accompany a profile or a setting. Just hover the pointer over any of the pop-up menus or the options to view a detailed description. For example, hover over any of the following text to see a description: Settings, Working Spaces, Ask When Opening, or Blend RGB Colors Using Gamma. You can make use of it when saving color settings by entering a description in the Color Settings Comment dialog box, which pops up after the Save dialog box closes.

Creating Custom CMYK Separation Settings

Photoshop kept the old CMYK engine for converting files when color management was introduced and mode changes handed over to profiles. However, it is rather tucked away in the Color Settings dialog box. Despite the popularity of profiles and tools and software for creating profiles, the old CMYK feature can be used to create custom CMYK separations that get the job done without extra cost. For example, if you need to print a four-color grayscale image, you can create a profile that uses a heavy GCR setting and use it to separate the file.

The Custom CMYK dialog box (Figure 12-4) is divided into two sections: Ink Options and Separation Options. The former lets you choose from a set of predefined inksets, such as SWOP, Eurostandard, or Toyo, or define your own by choosing Custom from the pop-up menu. In the Ink Colors dialog box (Figure 12-4), you can plug known ink values into the text boxes or choose by clicking a swatch and then selecting a color from the Color Picker.

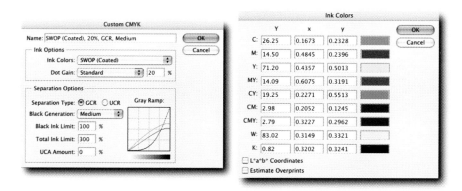

FIGURE 12-4: The Custom CMYK dialog box, accessed by choosing Custom from the CMYK working space pop-up menu in Color Settings, and the Ink Settings dialog box, accessed by choosing Custom from the Ink Colors pop-up menu.

You can also enter a dot gain percentage or define a custom dot gain curve for each plate if you have access to printed patches that can be accurately measured. To gain access to Dot Gain Curves, choose Curves from the Dot Gain pop-up menu.

The other section, Separation Options, enables you to define how the inks will be eventually laid down on paper. Here you can specify whether you favor GCR (Gray Component Replacement) or UCR (Under Color Removal) black generation. When you select GCR, the Black Generation pop-up menu becomes available and presents you with six choices that control the tonal areas in which the black ink replaces a colorant. One of the choices lets you define a custom black generation, but be aware that this requires considerable experience in evaluating images or, at the least, values provided by a printer.

The Black Ink Limit sets the limit of the ink laid in the darkest shadows. This can usually be left at 100% but may be lowered for newsprint stock. The Total Ink Limit takes into account the ink for all four plates. Both of these settings are highly dependent on the type of press, stock, and inkset. For example, values for high-quality sheetfed printing on coated stock can be as high as 300–340%, whereas for Web offset newsprint might be as low as 220–280%. The UCA Amount (Under Color Addition) values compensate for loss of ink density in neutral shadow areas when high GCR values are used. If the shadows look washed out, you can use small amounts of UCA to enrich them by adding back density.

To create a custom CMYK profile, take the following steps:

1. Choose Edit ➜ Color Settings, or Ctrl+Shift+K (Windows), ⌘+K (Mac OS).

2. In the Color Settings dialog box, choose Custom CMYK from the CMYK profile pop-up menu (the item is located at the top of the menu).

3. In the Custom CMYK dialog box, select ink options from the preset Ink Colors pop-up menu or specify your own inksets by choosing Custom from the same pop-up.

4. Enter a value for Dot Gain or click the pop-up menu, choose Curves, and then, in the Dot Gain Curves dialog box, enter values in the text fields for each plate or use the curve. Click the OK button.

5. Select black generation type: GCR or UCR. If you select GCR, choose from the pop-up menu a preset curve that defines which tonal areas will receive the treatment, or choose Custom and then alter the curve in the Black Generation dialog box.

6. Set values for Black Ink Limit, Total Ink Limit, and finally, if GCR was chosen at step 5, a value for UCA Amount.

7. Click the OK button to exit Custom CMYK.

8. Back in the Color Settings dialog box, click the CMYK pop-up menu and choose Save CMYK. Give the profile a descriptive name and save it in the default folder, which should be the folder in which your OS stores the profiles so that they can be seen by Photoshop.

Creating profiles using Custom CMYK is a highly skilled job and should not be undertaken lightly. Before you create a custom profile, talk to your service bureau or commercial printer and try to elicit as much information as possible to include in the profile.

Checking Files for Embedded Profiles

Before you send files to a client, it's usually a good idea to check them for embedded profiles in case of mismatches. For example, if sending CMYK files, you don't really want to include RGB files, or if sending files destined for the Web, you don't really want to send files in the Adobe RGB (1998) color space. It's also sometimes necessary to group files by their color space when batch processing files.

Unfortunately, Bridge does not include a sort-by-profile command. However, it does include a very powerful Find feature, and because one of the search criteria is Find by all metadata, it can be used as a substitute (Figure 12-5).

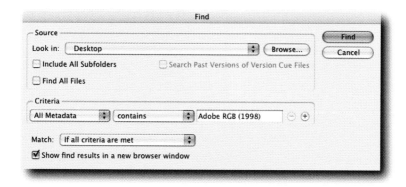

FIGURE 12-5: The Find dialog box in Bridge can be used to search files containing a specific color profile.

To use Find, choose Edit → Find, or Ctrl+F (Windows), ⌘+F (Mac OS). Select a folder from the Look in pop-up menu and other options as required. In the Criteria section of the dialog box, choose All Metadata from the first pop-up menu and Contains from the second and then enter the color space of the profile, for example, Adobe RGB (1998) or sRGB. Check the option at the bottom of the window to view the results in a new browser window or save it as a collection by selecting the Save As Collection button below the toolbar after the files have been found.

TIP If you didn't elect to view the results in a new browser window, the Find Results window will replace the current window. That can be a little disorientating because, at first, there is no obvious way to get back to the previous view. If you find yourself in that position, choose the previous folder from the Folders panel (not available in all workspaces unless you click the Show/Hide Panels button at the bottom left of the browser window) or select it from the Recent Folders list in the Look in pop-up menu, located at the top left of the Bridge window.

Viewing Gamut Warnings for Custom Profiles

Because not all output devices have the same color gamut, Photoshop includes the means to prewarn you of any colors that may not be seen or printed on your intended output device (Figure 12-6). However, there is one little caveat. Before Photoshop can alert you, you must have a profile for the output device, and the profile must be available in the View → Proof Setup submenu. Profiles are included for the current CMYK working space, separate CMYK plates, generic Macintosh and Windows monitors, and your actual monitor. However, before you can add a profile to the list, it has to reside in the folder where the OS keeps the ICC profiles. Windows stores the profiles in Windows\System32\Spool\Drivers\Color, and the Mac OS stores them in Library\ColorSync\Profiles.

FIGURE 12-6: The gray overlay, generated by the Gamut Warning command, clearly shows which colors will be clipped when the file is printed on a deskjet printer.

Assuming that you have already added the profile to the appropriate OS folder, take the following steps to add it to the Proof Setup menu:

1. Choose View ➜ Proof Setup ➜ Custom.

2. In the Customize Proof Condition dialog box, click the Device to Simulate pop-up menu and then select your custom profile from the list.

3. Select a rendering intent from the pop-up. Relative Colorimetric is commonly used. Unfortunately, you cannot choose it on a case-by-case basis. If you need to view warnings for more than one rendering intent, you will need to set up as many Custom Proof Conditions.

4. Check the Use Black Point Compensation option (this action maps the source and targets black points).

5. Check the Simulate Ink Black or Paper White option. If selected, the options affect the preview and not the print. Not all profiles support the options. If your paper contains a heavy amount of optical brightener, Paper White may give an incorrect preview. In that case, select only Ink Black.

6. Click the Save button, give the settings a memorable name, and save the profile in the default folder.

7. Back in the Proof Setup dialog box, the Custom Proof Condition name should change to your memorable name. Click the OK button to exit.

8. In the Proof Setup menu, the profile should also be selected, and you should be seeing a soft proof preview based on your custom profile.

9. There's just one more step needed to view the out-of-gamut colors: Choose View ➔ Gamut Warning or hold down Ctrl+Shift (Windows), ⌘+Shift (Mac OS) and press Y.

When the profile has been set up, there is no need to select Proof Colors to view a gamut warning; just select the profile in Proof Setup and then Gamut Warning. If the default warning overlay color doesn't stand out from your image, you can change the color and the opacity by opening Preferences ➔ Transparency & Gamut and choosing a color under Gamut Warning. Note that Proof Colors is a sticky command, so do remember to deselect it in order to return to your default working space preview.

NOTE When the Proof Colors command is not being used, by default, gamut warnings are based on the profile chosen in the CMYK working space in Color Settings.

Removing Colorcasts

Colorcasts can occur when you take a photograph in ambient light that has a different color temperature to the one your film is optimized for, or when the white balance on a digital camera is set for a different lighting condition. For example, the white balance is set to Tungsten but the ambient light happens to be daylight.

Removing colorcasts isn't always a desirable thing. For example, you would not want to remove it from an image shot at dawn or sunset. However, when the need does arise, Photoshop can do an excellent job. There is no single tool or command for removing colorcasts. However, there are a number of ways that you can approach the task at hand.

Three Ways to Correct a Colorcast

The following sections outline three popular ways to correct a colorcast: using Auto Color, Variations, or the Levels or Curves commands.

Using Auto Color

Using Auto Color is probably the quickest and dirtiest way to correct a colorcast. Simply choose Image ➔ Adjustments ➔ Auto Color and you are done color correcting. You are done even quicker if you use the keyboard shortcut Ctrl+Shift+B (Windows), ⌘+Shift+B (Mac OS) to call the command. However, Auto Color works on some images but not all. So, it can be a bit hit and miss (see the section "Using Auto Color Manually," later in this chapter, for more information).

Using Variations

The Variations command can also be used to correct colorcasts, but the main drawbacks to using Variations are the size of the thumbnails and the dependence on visual feedback only. Drawbacks notwithstanding, Variations can be used with great speed to adjust color and tone globally.

When you open the Variations panel (Image ➔ Adjustments ➔ Variations), you are presented with 12 thumbnails (Figure 12-7). This sight can be a little overwhelming at first, but when you are familiar with the layout, you can navigate around it without devoting too much thought. The panel is divided into three sections:

- The top-left section contains the Original and the Current Pick thumbnails. To the right are radio buttons that limit the adjustments to Shadows, Midtones, Highlights, or Saturation. Below them is a slider that controls the amount of adjustment (Fine applies the least adjustment and Coarse the most). You can elect to hide/show clipping by using the Show Clipping option.

- The bottom left section contains a Current Pick thumbnail surrounded by thumbnails that allow you to add more amounts of the six primary colors by clicking them. After you have added a color, you can subtract it by clicking its counterpart, located directly opposite. For example, click Blue to add and then click Yellow to subtract blue. The six primary colors, with their counterparts, are Red-Cyan, Green-Magenta, Blue-Yellow.

- The right section contains a Current Pick thumbnail and Lighter and Darker thumbnails above and below, respectively. Clicking them adjusts the tonal values.

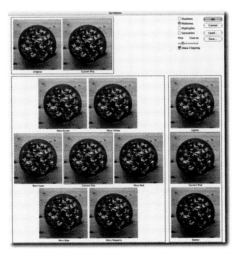

FIGURE 12-7: The Variations panel can be used to modify color and tone. Top left: Original and adjusted versions.

To adjust an image, set the Fine/Coarse setting to Fine (it's best to apply small adjustments). Start with Midtones and then adjust the Highlights and Shadows. Next, adjust the tone by using the Lighter or Darker thumbnails. Finally, adjust saturation as required. Save the settings if you have to correct a number of images shot under the same conditions.

Although you cannot use the Undo feature in the panel, you can revert back by clicking the Original thumbnail at any time.

Using Levels or Curves

Using Levels or Curves to correct colorcasts makes it possible to apply the adjustments through an adjustment layer. You can then use the eyedropper tools located in the dialog box, or adjust the curve if you use Curves instead of Levels. This method is a little more convoluted, but the upside is that it can provide more overall control and the option of changing your mind as many times as you like without altering the values of the underlying pixels.

To use the eyedropper tools in Levels or Curves, take the following steps:

1. Select the Eyedropper tool and set its option to Sample Size: 3 by 3 Average.

2. In the Layers palette, select the image layer.

3. Create a Levels/Curves Adjustment layer by clicking the Create New Fill or Adjustment Layer button.

4. In the Levels/Curves dialog box, double-click the Set Black Point eyedropper button (first one of the three inline eyedropper icons) to access the Color Picker. In the HSB (hue, saturation, brightness) section of the Color Picker, enter the following values: H0, S0, B5 (see the note toward the end of this section for more information). Click the OK button to close the Color Picker.

5. Drag the pointer through a deep shadow in the image (the advantage of using Levels is that you can find the deepest shadow or lightest highlight by holding down Alt (Windows), Opt (Mac OS), clicking the shadow/highlight input sliders, and moving them inward). See Figure 12-8.

6. Double-click the Set White Point eyedropper button (third one of the three inline eyedropper icons) to access the Color Picker once again. In the HSB section of the Color Picker, enter the following values: H0, S0, B95. Click the OK button to close the Color Picker.

7. Drag the pointer through a highlight in the image (make sure that it's not a specular highlight). See Figure 12-8.

8. Click the OK button to exit Levels/Curves.

9. Change the blend mode of the adjustment layer to Color (this action ensures that only the color is affected, not the tonal values).

A   B

FIGURE 12-8: A—Original showing where the Levels Set White Point (top), Set Gray Point (bottom right) and Set Black Point (bottom left) eyedroppers were used to neutralize the bluish colorcast. B—Corrected version.

After the shadows and highlights have been neutralized, the colorcast should disappear. If the image contains a colorcast in the midtones and also a gray object (perhaps a garment, furniture in an office, or a section of a building), you can also use the Set Gray Point Eyedropper tool (the middle one of the three inline eyedropper icons) in Levels or Curves. To use the tool, set its target color in the Color Picker by double-clicking the Set Gray Point button, and then in the HSB section of the dialog box, enter **H0, S0, B50**. Click the OK button to exit the Color Picker and then drag the tool across the gray object to neutralize the colorcast.

The Set Gray Point tool works slightly differently from how the Set White Point and Set Black Point tools do. It takes the luminance of the source color and the hue and saturation of the specified target color and then alters the gamma values for each channel in an attempt to map the colors to the source color, in the process eliminating colorcasts without altering the tonal values.

To avoid tonal clipping if applying the adjustment directly to a layer (not recommended; try to use adjustment layers at all times), immediately after leaving the Levels or Curves dialog box, choose Edit ➜ Fade Levels/Curves, select Color from the pop-up menu, and then click the OK button. Doing so ensures that only the colors, not the luminosity values, are affected in your image.

NOTE When you use the eyedropper tools in Levels or Curves, whatever their brightness values are set to in the HSB section of the Color Picker will be applied to the shadows and highlights, and clipping may take place. These values are usually set to H0 S0 B0 for the Set Black Point eyedropper and H0 S0 B100 for the Set White Point eyedropper, or equal amounts of 0 and 255 in the RGB text boxes, respectively. Lower the values to something like H0 S0 B12 for Set Black Point and H0 S0 B95 for Set White Point. That will ensure there is some detail in the shadows and highlights when the image is output to an offset printer.

Using Auto Color Manually

The Auto Color command, found under Image → Adjustments, can do a good job of adjusting an image and get you into the ballpark, but, more often than not, the result can disappoint. For that reason, if you have a fear of auto anything, you may be tempted to ignore the command altogether. However, if you dig a little deeper, you will find that the command also resides in the Levels and Curves dialog boxes; though chances are, if you ignored the menu command, you will also ignore the Auto button! After all, it does the same job—or so you may be led to believe by the layout of the buttons in the dialog boxes. The Options button right below the Auto button actually gives access not to options for Levels or Curves but for the Auto commands. After you click it, the Auto Color Correction Options dialog box opens, giving you manual control over Auto Color, Auto Levels, and Auto Contrast, and giving you the chance to redefine the default settings (Figure 12-9).

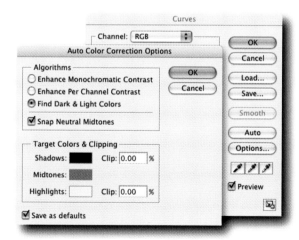

Figure 12-9: **The Auto Color Correction Options dialog box can be accessed from the Levels or the Curves dialog box by clicking the Options button.**

To use Auto Color manually, take the following steps:

1. Open an image containing a colorcast and make the image layer active by clicking it.

2. Open the Levels or the Curves dialog box; for this example, the Levels dialog box is being used.

3. In the Levels dialog box, click Options to open the Auto Color Corrections dialog box.

4. When you open the dialog box, the default algorithm is set to Auto Levels. To change it to Auto Color, select Find Dark & Light Colors and then check the Snap Neutral Midtones box.

5. In the Target Colors & Clipping section, enter zero for Clip percentages (the default can result in excessive clipping). You can exercise more control over the clipping values in the Levels dialog box by using the Shadow and Highlight sliders while holding down the Alt key to temporarily invoke threshold mode.

6. Next, check the Save as Defaults box and click the OK button.

7. In the Levels dialog box, hold down Alt (Windows), Opt (Mac OS) and click the Reset button. The preceding steps set Auto Color as a new default and undo the correction that was applied to the document.

8. Enter the Auto Color Correction Options dialog box once more by clicking Options.

9. In the Target Colors & Clipping section, click the Shadows color box to access the Color Picker and then use the text fields to alter RGB values, or drag the sampler in the color field and then move the color slider up and down to warm or cool the shadows. Do the same to the Highlights and Midtones if needed (Figure 12-10).

10. Click the OK button after you are satisfied with the changes. When the Save the new target colors as defaults? message appears, select No—unless, of course, you have many similar images to correct.

NOTE In the Auto Color Correction Options dialog box, Enhance Monochromatic Contrast does the same job as Auto Contrast, Enhance Per Channel Contrast does the same job as Auto Levels (the default setting), and Find Dark & Light Colors does the same job as Auto Color.

Correcting Images Exposed under Wrong Light Source

The following simulates removing a colorcast by converting to LAB mode and then using curves on the AB channels. However, you can use this method without leaving the original color mode. It's another quick-and-dirty method for removing a colorcast. After opening the document, take the following steps:

1. Select the Eyedropper tool and set its options to Size Sample 3 by 3 Average.

2. Drag the Eyedropper tool over the color you want to remove.

3. Make a new layer and fill it with the color that you just sampled (Edit ➜ Fill ➜ Use: Foreground Color).

4. Choose Image ➜ Adjustments ➜ Invert, or use the keyboard shortcut of Ctrl+I (Windows), ⌘+I (Mac OS).

5. Change the layer's blend mode to Color.

6. Lower the opacity of the layer to 50%.

That should get you into the ballpark. At step 2, you can also try duplicating the image layer, running the Blur ➜ Average filter and inverting the layer.

FIGURE 12-10: Before and after applying Auto Color.

NOTE Where appropriate, try to set neutral end points first by using the eyedroppers in Curves or Levels.

Saturating and Desaturating Images

Sometimes referred to as chroma, *saturation* is a measure of the purity and the vividness of a color. The degree to which a color is saturated depends on how different it is from gray at a given lightness. For example, colors that contain a high degree of gray appear less vibrant and less saturated and, therefore, are considered less pure. Colors that contain a lesser degree of gray appear more saturated and, therefore, are considered more pure.

Saturating Colors Selectively

When you need to saturate colors selectively, it's not always necessary to make selections or to create masks and then spend time refining them. You can do so by taking the following steps:

1. Create a Hue/Saturation Adjustment layer above your image layer.

2. Next, select the color that you want to saturate from the Edit pop-up menu in the Hue/Saturation dialog box.

Many users miss the controls available via the Hue/Saturation command, possibly because when they enter the dialog box, the eyedroppers and the color range slider controls are grayed out. However, as soon as you select a color from the Edit pop-up menu, a default color range is defined for you and the eyedroppers and the color range sliders spring to life (Figure 12-11).

  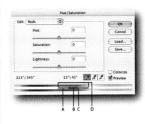

FIGURE 12-11: Left—Original image. Middle—Reds and yellows selectively saturated. Right—A breakdown of the Hue/Saturation adjustment slider: A—Adjusts color range without affecting fall-off; B—Moves the whole slider; C—Adjusts range of color component; D—Adjusts fall-off without affecting color range.

When the eyedroppers become available, you can define a color range with the first eyedropper by sampling in the image and then adding to it or subtracting from it by using the second and third eyedroppers, respectively. Furthermore, you can refine your selection by moving the color range sliders at the bottom of the dialog box. The two outside triangular sliders define how smooth or harsh the transition will be between the selected and nonselected colors.

Ten Ways of Desaturating an Image

The following section lists no fewer than 10 ways of desaturating an image. The list seems excessive but is included here to show how a little lateral thinking can unearth different methods for achieving, more or less, the same objective—in this case, desaturating an image locally or globally.

When looked at closely, the list also shows how methods, and not just the ones revealed in the following section but elsewhere, too, can vary in the degree of control that each one allows you to exercise over your image. For example, using the Channel Mixer to desaturate colors allows greater control than a mode change, but it doesn't allow for local control, whereas painting with the Brush tool set to Color mode allows for total control locally, and so forth. When you are aware of the fine nuances, you can make use of Photoshop's versatility, rather than be awed or overwhelmed by it.

The following hacks assume that you have a composite RGB image on its own layer open in Photoshop.

Method #1:

1. Apply a Channel Mixer adjustment layer.

2. When the Channel Mixer dialog box opens, select the Monochrome option from the bottom of the dialog box.

3. Set the mixer values to 60G, 40R, 10B (other weights can be used, as long as they add up to 100%; if they do not add up to 100%, tonal values will shift).

Method #2:

1. Copy the image layer to a new layer: Ctrl+J (Windows), ⌘+J (Mac OS).

2. Press D to set the foreground and background colors to default.

3. Select the Brush tool and a suitable brush tip.

4. On the options bar, set the brush's blend mode to Color.

5. Paint on the duplicate layer.

Method #3:

1. Select the area you want to desaturate (feather the selection).

2. Apply a Hue/Saturation adjustment layer.

3. In the Hue/Saturation dialog box, decrease the Saturation slider.

Method #4:

1. Double-click an empty part of the image layer.

2. When the Layer Style dialog box opens, select Color Overlay.

3. Choose Color from the Blend Mode pop-up menu.

4. Click the color box and enter **50** in the B text field of the HSB section of the Color Picker.

5. Click the OK button to exit Color Picker and then the Layer Style dialog box.

Method #5:

1. Create a new layer above the layer you want to desaturate.

2. Fill it with 50% gray (Edit ➜ Fill and then choose 50% Gray from the Contents pop-up menu in the Fill dialog box).

3. Click the OK button to exit.

4. Set the layer's blend mode to Color.

Method #6:

1. Make the image layer active.

2. Choose Image ➜ Adjustments ➜ Desaturate, or Ctrl+Shift+U (Windows), ⌘+Shift+U (Mac OS).

3. Choose Edit ➜ Fade Desaturate, or Ctrl+Shift+F (Windows), ⌘+Shift+F (Mac OS).

4. Play with the settings in the Fade dialog box.

Method #7:

1. In the Channels palette, select a channel with good contrast (try Green as a contender).

2. Choose Select ➜ All and then copy the content onto the clipboard.

3. Select the composite channel.

4. In the Layers palette, paste the contents. At this point, Photoshop creates a new layer and puts the contents on it.

5. Play with the Opacity or the blend modes of the new layer.

Method #8:

1. Press D to set the foreground and background colors to default.

2. Create a Gradient adjustment layer above the image layer.

3. In the Gradient Fill dialog box, select the Foreground to Background gradient from the Gradient pop-up menu. Click the OK button.

4. Set the layer's blend mode to Hue, Saturation, or Color.

Method #9:

1. Set the foreground color to 50% gray.

2. Select the Paint Bucket tool.

3. On the options bar, set the tools blend mode to Color.

4. Click the color you want to desaturate.

Method #10:

1. Select the Sponge tool and set its mode to Desaturate.

2. Choose a suitable brush tip from the options bar.

3. Drag across the areas you want to desaturate.

Replacing and Matching Colors

Replacing and matching colors in photographs is very often required by clients, sometimes for effect and at other times because two or more items in different images must have a matching color. If you happen to work with clients involved in textile or furniture, you might get almost daily requests to match fabrics. To make the task as painless as possible, Photoshop lets you replace colors by using masks, commands that do not require masks, layers, or tools. The following hacks walk you through just a few of the many methods that you can employ to replace and match colors.

Replacing Selected Colors in an Image

If you are presented with the task of changing a specific color in an image, for example, an item photographed for a catalog that the client wants to see presented in several colors, you can employ at least three methods.

- You can create a new layer above the image layer, change its blend mode to Color, and paint with the new color; this works but requires a steady hand or the use of masks and selections to prevent the brush strokes straying into unwanted territory.

- You can use the Color Replacement tool (hidden under the Brush tool). It works very similarly to the Background Eraser tool except that it changes the color of the sampled pixels instead of erasing them to transparency (see Chapter 11 for more on the Background Eraser tool).

- You can use the Replace Color command. This method requires very limited masking, or none, depending on image content, and a steady hand is not a prerequisite for using it.

Faced with a choice, try Replace Color first or combine the three methods.

To use Replace Color, take the following steps:

1. Duplicate the image layer (always a good idea to work on a duplicate layer).

2. Select the Eyedropper tool; set its options to Sample Size 3 by 3 Average and then sample the color that you want to change (if you forget this step, you can make amends in the Replace Color dialog box, see step 5).

3. Select the Lasso tool and create a rough marquee around the area containing the color that you wish to change (this step isn't necessary or desirable but can help prevent color changes taking place in unwanted areas).

4. Choose Image ➜ Adjustments ➜ Replace Color (Figure 12-12).

FIGURE 12-12: **Replacing colors, sans complex selections, by using the Replace Color command. In this example, the color of the flowers has been changed without having affected the background.**

5. In the Replace Color dialog box, you will see three eyedropper tools; the first one should be selected for you. Move the pointer into the document window and sample a target color if you did not do so at step 2. If you selected the target color at step 2, select the Add to Sample eyedropper tool and drag over any additional target colors. Likewise, use the Subtract from Sample eyedropper tool to refine the sampled colors. If you prefer, you can temporarily modify the Eyedropper tool by using Shift (to Add) or Alt (Windows), Opt (Mac OS) to subtract. The cursor does not change but the sample is added to or subtracted from, respectively. If you make a mistake, you have one undo to fall back on: Ctrl+Z (Windows), ⌘+Z (Mac OS).

6. Move the Hue slider to replace the sampled colors and then the Saturation and Lightness sliders to modify it, or click the Result color box and then select a color from the Color Picker.

7. Decrease the Fuzziness and then increase it until you see a good balance between the colors you want to change and similar, unwanted colors being added. Stop at that point and use the Add to Sample tool to add if need be. Keeping an eye on the selection in the proxy window can help to make a judgment call.

Depending on the image content, you may not be able to isolate a color completely. If that happens, use a mask to hide the unwanted replacement. This is another good reason to work on a duplicate layer and not the original layer.

Selectively Turning Elements to Black and White

You might have seen images that keep some elements of an image in color and turn everything else to black and white (Figure 12-13). Applied sparingly, the technique can help to focus the viewer's attention or help to create unique, memorable images. Now that your curiosity has been piqued, you may be wondering how to create the effect in Photoshop. As always, there are many ways of doing any one thing in Photoshop. Here's just one easy way:

1. In the Layers palette, make sure that the layer containing the image content that you want to alter is selected and then click the Create New Adjustment Layer button and select Hue/Saturation.

2. In the Hue/Saturation dialog box, bring the Saturation slider all the way down to zero and click the OK button to exit.

3. Press X to switch the foreground and background color boxes so that black becomes the foreground color.

4. Select a brush and a suitable soft brush tip (you can change the tip size by riding the square bracket keys and soften them by holding down Shift while you ride the keys). Make sure that the brush's dynamics are turned off from the Brushes palette menu, and then paint on the elements that you want to appear in color.

FIGURE 12-13: A Hue/Saturation layer created above the image layer, saturation set to zero, and then the clock masked to allow it to revert back to color.

As you paint on the mask, the colors will reappear as if by magic. If you make a mistake, change the foreground color to white (press X again to switch between the foreground and background colors) and then paint it out. When you paint on the mask with white, you basically reapply the Adjustment layer mask.

Applying a Multitone Effect to an Image

Not to be confused with multitoning a grayscale image by applying a duotone, tritone, or quadtone, the following method simply takes an RGB image and then applies an effect to it that appears to mimic a multitone image (see Figure 12-14 for an example).

FIGURE 12-14: A multitone effect applied to an RGB image by using a combination of a Hue/Saturation and Color Balance adjustment layers.

1. Create a Hue/Saturation adjustment layer above your image layer.

2. Desaturate the image by moving the Saturation slider to zero.

3. Create a Color Balance adjustment layer above the Hue/Saturation adjustment layer. Hold down Alt (Windows), Opt (Mac OS) as you click the Create New Fill or Adjustment Layer icon and change the blend mode to Color in the New Layer dialog box.

4. Play with the sliders in the Color Balance dialog box. When you enter the Color Balance dialog box, the Midtone radio button is usually selected by default. Select the appropriate radio button to confine the changes to Shadows, Midtones, or Highlights.

5. When you're satisfied with a look (you might need to go back and forth several times between Shadows, Midtones, and Highlight modes), click the OK button.

Matching Color between Two Images

The Match Color feature is useful for matching photos that have been shot under varying lighting conditions, or for matching the foreground subject to the background when compositing images. It can also be used for some very creative color adjustments!

To color match two images, open the images and then choose Image ➜ Adjustments ➜ Match Color. In the Match Color dialog box, select the image to which you would like to match the current image from the Source pop-up menu. Make sure that the Preview option is selected and then, if need be, play with the Image Options controls.

If the variation between the two images being matched is too extreme, make a selection in either the source or the target document before using the command and then choose the appropriate option under Image Statistics in the Match Color dialog box.

Figure 12-15 shows an example.

FIGURE 12-15: **Left—The target image. Right—The source image. Below—The color-matched result.**

307

Color Adjusting Quick Hacks

Here are some quick hacks to help you with your quest for that perfectly color adjusted image.

- **Setting the Sample Average for Eyedropper Tools.** When you use the eyedropper tools in modal dialog boxes, such as Curves, Levels, Replace Color, and so forth, if you've forgotten or need to reset the sample average, there's no need to quit the dialog box; just right-click (Windows), Ctrl-click (Mac OS) in the document window and then choose from Point Sample, 3 by 3, or 5 by 5 Average.

- **Sampling Colors from Documents on the Desktop.** The Eyedropper tool can sample colors not only from within the active document but also from other opened documents and even from the desktop.

  To sample a color from another document or the desktop, select the Eyedropper tool and click within the current Photoshop document window, but do not release the mouse button; instead, *drag* to the target area outside of the current document and, when the Eyedropper is over the color you wish to sample, release the mouse button.

NOTE The Sample Size selected in the options bar has a direct bearing on the accuracy of the sampled color. You can sample the color from a single pixel or let Photoshop arrive at an average from a 3×3 or 5×5 pixel area.

- **Loading a Swatch as a Background Color.** In the Swatches palette, when you click a swatch, it always loads as the foreground color. If you would rather it loaded as the background color, hold down Ctrl (Windows), ⌘ (Mac OS) and then click the swatch.

- **Using the Eyedropper Tool to Load Background Color.** When you use the Eyedropper tool to sample a color, it usually sets it as the foreground color. However, you can easily load it as the background color by holding down Alt (Windows), Opt (Mac OS) and then sampling.

- **Duplicating a Color Sampler in a Second Document.** If you need to place a color sampler in the same spot in a second document, provided that the two documents have the same pixel dimensions, employ this little workaround:

  1. Begin recording a new action.

  2. Place the color sampler in the first document.

  3. Stop the action.

  4. Select the second document and play back the action.

  Photoshop will create a new color sampler at the same x, y coordinates as in the first document.

Summary

Adjusting and correcting colors in Photoshop is quite an art form. It relies as much on the proper use of color management, calibrated equipment, and a consistent viewing environment as it does on personal taste. It can be a pleasurable art form or a chore, depending on your mastery of the various tools, commands, and techniques at your disposal in Photoshop. The key to mastering any art form is practice, practice, and practice some more. To that end, this chapter contains significant insights into the various tools, commands, and techniques required to master this fine and honorable art form.

chapter **13**

Creating and Editing Type

T ype in Photoshop and ImageReady is composed of mathematically defined vector-based outlines that describe the letters, numbers, and symbols of a given typeface. It is, therefore, resolution independent and can be viewed at any magnification, without fear of pixelation.

Photoshop includes four tools for creating type: Horizontal Type tool, Vertical Type tool, Horizontal Type Mask tool, and Vertical Type Mask tool (ImageReady includes only the one type tool). Actually, it's hard to imagine a use for the type mask tools because the normal tools create a mask automatically when one is required—for example, when you're placing type in an alpha or spot channel, or in a document in Indexed Color or Bitmap mode.

Type remains editable if saved in a format that supports layers. Furthermore, if the document is saved in a file format that preserves vector-based outlines, such as PSD, TIFF, PDF, or EPS, the type can be output to a PostScript printer at the resolution of the output device. However, if a file format does not support layers, such as JPEG, Indexed Color mode, Bitmap, and Multichannel, the type loses its editability and is automatically saved as rasterized type.

Creating Type

You can create three forms of type in Photoshop: point type, character type, and type on a path.

- **Point type** is created at the point where you click in the image. It is useful for entering a few words of text and can be horizontal or vertical.

- **Paragraph type** is created by enclosing it in a bounding box. It supports line wraps, leading, justification, indentation, Roman hanging punctuation, and hyphenation.

- **Type on a path** flows along the edge of a path, which can be open or closed.

Type is always created on a new layer except when the Horizontal or Vertical Type Mask tools are used; these two tools create a selection that then has to be filled with a color.

On the whole, creating and editing type in Photoshop and ImageReady are reasonably intuitive. This chapter looks behind the scenes and shows you the not so obvious in an effort to increase your productivity and streamline your workflow when creating, editing, and modifying type.

Specifying Paragraph Type Bounding Box Size

As noted previously, paragraph type needs a bounding box in order to support the various attributes needed to make the text flow. It's very easy to create a bounding box. Simply click in the document window, drag to set its size, and then let go. That's all there is to it. After it's created, you can alter its size by dragging one of the eight bounding box handles outward or inward. You can also place the I-beam cursor just outside the horizontal lines and drag when the cursor turns to a double-headed arrow, which it does when you either place the baseline indicator inside one of the bounding box handles or just outside the dotted horizontal line (Figure 13-1).

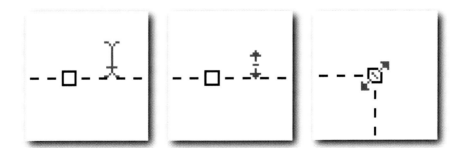

FIGURE 13-1: **A detailed view of the bounding box. The I-beam cursor, shown here in red for easier identification, changes shape to a double-headed arrow to indicate when the bounding box can be resized.**

You can specify the exact size of the bounding box either before you draw it or afterward. To specify the size before you draw it, hold down Alt (Windows), Opt (Mac OS) and click in the document window. This displays the Paragraph Text Size dialog box and anchors the top-left corner of the bounding box. Enter values for Width and Height and click the OK button. You can use all supported measurement units; for example, enter *px* for pixels or *cm* for centimeters and Photoshop will convert the values to the default units selected in Preferences ➜ Units & Rulers.

Alternatively, if you want to see the bounding box drawn before you define its width and height, hold down Alt (Windows), Opt (Mac OS) and then click and drag. The bounding box will be centered on the point where you clicked, and the Paragraph Text Size dialog box will appear after you release the mouse button. To constrain the bounding box to a square, add the Shift key to the keyboard shortcut.

While you're in type mode, text inside a bounding box can be transformed, scaled, rotated, skewed, warped, or flipped by transforming the bounding box (Figure 13-2).

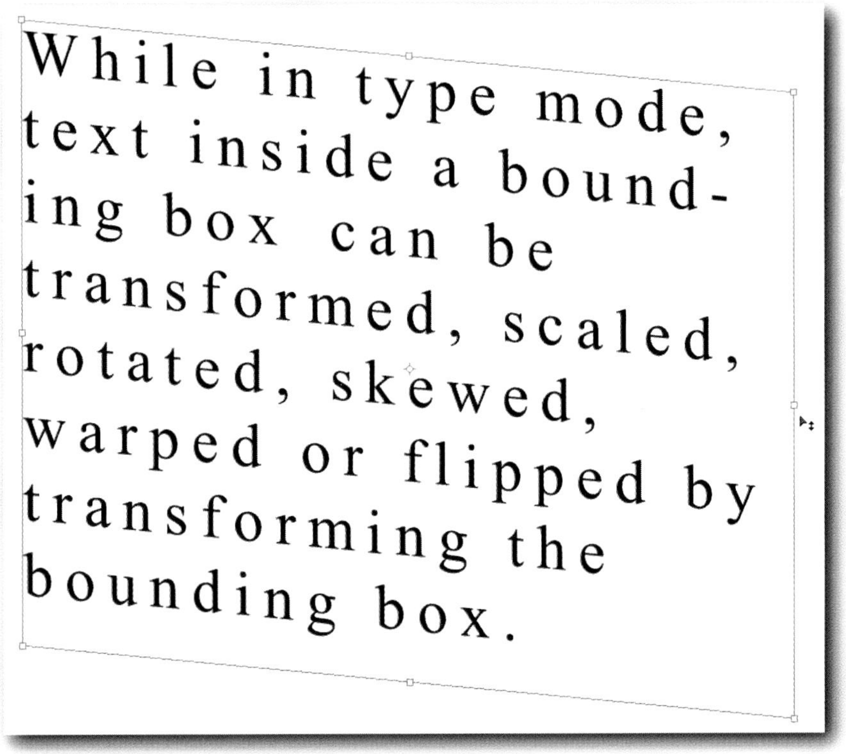

FIGURE 13-2: Transforming text by skewing the bounding box.

Exiting Type Mode Gracefully

There are just two ways to create type: click and type or click-drag and then type in the bounding box. However, after you have finished typing content, you can "commit" and exit type mode in one of several ways. Take your pick from the following:

- Press Ctrl+Enter (Windows), ⌘+Return (Mac OS) if you like to use a shortcut key to exit.

- Press the Enter key on the Numeric keyboard if you like a one-key solution.

- Click any layer tile or space in a palette.

- Choose another tool.

- Click the Commit Any Current Edits button that appears on the options bar whenever you enter type edit mode.

313

Typing on a Path

Actually, when it comes to typing on a path, Photoshop does not have a Type on a Path tool, as you might expect. Instead, it's assumed that you want to type on a path whenever you hover the Type tool over a path or inside a closed path, so the Type tool simply changes its behavior. To signify the change, the Type tool I-beam icon also changes its baseline indicator to a path or its boxed outline to an oval whenever it's in type-on-a-path mode, depending on whether it's over a path or inside a closed path. It's all very straightforward, after you know it (Figure 13-3). However, before you start tap-tapping, it may help to read the following pointers:

- Use simple, clean paths.

- If possible, don't use paths converted from a selection.

- Use Sharp anti-aliasing (the Smooth option will slow things down).

- Don't use the tool on a large file if you have limited resources. Instead, create the type in a smaller file, resample upward by using Image Size, and then drag the type layer into the larger file.

- Type flows in the direction that the path is created. This fact can be a great source of confusion. For example, if you draw an open-ended path from right to left and begin typing at the left end of the path, it will disappear!

- To create upside-down type, draw the path from right to left. If you create an open-ended path, start typing at the right end of the path. If you start typing at the left end of the path, the type will disappear into itself and you will have to move the start point to the right to see it.

The following pointers can also help when you modify type on a path:

- To reposition type after it has been committed, use the Direct Selection tool: Hover the pointer over the type until the icon changes to an I-beam plus an arrow and then simply drag in the direction in which you want to move the type (you can also click above the path to define a new start point).

- To reposition the type while you're in type mode, hold down the Ctrl (Windows), ⌘ (Mac OS) key and then drag the type to a new position (see preceding bullet point).

- To transform the path while in type mode, hold down Ctrl (Windows), ⌘ (Mac OS) and then modify the bounding box in the usual way: drag a bounding box handle or move outside and rotate the whole bounding box.

- To flip the type from above the path to below the path, drag downward with the Direct Selection tool; if the type is on a circle, you can flip it from outside the circle to inside, or vice versa.

As if that wasn't enough, you can modify the path using the path tools; the type will reflect the changes almost instantaneously. You can also apply layer effects to the type layer or the Warp Text command from the options bar (a Type tool must be selected, of course, before the Warp command can be accessed).

FIGURE 13-3: Type on a circular path.

Enclosing Type Inside a Custom Shape

One often overlooked attribute of the Type tool is its ability to type *inside* a path. For example, if you are drawing a comic strip, you can draw a speech balloon and then enter the text in the balloon and have the text automatically conform to the path boundary (Figure 13-4). The one proviso is the path must be a closed path. You can draw a closed path with the pen tools or use the Custom Shape tool. If you're using the latter, set its option on the options bar to Paths. That will enable you to draw paths and not filled shapes, though there is nothing to stop you from adding type inside a filled shape as long as the path is still active after you have drawn the shape.

NOTE You can activate a shape layer's path at any time by clicking its vector mask.

FIGURE 13-4: **Comic book speech balloons drawn with the Pen tool and then filled with type. (Script and art by Esther Jo Steiner.)**

Editing and Modifying Type

After type has been created, you can edit it or modify it *ad infinitum*. In fact, you have almost the same options in Photoshop that you have in a page layout program. You can kern and track, increase or decrease the leading, control justification and hyphenation, change font or color, and even check for spelling mistakes. Type can be converted to shapes or paths for editing. Point type can also be changed to paragraph type.

The following section explores in detail the options mentioned and also looks at how you can insert images into type, apply filters, and convert fonts to shapes, among other things.

Changing Type Attributes across Multiple Layers

If you have type on multiple layers and need to change its attributes across a number of layers, for example, to change the font type or transform all layers evenly, here's a quick and painless method:

1. Select the Type tool, but do not select any type in the document window.

2. Select all the type layers whose attributes you want to change.

3. From the options bar, change any of the following attributes: font, size, color, anti-aliasing, or text alignment.

Using the same method, you can even use the Warp Text command from the options bar, though not the Warp command that is available when you transform objects. Furthermore, you can change the options found in the Character and Paragraph palettes. For example, you can change the tracking of point type on several layers in one fell swoop.

Editing Type Using Keyboard Shortcuts

They say that nothing distinguishes a pro from an amateur as much as the use of shortcut keys. Although that kind of claim might serve only to make pros feel good about themselves and alienate the "recreational" users, keyboard shortcuts undoubtedly can save time and help increase productivity. If time is money for you and you do a fair amount of typing in Photoshop, the following keyboard shortcuts should help save a few pennies.

- **Selecting Type**
  - To select all the type in the bounding box, press Ctrl+A (Windows), ⌘+A (Mac OS).
  - To select all the type from the cursor *onward*, hold down Ctrl+Shift (Windows), ⌘+Shift (Mac OS) and press the Home End key.
  - To select all the type from the cursor *upward*, hold down Ctrl+Shift (Windows), ⌘+Shift (Mac OS) and press the Home Start key.
- **Filling Type**
  - To fill type with the *foreground* color, hold down Alt and press Backspace (Windows), Opt and press Del (Mac OS).
  - To fill type with the *background* color, hold down Ctrl and press Backspace (Windows), ⌘ and press Del (Mac OS).
- **Aligning Type**
  - To *left* align type, press Ctrl+Shift+L (Windows), ⌘+Shift+L (Mac OS).
  - To *center* align type, press Ctrl+Shift+C (Windows), ⌘+Shift+C (Mac OS).
  - To *right* align type, press Ctrl+Shift+R (Windows), ⌘+Shift+R (Mac OS).
- **Changing Font**
  - To *increase* the font size, highlight the text, hold down Ctrl+Shift (Windows), ⌘+Shift (Mac OS), and then press the *greater than* > arrow key.
  - To *decrease* the font size, highlight the text, hold down Ctrl+Shift (Windows), ⌘+Shift (Mac OS), and then press the *lesser than* < arrow key.

Kerning and Tracking Type

The terms *kerning* and *tracking* are often used in the wrong context. So, just to be absolutely clear: *kerning* adds or subtracts space between two characters, whereas *tracking* adds or subtracts an equal amount of space across a range of selected characters or words (Figure 13-5). If you need to kern or track, use the following routines:

To kern two letters:

1. Enter the cursor between the letters you wish to kern.

2. Hold down Ctrl+Alt (Windows), ⌘+Opt (Mac OS) and then:

  - To *decrease* the space between the letters, press the *Left* Arrow key, located by the numeric keyboard.
  - To *increase* the space between the letters, press the *Right* Arrow key.

To track a range of words:

1. Highlight the words you wish to track.

2. Press Ctrl+H (Windows), ⌘+H (Mac OS) to hide the highlight.

3. Hold down Ctrl+Alt (Windows), ⌘+Opt (Mac OS) and then:

   - To *decrease* the space between the highlighted words, press the *Left* Arrow key.

   - To *increase* the space, press the *Right* Arrow key.

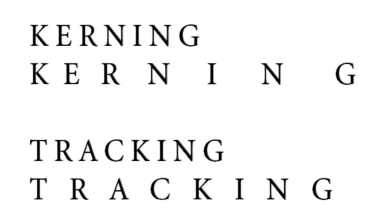

FIGURE 13-5: **Example of kerning and tracking.**

Increasing and Decreasing Leading

Leading is the space between two lines of type and measured from the baseline of one line to the baseline of the next line (Figure 13-6). It helps with readability and legibility of paragraph text.

The word *leading* comes from the time when compositors used strips of actual lead of varying thickness to set out the space between the lines of text. These days, the leading is much more precise and done automatically for you by word processors and page layout programs. In Photoshop, you can specify custom leading in units as small as pixels.

The amount of leading will depend on the font type, the size of the type, the column width, and whether the text is used in a heading or in a paragraph. Generally speaking, the rule of thumb is to set it to 120% of the point size (the default, or auto, setting). For example, if the font is set to 10 points, the leading should be set to 12 points.

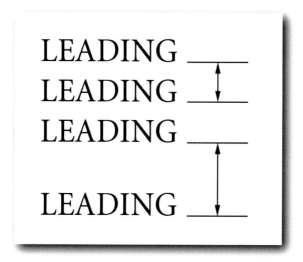

FIGURE 13-6: **Leading, measured from baseline to baseline.**

You can change the leading on a case-by-case basis. To do so, select the lines, or single line, that you want to affect and then choose a value from the Set the Leading pop-up menu in the Character palette. Next, enter a value in the text box or scrub by dragging the pointer left/right to the left of the text box. Alternatively, after selecting the lines, hold down Ctrl+Alt (Windows), ⌘+Opt (Mac OS) and then press the Up Arrow key to decrease the space or the Down Arrow key to increase the space.

Converting a Font to a Shape

Converting a font to a shape is one way of increasing your options for editing type. After a font has been converted, you can use the full force of the path editing tools to bend, warp, or distort individual letters in any which way you like. For example, you can use the Direct Selection tool to reposition anchor points and direction lines; you can use the Pen tool to add or subtract anchor points; and you can use the Convert Point tool to change smooth anchor points to corner anchor points.

319

You use not only the conventional fonts, such as Time New Roman or Geneva, but also Wingdings or symbols as the basis of a figure or shape, and then you can distort them to form something unique and original (Figure 13-7).

Furthermore, because the type is converted to a shape, if the layer has a style applied to it, the style will just follow the shape as you reposition/modify the anchor points or reshape the path. What's more, you can make changes to the style or apply a new style altogether.

How do you convert type to a shape? Create your type and choose Layer ➜ Type ➜ Convert to Shape.

FIGURE 13-7: **A wingding converted to a shape, modified with the Direct Selection tool and then a style added.**

Applying Filters to Vector Type

You may already know that it's not possible to apply a filter to type without first rasterizing it (see the section of quick hacks later in the chapter for information on how to rasterize type). You probably also know that the downside of rasterizing type is that you lose the ability to edit it and, consequently, any filter effect applied to the rasterized version. Well, here's one way to apply the filter straight to the vector type. Okay, you don't actually apply it to the type, but it will sure behave as if you have.

1. Create a new layer above the type layer.

2. Fill the new layer with the same color as the type (although some filters will work on a color fill layer, others might need the layer to be filled with 50% gray).

3. Alt-click (Windows), Opt-click (Mac OS) on the line that separates the two layers to create a clipping mask (Figure 13-8). Alternatively, press Ctrl+Alt+G (Windows), ⌘+Opt+G (Mac OS).

4. Apply a filter to the color or 50% gray filled layer.

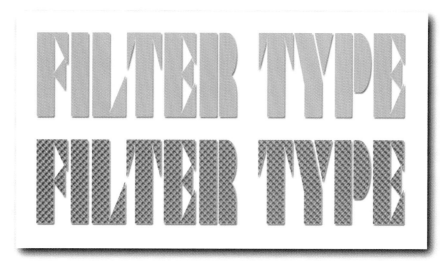

FIGURE 13-8: **The Halftone Pattern and Plastic Wrap filters applied to a type layer through a solid color, clipping layer filled with 50% gray.**

Now, when you change the text, font type, or size, the filter effect will not have to be reapplied—you can even warp the text or apply a Layer Style, or do both.

Restoring Rotated Type Back to Horizontal

There is no single button that you can press to restore manually rotated type back to horizontal. You could use the History palette to step back, but that's not always possible. The history may have dropped off the list, or going back to it might mean losing the steps that followed the transform. However, here's a little hack that will keep the last history and rotate the text back to the angle from which it was rotated:

1. Select the Measure tool and draw a vertical line from the base of the lowest part of the rotated type (Figure 13-9). Hold down the Shift key to constrain the line to a 90-degree angle.

2. Press Alt (Windows), Opt (Mac OS) and then drag the pointer from the base of the vertical line along the base line of the text. Holding down the modifier key puts the Measure tool into protractor mode.

3. Choose Edit ➜ Transform ➜ Rotate.

The text should rotate back to horizontal, provided that it was rotated clockwise. If it was rotated counterclockwise, a little modification is required. You need to draw the first measure line across the base of the type and then draw the 90-degree vertical line (Figure 13-9).

321

FIGURE 13-9: **Rotating type back to horizontal by using the Measure tool in protractor mode. Left—Protractor for type rotated clockwise. Right—Protractor for type rotated counterclockwise.**

The other good thing about rotating text this way is that any transforms or layer styles you applied to the type are preserved.

Inserting a Picture into Type

Do you need to insert an image into type, as they used to in the old greeting cards (Figure 13-10) and still do sometimes on some of the movie posters? The quickest way to do this in Photoshop, and the one with the least versatility, is to simply type over your image layer with the Type Mask tool and press Ctrl+J (Windows), ⌘+J (Mac OS), or choose Layer ➜ New ➜ Layer via Copy, and then turn the visibility off for the bottom layer by clicking the eye icon. This action clips the image to the type outlines and puts it onto its own layer.

The second way, close cousin to the previous method, is to type with the Type Mask tool but then click the icon Add Layer Mask at the bottom of the Layers palette. This creates a mask that you can manipulate and move. You also have the option of moving the picture; just remember to unlink the layer mask by clicking the link icon between the image and the mask thumbnails on the Layers palette. Note that you won't be able to add the mask if the image is on a Background layer. To promote a Background layer to a normal layer, double-click it to call the New Layer dialog box and then either rename it or accept the default and click the OK button.

The third way, and probably the most versatile, is to use a clipping mask as follows:

1. Make sure that your image is not on a Background layer.

2. Type your text with the normal Type tool.

3. Drag the type layer and place it below your image layer, or Ctrl+[(Windows), ⌘+[(Mac OS).

4. Create a clipping mask from the type layer by selecting the image layer and then choosing Layer ➜ Create Clipping Mask, or by pressing Ctrl+Alt+G (Windows), ⌘+Opt+G (Mac OS).

FIGURE 13-10: **An image seemingly inserted into type by positioning a type layer below an image layer and then using the layer's transparency to clip the image.**

Once again, you can manipulate either of the layers. For example, make adjustments to the image or apply a style to the type layer. If you use a style that includes an overlay, such as a color, gradient, or pattern, you will have to reduce the opacity of the effect; otherwise, it will mask the image. However, you can apply transforms and custom warps. Full warping can be applied only after the type has been rasterized (Layer ➔ Rasterize ➔ Type). Furthermore, you can convert the type to a shape and then manipulate it (see "Converting a Font to a Shape," earlier in the chapter).

Centering Type on a Layer

Should you need to center line type or paragraph type, take the following steps:

1. Select the Move tool.

2. Select the entire image (Select ➔ Select All), or Ctrl+A (Windows), ⌘+A (Mac OS). If you have a Background layer or a layer that fills the entire canvas, you don't need to do a Select All. Just select it along with the type layers and then execute the next step.

3. On the options bar, click the Align Vertical Centers button and then the Align Horizontal Centers button.

That should center the type nicely.

Applying Roman Hanging Punctuation

Ever wondered what the command Roman Hanging Punctuation in the Paragraph palette menu does? Wonder no more! The command determines whether punctuation marks fall inside or outside the margins for Roman Latin-based fonts. If the option is selected, single quotation marks, double quotation marks, periods, commas, apostrophes, hyphens, em dashes, en dashes, colons, and semicolons appear outside the margins (Figure 13-11).

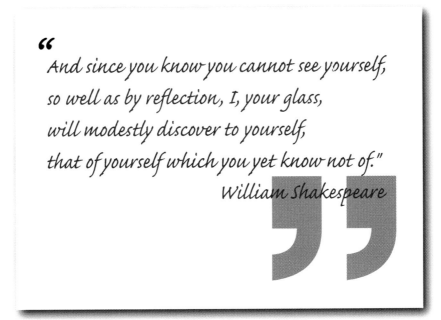

And since you know you cannot see yourself,
so well as by reflection, I, your glass,
will modestly discover to yourself,
that of yourself which you yet know not of."
William Shakespeare

FIGURE 13-11: **An example of Roman Hanging Punctuation.**

Creating Grungy Type

If you need to make grungy type and you're feeling artistic, you could rasterize the type layer, select a "grungy" brush from the preset folder, set its blend mode to Clear, and then paint on the rasterized type. If you're not feeling artistic or you're just not the artistic type, then the following method might just suit you.

1. Create a new document in grayscale mode.

2. Paint grungy lines, patterns, dots (whatever takes your fancy).

3. Save the file as a PSD to your hard disk.

4. Open the file containing the type you want to grunge, or create a new document and enter some type.

5. Duplicate the type layer (Layer ➜ Duplicate Layer) and turn off the original layer's visibility (the duping is only for backup purposes in case you need to go back to the original, editable type).

6. Rasterize the visible type layer (Layer ➜ Rasterize ➜ Type).

7. Select Filter ➜ Distort ➜ Displace (play with the settings later; just accept the default for now).

8. Click the OK button, at which point the Open dialog box should appear.

9. In the Open dialog box, select the grayscale PSD file you saved earlier.

10. Click the OK button, and your text is magically transformed (Figure 13-12).

FIGURE 13-12: Grungy type created by using a displacement map.

Those are the basic steps for creating grungy type. Try some variations by selecting different texture files from the ~\Adobe Photoshop CS2\Presets\Textures folder to displace the text. In addition, try the other distort filters and combine them with the text warp options.

Type-Related Quick Hacks

The following quick hacks are presented here to help you with your productivity and to forewarn you of pitfalls that you might encounter when creating, editing, or modifying type.

- **Type Behaving Badly.** If type is not behaving as expected, select it and then open the Character palette (Window ➜ Character). Next, choose Reset Character from the palette menu. The Type options should revert to default and all should return to normal. Paragraphs can be reset from the Paragraph palette menu.

- **Starting a New Line of Point Type.** If you want to create point type close to existing type, the Type tool assumes that you want to edit it and places the cursor in the existing type. To make sure that a new type layer is created, hold down Shift and then click; do likewise if the type hasn't been committed and you want to start a new line.

- **Viewing Selected Type Minus Highlight.** When you highlight text to change the font, the highlight makes it difficult to judge the suitability of the new font. Fear not! A little lateral thinking is what's required. You know how you can hide extras? Well, it turns out you can use the same keyboard shortcut of Ctrl+H (Windows), ⌘+H (Mac OS) to hide a highlight temporarily, which is ideal for seeing the new font more clearly.

- **Previewing Fonts.** In Photoshop, the font family and the font style menus on the options bar display a sneak preview of the available fonts. If the display size is too small for you, choose Preferences ➜ Type and then, from the Font Preview Size pop-up menu, select a preset size. If you want to see a full preview in the document window, make sure that the type layer is selected, Ctrl+H (Windows), ⌘+H (Mac OS) to hide a highlight temporarily, click in the font family text box on the options bar, and then use the Up and Down Arrow keys to scroll through the available fonts. To cycle through the styles, press Tab and after the style becomes highlighted, use the Up and Down Arrow keys. To jump to the end and beginning of the list, hold down Shift and then use the Up and Down Arrow keys.

- **Changing Type Orientation.** You can convert horizontal type to vertical type, and vice versa, by clicking the button Change the Text Orientation on the options bar. A type tool must be active for the button to appear on the options bar.

- **Copying and Pasting Text from a Word Processor.** Copying and pasting text from a word processor might seem straightforward but it confuses many people. Take the following steps if you want to join the know-it-all set! Select the text and copy it onto the clipboard. Before you do the pasting in Photoshop, select the Type tool and click in the image where you want the text to start flowing. Photoshop inserts the text at the point where the cursor is flashing.

- **Converting Point Type to Paragraph Type.** If you have created point type but then decide that you really should have created paragraph type—maybe because you need more justification options—rather than cut, create a new text layer, create a bounding box, and then paste, you can simply select the type layer and then choose Layer ➜ Type ➜ Convert to Paragraph Text.

NOTE You will need to manually remove the line returns created by point type before the text can wrap automatically in the text box.

- **Rasterizing Type Layers.** Some commands can be performed only on a type layer after it has been rasterized. More often than not, you will be told that the type needs to be rasterized and given the option to do so. However, for those rare occasions when you have to select the command, choose Layer ➔ Rasterize ➔ Type, or right-click (Windows), Ctrl-click (Mac OS) on the layer, not the thumbnail, and choose Rasterize.

- **Modifying and Editing Type.** You can access the commands for modifying and editing type at any time by right-clicking (Windows), Ctrl-clicking (Mac OS) on the type and then choosing from the contextual menu. The commands available in Photoshop and ImageReady differ greatly.

Summary

Type attributes can now be changed in Photoshop to such an extent that you very rarely have a need to use a page layout program for every job that requires superimposed type. You have precise control over kerning, tracking, leading, hyphenation, and justification. If you save the type as outline shapes, it can be output at high resolutions to a PostScript printer, thus ensuring crisp, jaggy free text. For an image-editing program, it has to be said, Photoshop does a pretty good job of creating and modifying type.

chapter 14

Hacking Camera Raw

amera Raw is a plug-in designed to process digital camera–originated raw files. It does this by using a combination of generic profiles, especially built for individual camera models and then hard wired into the plug-in, and tools and commands to modify the original camera settings, which it finds embedded in the raw file as EXIF data; these are settings such as exposure, white balance, saturation, sharpening, and contrast. Furthermore, it can correct for lens defects and reduce color noise, luminosity noise, lens vignetting, and color aberration. After the file has been processed, it can be opened in Photoshop if it requires further modification, or saved as a DNG (Digital Negative), TIFF, PSD, or JPEG, if it doesn't require any further modification.

So, what exactly is a *raw* file? As the name implies, it's made up of unprocessed raw data captured by a digital camera. When you take a photo with a digital camera, the light falling on each photosite on the sensor is recorded as a voltage level. This is true of cameras based on CCD (Charge-Coupled Device) and CMOS (Complementary Metal-Oxide Semiconductor). These voltages (analog) are then converted to ones and zeroes (digits) by the on-board analog-to-digital converter (ADC). Depending on the camera's output settings, the digitized information is processed by the camera and then saved either as a JPEG or a TIFF, or as raw censor data. When the information is saved as raw, the camera settings used at the time are also saved as EXIF data and can be used, or disregarded, when the file is processed on a computer using appropriate software, such as Camera Raw.

The advantage of saving the data in the JPEG file format is that the files can be compressed, and therefore, more images can be saved on the recording media and the data written more quickly. TIFF has no discernable advantage if the JPEG is saved as a full-quality image and minimum compression applied. It takes up more space on the recording media and takes longer to write.

The disadvantages of saving in the JPEG format are, one, that the settings applied to the raw data cannot be changed on a case-by-case basis and, two, that the compression applied can generate artifacts that cannot be eliminated. This compression can limit the use of the file severely, depending on the amount of compression applied. That said, the JPEG format is ideal for photographers who need to send their images by wireless technology and when time is of the essence, or if you are a consumer who is unlikely to want the very best quality or have no need to manipulate the photos in post.

In comparison to the JPEG format, the advantages of the raw format are almost limitless. Its only disadvantages are that it takes up more space on the recording media, takes longer to write, and has to be processed before it can be output (some cameras embed a JPEG that can be extracted, saving the processing step, but depending on the software, processing can be just, or almost, as fast). Its main advantage is that it can be processed to extract the maximum highlight and shadow detail recorded by the sensor, which may have been clipped when it was processed in camera. Furthermore, the color balance can be changed, chromatic aberration reduced or eliminated, and noise reduction algorithms applied manually. After being processed, the information can be output in 16-Bits/Channel mode and in a variety of color spaces, such as Adobe RGB (1998), sRGB, or ProPhoto RGB (some raw converters let you assign any color profile on your system, but Camera Raw is limited to just four color spaces, which is not as big a hindrance as first appears).

Why is there the need for processing a raw file if the information has already been digitized? The raw file doesn't contain any exposure or color information as such. It contains just the raw data, which has to be put through complex algorithms to construct an image that can faithfully represent the scene before the taking lens. Furthermore, digital cameras record data in linear increments, allotting more levels to the highlights than to the shadows. For example, if a camera uses 4,096 levels to record six stops of dynamic range, then the first stop, the darkest, is allotted 64 levels, the second 128, the third 256, the fourth 512, the fifth 1024 and the sixth, the lightest, the remaining 2,048 levels. By contrast, our eyes, and the devices we use to analyze incoming data, allot data in a nonlinear fashion. That's to say that the six stops are allotted the 4,096 levels equally so that the shadows, the midtones, and highlights all receive equal number of levels. Therefore, two things happen when you process a raw file. One, the raw data is demosaiced and an RGB color image constructed from the captured grayscale values (not applicable to raws from the Foveon X3 sensor, digital scanbacks, and multishot digital backs). Two, the data is converted into a nonlinear space and the image's brightness levels are replicated to represent the view as seen by the taking lens at the point of capture. That, in essence, is the *raison d'être* of Camera Raw.

Using the Camera Raw Dialog Box Effectively

For the sake of illustration, the Camera Raw dialog box can be divided into roughly two parts (Figure 14-1). Whereas the left side is given over to previewing and settings applied to the processed file, the right side contains the controls, settings, and readouts applied to the raw file. Additionally, if you open more than one file, their thumbnails appear as a Filmstrip on the left side.

FIGURE 14-1: The Camera Raw dialog box. A—The toolbar. B—Preview options: toggle preview, shadow clipping, and highlight clipping, respectively. C—RGB readouts under the pointer. D—Histogram. E—Settings menus, including Camera Raw menu. F—Tabs for all the adjustment panels. G—White balance controls. H—Tonal controls. I—Save, Open, Cancel/Reset, and Done buttons. J—Navigation buttons for Filmstrip mode. K—Workflow Options. L—Filmstrip. M—Toggle Filmstrip on/off. N—Synchronize button.

TIP You can widen the Filmstrip to increase the thumbnail size, close it by dragging on the dividing bar, or show/hide it by double-clicking it.

The Camera Raw dialog box offers easy access to all the controls and features. Although some are self-evident, others contain power that is not apparent at first sight. The following list looks behind the tools, controls, and menu items to give you the information you require to make the most of the Camera Raw dialog box.

- The **Toolbar** at the top of the dialog box contains the zoom and hand tools that you find in Photoshop for magnifying and scrolling the image preview (you can use the usual keyboard shortcuts if you don't like to use the tools).

■ The **White Balance tool** is used to set a custom white balance. To utilize it, drag it across a white element in your image (not a specular highlight, though) or gray element, such as an office chair that you know to be gray. If there was a colorcast present, it should disappear and the RGB readings become more equal (readings are displayed above the Histogram). Should the shadows retain a colorcast, the Shadow Tint control, located under the Calibrate tab, can be used. Moving the Shadow Tint slider to the left adds green; moving it to the right adds magenta.

One popular practice for white balancing an image involves shooting a color checker chart, such as the one sold by GretagMacbeth or the very popular Digital Gray Card and the Mini ColorChecker, under the same lighting conditions as the images you are trying to white balance and then using the White Balance tool on the gray patches. This technique is particularly effective when you are shooting in a studio under controlled lighting conditions.

■ The **Color Sampler tool** can be used to place nine color samplers on the image preview. This can help to make difficult color correction decisions. The readouts for the sample points appear above the image preview. You can clear all the samplers by clicking the Clear Samplers button or holding down Alt (Windows), Opt (Mac OS) and then clicking an individual sampler when the pointer icon turns to a scissors.

■ The **Crop tool** is used to crop the processed image before it's opened in Photoshop. This is extremely useful for cutting down the time it takes to export the file to Photoshop if your resources are limited. The crop is also remembered so that the next time you open the file in Camera Raw, it's applied automatically; Camera Raw adds a crop to the thumbnail in the Bridge window to indicate that a crop has been applied.

Furthermore, you can choose from predefined crop ratios from the Crop tool pop-up menu (to access the menu, click the Crop tool icon and hold down the mouse button) or define custom ratios by choosing Custom and then entering the values in the Custom Crop dialog box (Figure 14-2). As well as create custom ratios, you can also enter image dimensions in pixels, inches, or centimeters by choosing from the Crop pop-up menu. If you set custom to 600 × 600 pixels, don't expect the marquee to constrain to a fixed size of 600 × 600 pixels. In custom mode, the Crop tool works the same as the one in Photoshop when you enter values for width, height, and resolution, except that the resolution is set not in the Custom Crop dialog box but in the Workflow Options part of the Camera Raw dialog box. When you commit the crop, the marqueed preview is cropped (in this example, to 600 × 600 pixels), and the resolution set to the value defined in Workflow Options.

FIGURE 14-2: The Custom Crop dialog box, accessed from the Crop tool's pop-up menu, used to set custom crop ratios and image dimensions.

You can clear the crop by clicking the Crop tool icon, holding down the mouse button, and then selecting Clear Crop from the pop-up menu, or right-clicking (Windows), Ctrl-clicking (Mac OS) and then selecting Clear Crop from the contextual menu.

TIP If you want to resize an image larger than the preset sizes available in Workflow Options for your camera model, click the Crop tool icon, hold down the mouse button, and select Custom from the pop-up menu. Next, in the Custom Crop dialog box, choose a unit of measure from the Crop pop-up menu and enter the preferred image dimension in the text fields. You can enter a maximum of 10,000 pixels in each field, or 999.999 inches, or 999.999 centimeters. If you use inches or centimeters, the maximum size depends on the resolution set in Workflow Options. However, though it can vary, the maximum value that you can enter for width and height remains at 999.999. For example, if the resolution is set to 240 ppi and you enter 999.999 inches for width and height, the image will be upsized to 41.667 by 41.667 inches and 10,000 pixels by 10,000 pixels, and not 999.999 inches!

- The **Straighten tool** works very similarly to the Crop tool in as much as it defines a setting and applies the values when the file is opened in Photoshop. To utilize the Straighten tool, select it and then simply draw a line on the image preview. To clear the setting, either choose Clear Crop from the Crop tool pop-up menu or right-click (Windows), Ctrl-click (Mac OS) the image preview and then choose Clear Crop from the contextual menu. Camera Raw adds a crop icon to the image thumbnail in Bridge to indicate that the Straighten tool has been applied.

NOTE The settings applied by the Crop and Straighten tool do not affect the original raw file. They are kept separate from the original file, either in the central database or in the sidecar ".xmp" file, or in the DNG file if the processed file is saved in that format. Furthermore, in Filmstrip mode, the settings are applied to all the selected files when you commit the crop.

- The **Preview, Shadow, Highlight** checkboxes can be used to toggle the preview, and the warnings for shadow and highlight clipping. The keyboard shortcuts for toggling the options are P, U, and O, respectively. The shadow clipping warning, displayed in blue, is shown when all three channels lack detail. The highlight clipping warning, displayed in red, is shown when any one of the three channels lacks detail.

- The **Show Workflow Options** checkbox hides and shows options that apply not to the raw file but to the file output to Photoshop. Here you can assign a working space, bit depth, size, and resolution.

NOTE The way Camera Raw is designed does not allow you to choose from custom profiles; only one of the four built-in profiles can be assigned. If you have a reason to use another profile, choose ProPhoto RGB and then, in Photoshop, "assign" your profile. Alternatively, if you are unhappy with the generic profile for your camera, use the controls in the Calibrate tab to tweak it and then choose Save New Camera Defaults from the Camera Raw pop-up menu (click the black triangle button by the Settings pop-up menu to access the command).

- The **Histogram in Camera Raw** displays all three channels in color and shows overlapping values in white. The histogram is always based on the working space profile chosen in the Workflow Options of the dialog box and not a representation of the raw file. If you notice clipping caused by oversaturation, try selecting another working space (Figure 14-3). The ProPhoto RGB space has the widest gamut and should not show any clipping. However, if you expect to make further tonal adjustments, you should also select 16-Bits/Channel from the Depth pop-up menu.

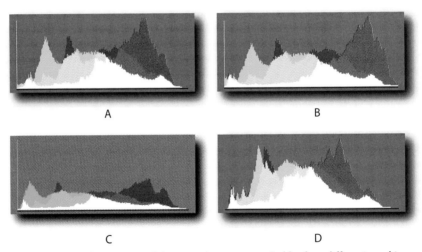

FIGURE 14-3: Four histograms of the same image generated by four different working spaces selected in the Workflow Options of the Camera Raw dialog box. A—Adobe RGB (1998). B—sRGB. C—ColorMatch RGB. D—ProPhoto RGB. Three of the working spaces show clipping of the green channel, but ProPhoto RGB shows no clipping.

- The **Adjust panel** contains a pop-up menu of presets for setting the white balance. These include As Shot, Auto, Daylight, Cloudy, Shade, Tungsten, Fluorescent, Flash, and Custom. More often than not, the As Shot or Auto setting does a very good job of setting the white balance. If the image looks too warm or too cold (Figure 14-4), too green or too magenta, you can use the Temperature and Tint controls to define a custom white balance.

- Moving the Temperature slider to the left counteracts a yellow/orange color-cast, induced by shooting under a low ambient color temperature, such as a household tungsten bulb or a candle flame.

- Conversely, moving the Temperature slider to the right counteracts a cold/blue colorcast, induced by shooting under a high ambient color temperature, such as a cloudy, overcast sky. Seen another way, moving the slider to the left adds blue and removes yellow/orange; moving it to the right adds red and removes blue.

- Moving the Tint slider to the left adds more green (removing a magenta tint); whereas moving it to the right adds more magenta (removing a green tint).

When you are happy with a custom white balance, you can save the settings from the Camera Raw menu and apply them to similar images from the Settings pop-up menu, or from the Edit → Apply Camera Raw Settings in Bridge (see the discussion of Settings later in the chapter).

FIGURE 14-4: **The Temperature and Tint sliders used to modify the White Balance.**

■ The **Exposure, Shadows, Brightness, Contrast, Saturation** sliders control the properties implied by their names. The Exposure slider reads in incremental values equivalent to f-stops. That's to say that a value of -1.0 is the equivalent of underexposing by one f-stop, whereas a value of +1.0 is the equivalent of overexposing by one f-stop. The Exposure and Shadow sliders should be used with care because they can easily clip data (move pixel values to 0, totally black, or 255, totally white). When you use them to make any adjustments, keep a watchful eye on the Histogram for spikes at either end. The Brightness slider differs in as much as it does not clip shadow or highlight detail but compresses it. The Contrast slider works very similarly to applying an S-shaped curve with the Curve command. It compresses the midtones more severely than the quarter and three-quarter tones and hardly affects the shadows and highlights.

The Exposure and Shadow sliders hide a little secret that, when known, can be very useful for adjusting these two properties. If you hold down Alt (Windows), Opt (Mac OS) while moving the slider, you can invoke threshold mode temporarily. This lets you see at what point on the scale the data begins to clip (Figure 14-5). When you know the point, you can accept it, back off a little, or clip it if the information isn't important. For example, it might just be noise in the shadows, in which case clipping it is safe. The clipped data is color coded so that you can see at a glance in which channel the data is being clipped. For the Exposure slider, the coding is as follows:

- White indicates clipping in all channels.
- Black indicates no clipping.
- Red, Green, Blue indicates clipping in the respective channels.
- Cyan indicates clipping in the Green and Blue channels.
- Magenta indicates clipping in the Red and Blue channels.
- Yellow indicates clipping in the Red and Green channels.

The threshold overlay coding for the Shadow slider is somewhat different:

- Black indicates clipping in all three channels.
- White indicates no clipping.
- Red indicates clipping in the Green and Blue channels.
- Green indicates clipping in the Blue and Red channels.
- Blue indicates clipping in the Red and Green channels.
- Cyan indicates clipping in the Red channel.
- Magenta indicates clipping in the Green channel.
- Yellow indicates clipping in the Blue channel.

FIGURE 14-5: Holding down Alt (Windows), Opt (Mac OS) while moving the Exposure slider in Camera Raw invokes Threshold mode to help you set the exposure. In this example, the green overlay indicates that the green channel is being clipped; the yellow overlay indicates that the green and red channels are both being clipped; and the white overlay indicates clipping in all three channels. The histogram (not shown here) also echoes the clipping.

- The **Detail panel** contains controls for applying sharpness and reducing luminance and color noise (sharpness can be limited to image preview from the Camera Raw preferences). The aforementioned noise can be produced by a number of factors but notably when high ISO settings are used or the image is underexposed and then shadow detail enhanced. Before applying either reduction control, zoom into the image preview in order to see the adjustments more clearly.

- The **Lens panel** is divided into two sections: Chromatic Aberration and Vignetting. The Chromatic Aberration sliders help to reduce complementary color fringing within the image; if it exists, fringing is usually noticeable at the detail edges (see Chapter 10 for more information).

  - To reduce red/cyan fringing, move the Fix Red/Cyan Fringe slider left or right, respectively. This adjusts the size of the *red* channel relative to the *green* channel, reducing the fringing in the process.

  - To reduce blue/yellow fringing, move the Fix Blue/Yellow Fringe slider left or right, respectively. This adjusts the size of the *blue* channel relative to the *green* channel, reducing the fringing in the process.

The Vignetting controls allow you to brighten any falloff around the perimeter of your image. The falloff can be attributed to the lens design, wide aperture setting, a lens hood, or a matte box wrongly adjusted. You can move the Amount slider to the right to lighten the dark areas or to the left to darken. The Midpoint slider lets you increase and decrease the area affected by the adjustment. Move it to the right to restrict the area of influence or to the left to broaden the area of influence.

- The **Curve panel** contains the means to apply a custom tone mapping. This is in addition to the tone mapping performed with the exposure, shadows, brightness, and contrast controls in the Adjust panel. On the surface, it works the way the familiar Curve command in Photoshop does. However, the operations are actually performed on the linear data in the background while the curve is plotted in a 2.2 gamma working space to make it easier to use. Furthermore, when the linear curve is modified, the input and output settings are concatenated with the settings applied by the brightness and contrast controls in the Adjust panel and then processed in a single step.

Camera Raw ships with a Linear, Medium Contrast (the default), Strong Contrast, and Custom curves. You can modify the default curve or select Custom from the Tone Curve pop-up menu and then modify it. Just as you can with the Curve in Photoshop, so you can add and delete anchor points by clicking the curve or Ctrl-clicking (Windows), ⌘-clicking (Mac OS) in the preview to add a corresponding anchor point. To delete anchor points, drag them out of the curve window, Ctrl-click (Windows), ⌘-click (Mac OS) the anchor point, or select Linear from the Tone Curve pop-up menu.

- The **Calibrate panel** contains further controls for improving the image. For example, if you find that the generic profile for your camera is not providing expected results, the skin tones may be too saturated or the shadows contain a tint, you can use the hue, saturation, and tint controls to modify the generic, built-in profile of your camera. When modified, the generic profile can then be saved as a new Camera Raw default from the Camera Raw menu and applied automatically each time you open a raw file.

  However, modifying the generic profile by eye can lead to errors (the viewing conditions, the state of your monitor, and the monitor profile can all confound any errors). Tom Fors has written a script that can automate the process and does away with the need to make decisions based on visual feedback. It requires you to capture a 24-patch GretagMacbeth color checker in raw mode with your digital camera and then use the script to automatically arrive at settings that can be plugged into the Camera Raw dialog box and then saved as a new Camera Raw default. You can find the script and instructions on how to use it, including a QuickTime movie, here: `http://fors.net/chromoholics/`

  Although the controls in the Calibrate panel are designed to modify the generic, built-in profile of your camera, there is nothing to stop you from using them in conjunction with the controls in the Adjust panel to modify the current image and then fine-tune by applying a custom tone curve. When you are happy with a look, you can save the current settings from the Camera Raw menu and then apply them to other images from the Settings menu or the Edit ➜ Apply Camera Raw Settings submenu in Bridge.

- The **Open, Save, Done, Cancel/Reset** buttons allow you to open the processed raw data in Photoshop for further editing and saving. The raw file is not modified; instead, the applied settings are saved either in the central database or in a sidecar file, depending on the options specified in the Camera Raw Preferences. Clicking the Save button takes you to the Save Options dialog box (Figure 14-6), where you can save the file as a Digital Negative (DNG), TIFF, JPEG, or Photoshop (PSD) file. Holding down Alt (Windows), Opt (Mac OS) suppresses the Save Options dialog box and saves the file in whatever settings were used last. When Photoshop hosts Camera Raw and the Alt/Opt key is held down, the Open button changes to Open Copy. This can be very useful when you need to open a modified copy but do not want to overwrite the old settings with the current settings. The Done button closes Camera Raw and either saves the current settings or overwrites old settings previously applied to the raw file. The Cancel button, as in many other dialog boxes, changes to the Reset button when you hold down Alt/Opt. Clicking it resets all the settings in the dialog box.

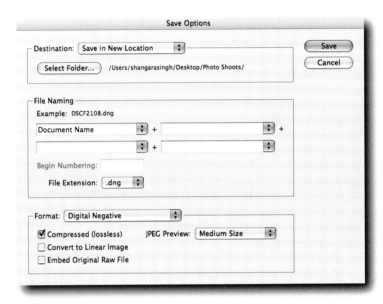

FIGURE 14-6: The Save Options dialog box, accessed from Camera Raw.

■ The **Filmstrip mode** is invoked automatically when you open a group of raw files simultaneously. When the selected files are read, their thumbnails are displayed in a filmstrip-like fashion down the left side of the dialog box and the preview for the currently selected thumbnail to their right. You can scroll the thumbnails using the scroll bar or use the arrow buttons below the preview to navigate to the next/previous file (Figure 14-1).

You can apply settings to each file on a case-by-case basis or en masse. To apply settings to a single file, select a thumbnail and then use the sliders in the panels or choose settings from the Settings menu. To apply settings en masse, select the thumbnails by using the usual file selection methods, or click the Select All button above the thumbnails or Ctrl+A (Windows), ⌘+A (Mac OS). Next, choose the settings as mentioned previously or click the Synchronize button to invoke the Synchronize dialog box; then, either pick and choose the settings you want to apply by selecting the checkboxes or choose an item from the pop-up menu. For subsequent invocations of the Synchronize dialog box, if you want to apply the same settings, you can suppress the dialog box by holding down Alt (Windows), Opt (Mac OS) while you click the Synchronize button.

TIP To synchronize the preview magnification for a number of files, select the thumbnails and then double-click the Zoom tool icon (sets magnification to 100% for selected files), or double-click the Hand tool (sets magnification to Fit in View). Alternatively, after selecting the thumbnails, use the Set Zoom Levels controls at the bottom left of the preview. Likewise, to scroll all the images simultaneously and in synch, select the thumbnails and then use the Hand tool.

- The **Settings** pop-up menu and the Camera Raw menu next to it tend to confuse many people. This may be because both menus feed off each other. For example, you can save the current settings from the Camera Raw menu but then must access it from the Settings menu. Likewise, to delete a setting from the Settings menu, you must do it from the Camera Raw menu, even though it's not a global Camera Raw setting. To dispel some of the confusion, the next part of the chapter takes a look at the Camera Raw menu first (accessed by clicking the black triangle button) and then at the Settings menu so that you can see how the items relate to each menu.

At the top of the Camera Raw menu are the commands to load, save, and delete settings. These commands are self-explanatory apart from the fact that the settings you load, save, or wish to delete all appear in the Settings menu. However, the Export Settings command does need a little elucidation. If you elected to save the settings in a central database, as opposed to sidecar files, the Export Settings command provides the opportunity to generate sidecar files from the central database. You may wish to do that if, for example, you are moving your raw files to another computer or archiving onto a CD or DVD. You are not limited to exporting the settings for a single file; you can export the settings for any number of files selected in Filmstrip mode.

The Save New Camera Raw Default command replaces the built-in Camera Raw Default generic profile for your camera. When you select the command, current settings in all the panels are included in the new default profile. This can be useful, for example, if you do not want Camera Raw to apply auto adjustments, which it does by default to create a cache and to preview any opened file. After turning off the auto adjustments, either from the Camera Raw menu or by pressing Ctrl+U (Windows), ⌘+U (Mac OS), select the Save New Camera Raw Default command. The default profile is not overwritten; you can return to it at any time by selecting Reset Camera Raw Default from the same menu.

NOTE You can use multiple undos in Camera Raw by using the keyboard shortcuts Ctrl+Alt+Z (Windows), ⌘+Opt+Z (Mac OS). If the shortcut doesn't work, check the keys assigned in the Keyboard Shortcuts dialog box.

Camera Raw Preferences and Settings

There are two ways to access Camera Raw Preferences. In Bridge, Windows users can choose Edit→Camera Raw Preferences, and Mac OS users can choose Bridge→Camera Raw Preferences. Alternatively, open a raw file in Camera Raw, click the black triangle button (located by the Settings pop-up menu) to access the Camera Raw menu, choose Preferences, and then set your preferred options. The following list examines each preference in more detail (Figure 14-7).

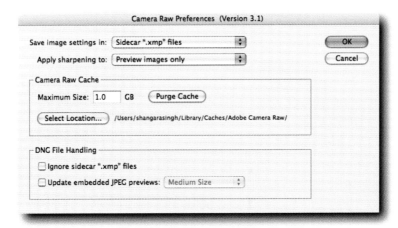

Camera Raw Preferences (Version 3.1)

Save image settings in: [Sidecar ".xmp" files ▼]   (OK)

Apply sharpening to: [Preview images only ▼]   (Cancel)

Camera Raw Cache

Maximum Size: [1.0] GB   (Purge Cache)

(Select Location...) /Users/shangarasingh/Library/Caches/Adobe Camera Raw/

DNG File Handling

☐ Ignore sidecar ".xmp" files

☐ Update embedded JPEG previews: [Medium Size ▼]

FIGURE 14-7: **The Camera Raw Preferences dialog box.**

- From the Save Settings In pop-up menu, you can tell Camera Raw where to save the custom setting applied to a raw file. The default location is Camera Raw database. This ensures that the settings are saved in one central file on your hard drive. When this option is selected, Camera Raw can always find the settings applied to the raw files, even if a file is renamed or moved. The other choice is Sidecar ".xmp" Files. This setting ensures that the sidecar files move automatically with the raw file, provided that you use Bridge to move the raw files (see "Managing Caches and Sidecar Files," later in the chapter).

- From the Apply Sharpening To pop-up menu, you can tell Camera Raw to apply sharpening to the preview only or to all processed images opened or saved from Camera Raw.

- In the Camera Raw Cache section, you can set the maximum size of the cache (the default is 1GB), purge the current cached data, and set the location of the cache, which should be a local hard drive.

- The DNG File Handling section (available only if you have updated Camera Raw 3.0 to 3.1) has two checkboxes. When you select Ignore sidecar ".xmp" Files, doing so tells Camera Raw to ignore the settings in sidecar files that have the same name as the proprietary raw but have the DNG extension appended; Photoshop CS and Photoshop Elements 3 both write sidecar files for raws and DNGs, whereas Photoshop CS2 writes sidecar files for raws only. The option stops Camera Raw from updating the sidecar files for the DNGs in the unlikely event of a folder's containing sidecar files for both formats.

The Update Embedded JPEG Previews option tells Camera Raw 3.1 to update the embedded JPEG preview in the DNG file. Selecting it can be helpful in making judgments about the content of the DNG file, but the downside to it is a speed hit when you save the file. You can leave the option unchecked and update the previews at a later date by invoking the Export Settings command from the Camera Raw menu. You will be presented with the Export Settings dialog box, which gives you the option of updating and specifying the size of the preview (Figure 14-8). To skip the dialog box, hold down Alt (Windows), Opt (Mac OS) before you select Export Settings, and Camera Raw will defer to the settings in the dialog box that were present the last time you saved a DNG file or exported the settings.

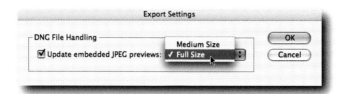

FIGURE 14-8: **The Export Settings dialog box lets you decide whether you want to update embedded previews in DNGs and makes it possible to choose between Medium and Full Size. Whereas the Medium Size option embeds only a medium-sized JPEG, the Full Size option actually embeds both sizes so that applications can pick and choose.**

Managing Caches and Sidecar Files

Cache files are used by both Bridge and Camera Raw to speed the process of viewing and of loading files into memory.

Bridge uses two files to store information, one to store previews and thumbnails and the other to store information about rotations, labels, and ratings. It can store these files in a central database or distribute them to the viewed folders (including the desktop).

Camera Raw uses cache files to store pre-parsed raw data of the most recently processed raw file so that it can load it faster the next time you open it in Camera Raw. It also uses them to help rebuild previews in Bridge when you make changes to the settings in Camera raw. Furthermore, when Camera Raw is used in filmstrip mode, the cached files are used to help speed the process of switching between the opened raw files.

Camera Raw keeps track of any settings applied to a raw file and can store the information either in a central database (distinct from the cache), or as sidecar ".xmp" files alongside the raw files. When you want to export the applied settings and the information cannot be embedded into the file, you can generate sidecar ".xmp" files from the central database (however, the Camera Raw settings can be embedded in the DNG format, doing away with the need for sidecar files).

The cache files that Bridge creates are negligible in size, but the cache files that Camera Raw creates are approximately 4.2MB each. These can soon add up, and the default ceiling of the cache size can soon be reached if you view enough raw files. This default size of 1GB holds the preparsed raw data for approximately 200 raw files. If you regularly edit more than 200 raw files, you might want to increase the size limit from Camera Raw preferences (see the previous section, "Camera Raw Preferences and Settings").

TIP You can safely delete the Camera Raw cache without fear of losing any valuable information. However, the uncached raw files will take longer to load into memory next time you open them.

Opening and Saving Raw Files

Opening raw files from Bridge or Photoshop is straightforward: You can use the commands on the File menu or the contextual menu. However, you do have a choice of whether you want Bridge or Photoshop to host Camera Raw. This can make a lot of difference to your workflow. To give some examples, if you open a raw via Photoshop first, you can then open another raw via Bridge. While you edit a raw via Photoshop, Bridge can be busy creating a cache for files that you have just downloaded from your digital camera. Conversely, while Photoshop is busy creating a Web Photo Gallery, you can process raws via Bridge at the same time.

- To open a raw and have Bridge host Camera Raw, select a thumbnail and then choose Open in Camera Raw from the Bridge File menu, or Ctrl+R (Windows), ⌘+R (Mac OS). If you have the option Double-Click Edits Camera Raw Setting in Bridge set in Preferences, you can, of course, double-click a thumbnail or a preview to open the file.

- To open a raw and have Photoshop host Camera Raw, select a thumbnail and then choose Open from the Photoshop File menu, or select a thumbnail in Bridge and then Ctrl+O (Windows), ⌘+O (Mac OS). Alternatively, in Bridge, select the file's thumbnail and then from the contextual menu choose Photoshop CS from the Open With submenu (this method also works with the preview). You can also drag a thumbnail to a Photoshop shortcut (Windows) or alias (Mac OS). If the focus is on a thumbnail, you can also press Enter (Windows), Return (Mac OS).

- To open a raw from Bridge, have Photoshop host Camera Raw, and minimize Bridge at the same time, select a thumbnail and then press Alt+Enter (Windows), Opt+Return (Mac OS).

Saving raw files from Camera Raw can be done in one of two ways: You can either open the processed file into Photoshop, apply adjustments to it, and then save it in any of the supported formats, or you can save it straight out of Camera Raw by clicking the Save button. If you choose the latter route, you can save in one of the four supported file formats: Digital Negative (DNG), JPEG, TIFF, or Photoshop (PSD). The Save Options dialog box also lets you rename the file, using batch renaming options and options for each file format (Figure 14-6).

The following list contains some of the advantages of converting raw files to DNG from the outset and including such a step in your workflow:

- Depending on the choices you make in the DNG converter dialog box, you can decrease the file size by as much as half without any data loss. For example, 12MB raw files from a Fuji FinePix S2 Pro are reduced to just 5.8MB. This can help to conserve space on CDs and DVDs when you create archives.

- If you do not wish to delete the original raw file because it contains proprietary information that you think you might need in the future, you can include it in the DNG and extract the raw at a later date. This will add approximately 3MB to the file size.

- When you process a DNG in Camera Raw, it saves the settings in the file, eliminating the need to store them in a sidecar file or a central database and thus making it easier to manage your archives.

- If you work with multiple digital cameras, you can consolidate all the formats into one manageable format.

- Should your camera manufacturer cease to support its proprietary raw format, you will still be able to process the DNG in one of the third-party converters, such as Camera Raw, Capture One, or Rawshooter Essentials.

Using Image Processor to Batch Process Raw Files

If you have a folder full of raw files that you wish to save as JPEGs, PSDs, or TIFFs, you can use the Image Processor to help speed the work. To do so, select the files in Bridge and then choose Tools ➜ Photoshop ➜ Image Processor. Before you make the selection, either apply Camera Raw settings to all the files you want to process or have the Image Processor show the Camera Raw dialog box for the first file, define the settings, and have them applied to all the subsequent files. If you elect to open Camera Raw, press the Open button to proceed.

NOTE If no settings have been applied to the raw files, the default Camera Raw settings are applied to all selected files.

If you wish to apply sharpening, or any other effects, such as frames or embossing a copyright notice, you can choose an action set and an action from the pop-up menus at the base of the dialog box. The action must reside, of course, in your Actions palette before it will register in the pop-up menus. You can also assign a copyright notice by filling in the Copyright Info text box. If you do, the notice will be recorded as metadata and not visibly stamped on the image.

Use the Save button to save the current settings if you are likely to make use of them in future batches.

Camera Raw Quick Hacks

The following quick hacks are presented here to help you work more efficiently in Camera Raw.

- **Turning Off Auto Adjustments.** If you like to see your images in their As Shot state, the auto adjustments for Exposure, Shadows, Brightness, and Contrast, located under the Adjust tab, can be turned off either by choosing Use Auto Adjustments from the Camera Raw menu or by pressing Ctrl+U (Windows), ⌘+U (Mac OS) while in the dialog box. To turn the auto adjustments off permanently, create a new default by selecting the Save New Camera Raw Default command. You can return to the auto default by selecting Reset Camera Raw Default from the same menu.

- **Bypassing the Camera Raw Dialog Box.** The Camera Raw dialog box is automatically suppressed when you create a Web Photoshop Gallery or Contact Sheet directly from raw files. However, there are occasions when you want to open a raw in Photoshop but do not want to see the Camera Raw dialog box. To suppress the dialog box, in Bridge, select the raw file(s) and then press Shift+Enter (Windows), Shift+Return (Mac OS).

- **Applying Existing Camera Raw Settings.** If you like the settings applied to a raw file and you want to apply them to other raw files, you have two choices. One, save the settings when the file is open in Camera Raw and then apply them from the Edit ➜ Apply Camera Raw Settings submenu in Bridge; two, copy the settings by selecting Copy Camera Raw Settings from the same submenu and then choose Paste Camera Raw Settings, again from the same submenu.

  The commands are also available from the contextual menu and as keyboard shortcuts: Ctrl+Alt+C (Windows), ⌘+Opt+C (Mac OS) to copy and Control+Alt+V (Windows), ⌘+Opt+V (Mac OS) to paste.

- **Applying Custom ICC Profiles.** Custom ICC profiles cannot be chosen directly in Camera Raw. If you want to apply a custom profile, assign ProPhoto RGB in Camera Raw and then, in Photoshop, assign your custom profile from the Edit menu.

TIP Should you decide to apply sharpening through an action, remember to check the Camera Raw Preferences. If you have elected to apply sharpening to all files, you may end up applying sharpening twice. Furthermore, if you elect to resize downward and Bicubic Sharper is the default Image Interpolation algorithm chosen in Photoshop Preferences, it, too, will apply some sharpening.

- **Rotating Images in Camera Raw.** You can use the rotate icons in the toolbar in the Camera Raw dialog box to rotate the preview or use the keyboard shortcuts Ctrl+[(Windows), ⌘+[(Mac OS) to rotate counterclockwise; substitute the [bracket key for the] bracket key to rotate clockwise. When you open the processed raw or click Done, the rotation is saved in the Bridge cache for future reference.

- **Generating Sidecar ".xmp" Files from Camera Raw Database.** If you have been using a central database to store the Camera Raw settings and want to extract them and distribute them to their respective folders, open the files and then choose Export Settings from the Camera Raw menu. This copies the settings from the database and creates sidecar ".xmp" files.

- **Removing Applied Camera Raw Settings.** Applied Camera Raw settings travel with the raw files when saved as sidecar ".xmp" files and moved in Bridge. If the settings are stored in the central database, they stick to the files even if the file is renamed. However, suppose that you want to start fresh? In that case, choose Clear Camera Raw Settings from the Edit ➜ Apply Camera Raw Settings submenu or from the contextual menu.

- **Speeding up Preview Redraw in Camera Raw.** The rate at which Camera Raw redraws previews can be influenced by the magnification factor. Below 50% magnification, Camera Raw does not include some of the algorithms and, therefore, can redraw faster. If you are experiencing slow redraws while using a very large monitor set to a high resolution, or using a high magnification factor, or using the Fit in View magnification level, the remedy is to reduce the size of the Camera Raw dialog box.

- **Recovering Lost Highlights.** Camera Raw is very good at recovering lost highlights. When other raw converters will give up if data is clipped in one of the channels, as long as two channels contain data, Camera Raw can usually recover highlights. Start by reducing the exposure; hold down Alt (Windows), Opt (Mac OS) to invoke threshold mode to see the clipping, or press O to turn on the highlight clipping preview. Next, raise the Brightness value to compensate for any darkening caused by the Exposure adjustment. Apply a tone curve from the Curve panel to fine-tune.

Summary

For something classed as a plug-in, Camera Raw is a very deep application, as can be seen by the ground covered in this chapter. Unfortunately, in the past, it has had some bad press because it appeared from the image previews that it wasn't doing a good job. In fact, it was simply showing the image, warts and all, and not suppressing unwanted artifacts, such as noise in the shadow areas, or applying a tone curve that boosted saturation, something proprietary raw processors tend to favor.

To counter the bad press, Camera Raw 3.0 introduced auto adjustments. Fortunately, they can be turned off by anyone who wishes to see his or her images with As Shot settings. If, however, you are somewhat overwhelmed by all the controls, don't be afraid to use auto adjustments. They can do a pretty good job of processing, which you can accept, reject, or use as a platform for jumping off to more ideal adjustments.

chapter **15**

Automating Tasks

Although learning to automate tasks in Photoshop may not bring more excitement into your life or make you more creative, it will alleviate the sheer mind-numbing boredom generated by the repetitive task disorder and, instead of your being used by Photoshop, elevate you to the lofty position of one who uses Photoshop.

Photoshop has a dual personality. It can be your ally one minute and your enemy the next. When you use it creatively, it sings to you, but when you have to process hundreds of images that require the same one or two parameters to be changed, it can turn on you and drive you straight into the arms of the repetitive task disorder. When that happens, actions are the allies you need to rescue you.

Actions can perform tasks automatically and save time, effort, and wasted energy. For example, if your boss says convert hundreds, or even thousands, of images to another file format or color space, actions can take the tedious repetition out of the task and free you to do other more exciting tasks, or even slink off work early.

Furthermore, actions can record not only simple operations, such as resizing or changing modes, but also very complex tasks. Learn to use actions and you have learned to use Photoshop, instead of letting it use you.

Creating, Saving, and Playing Actions

Creating an action couldn't be simpler. You create a new action set, create a new action, start recording, execute the tasks in Photoshop that you want to record, and stop recording. Couldn't be any simpler, really. No need to perform mental gymnastics or learn a complex programming language. So, why the need for a whole chapter devoted to actions? As always, there are a few qualifications, warnings, cautions, and secret handshakes attached to any activity in Photoshop. With that in mind, before proceeding any further, here is a quick overview of actions:

In Photoshop, actions reside inside action sets, which in turn reside in the Actions palette (ImageReady has a slightly different arrangement in that it doesn't use sets for organizing actions). The sets can be renamed and moved but cannot be placed inside another set. The action inside the set, on the other hand, can be moved in the same set or to another set. These sets can be saved out of the Actions palette, backed up onto your hard drive or any backup media, and reloaded as required. Single actions can be saved by moving or copying them into a new set and then saving the set.

You can play an action one at a time or create an action that calls another action from the Actions palette. The ability to call other actions opens a number of workflows. For example, you can have one action that sharpens an image and then create another one that converts an image to another format, such a JPEG, and then plays the sharpening action. This way, you can use the sharpening action on its own or combined with a change in file format. Actions can also be played in a Batch command to process images, for instance, resizing a folder of images to a specific size or converting to another color space.

Creating an Action

The Actions palette is where all the action takes place (pun intended). Before creating an action, it's worth taking a brief look at the Actions palette and menu (Figure 15-1).

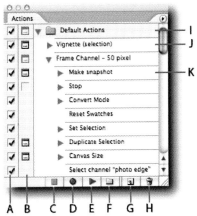

FIGURE 15-1: **The Actions palette. A—Checkbox column for excluding steps and turning off actions. B—Modal column for hiding and showing dialog boxes; a red modal dialog box indicates that one or more of the modal dialogs have been turned off in the set or action. C—Pause. D—Record. E—Play. F—New set. G—New action. H—Trash. I—Actions set. J—Action. K—Action step.**

The palette has at its base buttons for creating and playing actions and two columns to the left of the action tiles for modifying recorded steps. The first column is used to turn off actions and to exclude action steps. This can be very useful when you want to play only selected steps from an action, which otherwise would require editing the action or recording it again. For example, an action that resizes and sharpens an image may be played back to resize the image and exclude the sharpening by simply deselecting that step, or steps.

CAUTION Actions are linear by design; they rely on previous steps, and deselecting a step may disable the action.

The second column is used to control modal steps recorded in an action. What exactly is a modal step? If the column contains an icon of a dialog box, the action will pause after executing a command and expect you to either change the recorded values, to accept them, or to use a modal tool (one that requires you to click the OK button). However, if you are happy with the recorded values and you do not want the action to pause, you can do so by clicking the icon. The icon will disappear, leaving an empty embossed box, and the action will continue without pausing at that juncture. Clicking in an empty embossed box has the opposite effect. It enables a modal dialog or command.

CAUTION When you turn off *all* the modal controls for a set or single action by clicking the dialog box icon at the head of the set or single action, proceed with caution. The reason for the warning is because *all* the modal controls are disabled and the previous order is not restored when you click in the modal box to turn the controls on again. Furthermore, in case you are wondering why some of the dialog box icons at the head of an action set or action are colored red, it's to indicate that one or more of the modal steps have been disabled.

Next, take a look at the Actions palette menu. It contains some commands that are self-explanatory, such as New Action, Start Recording, and so forth, but others, such as Delete and Insert Stop, could benefit from a little elucidation (Figure 15-2).

The Delete command deletes selected items; these can be actions steps, actions, or sets. The Clear All command deletes all loaded action sets from the palette. However, neither command deletes the source sets on the hard drive. If you make a mistake and accidentally use the commands, you can invoke Edit➜Undo, or Ctrl+Z (Windows), ⌘+Z (Mac OS) to restore the deleted items. However, it is limited to only the one undo.

The Insert Stop command is very useful for reminding yourself of some information before continuing to the next step or informing other people of some crucial information if you intend to share an action. Stops are particularly useful at the beginning of an action when you use them to forewarn users of requirements to play the action successfully—for example, informing users that they must select a portion of an image before proceeding to the next step. Try to keep the stops to a minimum. Too many stops can just irritate people if they have to keep clicking to dismiss the dialog box.

The Insert Menu Item command is useful for applying commands that cannot be recorded as a step. For example, you cannot record a zoom-in step, but you can insert View➜Zoom In. Likewise, you cannot toggle palette views and record the step, but you can select Insert Menu Item and then choose a palette from the Window menu. When the action is played, the step will show a hidden palette or hide a visible palette. The command is also useful for assigning function keys to frequently used filters. For instance, create a new action, assign a function key in the New Action dialog, select Insert menu Item, and choose a filter, such as Smart Sharpen, or another command altogether, such as Image → Duplicate if you dupe a lot of documents, and then stop recording. Play back the action by pressing the assigned key. No more clicking or zig-zagging to select menu items!

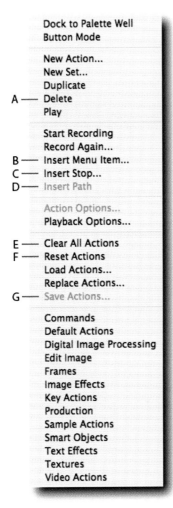

FIGURE 15-2: The Actions palette menu contains some commands that can benefit from a little clarification: A—Deletes loaded actions from the Actions palette; leaves the source actions untouched; B—Inserts menu commands that cannot be included in an action by selecting them the conventional way; C—Inserts a message, a stop, or both; D—Inserts completed paths from the Paths palette; E—Clears all the loaded actions from the Actions palette; leaves the source actions untouched; F—Clears all the loaded actions and default actions set; G—Saves an action set, not a single action; not available unless a set is selected.

The Insert Path command is used to insert a completed path. The path can be one that you have drawn with the pen tools in Photoshop or imported from a vector program, such as Illustrator or FreeHand. The command is usually grayed out until you either create a path with the shape tools (including the Custom Shape tool) or activate a work or saved path in the Paths palette.

NOTE Paths created with the shape tools, including the Custom Shape tool, are automatically included as you draw them while recording an action, but paths drawn with the pen tools must be completed paths and then the Insert Path command used to include them in an action.

Having taken in all the preceding information, you can create a very basic action that takes on board some of the aforementioned warnings and caveats and puts the theory into practice. The following steps chart how to create a new document, make a selection, fill it with a gradient, apply the Pointillize filter, and then view the document in full screen mode.

1. In the Actions palette, click the Create New Set button at the base of the palette, or select an existing set to nest the new action inside it and skip the next step.

2. Name the set in the New Set dialog box and click the OK button.

3. Click the Create New Action button.

4. In the New Action dialog box, name the action and assign a keyboard shortcut from the Function Key pop-up menu. Choose a color from the Color pop-up (this affects only the Button mode view and not the List mode view).

5. Click the Record button to exit the dialog box and to start recording.

6. Create a new document by choosing File ➔ New. The document can be any size, as long as it's in RGB color mode.

7. From the Actions palette menu, select Insert Stop. Type a message that says something like the following: Create a marquee with the Rectangular Marquee tool, fill it with a gradient, and press the Play button in the Actions palette when done (Figure 15-3).

FIGURE 15-3: **The Record Stop dialog box allows you to enter a message and to stop the action while a user performs a task. Selecting the Allow Continue checkbox permits the action to continue automatically after pressing Enter (Windows), Return (Mac OS).**

NOTE Do not select Allow Continue because, in this case, the user must continue manually. Click the OK button to exit the dialog box.

8. Create a marquee with the Rectangular Marquee tool and use the Gradient tool to fill it with a gradient of choice.

9. Select Filter ➜ Pixelate ➜ Pointillize and accept the default cell size setting or define another size.

10. Choose Select ➜ Deselect, or Ctrl+D (Windows), ⌘+D (Mac OS).

11. From the Actions palette menu, choose Insert Menu Item.

12. Choose View ➜ Screen Mode ➜ Full Screen Mode and press the OK button to exit the dialog box.

13. Click the Stop Playing/Recording button.

You should have an action that has all the checkboxes selected, a red modal icon by the side of the action name, and a normal modal icon by the side of the Stop step (Figure 15-4). Play back the action. Try deselecting the checkboxes and the modal controls by clicking in the respective columns to see how they affect the action. Click in the empty modal boxes by the side of the Make and Pointillize steps. This very simple exercise should give you a good grounding for creating an action. When you feel confident, try creating actions that are increasingly complex.

FIGURE 15-4: **The Actions palette showing the recorded action steps, the checkboxes, and the modal dialog box controls where applicable.**

Now, there are limitations imposed on what can and what cannot be recorded by an action and by what can cause an action to fail on the other platform because of compatibility issues.

Generally speaking, painting strokes, creating paths, changing magnification, and scrolling cannot be recorded. Of all the tools in the Toolbox, only the following can be included:

- Spot Healing and Healing Brush tools

- Brush tool

- Color Replacement tool

- Clone Stamp and Pattern Stamp tools

- History and Art History Brush tools

- Eraser and Background Eraser tools

- Blur, Sharpen, and Smudge tools

- Dodge, Burn, and Sponge tools

Furthermore, although completed paths can be inserted into a document by an action, the individual steps that go into creating a path cannot be recorded. Although zooming and scrolling steps cannot be recorded, the items Standard Screen Mode, Full Screen Mode With Menu Bar, and Full Screen Mode, found in the View ➜ Screen Mode submenu, can be recorded.

When you are creating actions destined to play on a machine other than the host machine, you might face some compatibility issues. An action recorded on one computer using an Open or Save command is guaranteed to fail on another computer because of differences in the path and folder structure, regardless of platform. An action that includes custom brushes, shapes, textures, patterns, presets, and so forth that reside only on the host computer is likely to cause the action to fail when played back on a client computer. The workaround, of course, is to package custom items with the action and include instructions to load them prior to playing the action. An action that uses a special font to create a text layer is likely to fail if that font is not available on the client machine. Avoid selecting a layer or a channel directly because when the action is played on another file, Photoshop will look for the layer by name and if it doesn't find it, the action may fail. Instead, use keyboard shortcuts to select next or previous layer or channel. To select layers, use Alt+[or] (Windows), Opt+[or] (Mac OS). To move layers, use Ctrl+[or] (Windows), ⌘+[or] (Mac OS). To select channels, use Ctrl+1, 2, 3, 4, and so forth (Windows), ⌘+1, 2, 3, 4, and so forth (Mac OS).

Including a Safety Net in a New Action

When you create a new action for an unknown user, or even yourself, it's always a good idea to include a Create New Snapshot command from the History palette menu at the head of the action. Doing so acts as a safety net if the user needs to revert to the step before the action was played. To widen the safety net, include a message by using the Insert Stop command from the Actions palette menu so that the user is made aware of the snapshot.

A safety net might be needed because the number of steps in the action might exceed the maximum number of history states the user has specified in Preferences, resulting in the action's overwriting the existing history states so that the user is unable to revert back to the step before the action was played. Furthermore, the user may not even have the Automatically Create First Snapshot history option enabled and find that he or she cannot even revert to the original state. Moreover, guess who the user will blame for that sticky situation?

An Action for All Image Dimensions

One downside of recording an action is that it records coordinates of placed or moved objects according to the units of measurement specified in Preferences. This can be a blessing when actions are played on documents having the same canvas dimensions as the one used to create the action, or a disaster when the action is played on documents of varying canvas dimensions. For example, if the unit of measurement is set to pixels, centimeters, or inches when you record an action, then the placed or moved object will not position itself relative to the original document's canvas dimensions. An object placed in the center of a document canvas while you were recording the object will end up to one side of center if the target document's dimensions are smaller or larger.

The solution is to open Preferences and then, in the Units & Rulers screen, set your Rulers in the Units section to read in percentages. You can do this before you create the action or as the first step in the action. Doing so ensures that all commands which record positioning and measurement are recorded and applied relative to the original canvas size when the action is played on another document.

Including Conditionals (ImageReady)

ImageReady has extended the actions' boundaries beyond Photoshop's linear dash to the finishing line by introducing conditionals. A *conditional* forces the action to take a slight detour. When a conditional is selected, the next step is executed only if all the specified conditions are met. For example, if you are importing lots of images into a Web Photo Gallery but the folder you are importing from contains images that are too large, you can use a conditional in your action that looks at all the files, checks their size, and then changes only the files that are too large.

To insert a conditional in an action, take the following steps in ImageReady:

1. Initiate a new action and then click the record button at the base of the Actions palette.

2. Choose Insert Conditional from the Actions palette menu, or click the Insert a Step button and then choose Insert Conditional.

3. In the Conditional dialog box (Figure 15-5), choose one of the following Conditionals from the If the Following Condition Is Met pop-up menu:

   - Always
   - Never
   - Ask
   - Image Aspect Ratio
   - Image Width
   - Image Height
   - Layer Count
   - Layer Type
   - Layer Name
   - Document Name

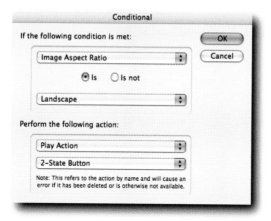

FIGURE 15-5: The Conditional dialog box, used to specify
a preset conditional logic.

4. After you have selected a Conditional, specify a property from the available list.

NOTE If you choose Always, Never, or Ask at step 3, you will not be able to select one of the other Conditionals.

5. From the Perform the Following Action" First pop-up menu, select an action and then specify a value or choose an item from the second pop-up menu.

6. Click the OK button.

With luck, in the next version conditionals will make an appearance in Photoshop. Unfortunately, for the time being, at least, they are confined to ImageReady and, regrettably, ImageReady actions are not supported by Photoshop, and vice versa.

Converting History Steps into Action Steps (ImageReady)

ImageReady has another neat option that Photoshop lacks: You can easily convert your history steps into a new action or insert them into an old action. To convert the history steps into a new action, here's what you need to do:

1. Have the Actions palette and the History palette open side by side.

2. Start recording an action and then stop recording so that you end up with just a tile containing the action title without any steps recorded.

3. Drag the history step tiles one by one "into" the action. You do that by placing the step just below the action tile. When you see a black line with inward-pointing arrowheads appear, let go. Repeat the process as often as necessary.

That's it! Remember to save your action to safeguard it against loss.

Creating Unconventional Actions

To round off the "Creating, Saving, and Playing Actions" section, here is an example of an action used to overcome a limitation. Suppose that you want to apply an existing Curves Adjustment layer to a number of documents by dragging and dropping it into the open documents. You will soon find that the move cannot be included as a step in an action. Here is a little workaround that you can use to produce the same result:

1. In the Layers palette, double-click the icon of the Curves Adjustment layer that you want to "drag" into another document.

2. When the Curves dialog box pops up, click the Save button and save the current settings as an .acv file to a folder you are unlikely to rename, move, or delete.

3. Start recording your action.

4. Open a dummy document and create a new Curves Adjustment layer.

5. Double-click the Curves Adjustment layer icon and then, in the Curves dialog box, use the Load button to load the earlier saved .acv file.

6. Click the OK button to exit the dialog box.

7. Save and close the document.

8. Stop recording.

Now, use the newly created action in a batch command to apply the same Curves Adjustment layer to a folder of files. It goes without saying that you can apply the preceding method to any Adjustment command that has a Save button in its dialog box.

The preceding example is provided to show what a little lateral thinking can achieve. Photoshop can be a nightmare to master because of the many ways that you can perform a task, but that's also something you can exploit to your advantage.

CAUTION Actions that contain the location of a file may need to be modified because the information is often platform- or OS-specific, or both.

Saving Custom Actions

If Photoshop closes unexpectedly for any reason, any custom actions in the Actions palette will be lost. That's because Photoshop keeps track of the actions in a file called Actions Palette.psp and updates the file when it closes normally. If you have spent time creating a complex action, it's imperative that you save it before you become a victim of the unexpected.

Now that you've been warned to save an action, you won't take long to realize that you cannot actually save actions, per se, from Photoshop. That's because you can save only action sets. This stymies a number of people when they select an action and then try to save it by choosing Save Actions from the palette menu, only to find the item grayed out. The solution is obvious when you know that only action sets can be saved. Therefore, select the action set, not the action, choose Save Actions from the palette menu, and then follow the save steps.

The default location for storing actions is `~\Adobe Photoshop CS2\Presets\Photoshop Actions`. Action sets located in this folder can be loaded from the Actions palette menu without your having to use the Load command and then navigate to the action set.

If you need to save a single action (for example, to send to someone), create a new set and then either drag the action into it or copy it by holding down Alt (Windows), Opt (Mac OS) while you drag it into the set. Select the set and then save it by choosing Save Actions from the palette menu.

TIP If you have spent time, effort, and energy creating custom actions, save them away from the Photoshop Actions folder; otherwise, you might lose them during a reinstall. If possible, you should save them on removable media.

Saving Actions as Droplets

After action sets have been created, you can use actions as the basis of a Droplet. A *Droplet* is a small executable. You can drag files or folders onto it, have Photoshop launch, and have the action play out the steps. You can store the Droplets anywhere on your hard drive but probably the desktop or a folder on the desktop is the best place for quick access. Furthermore, because a Droplet is an executable, you can use your OS's Open With command to open a file and to execute the action steps.

To create a Droplet, take the following steps:

1. In Photoshop, make sure that the action you want to convert to a Droplet is residing in the Actions palette.

2. Choose File ➔ Automate ➔ Create Droplet.

3. In the Create Droplet dialog box (Figure 15-6), give the Droplet a descriptive name and choose a location where you would like to save the Droplet.

4. In the Play section of the dialog box, select the set and the action.

5. Select the options from the checkboxes:

   ▪ **Override Action "Open" Commands** if the action contains an Open command.

   ▪ **Include All Subfolders** if you want to drop a top-level folder on the Droplet and have it process the files in the subfolders.

   ▪ **Suppress File Open Options Dialogs** if you do not want to see any Open dialog boxes.

   ▪ **Suppress Color Profile Warnings** if you want Photoshop to ignore any warnings about color profiles.

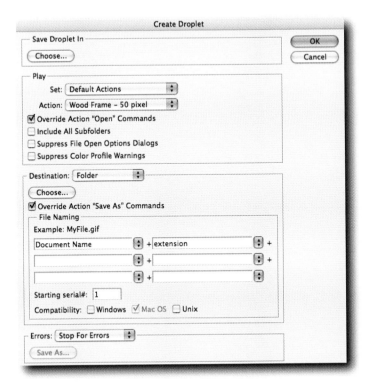

FIGURE 15-6: The Create Droplet dialog box, accessed from the File ➔ Automate menu, can be used to create a cross-platform executable from an existing action.

6. From the Destination pop-up menu, choose:

   ■ **None** to leave the files open without saving changes (unless the action contains a Save command).

   ■ **Save and Close** to save files in the current location (original files will be overwritten).

   ■ **Folder** to save the files to a specified folder.

7. Select Override Action "Save As" Commands if the action contains a Save As command.

8. If you opted for Folder at step 6, choose options for renaming processed files in the File Naming section. As you select an option, you can see from the Example name above the text fields just how your file will be renamed. You can choose elements from the pop-up menus or enter text in the fields.

9. From the Errors pop-up menu, choose Stop for Errors or Log Errors To File. If you select the latter, specify a location for the log file by clicking the Save As button.

10. Click the OK button to generate the Droplet.

After you have created the Droplet, remember to test it by dropping duplicated files onto it.

Droplets are cross-platform compatible, but you need to observe the following provisos before you can use them on the other platform. If you are Windows based and you want to use a droplet created on the Macintosh, make sure that it has the .exe extension appended to the filename so that Photoshop can see it. If you are Macintosh based and you want to use a droplet created on a Windows machine, drop it on the Photoshop alias to initialize it.

Saving Actions as Text Files

If you need to print all the steps in an action, you can save it as a text file and then print it. Unfortunately, you cannot edit the text file and then load it back into Photoshop (see "Editing and Managing Actions," later in the chapter).

In Photoshop, take the following steps to save an action as a text file:

1. Select the action set in the Actions palette.

2. Click the black triangle button to access the palette menu.

3. Hold down Ctrl+Alt (Windows), ⌘+Opt (Mac OS).

4. Choose Save Actions.

5. Give the file a memorable name, choose a location, and save the file.

Photoshop saves all the action sets in the Actions palette as a single text file. There is no way of saving a single action set other than by removing all the unwanted sets from the palette first by using the Delete command or Trash button. Do make sure that you have saved all the sets before embarking on a palette clean-up operation!

In ImageReady, you can simply choose Save Action from the palette menu; there is no need to hold down any modifier keys. ImageReady always saves the file as an ActionName.isa file, regardless. However, you can edit it in a text editor and, in contrast to the file saved from Photoshop, reload it back into ImageReady.

Playing Back Actions

To play the complete action without having to mouse down to the Play button, hold down Ctrl (Windows), ⌘ (Mac OS) and then double-click the action name.

To play back a single command, select it in the Actions palette and then Ctrl-click (Windows), ⌘-click (Mac OS) the Play button at the base of the palette. Alternatively, press Ctrl (Windows), ⌘ (Mac OS) and then double-click the command.

You can also elect to play an action a step at a time or to pause a set number of seconds and then continue to the next step. To do so, select Playback Options from the Actions palette menu. In the Playback Options dialog box, select an option (Figure 15-7). This can be very useful for debugging an action or for learning how actions are constructed.

FIGURE 15-7: **In the Playback Options dialog box, accessed from the Actions palette menu, you can elect to play an action a step at a time or pause for a given number of seconds.**

NOTE In Photoshop, you must select the tile with the action name, not the set name, to play an action.

Playing Actions in Button Mode

The Actions palette has two view modes: List and Button. Each one has pros and cons.

- **List mode** contains the checkbox and modal columns and the option of organizing actions into sets, as well as the all-important buttons for creating new actions and deleting unwanted actions from the palette.

- **Button mode** is useful for playing actions with one click. However, you cannot play individual commands if they were excluded in List mode. They won't execute in Button mode. This also applies to modal controls. If a modal control is enabled, the action will stop at that point. If it is disabled, the action will continue without a pause.

  Button mode is also useful for distinguishing sets by assigning colors. However, you cannot rearrange actions in Button mode; to do that, you must view in List mode.

Playing Automatically

You can tell Photoshop to play an action automatically when a specified event occurs. The event can be anything, from opening, saving, or exporting a file to starting the application or printing a document. Photoshop ships with sample events, but you can add your own if you know how to write scripts, or simply download them from the Internet; it's only a matter of time before people write more events and share them via Internet sites. For that reason, it's always worth the occasional visit to the Adobe Studio Exchange to see whether any new scripts have been added recently (http://share.studio.adobe.com).

To specify an event, take the following steps:

1. Choose File → Scripts → Scripts Events Manager.
2. Select Enable Events to Run Scripts/Actions at the top of the dialog box (Figure 15-8).

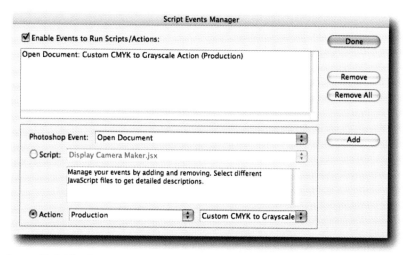

FIGURE 15-8: The Script Events Manager dialog box. Here you can associate an action or a script with an event, such as opening a document, printing a document, and so forth.

3. From the Photoshop Event pop-up menu, choose an event.
4. Select the Action radio button and then choose an action set from the pop-up menu.
5. Choose an action from the action pop-up menu.
6. Click the Add button (to remove an event, select it and then click the Remove button).
7. Click the Done button to exit.

You can add a script just as easily as an action by selecting the Script radio button instead of the Action radio button and choosing a script from the pop-up menu.

Although an action set must reside in the Actions palette before you can select an action from it, you can browse from the Script pop-up menu to add a script.

Using Actions in Batch Mode

Actions can be used to process images in batches by eliciting the help of the Batch command (File → Automate → Batch, or in Bridge Tools → Photoshop → Batch). This method of using actions opens a number of possibilities:

- Importing files from a digital camera or a scanner, provided that it possesses an acquire plug-in module that supports actions

- Processing open images or a folder full of images

- Processing single folders or nested folders

The Batch dialog box is not the easiest of dialog boxes to comprehend. Although options such as Include All Subfolders are easy to understand, the override and suppress options (Figure 15-9) seem to cause the most confusion. The following breakdown of all the commands, starting at the top of the dialog box, should help to unravel some of the confusion:

- In the **Play** section, you can select an action set from the Set pop-up menu; just below it, you can select an action from the chosen set. The set must, of course, reside in the Actions palette.

- In the **Source** section, you can select a source from the pop-up menu. This can be a folder, a digital camera or scanner acquire module, all opened files, or Bridge.

  - If you select **Folder**, you can navigate to it by clicking the Choose button.

  - If you select **Import**, you can select an acquire plug-in module from the pop-up menu.

  - If you select **Opened Files**, there is nothing to select.

  - **Bridge** is available only if you select Batch from the Bridge Tools → Photoshop submenu. If no files are selected, the batch is performed on the current folder.

- The **Override Action "Open" Commands** option refers to any Open commands recorded in the action. Select the option only if you wish to honor the Open commands recorded in the action. Deselect it to open mixed file formats or to open files when the action does not include the Open command.

- Select **Include All Subfolders** if you want to process files in the source folder and any nested folders. You can make shortcuts (Windows), aliases (Mac OS) for folders outside the source folder and drop them into it. They will be treated as though they are nested folders.

- Select **Suppress File Open Options Dialogs** to hide any Open dialog boxes. For example, use it to hide the Camera Raw dialog box when opening raw files. The option will also suppress dialog boxes for other file formats, such as EPS and PDF, which you may need to see. So, select it wisely.

- Select **Suppress Color Profile Warnings** to hide the Profile Mismatch, Missing Profile, and Paste Profile Mismatch dialog boxes.

- In the **Destination** section of the dialog box, you can choose between None, Save and Close, and Folder from the pop-up menu.

  - **None** leaves the files open after they have been processed. This can consume a lot of resources depending on the number of files being processed. Select it wisely.

  - **Save and Close** overwrites the original files. You may wish to do that on occasion, but the safer habit is not to use this option before your third cup of coffee.

  - **Folder** lets you select a destination folder. Click the Choose button to specify the location for the processed files. This is probably the safest course. If you choose this option, the File Naming section lets you rename the process files. You can select options from the pop-ups or enter custom text in the text fields. Just below the section name, Photoshop shows you an example of the filename as you select different parameters.

- **Override Action "Save As" Commands** is similar to the Override Action "Open" Commands option. It overrides instructions in the Save As steps that you might have recorded in the action. Turn this option on to ensure that the processed files are saved to the destination folder selected in the Batch dialog box and not the destination recorded in the action.

- You can log any errors or stop the batch by selecting **Log Errors To File** or **Stop For Errors** from the Errors pop-up menu. If you select Log Errors To File, click the Save As button to specify a location for the log file.

  It's imperative to verify that the settings in the Batch dialog box are producing the results you want by testing a few duplicated files before embarking on a time-consuming batch process.

In addition to using actions via the Batch command, you can also use them in the Image Processor (File ➔ Scripts ➔ Image Processor, or in Bridge, Tools ➔ Photoshop ➔ Image Processor). The main difference between the two commands is that the Image Processor can function with or without an action. You can also save the settings and load them at a later date.

Actions versus Scripting

The majority of the tasks carried out in Photoshop can be recorded in an action. The tasks that cannot be recorded can be circumvented in most cases. All it requires is a little lateral thinking and the time to think through the problem.

However, actions cannot cope with situations requiring conditional logic, such as "If the horizontal file dimensions equal 650 pixels, then rotate file counterclockwise or else rotate clockwise." At present, scripting is the only answer; although ImageReady includes some predefined conditionals, actions created in ImageReady are not compatible with Photoshop.

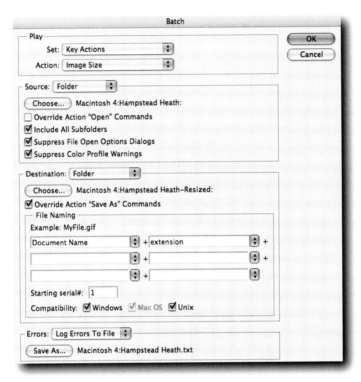

FIGURE 15-9: The Batch dialog box set to run an action that resizes images and then puts them into a different folder.

Unfortunately, in contrast to actions, scripting does require knowledge of JavaScript, AppleScript, or Visual Basic and is not, therefore, as popular as actions: Witness the proliferation of free custom actions on the Internet as opposed to the scarcity of freely available scripts. The situation might change in the future; in the meantime, if you wish to use conditional logic, your best recourse is to learn one of the required languages. JavaScript is preferable because it is cross platform, whereas AppleScript and Visual Basic are platform specific.

In addition to using conditional logic within Photoshop, you can also use OLE Automation (Windows), AppleScript (Mac OS) to control it externally. External automation allows scriptable applications to perform and share tasks. For example, you could batch process images in Photoshop and then send them to a client using a scriptable application. Photoshop ships with AppleScript Reference Guide, JavaScript Reference Guide, Photoshop Scripting Guide, and Visual Basic Reference Guide. You can find these scripting guides in the ~\Adobe Photoshop CS2\Scripting Guide folder.

Editing and Managing Actions

It's good to know that actions aren't sacrosanct and that they are amenable not only to change but also to herding and even migration. You therefore can edit the actions, rearrange them in the Actions palette, export them to your hard drive, distribute them for the sheer pleasure that comes from being generous, or levy a charge and watch the dollars roll in.

Changing Recorded Values and Adding Steps

If you don't like a recorded value in an action that you downloaded off the Internet or previously recorded yourself, you can record over the old values and include new ones without having to record the whole action again. For example, say that an action performs several commands before it saves the file as a JPEG with a quality level of five. However, you want to save the file as a JPEG with a quality level of 10. Well, you can record over just the command that sets the quality level without upsetting the other commands (if you need to replace a step, as opposed to changing a value, see the end of this section).

To replace a recorded value, take the following steps:

1. Make sure that the Actions palette view is set to List mode and not Button mode (you can select display modes in the Actions palette menu).

2. Unfurl the action steps by clicking the triangle next to the action's name.

3. Double-click the command that you want to change (at this point, Photoshop starts recording).

4. Change the values as required and OK the dialog boxes.

5. If you are happy with the new values (you can double-check them by unfurling the step), select the set and save the action (see "Saving Custom Actions," earlier in the chapter).

CAUTION If you are modifying a Save command in an action, work on a dummy file, because Photoshop will have to go through the steps of saving to record over the old settings; otherwise, step back in history. To be on the safe side, working on a duplicate or a new document is always a good idea.

Adding a step after an action has been recorded is as basic as recording an action, and simpler than you might imagine. To do so, select the step after which you want to insert the new step, click the record button, perform the steps in Photoshop, and stop recording. Alternatively, record the steps in a new action and when you are happy with them, drag and drop into the action you want to supplement.

Editing Droplets

After you have saved an action as a Droplet, you cannot modify it in any way. If any modification is required, you must make it to the action and then resave it as a Droplet. This is not a problem in the normal course of events. However, suppose that you are faced with an abnormal situation because you have either mislaid the original action or deleted it and just need to modify a step or two? What else can you do apart from rewrite the entire action? Here is a little hack that you can employ to extract the action and save perhaps hours of work:

1. From the Actions palette menu, choose Playback Options.

2. Choose Step by Step or, better still, choose Pause For and enter **55** in the seconds text field. You don't really need that many seconds, but because it costs the same, you may as well buy as much time as you can afford (you may be able to afford more time, but Photoshop sells you only a maximum of a minute).

3. Run the droplet by dropping a file on it. Make sure that it's not a valuable file; just in case, play safe and work with a copy. You can dupe files easily in Explorer (Windows) or Finder (Mac OS) by holding down Alt (Windows), Opt (Mac OS) and dragging the file to a new location within the window. Photoshop will create a Droplet Set in the Actions palette while it runs the action in the droplet.

4. Hold down Alt (Windows), Opt (Mac OS) and drag the Droplet Set to a new location in the Actions palette. Photoshop will create a duplicate and rename it Droplet Set copy.

5. Stop the action contained in the droplet by clicking the Stop Playing/Recording button at the base of the palette. OK any ensuing warning dialog boxes.

Now, open the Droplet Set copy set, edit it any which way you like and then save it again as a droplet (see "Saving Actions as Droplets," earlier in the chapter). If you want, you can rename it and store it as an action. Just remember to save the action set in case Photoshop quits on you.

Loading

Photoshop and ImageReady treat actions slightly differently when it comes to storing and loading. Although both ship with preloaded and preinstalled actions, Photoshop stores its preinstalled actions in the ...\Adobe Photoshop CS2\Presets\Photoshop Actions folder, whereas ImageReady stores them in the application package itself. In Photoshop, action sets stored in the Photoshop Actions folder appear as items in the Actions palette menu. You can load them at any time by simply selecting the set name from the palette menu, thus bypassing the Load command.

You are not confined to loading one of the available actions from the palette menu. You can load actions from anywhere on your hard drive or from a storage media. However, if you want custom actions to appear as an item in the Photoshop palette menu, you must deposit them in the Photoshop Actions folder and restart Photoshop.

TIP   Mac users can load an action by making sure that Photoshop is running and then double-clicking the action file.

Furling/Unfurling Actions the Easy Way

Some actions can be complex beasts and contain many steps. If you want to inspect such an action (you must be in List mode and not Button mode to see action steps), it can get tedious very fast having to open each step by clicking the triangle at the head of each command. You can avoid the tedium by using the following keyboard shortcuts to furl and to unfurl all the steps:

- **To furl/unfurl a single action:** Alt-click (Windows), Opt-click (Mac OS) the triangle at the head of the action.

- **To furl/unfurl all the actions in a set folder:** Alt-click (Windows), Opt-click (Mac OS) the triangle next to the actions set folder.

Summary

When it comes to taking the chore out of repetitive chores, actions are hard to beat for the ease with which they can be created and played back singularly or in an automated batch command. What's more, actions are easy to modify, duplicate, back up, and restore. You can share them easily because of their small file size and, for the most part, their compatibility between different workstations and platforms.

Learning to use actions is not difficult. Neither is learning to "write" actions difficult. In either case, a formal computer programming background is not required, just a little perseverance and the time and inclination to experiment.

chapter 16

Outputting to Print

Y ou could see the process of outputting your masterpieces to print as the last line of defense before the critics, or clients, pounce on you from all four points of the compass, or as a validation of the many hours spent in front of a hot screen.

All the hard work you put into color correcting, adjusting, and editing will either bear fruit or lead to frustration and depression when the image finally emerges from the deskjet, or when you turn the pages of a magazine or view a billboard that features your masterpiece.

Yes, there are many traps lying in wait for the unwary Photoshop user. Whether you output to a local deskjet, a Fuji Frontier, a Durst Lambda, or an offset Web press, they all have their pits and moats that you can easily fall into.

However, there are some basic precautions that you can take to defend yourself and to avoid the pits and moats. Some precautions are just based on common sense, but others rely heavily on secret handshakes and wormholes found by hours clocked in front of Photoshop and are presented here for your protection and to guide you through the land of the critics and the hard-to-please clients.

Preparing Images for Printing

If you send your image to three desktops and three offset printers, you will very likely get back three different prints. Even if you send a file to two deskjets made by the same manufacturer and the same model number, it's highly unlikely they will produce identical color or tone. Therefore, images need to be optimized for the output device. To do that, you must know the characteristics of the output device or, in the case of an offset printer, the characteristics of the proofing device. You can do this in two ways: either by producing a hard proof or by using an ICC profile. The latter method is becoming increasingly popular, not just in the case of deskjet printers but also of the proofers for the offset printers (though hard proofing is still widely used for offset printing).

Appropriately, the more preparation you put into the file, the closer the end result will be, though profiles make some of the work unnecessary. However, to produce "accurate" results, you need to incorporate color management into your workflow (see Chapter 12 for more information on how to use profiles). Briefly, you need to work with a calibrated and characterized monitor, consistent viewing conditions, and custom profiles for the output device or proofer. Without these fundamental aids in place, any image preparation you do is likely to produce inconsistent results. Before you embark on time-consuming procedures, it's usually a good idea to gather all the information you possibly can from your service bureau or commercial printer. This can include but isn't confined to Color Settings in Photoshop, profiles for any color-managed devices in a chain or at the end of the chain, and delivery methods, which can include providing files in CMYK mode to RGB mode to PDF/X standard.

Soft Proofing Images in Photoshop

The Proof Colors feature in Photoshop allows you to predict with a great deal of accuracy how the document that you are viewing will look when output to a printer. The feature works by taking the profile for your color working space and the profile for your output device, such as a deskjet printer (but it can just as easily be a monitor), doing some complex math in the background, and generating a preview of how the print will look eventually when output from the elected output device while using the elected profile. The preview represents as close a match as possible, considering that the monitor transmits light to create a preview whereas a print absorbs and reflects light. The quality of the preview depends on the profile used, the accuracy of your monitor, and the viewing conditions.

By default, when you invoke the Proof Colors command, Photoshop selects the CMYK working space that you have elected in Color Settings. However, the feature would have a very limited application if that was all it could do. You can, in fact, soft proof almost any device that can be described by a profile.

However, before you can set up custom conditions, you must make sure that the profile for the device you want to soft proof is in the folder where ICC profiles are normally stored by your operating system. If you are not sure of their location, do a search on your hard drive for the extensions .icc or .icm. Note that if you add the profile while Photoshop is running, you will need to relaunch the application before it can see the profile. Having stored the profile correctly, take the following steps to set up a custom condition in Proof Setup:

1. Choose Custom from View ➜ Proof Setup.

2. In the Customize Proof Condition dialog box, select your printer profile from the Device to Simulate pop-up menu.

3. Choose Preserve RGB Numbers (or CMYK if the profile describes a CMYK device) only if you want to simulate how colors will appear without being converted. For example, if the device you want to simulate is your deskjet, select it to see how the file will print if you forgo a conversion to the elected profile. The option is available only if the selected profile's color space matches the image being soft proofed.

4. Choose a rendering intent. Leave it on Relative Colorimetric unless you have a specific reason or need to favor another intent. Relative Colorimetric is commonly used. Unfortunately, you cannot choose rendering intents on a case-by-case basis. If you need to soft proof more than one rendering intent, create a Custom Proof Condition for each intent.

5. Select Black Point Compensation (on by default). The option allows the black point of the source and the target profiles to be mapped when a document is converted.

6. Select Simulate Paper Color to imitate the white of the paper (not all profiles support the option).

7. Choose Simulate Black Ink to imitate the intensity of the black, as produced by the printer (not all profiles support the option).

NOTE Simulate Paper Color and Simulate Black Ink affect the preview only and not the print.

8. Select Save to save the settings in a PSF file in the default folder and then OK to exit the dialog box.

Having seen your preview, make sure that you return to normal view by selecting View ➜ Proof Colors, or Ctrl+Y (Windows), ⌘+Y (Mac OS). Whichever method you use, make sure there is no tick next to View ➜ Proof Colors.

Sharpening Images

Sharpening is the act of creating the illusion of a sharply focused image. It's also a very important aspect of the workflow from capture to print. However, it is easy to either oversharpen and see crunchy images with distracting white lines accompanying the detail edges, or to not sharpen enough and see soft, mushy images that lack focus (see Chapter 11 for more information on sharpening).

Here are some pointers to bear in mind when sharpening images that are destined for print output:

- Sharpening should take place before shadow and highlight end points are set, which should be the last step in the image optimization workflow. If you sharpen after the end points are set, their values may alter (see the next section, "Setting the Shadow and Highlight End Points").

- When you evaluate sharpening for output to an offset printer, view at 50% or 25% magnification. Generally speaking, images destined for offset printing require more sharpening than images destined for digital printing.

- Don't sharpen before downsizing an image. If you are not sure of the final layout size and you have to downsize, use the Bicubic algorithm in Image Size, not Bicubic Sharper because that will add some sharpening, and inform the person handling your images that they have not been sharpened. Ideally, you should know the final size, downsize the image, sharpen, and then set the end points, but this sequence is often not followed because of budget constraints or lack of communication between supplier, designer, and service bureau.

These general rules will help you sharpen your images destined for print output, and you will get more comfortable with these techniques with experience.

Setting the Shadow and Highlight End Points

Setting the shadow and highlight end points is not necessary when outputting to a color managed printer. This is taken care of for you by the CMM (Color Management Module) when the file is converted from the working space, or the tagged working space, to the color space as described by the ICC profile for the printer.

When you're outputting to an offset printer whose characteristics are known, setting the shadow and highlight end points ensures that the important shadow and highlight detail is brought into the printable range of the press (Figure 16-1). For example, if you know that a press cannot hold detail in the highlights above level 243 (a 5% dot), and the image contains important highlight detail at level 250, you can set the highlight output slider to level 243, thus ensuring that the detail will print safely. Similarly, if the press cannot hold detail in the shadows below level 13 (a 95% dot) and you have important shadow detail below that level, raise the shadow output slider to level 13, thus ensuring that the shadow detail will print safely. To read dot percentages in the Info palette (Windows ➔ Info), set the second readout to Grayscale (click the eyedropper icon and choose Grayscale from the pop-up menu).

A

B

FIGURE 16-1: A—Before shadow and highlight end points were set. B—After shadow and highlight end points were set to compress detail and to bring the end points within range of the printer.

375

NOTE Commercial printers can actually print a flat-color tint of 3% or a 100% solid-color. The 5% and 95% dot gain settings are strictly to make sure that the highlights and shadows retain some detail in continuous tone images.

To set shadow and highlight end points, you need to identify the end points in the image, set down color samplers, and then compress the data by using the Output Levels sliders. To do so, take the following steps:

1. Make sure that the Info palette is in view and the secondary reading set to read Grayscale.

2. Create a Levels adjustment layer above the image layer by clicking the Create New Fill or Adjustment Layer button at the base of the palette and then selecting Levels.

3. In the Levels dialog box, move the highlights *Input Levels* slider all the way to the left. Move it back until you see the shadow detail that you want to ensure prints with a halftone dot.

4. Hold down Shift and click the shadow detail to set down a Color Sampler.

5. Move the highlights *Input Levels* slider back to where it was, or hold down Alt (Windows), Opt (Mac OS) and then click the Reset button. You can also find the shadow and highlight detail by holding down Alt (Windows), Opt (Mac OS) to invoke Threshold mode temporarily while you move the shadow and highlight sliders. However, it's not possible to set down a Color Sampler while in Threshold mode.

6. Repeat the preceding steps with the shadows *Input Levels* slider to identify the highlights and to place a Color Sampler on the highlight detail that you want to ensure prints with a halftone dot.

7. Having identified the important shadow and highlight end points, click in the shadows *Output Levels* textbox (located above the gradient bar). Next, hover the pointer over the color sampler for the shadows till the two icons blend and then ride the Up Arrow key while watching the K values. Stop when the value reads 95%.

8. Repeat the step for the highlights *Output Levels* so that the K values for the highlights reads 5% in the Info palette.

9. Click the OK button to exit the dialog box.

You have just set the shadow and highlight end points without damaging the file. Should you need to repurpose the file, for example, for printing on a press with a more porous paper and therefore a higher dot gain, simply turn the visibility off for the Levels adjustment layer, create another Levels adjustment layer, and follow the preceding steps to enter new values.

Avoiding Posterization and Banding

When RGB files in 8-Bits/Channel mode containing out of gamut colors are converted to CMYK, posterization can occur, resulting in a blotchy, mottled appearance. This is the result of large blocks of RGB colors mapping to a small block of CMYK values (Figure 16-2).

FIGURE 16-2: **Left—Original image. Right—Converted to 256 colors to highlight posterization.**

Posterization can also occur when an image has been edited overzealously, particularly an image in 8-Bits/Channel mode, which supports only 256 levels per channel and therefore cannot afford to lose too many levels—for example, if an image was underexposed at the capture stage and extreme Levels or Curves moves are required to "rescue" the information in the shadows. The transitional areas, lacking adequate number of levels to describe them, are easy prey to posterization. It should be noted that a loss in levels doesn't automatically result in posterization; most images can cope with some loss of data but gradients, or areas containing transitional data, such as skin tones, are particularly prone to posterization.

Banding occurs when an RGB file in 8-Bits/Channel mode containing generated smooth gradients, or blurred or feathered areas is converted to CMYK or output to a low-resolution printer.

One way to avoid posterization is by editing in 16-Bits Channel mode or a wide-gamut working space (or both), such as ProPhoto RGB. Color and contrast edits can usually benefit from being edited in 16-Bits/Channel mode because the mode supports 45,536 possible discreet levels per channel. However, images that have been converted from 8-Bits/Channel mode or a smaller working space will not benefit by being converted to 16-Bits/Channel mode or a working space with a wider color gamut.

Another way to avoid posterization is by using adjustment layers, which can prevent data loss because the settings in the adjustment layers are applied only once (see Chapter 6 for more information on adjustment layers).

Adding noise to gradients, blurs, and retouched areas can also help to avoid, or minimize posterization. To add noise:

- When using the Gradient tool, select Dither on the options bar.

- In Color Settings, select Use Dither (8-bit/channel images). This can help reduce posterization when you're converting images in 8-Bits/Channel mode.

- Create a new layer and fill it with 50% gray. Change its blend mode to Overlay. The gray fill should disappear and you should not see a difference. Next, use the Add Noise filter (Filter ➝ Noise ➝ Add Noise). The filter gives you the option of specifying the Amount and Distribution (Uniform or Gaussian) and whether to add chromatic noise or monochromatic.

- Apply monochromatic noise to Images in RGB mode; it's usually less noticeable than chromatic noise.

After you have applied the noise to a layer filled with 50% gray, or a duplicate layer, you can use the Opacity slider to decrease the clarity. You can also exclude the noise from the extreme shadows and highlights by invoking Blend If (Layer ➝ Layer Styles ➝ Blending Options, or double-clicking the layer tile). In the dialog box, use the Underlying Layer sliders, which can be split by holding down Alt (Window), Opt (Mac OS) to gently ramp the transitional levels, limiting the noise to specific levels.

Images in CMYK can often benefit from having the noise applied to one or two channels, with Distribution set to Gaussian, rather than the composite channel. This is because not all channels suffer equally from posterization, so a more holistic approach can be taken to solve the problem. An added bonus of adding noise to one or two channels is it may not be as noticeable as noise added to all the channels.

Other solutions include the following:

- Lowering the LPI (Lines Per Inch) and the resolution. For example, if the resolution was 300 ppi for a 150 lpi screening, lower it to 225 ppi. If that doesn't work, try lowering the LPI to 133 and the resolution to 200 ppi (effectively using a 1.5 × LPI formula to arrive at the resolution, instead of 2 × LPI: 150 lpi × 2 = 300 ppi).

- If a gradient is banding, recreate it in CMYK mode instead of creating it in RGB and then converting to CMYK. Alternatively, decrease the number of discreet shades by editing the gradient.

- Try assigning a smaller gamut color space as an intermediary step. For example, if working in Adobe RGB (1998), assign sRGB and then convert to CMYK. You will lose some of the color vibrancy, but the risk of posterization and banding ought to be reduced.

Printing Vector Data at Printer Resolution

If a document includes type or shapes and you prepare it for print by flattening it and then saving the file as a TIFF, the type and shapes will print only to the resolution of the file. This could result in jaggy type and unclean shape outlines. To prevent that from happening, save the file as

Photoshop PDF, EPS, or DCS 2.0 without flattening it and make sure that you select Include Vector Data in the EPS Options and DCS 2.0 Format dialog boxes. This action ensures that the vector data are saved as outlines and consequently output at the image setter's resolution, which can be as high as 2400 dpi, whereas the file's resolution may be only in the region of 240 to 300 ppi.

NOTE InDesign can import PSD files but will rasterize any included vector data. However, it will not do so if the file is a PDF. If the vector data are destined for an older page layout program, save as EPS or DCS 2.0.

If saving in the EPS or DCS 2.0 formats, you can also specify an encoding method from their dialog boxes (though it does not have a bearing on how the vector data are printed). There are three to choose from: ASCII, Binary, and JPEG. ASCII uses more bytes to describe the data than Binary but is supported by a greater number of PostScript-enabled devices. Binary is more popular because it takes up less space. If your PostScript device does not support Binary, you can try ASCII85, which is more compact than ASCII and preferable if you are unsure whether the PostScript device you are sending to supports the encoding method. The third choice, JPEG, is the most compact of the three but is also a lossy compression. However, because the compression is minimal, you might be hard put to notice it in print. To be absolutely sure, ask your service bureau or commercial printer which encoding method it recommends, and do some tests for JPEG encoding. Note that JPEG encoding is supported by PostScript level 2 and 3 printers only.

If you send a file directly from Photoshop to a local printer that supports PostScript, Photoshop can also output the vector data as outlines, which will print at the printer's resolution. To do so, make sure that Include Vector Data is selected in the Print with Preview dialog box (to be precise, it's actually labeled Print but is invoked from the File → Print With Preview command). To access the option, choose Output from the pop-up menu below the preview thumbnail (click the More Options button if it's not available). You may also choose an encoding method from the pop-up menu.

Four-Color Grayscale Printing

When you print an image in Grayscale mode on an offset printer, the print will very likely lack shadow density because of the single ink used to print all the tonal variations. Although a grayscale image can contain up to 256 discreet levels, an offset printer can reproduce approximately only 50 levels per ink, which means that the image will not look as smooth as one printed with two, three, or four inks. It will also appear coarser compared to any four-color images printed next to it owing to the use of a single screen, which makes the halftone dot pattern easier to discern. To overcome these shortcomings, you can convert the grayscale to CMYK and thereby make use of four inks, which will ensure more tonal variations in the shadows, produce richer blacks, and appear less coarse owing to the use of four combined screen patterns, which form a less discernible rosette pattern.

If you do decide to use CMYK to print your grayscale image, it's very likely to print with a colorcast when it's "impositioned" on film with other color images, which may require an ink combination that favors one of the CMY inks more than the others. To overcome this problem, you can use a custom color separation that removes some of the inks by adding a heavier GCR setting, ensuring that more of the image detail is contained in the black plate than would be with a normal separation and just a skeleton mix of CMY inks. The use of a heavy GCR effectively negates any hue shifts introduced by the press (Figure 16-3).

FIGURE 16-3: A grayscale image printed using CMYK and a heavy GCR setting.

To create a custom separation in Photoshop for a four-color grayscale, take the following steps:

1. Create a duplicate of your image (Image ➜ Duplicate) and close the original.

2. Convert the duplicate to Grayscale if it is in RGB mode.

3. Choose Edit ➜ Convert to Profile.

4. In the Convert to Profile dialog box, choose Custom CMYK from the Profile pop-up menu, located under Destination Space.

5. In the Custom CMYK dialog box (Figure 16-4), choose a suitable Ink Colors set from the pop-up menu. For example, if you're printing on coated stock on a sheetfed offset printer in the United States, choose SWOP (Coated).

6. In the Separation Options, select GCR and choose Heavy from the Black Generation pop-up menu.

7. Reduce the Black Ink Limit to 90%, Total Ink Limit to 290–295% (this will vary depending on press conditions), and increase UCA to 5%.

8. Click the OK button to exit dialog box and click again to exit the Convert to Profile dialog box.

9. Save the image as a TIFF.

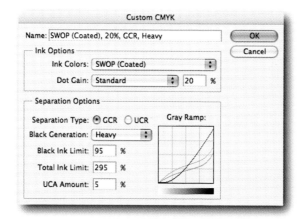

FIGURE 16-4: **The Custom CMYK feature used to create a bespoke-heavy GCR profile for separating a four-color grayscale image.**

The preceding settings should *not* be regarded as suitable for all images and all press conditions. There is no substitute for producing proofs on the device allied to the offset printer.

Owing to the heavier than usual GCR used in a CMYK file, it might be a good idea to flag the file so that your service provider or commercial printer is made aware of your intentions.

Using Spot Colors

Spot colors consist of inks premixed to an exacting standard. They are primarily used when CMYK process inks cannot produce a given color or an effect, such as metallic ink or varnish, or color consistency is required, such as when a corporate logo needs to be printed with the exact same hue on different printing devices. Spot colors can also be used to print two- or three-color jobs when a budget is limited. Furthermore, spot colors can be used in addition to CMYK colors to create interesting color combinations.

To use spot colors in Photoshop, you can either create spot channels or use Duotone mode. This section looks at both methods because both can have their use.

To create a spot channel, take the following steps:

1. From the Channels palette menu, select New Spot Channel.

2. In the New Spot Channel dialog box, specify a name for the color if you know it or use the color box in the Ink Characteristics to open the Color Picker, select Color Libraries, and then choose a color (Figure 16-5).

   You can choose an ink manufacturer from the Book pop-up menu and then a color from the manufacturer's published swatches. There are seven ink manufacturers included. If you know the swatch number, you can type it on the keyboard, but you need to be quick; otherwise, the sequence will jump by the hundreds, corresponding to the last key press!

3. Click the OK button and then, in the New Spot Channel dialog box, the OK button once more.

4. Include the text or logo, or whatever, in the Spot Channel. You can, if you want, type the text and select it before you access the New Spot channel. To select text, Ctrl-click (Windows), ⌘-click (Mac OS) the thumbnail in the Layers palette.

5. Save the document as a PSD or a PDF if placing it directly in an InDesign or Illustrator document; if placing in older layout programs, save it in the DCS 2.0 format.

NOTE Placed PDF files will not show up correctly unless the Overprint Preview item is selected in the View menu.

CAUTION Do not expect the print to match the Pantone spot colors you pick in Color Libraries. The on-screen colors are only simulations. If you need to match spot colors to printed colors in your project, use an appropriate printed swatch book to pick the colors, such as the series of Pantone solid color swatch books.

The spot channels print over the top of the composite image and in the order they appear in the Channels palette. For instance, the spot color in the channel at the top of the stack will print over the top of all the spot colors used. Furthermore, spot colors do not knock out the image; instead, they overprint. Knock-outs and trapping need to be done manually.

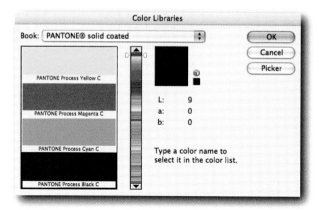

FIGURE 16-5: **Choosing a spot color from the Color Libraries, accessed from the Color Picker.**

NOTE The solidity setting in the New Spot Channel and the Spot Channel Options dialog boxes applies only to the preview and not the printed separations, unless you output the file to a composite color printer, in which case the spot color will print at the opacity indicated by the Solidity setting. Be aware that previews may not give an accurate idea of the spot color owing to many of the spot colors' being outside the gamut of most monitors.

If you need to apply a tint to an image using a spot color, Duotone mode is recommended. You can apply up to four spot colors, one for each plate. To do so, take the following steps:

1. Convert your image to Grayscale mode and then to Duotone mode from the Image → Mode submenu. Alternatively, convert the image to grayscale using other known methods, such as by using the Channel Mixer or Calculations or by converting to Lab and using the L channel to convert to Grayscale mode.

2. In the Duotone Options dialog box (Figure 16-6), select a type from the pop-up menu. There are four choices: Monotone, Duotone, Tritone, and Quadtone.

3. Click the color box and choose a color from the Color Libraries. Alternatively, type the color swatch's name in the text field.

4. Click the curve box to apply a custom Duotone Curve (see the explanation ahead).

5. Save the document as a PSD or a PDF if placing it directly in an InDesign or Illustrator document; if placing in older layout programs, save it as an EPS.

The Duotone Curves do not affect the actual underlying grayscale image; instead, they control how the inks are laid down when you print the image. If anything, they behave more like Curves applied through an adjustment layer. You can change them any number of times without fear of altering the original image. This also means that you can repurpose an image any number of times.

383

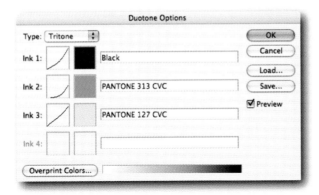

FIGURE 16-6: **The Duotone Options box, used to select spot colors and custom Duotone Curves.**

TIP Having created a Duotone image using the above method, you can convert it to CMYK for process printing. This is more desirable than creating a "fake" Duotone in a page layout program, though it may not be as fast.

Using a PDF/X Standard Workflow

The PDF/X standard (Portable Document Format Exchange) is a subset of Adobe's ever-popular PDF file format. It is designed with one purpose in mind: to deliver graphic files for print in as robust a format as possible, one that requires little or no intervention between dispatch and output. For example, if you were to send a QuarkXPress, InDesign, or a PDF document to a service bureau or a client, it's possible to alter it accidentally, or intentionally, with unpredictable results. Sending the files in one of the PDF/X standards can ensure that files are output as intended, without any intervention from third parties. Access can be limited by using 128-bit RC4 encryption. Currently, there are two popular standards for delivery: PDF/X-1a and PDF/X-3.

- **PDF/X-3** is an ISO standard for delivering graphic content. It allows the use of color management and device-independent color (CIE Lab, ICC-based color spaces, CalRGB, and CalGray), in addition to CMYK and spot colors. This standard is recommended when press conditions are not known or you intend to print the file on various output devices. Profiles are automatically embedded at the save stage.

- **PDF/X-1a** requires all fonts used in the publication to be embedded, appropriate bounding boxes to be specified, and the color to appear as CMYK, spot colors, or both. Furthermore, the aimed printing conditions must be described. This standard is recommended when the press conditions are known and no further color management is required. When this standard is selected, colors are converted to the destination color space and profiles are not embedded.

To save a file in PDF/X, take the following steps:

1. In the Save dialog box, select Photoshop PDF, give the file a name, and then click the Save button.

2. When the Save Adobe PDF dialog box pops up (Figure 16-7), choose an option from the Adobe PDF Preset.

3. Choose a standard and a compatibility option.

4. Type a message in the General Description text box.

5. Specify options for thumbnails and Fast Web Preview and indicate whether you want to preview the PDF after saving.

6. Work through the options for Compression, Output, and Security.

7. View a summary and then click the Save PDF button to save and exit.

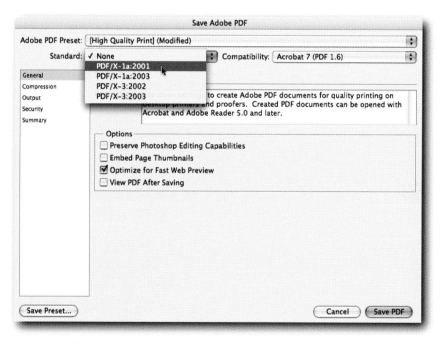

FIGURE 16-7: **The Save Adobe PDF dialog box lets you choose from four preset PDF/X standards, which you can modify and save as custom presets.**

If you are unsure which options to select, talk to your commercial printer or service bureau or visit its Web site and download instructions. Most of the larger concerns upload instructions on how to deliver files that you can download.

Rotating Images—a Ripping Question

If you are placing images in a page layout program—such as InDesign, QuarkXPress, or PageMaker—and rotating them, it can be more economical to rotate the images in Photoshop because the RIP (Raster Image Processor) will then have less work to do when it processes the image, especially if it's a large EPS file. Having said that, modern RIPs do not suffer too much from memory issues; therefore, consider rotating the images when outputting to an older device. To do so, take the following steps:

1. In your page layout program, make a note of the image's rotated angle and whether it was rotated clockwise or counterclockwise.

2. Open the image in Photoshop and choose Image → Rotate Canvas → Arbitrary.

3. In the Rotate Canvas dialog box, enter the degree of rotation in the Angle text field and select °CW or °CCW.

4. Click the OK button to accept the rotation.

5. After the document has been saved, update the link in the page layout program.

Rotating the canvas this way will either add white to the background or transparency if the image is on a normal layer, which is something you will have to take into consideration.

NOTE Images rotated 90 or 180 degrees in a page layout program do not benefit from being also rotated in Photoshop, so you may as well let the RIP do the grunt work.

Printing from Photoshop

Photoshop has several commands for outputting images to a desktop printer, each leading to a different dialog box that enables you to specify options or to print using last-used settings. All the printing commands are accessible from the File menu and, apart from Print Online, via keyboard shortcuts.

- **Page Setup** takes you to the printer driver dialog box, where you can specify page properties, such as size, orientation, custom size, and printer model if you have more than one printer installed.

- **Print with Preview** takes you to a dialog box that offers a plethora of options. In the dialog box, you can specify color management settings and output parameters, parameters such as position, scale, custom half-tone screening, and transfer functions. Furthermore, you can limit printing to selected areas and include information such as crop marks and labels. This is probably the dialog box you will use most.

- **Print** takes you straight to the printer driver's Print dialog box, where you can choose printer settings before printing.

- **Print One Copy** prints one copy of the image without showing any dialog boxes. The last-used settings in Print with Preview, Page Setup, and the printer's Print dialog box are applied.

■ **Print Online** requires you to create an account with OFoto, a Kodak-owned company. After the account is opened, you can order prints online and have them delivered to your door. You need to save your images as JPEGs, which you can drag and drop to upload.

Print with Preview

The Print dialog box (Figure 16-8) contains the most options and is the one most likely to confuse or bewilder the unwary user. The first thing to know is that the dialog box is actually called Print, not Print with Preview (not to be confused with the printer driver dialog box, which also tends to be called Print).

FIGURE 16-8: The Print with Preview dialog box, showing options for Color Management. The options have been chosen to print a grayscale image on fine art paper using Lysonic inks.

The dialog box has three views: a compact view that contains just a thumbnail; Position; and Scale Print Size options. Selecting More Options reveals choices for Color Management and Output. Each can be accessed from the pop-up menu below the thumbnail. The pop-up is sticky, meaning that whichever option is chosen will be remembered the next time you access the dialog box, provided that you do not cancel after making a choice.

Color Management

When Color Management is selected, you can select Document or Proof from the Print section of the dialog box. Selecting Document ensures that the numbers in the document are converted to the current profile, which can be a working space or an embedded profile, before it is sent to the printer driver. Under Options, you can specify Color Handling from the pop-up menu. Let Printer Determine Colors is the default. When this option is selected, Photoshop doesn't do a color conversion but instead hands off the information to the printer driver. Although this method requires the least effort to understand what's happening behind the scenes, the chances of the monitor preview's matching the print are very minimal. You can increase your chances if you convert the document to sRGB before entering the Print with Preview dialog box.

When you select Let Photoshop Determine Colors from the Color Handling pop-up menu, Photoshop lets you choose a custom or generic printer profile from the Printer Profile pop-up menu. Choosing a *printer profile* can increase your chances of matching the monitor preview to the print, especially if you use a custom profile for your paper and ink combination and your monitor is calibrated and characterized. At this stage, Photoshop knows the color space of the document and the color space of the printer but needs to know which rendering intent to use to convert from one space to the other, so, the Rendering Intent pop-up menu is enabled when you select Let Photoshop Determine Colors. Choose Relative Colorimetric (recommended overall) or Perceptual for continuous tone images. The former clips out-of-gamut colors but does not alter the in-gamut colors, whereas the latter preserves the relationships between the in-gamut colors, avoids clipping, but may desaturate some colors. Unfortunately, at this stage there is no means of judging which is the better option because the thumbnail preview does not update and the dialog box does not talk back to the document preview.

Having gathered all the information it needs, Photoshop then converts the document to the custom or generic profile selected in the Printer Profile pop-up menu and sends the numbers to the printer driver on the fly. At this point, Photoshop more or less drops out of the loop. The printer driver takes over, converts the numbers to CMYK, and uses the settings in the driver dialog box to create the print. There is one more tiny detail that you need to know if you want to ensure accurate color. You must turn off color management in the printer driver dialog box; otherwise, two conversions will take place and produce unpredictable results.

If you have been soft proofing, selecting Proof ensures that the numbers in the document are converted to the preset selected in View ➜ Proof Setup. After Proof is selected, you can accept the current preset selected in Proof Setup or choose another from the Proof Setup Preset pop-up menu, which is grayed out until you select Proof.

If all this seems like a great deal to remember, hold the mouse button over the options to read a description.

NOTE The descriptions for the speech balloon changes depending on the option selected in the Color Handling pop-up menu.

Output

Selecting Output from the pop-up menu, located below the thumbnail, reveals options that apply to offset printing as well as to printing directly from Photoshop. From this section of the dialog box, you can print a variety of information along with your print. For example, Crop Marks, Labels, Description, and Background color are just a few useful options that you should know are available (Figure 16-9).

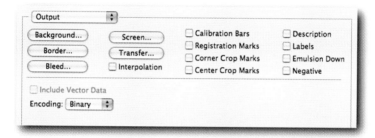

FIGURE 16-9: **Detail view of the Options section of the Print with Preview dialog box.**

- **Background** prints a color outside the image area. To use this option, click the button and then select a color from the Color Picker.

- **Border** prints a black border around the image. To use this option, click the button, choose a unit from the pop-up menu, and then enter a value in the text field. The maximum border allowed is 0.15 inch, 3.50 mm, or 10 points.

- **Bleed** prints crop marks inside the image so that you can trim it accurately. The maximum bleed allowed is 0.125 inches, 3.18 mm, or 9.01 points.

- **Screen** lets you specify a custom screen frequency and halftone dot shape for printing process colors. This option should be used with care; consult your service bureau or commercial printer before specifying custom screen options.

- **Transfer** lets you specify a custom curve for each plate. You can use transfer functions to repurpose a file for different printing conditions. If used, notify the recipient of the curve's existence. Although the curve may be saved in most of the file formats supported by Photoshop, to apply transfer curves to images output via a page layout program, you need to save the file as an EPS and check the Include Transfer Function in the EPS Options dialog box.

The Load and Save buttons have two functions. Holding down Alt (Windows), Opt (Mac OS) changes the Save button to a ->Default button that can save the current curve as the default. The Load button changes to a <-Default button that can apply the default curve. The <-Default button can be used to restore the curve, as long as you have not set a new default, in which case, dragging the anchor points out of the curves window restores it.

- **Interpolation** resamples a low-resolution image automatically while printing. For the function to work, a PostScript printer must support interpolation.

- **Calibration Bars** prints an 11-step wedge for a grayscale image and a gradient tint bar for a CMYK image, one for each plate.

- **Registration Marks** prints marks that you can use to align color separations.

- **Corner Crop Marks and Center Crop Marks** print marks for trimming the page.

- **Description** prints a caption underneath your image. You must enter the description in the File Info dialog box for this function to work.

- **Labels** prints the filename above the image for easy identification.

- **Emulsion Down** reverses the way the image is printed on film. Normally, images printed on paper have the emulsion facing you but images printed on film are printed with the emulsion facing away from you.

- **Negative** inverts the entire image. Separations printed directly to film in the United States are usually negative, but in countries in Europe, and some countries outside Europe, the practice is to print positive separations. If you are required to supply film separations, check with the print shop to see how they prefer the film: negative emulsion, facing or away; positive emulsion, facing or away.

Printing Multiple Images on a Single Page

It may not be obvious at first sight, but the Picture Package lets you print different images on one page. You may think that you can't do it because when you select a file or folder under Source the Picture Package shows either multiple versions of the selected file or of the first file in the specified folder. To select different files, take the following steps:

1. Make sure that no documents are open or the Picture Package will use them as the source files (you can, of course, take advantage of this feature by opening only the documents you want to include in the picture package).

2. Choose Picture Package from the File ➜ Automate submenu or from the Bridge Tools ➜ Photoshop submenu.

3. In the Picture Package dialog box (Figure 16-10), select a Page Size, Layout, Resolution, Color Mode, and any information under Document.

4. Use the Content pop-up menu under Label to specify any information from the File Info dialog box that you want to print.

5. Click the thumbnail placements to the right of the window and then select a file (unfortunately, you cannot use drag and drop). Photoshop will open the file, resize it, and update the preview window.

6. Click the OK button to create the picture package.

7. Save the picture package or send it down the pipe to your printer.

FIGURE 16-10: **Contrary to first impressions, the Picture Package feature can be used to print more than one image.**

If you are not happy with the default layouts, you can define your own. To do so, click the Edit Layout button, make your choices, and then save the custom settings (Figure 16-11). You can define custom Image Zones by deleting all current zones and then adding new ones. To resize and reposition the zones, click a new zone to reveal the bounding box handles and then drag to resize; alternatively, enter a value in the text fields. Remember, you can enter the cursor in the Size and Position text fields and then ride the Up and Down Arrow keys for values that are more exact.

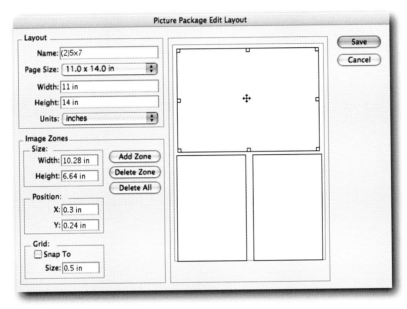

FIGURE 16-11: **You can edit the Picture Package layout by clicking the Edit Layout button and then defining custom image zones.**

Printing Selected Channels

There are times when you do not want to print all the channels in an RGB image. Although you can print individual layers easily by turning off the visibility of the layers you do not want to print, you cannot use the same method with RGB channels. If you try to print this way, the visible channels will just print as grayscale separations.

There are three methods that you can use for printing less than the default RGB channels. The first method destroys the information in the nonprinting channel, whereas the second and third preserve the information and give you the option of changing your mind at a later date.

The Fill Method

In this method, you fill the channel that you do *not* want to print with black. To do so, press D to set the foreground and background colors to default. Highlight the channel that you do not want to print. Choose Edit ➜ Fill and then, in the Fill dialog box, select Use: Foreground Color under Contents and click the OK button. Alternatively, use a keyboard shortcut. For example, Shift+Backspace (Windows), Shift+Delete (Mac OS) to call the Fill dialog box or Alt+Backspace (Windows), Opt+Delete (Mac OS) to fill without recourse to a dialog box.

TIP   If you use this method, make sure that you either create a new history snapshot or have sufficient history steps to revert.

The Channel Mixer Method

Use the Channel Mixer to achieve the same result while preserving the information in the channel(s) that you do not want to print. In this example, the green channel is being printed.

1. Create a Channel Mixer adjustment layer above your layers.

2. Move the slider for the Red channel to zero or sliders for the Green and Blue channel to -200%. This fills the Red channel with black.

3. Select the Blue channel from the Output Channel pop-up.

4. Move the slider for the Blue channel to zero or sliders for the Red and Green channel to -200%. This fills the Blue channel with black.

5. Click the OK button and print.

When you have finished printing, simply delete the Channel Mixer adjustment layer or turn off its visibility to restore the information in the channels.

The Blending Options Method

Double-click on a layer tile, hold down Alt (Windows), Opt (Mac OS) if you are double-clicking a layer name to access the Blending Options, or choose Layer → Layer Style → Blending Options. Next, in the Layer Style dialog box, turn off the channel(s) in the Advanced Blending section that you do not want to print. You can turn the channel(s) back on by accessing the dialog box again.

Printing a Folder Full of Images

Next time your boss asks you to print a folder full of images, don't panic or feign illness and hope that he or she will ask a colleague to do it. You can batch print in one go any number of folders and justifiably ask for a raise in doing it in record time or put a Do Not Disturb sign on your office door and play some golf while Photoshop does the hard work.

Before you can batch print, there are two things you must do:

- One, create a preset in the printer driver dialog box.

- Two, create an action that opens an image, sets options in the Print with Preview dialog box, selects the preset in the printer driver dialog box, and then sends the file to the printer.

To create a preset in the printer driver dialog box and the necessary action, take the following steps:

1. Have a dummy file open and then choose File → Print.

2. In the Print dialog box, create a preset, save it, and cancel out of the dialog box.

3. In the Actions palette, begin recording a new action (see Chapter 15 for information on creating actions).

4. Choose File ➜ Print with Preview and select the appropriate settings (see the "Print with Preview" section, earlier in the chapter).

5. Select Page Preset, the appropriate settings, and then click the OK button to apply and exit.

6. Back in the Print with Preview dialog box, select Print.

7. In the Print dialog box, select the preset you saved earlier.

8. Select Print.

9. Choose File ➜ Close.

10. Stop recording.

11. In Bridge, rotate your images so that all of them have the same orientation as the option you selected in the Page Preset dialog box (step 5).

12. Create shortcuts (Windows), aliases (Mac OS) for all the folders that you want to print and drop them one at a time into the other folders so that you form a daisy chain that ends with the top-level folder. If you are printing the contents of only one folder or your folders are already arranged in a hierarchical order, you obviously do not need to create shortcuts/aliases.

13. Having got the preparation out of the way, you can now start the actual batch: Choose File ➜ Automate ➜ Batch.

14. In the Batch dialog box, the action you just created should be selected for you in the Play section of the dialog box. If not, select it.

15. Select a Source folder (the top-level folder in the daisy chain or hierarchy).

16. Check the following commands: Override Action "Open" Commands, Include All Subfolders, Suppress File Open Options Dialogs, Suppress Color Profile Warnings.

17. Choose Destination: None.

18. Check Errors: Log Errors to File and then select a location for the log. If you intend to stay by the computer, select Stop For Errors.

19. Make sure that plenty of paper is in the tray and press the OK button.

With a bit of luck, all should go smoothly and you can enjoy a well-earned break. If not, check the log and make any adjustments.

CAUTION Not all printer driver settings can be recorded in an action. Make sure that they are set as per the recorded action by printing one file.

Printing Quick Hacks

Here are some quick hacks to help you avoid some printing pitfalls and to add to your printing options.

■ **Printing Selected Portions of a Document.** If you need to print only a small portion of your document—for example, to save paper—there's no need to crop the document, print it, and then undo, or dupe it, crop it, and then print. Just draw a marquee around the portion that you want to print and then select Print Selected Area in the Print with Preview dialog box. You can find it under Scaled Print Size. The option becomes available only if you have a rectangular or square selection active in the document.

■ **Printing Single Plates from CMYK and Duotone Documents.** If you are working with CMKY or Duotone documents and you need to output the channels as separate pages, you can do this directly from Photoshop. To do so, in the Print with Preview dialog box, choose Separations from the Color Handling pop-up menu. The menu is available only when you are in the Color Management section of the dialog box and Document is selected in the Print section of the dialog box.

■ **Centering Images on the Printed Page.** When you print from Photoshop, the image doesn't always appear in the center of the page. This confuses many users because they can see that the Center Image in the Print with Preview dialog box is selected (the default) but find that it has no effect.

This is because Photoshop centers the image with respect to the margin defined by the printer driver and not with respect to the paper's edge. The default margin is usually uneven, being wider at the leading edge, forcing the image to print higher toward the top and appear off-center.

If your printer driver supports printing to the paper's edge (that is, with no margins), you can define a custom page size in the Page Setup dialog box that has no margins and use it to print all documents that require the image to be centered (Figure 16-12). Photoshop will still center the image in respect to the margin, but because it overlaps the paper's edge, the image will appear to center with respect to the paper's edge.

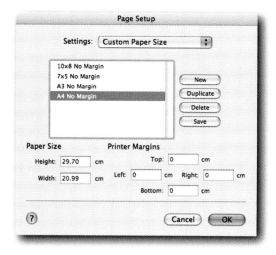

FIGURE 16-12: **Custom Paper Size dialog box, accessed from the Page Setup dialog box for an Epson inkjet printer.**

395

- **Automatically Scaling Images to Fit Media.** If you see a warning saying that your image is larger than the paper's printable area when you select Print, you can either click Cancel and choose a custom paper size with no margins from the Page Setup dialog box (if your printer driver supports no margins) or select Scale to Fit Media from the Scaled Print Size section of the Print with Preview dialog box and let Photoshop do the resizing for you.

- **Adding File Names to Prints.** To add a filename to a print for easier identification, select Labels in the Print with Preview dialog box, under Output. Photoshop will add the filename above the image. Just be aware that the option is sticky and will persist if you print any more files in the same session.

  If you have a number of files that can benefit from the filename's being printed, record an action that opens a file, selects Labels, prints, and closes the file. You can then use the action in a Batch command on a folder or selected files in Bridge.

Summary

Whether you're printing from Photoshop or from another application, the path is not a smooth one by any means. Nevertheless, the outputting to print hacks you have learned should go some way toward smoothing the bumps and filling some of the craters you are likely to encounter on the path to that final goal: the print.

However, do bear in mind that the print is heavily dependent on the judgment calls you make while editing, and those in turn are dependent on not only calibrating and characterizing your screen but also your printer. Bringing both online will save you wasted hours, frustration, and a fortune in expensive materials.

If you have been putting off the evil day, now is a good time to pluck up courage, bite the bullet, take the bull by the horns, and invest in color-management tools (see Chapter 12 for more details). With the right tools, monitor, printer, ink, and paper combination, you should be able to provide aim-prints as guides to your commercial printer and proofs to your clients that instill confidence not only in your editing abilities but also in the consistency and reliability with which you can produce prints.

chapter **17**

Outputting to the Web

It's no exaggeration to say that the World Wide Web has brought about the biggest publishing revolution since the invention of the printing press. The upside is that anyone can now publish, and the downside is that nearly everyone does! Because there are very few standards and new ones are being invented almost daily or old ones broken, it's left up to the publisher to avoid the pitfalls and to successfully navigate through the standards maze.

Some of the chaos is the inevitable result of forcing the WWW to be what it was never intended to be: a soft version of the hard publications. Designers are constantly striving to create visually pleasing publications using a language (HTML) that was primarily intended to carry only cold, faceless streams of hard facts, and succeeding against all expectations by employing various hacks to overcome the limitations of the language and the hardware used to view the online publications.

Editing and Preparing Images for the Web

When you publish on the WWW, as far as graphics are concerned the biggest hurdle that a publisher needs to clear is the lack of faithful color reproduction. Your publication is inevitably going to be seen on a monitor and, sadly, very few monitors are characterized, that is, have had their white point, brightness, contrast set to a standard. That means that your graphics will end up looking darker or lighter, biased toward one color or another, more saturated or less saturated than they appeared on your monitor; basically, the online "printed" versions bear little resemblance to the originals.

The size of the graphic matters, too, because not all "readers" are equipped with fast connections. Two factors control size: the number of pixels and the bits used to describe the color of those pixels. To reduce file size, you have to either reduce the number of pixels or sacrifice color fidelity by reducing the number of hues. In most cases, you will have to do both: reduce size to a few hundred kilobytes and use some means of compressing or shedding some of the colors.

The hacks in this section can help you sidestep some of the pitfalls, clear some of the hurdles, and accelerate your workflow.

Taking the Guesswork Out of Resizing

When you include an image in a Web page, it sometimes takes a number of tries before you can settle on a final size. Rather than rely on trial and error, here is a hack that you can employ. It does away with all the guesswork and goes right to the heart of the problem: matching the resized image and the on-screen preview.

1. Set your monitor resolution to 1024×768. You don't need to do this, but because most Web sites are designed with this resolution in mind, it's a good idea to work at the same resolution as the one used by the average surfer.

2. In the Navigator palette, use the Zoom slider to resize the on-screen preview until it looks right to you.

3. Highlight the Zoom slider magnification percentage value and then copy it onto the Clipboard.

4. Open the Image Size dialog box (Image ➜ Image Size) and make sure that the checkboxes for Constrain Proportions and Resample Image are selected.

5. Select Percent from the Width pop-up menu, located under Pixel Dimensions, not Document Size.

6. Paste the Clipboard contents into the Width text field.

7. Click the OK button to exit Image Size.

8. Double-click the Zoom tool icon to view actual pixels, or select View ➜ Actual Pixels.

Your resized image's dimensions should match the on-screen view that the Navigator palette generated in step 1. No more wasted guesswork. Save that for next week's lottery!

Creating Irregular Shaped Image Maps

Image maps are used in Web pages to define areas of an image that a user can click in a browser to navigate to a specified URL. For example, a map of the world can have each country defined by a discrete image map and each image map linked to a different URL. When users click a country's outline, they are taken to the Web site related to that country.

In ImageReady, you can use the Rectangle, Circle, and Polygonal Image Map tools to define sections of an image as discrete image maps. However, if a map needs to encompass the entire layer content, you are better off using the New Layer Based Image Map command from the Layer menu. Layer based image maps provide a lot more flexibility because, when the content changes dimensions, the image maps automatically change in concert (the content can be regular, as in square or rectangular, or totally irregular).

To create irregular shaped image maps, take the following steps:

1. Make sure that the Image Map palette is in view (Window → Image Map). See Figure 17-1.

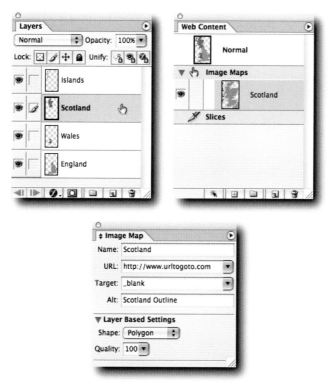

FIGURE **17-1:** The Layers, Web Content, and Image Map palettes show the progress of a new layer-based Image Map. Here, the outline of the content on the selected layer (Scotland) is being used as an Image Map to jump to when a user clicks it in a browser.

2. Select the layer that you wish to define as an image map.

3. Choose Layer → New Layer Based Image Map Area.

4. In the Image Map palette, insert/select the following information:

In the URL text field, insert the address to go to when the image map area is clicked in a browser.

399

In the Target text field, specify how you want the link to be displayed:

- **_blank**—To leave the original browser window open and display the linked page in a new window
- **_self**—To display the linked page in the open window
- **_parent**—To display the linked page in the current parent frameset
- **_top**—To remove the current frames and to display the linked page in the entire browser window

In the Alt field, enter a text description of the image (this can help visually impaired people who are using special software to surf and to navigate).

From the Shape pop-up menu, select Polygon; to conform the map more closely to the layer content, increase the Quality threshold from the pop-up slider or enter a higher value in the text field.

To preview in your default Browser, click the Preview in YourBrowser button in the Toolbox or Ctrl+Alt+P (Windows), ⌘+Opt+P (Mac OS).

TIP You can hide/show the Image Map's visibility by pressing A on the keyboard.

In-Betweening

Tweening is shorthand for in-betweening. It describes a process used by traditional animators to depict the practice of inserting frames between two images to give the appearance of a smooth transition from the first to the last frame in a sequence with minimal redrawing (only the parts that change are redrawn).

If you need to fade out an animation, rather than duplicate 10 frames and change their layer's opacity from 100% to 0% in steps, use the Tween command to create a smooth fade automatically. To do so, take the following steps:

1. Duplicate the frame (don't select any other frame).

2. Set the opacity of the duplicated frame's layer to 0%.

3. Select Tween from the Animation palette menu or click the Tweens Animation Frames button at the base of the palette.

4. In the Tween dialog box, select:
   - Tween With: Previous Frame (the default selection)
   - Frames to Add (accept the default)
   - Layers, select All Layers
   - Parameters, select Opacity

5. Click the OK button.

Play back the animation and admire the smoothness of your fade. If it's jerky, undo and add more frames; bear in mind that each extra frame adds to the file size, which in turn will add to the download time when the animation is played back on the Internet.

The Tween command is not limited just to creating smooth fades by varying the opacity of successive frames; you can also choose layer position and applied effects in the Tween dialog box (Figure 17-2).

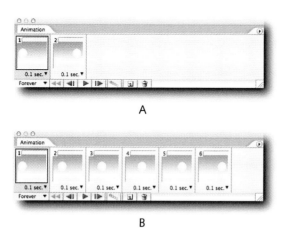

A

B

FIGURE 17-2: The Tween command automatically generates frames to fill in gaps. In this example, six frames were added to make the ball slide across the frame.

TIP   If you like to use keyboard shortcuts, here's a nice one for starting and stopping animations in ImageReady. To start an animation, hold down Shift and press the Spacebar. To stop an animation, either repeat the shortcut or press the Esc key.

Copying Hexadecimal Colors

If you are using hexadecimal colors in an HTML editor and need to convert the RGB color values in your Photoshop document to hexadecimal, you can set the Color palette to read in hexadecimal values from the palette menu. To copy the color values, select Copy Color as HTML from the palette menu.

In ImageReady, the Info palette displays the hexadecimal values next to the RGB values by default. In Photoshop, you can change the reading by selecting Palette Options from the palette menu and then choosing Web Color for one of the readouts; alternatively, click one of the eyedropper icons and then choose Web Color from the pop-up menu.

If the Eyedropper tool is selected, you can also right-click (Windows), Ctrl-click (Mac OS), use the contextual menu to copy any color under the pointer as hexadecimal values, and then paste into your HTML editor, or text editor. This contextual menu is also available when you are working in the Color Picker (Figure 17-3). Just hover the pointer over the document window and right-click (Windows), Ctrl-click (Mac OS) to access the Copy Color as HTML command.

FIGURE 17-3: **You can copy a color as hexadecimal values while working in the Color Picker by using the contextual menu in the document window.**

Two points to bear in mind: One, wherever you rest the pointer defines the source of the color; two, the Eyedropper Sample Size setting has a direct bearing on the sampled color. For example, if it's set to Point Sample, you may think that you are sampling from a patch of color when in fact you might be sampling a stray pixel. Therefore, unless you can see the actual pixel you are sampling, it's safer to set the Eyedropper tool to Sample Size: 3 × 3 Average, which you can do from the contextual menu.

Blending GIFs into Backgrounds

One of the advantages of using the GIF file format is its support for transparency. However, the GIF file format and the less popular PNG-8 support only single-level transparency, which means that pixels of a given color are either opaque or transparent. The PNG-24 file format does support multilevel transparency but, because it's not supported by all browsers and also creates comparatively large files by necessity, is rarely used on the Web.

To overcome the multilevel transparency limitation, you can use a matte color that will allow you to blend the edges of the transparent areas with a background color. By default, when you include transparency, a white matte is added to the edges of transparent pixels. This can work fine if the Web page's background is a light color. However, against a darker background, the matte color becomes obtrusive (Figure 17-4).

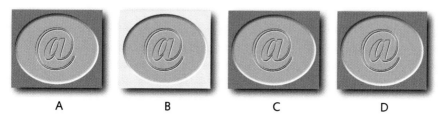

A   B   C   D

FIGURE 17-4: A—A button saved with transparency and Matte: None. The edge is not anti-aliased and shows signs of jaggedness. B—Same button saved as a GIF with transparency and default matte color and then placed in an HTML page. Against a lighter background, it works fine. C—However, placed on a darker background, the white fringing is clearly visible. D—Same button saved with a matte color that matches the background color of the HTML page. The button blends perfectly into the background.

To save a GIF in Photoshop with transparency and a suitable matte color, take the following steps:

1. Select a layer containing transparency. Deselect layers containing a background color; otherwise, Photoshop assumes that you want to use the background color as the matte color.

2. Choose File ➜ Save for Web.

3. In the Save for Web dialog box, select GIF from the Preset pop-up menu, or from the Optimize File Format pop-up menu. At this point, the Transparency and the Matte options should be automatically selected for you.

4. To see the matte color, select the Optimize tab in the preview window.

5. Choose a matte color from the Matte pop-up menu. If you want to specify a color as a hexadecimal value, choose Other, and then, in the Color Picker, enter the value in the text field marked with the hash sign (#).

6. Click the Save button or the browser button at the bottom of the dialog box to view the GIF against the matte color.

The steps are very similar in ImageReady except for the fact that you use the Optimize palette rather than Save for Web, and you must have the Optimize tab selected in the document window to view the matte color.

CAUTION   Mattes cannot be used if the Color Table palette is used to drop colors to transparency. In Photoshop, the Color Table palette is located in the Save for Web dialog box. In ImageReady, it's accessed from the Window menu, as are all palettes.

Applying Weighted Optimization

When you need to keep the file size down and quality up, Photoshop includes a little technique called Weighted Optimization that allows you to vary the optimization settings locally by clever use of masks. For example, if you need to upload a graphic that contains important text, you can mask the text and apply strong optimization settings to the background only, thus ensuring that the text stays nice and crisp, while the unimportant, or less important, background receives the necessary optimization needed to keep the file size down (Figure 17-5).

Using Weighted Optimization, you can control the amount of dithering and color reduction applied to GIF and PNG-8 files, the dithering to WBMP files, the lossiness to GIF files, and the quality level for JPEG files.

The technique works by using a black mask to protect the important areas, which then receive the least dithering, lossy settings or quality amount, and a white mask to define the unimportant areas, which then receive the most dithering, lossy settings and least quality. File size is reduced while the appearance of a higher-quality image is maintained.

To apply weighted optimization, take the following steps:

1. Make sure that your document contains an alpha channel mask, type, or shape layers; masks are created automatically for the latter and you need only select them in the appropriate dialog boxes.

2. In Photoshop, choose File ➜ Save for Web, or Ctrl+Alt+Shift+S (Windows), ⌘+Opt+Shift+S (Mac OS). In ImageReady, use the Optimize palette.

3. Depending on which optimization setting you want to apply, click the mask button, located next to the Selective, Lossy, and Dither text fields for GIFs or the Quality text field for JPEGs; WBMP contains just the one control for Dither.

4. In the pop-up dialog box, select a mask or select an alpha channel from the Channel pop-up menu. For example, to apply minimum quality level to a background and maximum to text while saving the file as a JPEG:

   a. In Save for Web, click the mask button next to the Quality pop-up slider.

   b. In the Modify Quality Setting dialog box, select Use: All Text Layers, All Vector Shape Layers if the file contains shapes layers, or an alpha channel that you created before entering the dialog box.

   c. Use the Quality sliders to control the amount of quality to apply to the masked (black) and unmasked (white) areas of the image (Figure 17-5).

A

B

C

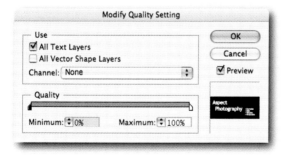

D

FIGURE 17-5: GIFs, JPEGs, and WBMP files can benefit from weighted optimization. In this example, optimization was applied equally (A) to text and background, (B) to the background only and (C) to neither.

Creating Galleries and QuickTime Movies

Web Photo Galleries allow you to exhibit your work on the Web and to receive feedback from clients. Photoshop ships with HTML and Flash templates that you can use to create a style that suits your visual and practical needs.

If you like a style but wish to customize it, for example, by replacing the default banner with your banner, you can open the template in a text editor or an HTML editor and make the necessary modifications.

Although this feature is not blatantly obvious at first, ImageReady has the means to create and edit QuickTime movies; these, too, can be streamed and published on the Web.

Web Photo Galleries

You can create a Web Photo Gallery from Bridge or Photoshop. Creating a WPG from Bridge has one advantage: You can choose which images in a folder to include and which to exclude.

To create a gallery from Bridge containing selected images and a feedback form, take the following steps:

1. Select all the images that you want to include in the gallery. You can use the usual selection methods for including and excluding files—Shift-click for contiguous selection and Ctrl-click (Windows), ⌘-click (Mac OS) to take from or add to a selection—as well as the commands from the Edit menu.

2. Label them or rate them and then use the Filter menu on the toolbar to view only the rated/labeled files (see Chapter 4 for more on rating and labeling files).

3. Arrange the files in the order that you want to see them in the gallery (you can drag them to a new position). If the gallery order is not important, skip this step.

NOTE Dragging a file to a new position automatically selects Manually in the View ➜ Sort menu. You will not be able to use the Refresh command until you select another command from the menu.

4. Choose Tools ➜ Photoshop ➜ Web Photo Gallery.

5. In the WPG dialog box, choose a style that contains a feedback form from the Styles pop-up menu, or another style, and then skip the next step.

6. Enter the e-mail address in the text field that you want to display as the contact address for the gallery.

7. In the Source Images section, choose a Destination folder for the gallery.

8. In the Options section, choose the following items from the pop-up menu: General, Banner, Large Images, Thumbnails, Custom Colors, and Security; then, fill in the text fields below.

9. Click the OK button to create the gallery.

The gallery will be displayed in your default browser after it has been created.

If you know advanced HTML, you can customize the templates for the preset styles in an HTML or text editor. You can find the templates in the `~\Adobe Photoshop CS2\ Presets\Web Photo Gallery` folder.

Each template contains HTML code and tokens. Tokens are text strings used by Photoshop to replace corresponding options in the WPG dialog box and can be added to a template. For a list of tokens that can be used, refer to Chapter 20 in the User Guide. Alternatively, type *Web photo gallery style tokens* into the Search field of the Adobe Help Center for Photoshop CS2.

NOTE If you want to create a WPG from a folder, select it from the Folders palette in Bridge or, alternatively, invoke the WPG command from within Photoshop.

Flash Photo Galleries

Photoshop ships with two Flash photo galleries: Flash—Gallery 1 and Flash—Gallery 2. You can create one in the same way as you can an HTML gallery by selecting one of the styles from the Styles pop-up menu in the Web Photo Gallery dialog box.

There are no controls in the Web Photo Gallery dialog box for selecting an audio file or changing the parameters of the Flash galleries. If you want to do either, you can employ a little workaround:

- To include an audio file with the gallery, name your mp3 file `useraudio.mp3` and place it in the selected style folder in the `~\Adobe Photoshop CS2\Presets\ Web Photo Gallery\Flash—Gallery 1`, or `Flash—Gallery 2` folder before you create the gallery or in the gallery folder after you have created it.

- To change the parameters manually, open the `galleryconfig.xml` file in a text editor: Notepad (Windows), TextEdit (Mac OS). You can find the file in the style folder for the gallery (see the paths mentioned previously).

After a gallery has been opened in a browser, you can navigate back and forth among the images by using the control strip that appears in the lower-right corner of the Web page. You can also use it to toggle audio on/off and start a slide show; alternatively, use the Left and Right Arrow keys, located by the numeric keypads, to move back and forth.

QuickTime Movies

Though just about everyone has heard about QuickTime, not everyone knows that you can create QuickTime movies in ImageReady from your animation without investing in expensive plug-ins. You can also open or place existing QuickTime movies as animations and then modify the frames. When you place a QuickTime, you can specify the range of frames to import or select the range by holding down the Shift key and then moving the slider on the controller bar. So, if you want to save your animation as a QuickTime movie, take the following steps:

1. Choose File ➜ Export ➜ Original Document.

2. Choose QuickTime Movie from the Save As Type menu (Windows), or Format menu (Mac OS).

3. In the Export Original dialog box, select Format: QuickTime Movie and click the OK button.

4. When the Compression Settings dialog box pops up, click the Options button and tick the Optimize for streaming checkbox if you intend to stream the movie.

5. Click the Save button.

That's it! You have just saved the animation as a QuickTime movie.

NOTE On the PC, the QuickTime Movie format is available only if QuickTime is installed on your computer (you can download it for free from www.apple.com).

Outputting to the Web Quick Hacks

The following quick hacks cover some essentials for optimizing images for the Web, as well as some insights into creating and editing slices.

- **Matching Colors in Save for Web.** If you work in a wide-gamut color space, such as Adobe RGB (1998) or ProPhoto RGB, the colors will not match the preview in Photoshop when you preview the file in Save for Web. This is because the preview in Save for Web is not color managed and mimics the Web.

  The majority of the browsers do not support ICC profiles and assume a color space that is closer to sRGB and, for that reason, so does Save for Web; consequently, your image will appear dull and desaturated compared to the preview in Photoshop. To avoid this pitfall, *convert* to sRGB by using the Convert to Profile command in the Edit menu. This way, when you send your graphics out into the great big ether, they will have some protection against the philistines viewing your publication.

- **Optimizing to a Given File Size.** Should you need to optimize a document to a predetermined file size, you can do it in Photoshop and ImageReady. In Photoshop, choose File ➜ Save for Web. In the dialog box, click the triangle button (located to the right of the Settings pop-up menu) and choose Optimize to File Size from the pop-up menu (Figure 17-6). To do the same in ImageReady, select Optimize to File Size from the Optimize palette menu.

- **Resizing and Exporting Transparent Images.** If you are unsure how to resize an image or how to include transparency in a GIF, Photoshop includes assistants that can help you walk through the steps. You can access both assistants, Resize Image and Export Transparent Image, from the Help menu. Bear the following points in mind when using assistants:

  - When you use either assistant, your original image is left untouched; the assistant instead creates a duplicate for you to save.

  - When you use the Resize Image assistant, it gives you the option to preview the on-screen size before accepting the new size.

  - For you to save transparency, an image must either include transparency or have a selection active before the assistant is invoked.

FIGURE 17-6: **Photoshop's Optimize To File Size dialog box, accessed from the Save for Web dialog box menu.**

- **Reducing JPEG File Size.** There's a direct correlation between sharpening an image, increased file size, and the JPEG format: The more sharpness you apply, the larger the file size will be in kilobytes when you come to output it as a JPEG. If sharpening increases file size, then the opposite is also true: blurring an image can dramatically reduce its file size. Therefore, to keep JPEG file sizes low, select the unimportant areas of your image (for example, the background), feather the selection, and apply a slight blur before you enter the Save for Web dialog box.

- **Preventing Go-Slows on the Web.** Sometimes, images destined for the Web aren't trimmed as closely as they could be if a little bit more care were applied or the grueling schedules were a tad bit less grueling. Fortunately, Photoshop includes a little feature specifically to help you trim the excess fat from your Web-bound images. It's called Trim, oddly enough, and you can access it from the Image menu (Figure 17-7). The command lets you crop your Web graphic as tightly as possible and produce the smallest possible file size. Therefore, if you are the conscientious type and want to help reduce the go-slows on the World Wide Web, you now know which command to use.

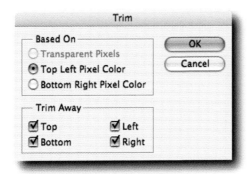

FIGURE 17-7: **The Trim command, accessed from the Image menu, can be used to shed surplus fat from overblown files.**

409

- **Copying Slices in ImageReady.** If you have sliced an image in Photoshop and need to duplicate the slices in another document, you really have no choice but to roll up your sleeves, grab the Slice tool, and slice the new document. You could record the whole process as an action and then run it on the new document, but that's not always feasible.

  To save time, open the documents in ImageReady, select the slices, and then copy and paste into the new document. You can select slices by choosing Select All User Slices from the Slice menu, or Ctrl+Shift+A (Windows), ⌘+Shift+A (Mac OS). Having copied the slices, choose Paste Slices from the Edit menu or Ctrl+V (Windows), ⌘+V (Mac OS).

- **Growing Slices Automatically.** A slice created from a layer encompasses all the pixels on that layer and, therefore, can grow and shrink automatically as the data on the layer is transformed or moved. For example, if you create a button on a layer and then create a layer-based slice and change the style of the button by adding a drop shadow, the slice will grow to accommodate the extra pixels. If you reposition the elements that make up the button, the slice will readjust accordingly.

  To create a layer-based slice in ImageReady or Photoshop, select a normal layer (cannot be a Background layer) and then choose Layer ➜ New Layer Based Slice.

  If you need to move, resize, or edit a layer-based slice manually, you must first promote it to a user slice. To do this in Photoshop, select the Slice Select tool and then click the Promote to User Slice button on the options bar. In ImageReady, choose Slices ➜ Promote to User Slice.

  The Slice tools are practically the same in Photoshop and ImageReady. However, it's easier to slice an image in ImageReady because of its ability to create slices from selections and guides, the dedicated Slice menu, and the ability to create slice sets that can be turned on and off.

- **Moving and Resizing Slices Precisely.** After slices have been created, they can be moved and resized with great precision. To do so, simply double-click with the Slice Select tool on the slice to bring up its Slice Options dialog box (if the Slice tool is active, hold down Ctrl (Windows), ⌘ (Mac OS) to toggle to the Slice Select tool). Enter the required location or size in the X (Horizontal) and Y (Vertical), or Width and Height text fields, respectively (Figure 17-8).

- **Preventing Clashes with Image Content.** If the slice borders are difficult to see in the document window because they blend into the background, you can change the color from Preferences ➜ Guides, Grids & Slices. You can also turn off the slice numbers by deselecting Show Slice Numbers from the same dialog box screen.

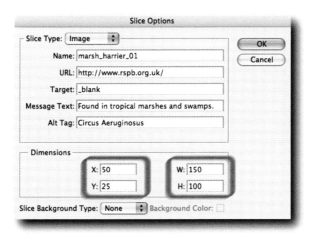

FIGURE 17-8: **The Slice Options dialog box; accessed by double-clicking a slice with the Slice Select tool.**

■ **Slicing Images Evenly.** Need to slice an image evenly into squares or rectangles? Well, there is no need to do complex math or spend hours creating guides and then slicing the image along them. Instead, take the following steps and let Photoshop and ImageReady do the work for you:

1. Choose the Slice Select tool from the Toolbox.

2. Click in the document window to select the slice that encompasses the canvas. This also activates the buttons on the options bar in Photoshop.

3. Click the Divide Slice button (In ImageReady, choose Slices → Divide Slice).

4. In the pop-up dialog box (Figure 17-9), decide how you want to divide the main slice and enter the required measurements in the appropriate text field.

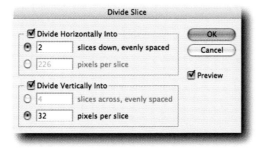

FIGURE 17-9: **Slices can be divided evenly without recourse to complex math in the Divide Slice dialog box.**

411

5. Click the OK button to exit and to accept the division.

As you enter a value, the new slices should appear in the main document window. If they do not, make sure that the Preview option under the Cancel button is selected.

Summary

There can be little doubt that Internet publishing will continue to make strides. Already, tools such as Flash, SVG (Scaleable Vector Graphics), and CSS (Cascading Style Sheets) have given the designer a means of either controlling or bypassing HTML deficiencies. However, traditional graphics and plain HTML still form a large part of Internet publishing, and learning to grapple with their limitations can enhance the look of your publication and the surfing experience of the users who read your online publications.

chapter **18**

Exploiting Filters and Photoshop Flexibility

Compared to other image editors on the market, Photoshop does not include too many auto commands or walkthrough wizards. However, as emphasized throughout much of the book, it makes up for this lack by giving the user the flexibility to perform almost any task in numerous ways.

Whether this flexibility has come about by accident or design is neither here nor there. The important thing is that you can take advantage of it by throwing a little lateral thinking into the mix and, consequently, overcome almost any image-editing problem, or conjure up new techniques and workflows. The hacks discussed in this final chapter give just an indication of what is possible, but first a word or two about using filters.

Hacking Filters

There are literally thousands of Photoshop filters that you can purchase or download for free from the Internet. The filters are designed to cover a variety of functions, ranging from filtering a file with preset settings, to adding ornamental edges, to analyzing a file scientifically.

Photoshop ships with no fewer than 105 filters, plus four panels that are also classed as filters. You can use the filters to create artistic effects or fake photographic effects, or to optimize images for output. As far as usage goes, these filters can be split into four broad categories:

- The standalone panels, such as Extract, Liquify, Pattern Maker, and Vanishing Point; used to extract, distort content, create custom patterns, and clone in perspective, respectively

- Those that can be applied through the Filter Gallery, such as Colored Pencil, Bas Relief, Grain, and so forth; used to create artistic effects

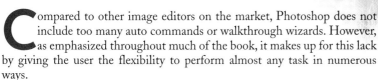

in this chapter

- ◗ Filtering a layer nondestructively

- ◗ Working with the Lighting Effects filter

- ◗ Creating printable grids

- ◗ Creating backgrounds

- The filters that have their own dialog boxes and can accept custom settings, such as Lens Correction, Smart Sharpen, and High Pass; used to optimize files for output

- The filters that don't have customizable settings, such as Despeckle, Sharpen Edges, Blur, and so forth; used to apply default settings for quick optimization

Some of the filters are very memory hungry and can take considerable time to calculate and to apply settings, especially when the allocated RAM has been consumed and efficiency is well below 100% or you are working on large files in 16-Bits/Channel mode. In those circumstances, you can take some evasive measures before you apply a filter: purge clipboard, purge histories, close Bridge (and other applications and utilities not being used currently, such as a browser or e-mail client), increase the amount of available RAM, or reduce number of fonts and plug-ins. Decreasing or increasing the filter settings can also help. For instance, if you are using Palette Knife, decrease the Stroke Size or increase the Stroke Detail.

TIP Selecting a part of an image and applying the filter can also help to gauge an effect before applying it to the full image.

Applying RGB Filters to CMYK Files

A number of Photoshop filters work only on images in RGB color mode. So, what do you do, for example, if you want to apply the Stylize ➜ Glowing Edges filter to an image in CMYK color mode? Your first thought might be to change the color mode to RGB and then back again to CMYK. However, mode changes are usually not recommended while you're editing an image and should be preformed only as a last resort, or as a necessary step in a technique that will off-set the damage that may be done by the mode change.

Here's a little workaround that you can use that bypasses the need for a mode change.

1. In the Channels palette, select one of the channels.

2. Apply the filter, select another channel, and then use the keyboard shortcut Ctrl+F (Windows), ⌘+F to apply the filter again.

3. Apply the filter this way to all four channels.

Now when you click the composite channel, you will find that the filter has been applied to the image as a whole and you have avoided a color mode change.

CAUTION Not all filters can be used this way and achieve the same results as though the filter had been applied to the composite channel. This is especially true of filters that modify pixels randomly.

Reapplying Filter Settings

To reapply a filter using the previously used settings without first having to call the dialog box from the filter menu, press Ctrl+F (Windows), ⌘+F (Mac OS). The shortcut works for only the last used filter. If another filter has been used in the meantime, you have no choice other than to select the filter again from the filter menu. If you need access to the last used filter and its dialog box, including the last-used setting, press Ctrl+Alt+F (Windows), ⌘+Opt+F (Mac OS).

Filtering a Layer Nondestructively

When you apply a filter to a layer, the pixels change value and cannot be reverted without undoing all the edits that followed in its wake. The following workaround applies the filter to a layer that can be positioned anywhere in the layer stack and acts as a poor man's adjustment layer.

1. Create a new layer above the layer to which you want to apply a filter effect.

2. Fill it with 50% gray pixels (Edit → Fill → Contents Use: 50% Gray).

3. Set its blend mode to Overlay so that only the filter effect interacts with the layer below.

4. Apply the filter (Figure 18-1).

FIGURE 18-1: The Graphic Pen filter applied to a layer filled with 50% Gray, the layer's blend mode set to Overlay, duplicated and flipped horizontally and the opacity lowered to 50%.

415

This way of applying a filter makes it possible to modify the filter effect further by:

- Using a layer blend mode other than Overlay
- Duplicating the layer and then changing its blend mode
- Reducing the layer's opacity
- Using the Blend If options found in the Layer Style dialog box
- Turning the layer's visibility off if the effect is no longer required

Unfortunately, not all filters listed under the Filter menu can be applied this way. However, applying textures via the Texturizer filter works extremely well. The results will also differ from applying the filters directly to a layer, which is something to bear in mind.

There is one other method you can use to apply a filter nondestructively, but it can be used only in the current session. It involves the use of Smart Objects.

1. Select the layer to which you want to apply a filter effect.
2. Choose Group into New Smart Object from the Layers palette menu.
3. Double-click the layer thumbnail. Photoshop will open a temporary PSB document containing the layer content (you cannot apply a filter directly to a Smart Object, but you can to the PSB document).
4. Apply the filter to the PSB document and save it. When you save the PSB document, Photoshop applies any changes you made to it to the parent file.

As long as you do not close the PSB document, you can revert it using its histories, apply another filter, and then save it again to apply the filter to the parent document. You can do this as many times as you like without fear of damaging the original content.

TIP You can also use this technique to apply a filter to a shape layer without having to rasterize it first. To do so, after creating a 50% gray layer above the shape layer and changing its blend mode to Overlay, clip it by holding down Alt (Windows), Opt (Mac OS) and then clicking the dividing line between the two layer tiles.

Placing a Lens Flare Precisely

The Lens Flare filter lets you simulate flares caused by light sources shining directly into the camera lens. You can place the lens flare pretty accurately by moving the crosshair in the filter's proxy window (Figure 18-2). However, if you need to place it more precisely, take the following steps:

1. Place the pointer where you would like to center the lens flare and make a note of the X, Y readings in the Info Palette.
2. Select the layer you wish to apply the filter to and then choose Filter ➜ Render ➜ Lens Flare.

3. When the Lens Flare dialog box opens, hold down Alt (Windows), Opt (Mac OS) and click anywhere in the Lens Flare proxy window to access the Precise Flare Center dialog box (Figure 18-2).

4. Enter the X and Y coordinates that you noted earlier.

5. Click the OK button to exit the Precise Flare Center dialog box.

6. Click the OK button in the Lens Flare dialog box. After you exit the Lens Flare dialog box, you will see the lens flare placed precisely where you specified.

TIP You can also control the placement of a flare by applying the Lens Flare filter to a layer filled with black and then changing the layer blend mode to Screen. Depending on the shape and size of the flare, you may see some sharp cutoff using this method when you move the flare.

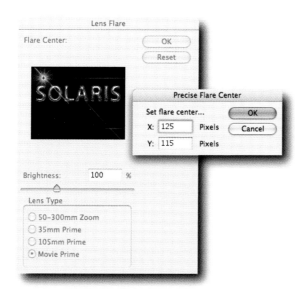

FIGURE 18-2: **Lens flare pop-up dialog box used to place a flare precisely.**

Creating Seamless Patterns

Need to make seamless patterns for tiling Web page backgrounds or for filling in areas when repairing photographs? You can do it painlessly in Photoshop by using the often-overlooked Pattern Maker filter. To create a seamless pattern, just take the following steps:

1. Use a marquee tool to select a portion of your image (this will form the basis of the pattern) and then copy it onto the clipboard.

2. Create a new layer (if you don't, the new pattern will replace the content of the currently active layer).

417

3. Choose Filter ➜ Pattern Maker.

4. In the Pattern Maker dialog box, check the box Use Clipboard as Sample.

5. Next, click the Use Image Size button and then the Generate button. You can click the Generate button as many times as you like to generate another random pattern based on the current settings.

6. When you're satisfied with the pattern, click the OK button to fill the currently active layer with the pattern.

The dialog box contains a number of settings that you can work your way through. The Offset setting determines the amount of offset for each tile; the Smoothness determines the smoothness of the tile edges; the Sample Detail setting determines the size of the image sampled for each tile (the higher the setting, the more detail included in the tile). The video buttons at the bottom of the Tile History section allow you to view all the iterations. The Save button is very useful. Any tiles you save are added to the Pattern Picker palette and may be used by any tool or command that can make use of a pattern, such as Pattern Stamp tool or Layer Style.

Working with the Lighting Effects Filter

The Lighting Effects filter adds depth to an image. It does this in two ways: by varying the lighting intensity and its quality across the image's surface and by adding a bevel and emboss effect using the information in an alpha channel. The filter works only on RGB images in 8-Bits/Channel mode.

The filter dialog box (Filter ➜ Render ➜ Lighting Effects) is divided into five sections (Figure 18-3):

- In the Style section, you can select from a number of preset styles from the pop-up menu. You can also add your own by saving customized settings, or delete the current style.

- In the Light Type section, you can choose between a spotlight, directional, or omni type from the pop-up menu and specify its intensity and focus by using the sliders. You can change the color of the light by clicking the color box (white by default) and then selecting a color in the Color Picker dialog box.

- In the Properties section, you can modify the quality (how the light reflects off surfaces), the exposure, and the ambience (whether the light source is diffused by ambient light and to what extent). As with Light Type, you can modify the color by clicking the color box and then choosing a color in the Color Picker dialog box.

- In the Texture Channel section, you can elect to apply a surface texture by selecting a channel and vary the depth and height by using the Height slider.

- To the left is a small proxy window for previewing and, below that, a button for adding new lights and the Trash icon for deleting lights by dragging them onto it (you can't select a light and click to delete; that method for deleting isn't available).

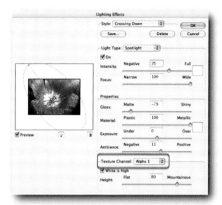

FIGURE 18-3: The Lighting Effects dialog box. Left. Original image. Right. The image copied into a new alpha channel and then selected from the Texture Channel pop-up menu in the Lighting Effects dialog box.

Bear the following pointers in mind when you work in the dialog box:

- To add a new light source, click the light bulb icon and then drag it into the preview window, or press Alt (Windows), Opt (Mac OS), click an existing light, and then drag to make a copy.

- To delete a light, click it and then press Backspace (Windows), Del (Mac OS), or drag it onto the Trash icon.

- You can reposition a light source by clicking the point in the center of the beam and then dragging to a new position.

- To widen, narrow, or rotate a beam, click the square gray handles on the side and then drag outwards or inwards.

- To jump from one light source to another, press Alt+Tab (Windows), Opt+Tab (Mac OS).

The Smart Way to Find Edges

If you use the Find Edges filter to create selection edges for sharpening images or for creating watercolors, you may want to investigate the possibilities of Smart Blur. Contrary to what the name may imply, the Smart Blur filter can be used to find the edges and can sometimes produce better results than the Find Edges filter (it also contains options whereas Find Edges is a take-it-or-leave-it filter).

To find the edges in an image, open the filter dialog box (Filter ➜ Blur ➜ Smart Blur), click the Mode pop-up menu and choose Edge Only, or Overlay Edge, and then select a Quality level from the pop-up above it. As the names imply, choosing Edge Only creates edges and replaces the image detail with black, which can be knocked out quite easily by changing the blend mode to screen or by using the Blend If sliders in Blending Options; if you want to play with the edges, you may wish to work on a duped layer. Choosing Overlay Edge superimposes the edges on the image (Figure 18-4).

FIGURE 18-4: In this example, the image layer was duped, the Smart Blur filter applied (Radius 3.0; Threshold 25.0; Quality: High; Mode: Edge Only). Next, the Rough Pastels filter was applied and the layer blend mode set to Darken. The image layer was duped and positioned at the top of the stack, its opacity reduced to 12% and Blend mode set to Hard Light.

Taking Advantage of Photoshop Flexibility

Photoshop's tools and commands lend themselves to exploitation because of their versatility. This versatility often causes much confusion and gnashing of teeth by new or infrequent users. However, by including a little lateral thinking, that versatility can be used as a catalyst by the imaginative user. The following hacks are included to whet your appetite for experimentation; use them as a springboard to greater things.

Creating Printable Grids

Although you can create a grid overlay in Photoshop and ImageReady, you cannot edit it or print it. To create an editable/printable grid, you have to apply some of that legendary Photoshop versatility. Here's one approach:

1. Create a new transparent layer.

2. Use the Rectangular Marquee tool to create a black cross with equal sides. Color it if you like or leave it black and color it later.

3. With the Rectangular Marquee tool active, hold down Alt+Shift (Windows), Opt+Shift (Mac OS) and draw a square selection from the center of the cross (Figure 18-5).

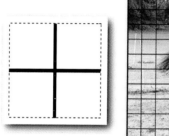 

FIGURE 18-5: A printable grid defined from a cross on a transparent layer and then applied through a Pattern Overlay command in the Layer Style dialog box.

4. Choose Edit → Define → Pattern and call it Grid Pattern.

5. Create a new, blank layer.

6. Choose Edit → Fill and then Contents → Use: Pattern → Custom and select the Grid Pattern that you saved in step 4.

7. Click the OK button.

To fill a layer with a grid pattern and to have the option of scaling the grid, you can choose Layer → Style → Pattern Overlay (or a Pattern Adjustment layer) at step 6 and then use the Scale slider to expand and contract.

Creating Space Age Grids

This approach to creating a grid pattern can be adapted to create backgrounds and effects, for example, lightning bolts, ocean or pond surfaces, and the like. You start with an empty layer, fill it with clouds, and then build on that base by using filters, adjustments, and layer stacking (see Figure 18-6 for the end result).

1. Make new document.
2. Press D to reset foreground and background swatches.
3. Fill with clouds: Filter ➜ Render ➜ Clouds.
4. Apply the Mosaic filter: Filter ➜ Pixelate ➜ Mosaic. Set the cell size to 60, or experiment.
5. Apply Auto Levels: Image ➜ Adjustments ➜ Auto Levels.
6. Apply filter Glowing Edges: Filter ➜ Stylize ➜ Glowing Edges. Set Edge Width to 1, Brightness to 7, Smoothness to 6, or play with the settings. Click the OK button.
7. Make a new layer.
8. Set foreground color to R56, G77, B204, or another color of choice, and fill the new layer.
9. Change the blend mode to Color.

Creating a Grayscale Step Wedge

Sometimes, having an on-screen grayscale step wedge as a visual reference can be very handy when correcting an image. It can also be used as a quick test image to see whether a monitor is overcontrasted or contains a colorcast. Furthermore, you can print it and see how your printer is laying down ink at the various steps. Grayscale step wedges can also help when you're learning how to use the Blend If commands (see Chapter 6 for more information on Blend If). To create a 17-step grayscale wedge, take the following steps:

1. Create a new RGB document.
2. Press D to set the foreground and background color swatches to their default black and white, or click the Default Foreground and Background Colors icon in the Toolbox.
3. Select the Gradient tool and then press Enter (Windows), Return (Mac OS) to open the gradient picker.
4. Double-click the first gradient to select it (it should be a foreground to background gradient). Double-clicking should also dismiss the gradient picker.
5. In the Options bar, select Linear Gradient by clicking the first of the five inline icons next to the gradient picker. Make sure that the Dither option is *not* selected.
6. Fill the current layer with a linear gradient by dragging the tool from the left edge to the right edge of the document.
7. Choose Image ➜ Adjustments ➜ Equalize.
8. Finally, choose Image ➜ Adjustments ➜ Posterize and enter a value of 17 in the Levels input field.
9. Click the OK button.

You have just created a 17-step grayscale wedge (Figure 18-7). Save it as a TIFF for future reference.

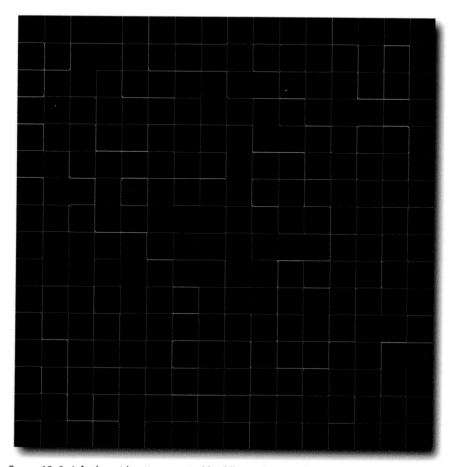

FIGURE 18-6: A funky grid pattern created by filling a layer with clouds and then using the Mosaic and the Glowing Edges filters.

FIGURE 18-7: A 17-step grayscale wedge made for reference.

The dither option for the Gradient tool is good for print reproduction (although extra, more visible noise often needs to be added as well). However, adding dither will increase the file size, which you may wish to take into consideration if outputting to the Web.

Creating Backgrounds

One of the pleasures of working in Photoshop comes from transforming images by changing backgrounds. This can be something as mundane as substituting a dull, overcast or overexposed sky with one from a library that sings of blue skies or skimpy cumulous clouds, or substituting the background with an abstract background. Alternatively, it could involve creating a design from the ground up and require an original background.

Creating original backgrounds in Photoshop is very easy by using a combination of tools, fills, and filters plus a little lateral thinking. This hack takes the Gradient tool and shows you how to create original abstract backgrounds and endless variations by simply changing the tool's blend mode (Figure 18-8 shows an example of this technique; including a few variations).

1. Create a new document in RGB mode.

2. Select the Gradient tool and then select its Linear Gradient option.

3. Select a gradient from the gradient picker.

4. Drag the tool from the left edge to right edge in the document window to apply a linear gradient.

5. Change the tool's blend mode to Difference.

6. Apply the same gradient again but in another direction (experiment is the byword here).

7. Apply Auto Levels (Image ➜ Adjustments ➜ Auto Levels).

8. Fade Auto Levels from the Edit menu (use your judgment).

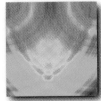

FIGURE 18-8: These backgrounds were created with the preceding technique, but it was varied slightly by using the Gradient tool in Reflected Gradient, Radial Gradient mode and by throwing other ingredients into the mix, such as the use of Difference Clouds and the Wave filter to apply some distortion.

Creating Fancy Photo Frames

If you need to create frames/borders around your images (Figure 18-9), you can invest in a plug-in and save yourself a lot of time (PhotoFrame from Extensis and Photo/Graphic Edges from Auto FX Software are highly recommended). However, if you can't invest money but can invest time, you can create your own artistic frames/borders without too much difficulty. Here's just one technique; you can easily modify it when you know the thinking behind it:

1. Create a new layer above your image layer.

2. Make a selection around your image with the Rectangular Marquee tool (use the Elliptical Marquee tool if you want to create vignettes, or turn your selection into a border by choosing Select ➜ Modify ➜ Border).

NOTE Borders created using the Border command have a limit of 200 px and are anti-aliased. Press Q to view the effect of the anti-aliasing.

3. Press Q to Invoke Quick Mask mode and apply a distortion filter to the selection, such as Filter ➜ Distortion ➜ Ocean Ripple.

NOTE You can apply most filters; just experiment with different ones after you know the basic steps.

4. Press Q once more to exit Quick Mask mode.

5. Press Ctrl+Shift+I (Windows), ⌘+Shift+I (Mac OS), or choose Select ➜ Inverse to inverse the selection.

NOTE This step is not necessary if the Border command is used in step 2.

6. Select a foreground color of your choice and then choose Edit ➜ Fill to fill with the foreground color.

Because you created the frame on its own layer, you can apply Layer Styles to it. Try the different effects: Drop Shadow, Satin, Stroke, Pattern Overlay, and so forth.

FIGURE 18-9: A fancy frame created by using a selection, applying the Ocean Ripple filter in Quick Mask Mode, and then adding a Layer Style for good measure.

Summary

With luck, the preceding hacks have whetted your appetite for exploring Photoshop's potential to be here, there, and everywhere when it comes to problem solving or providing tools and commands that can be used in ingenious and, almost, devious ways. If your appetite is indeed whetted, set aside some time and just play in Photoshop. Doing so will pay dividends in the future, usually in ways you could not have imagined or at crucial times when the clock is ticking and the commissioning editor or the client is breathing down your neck. Playing in Photoshop will allow you eventually to solve problems in unique ways, or forestall them before they have had the chance to raise their heads above the parapet.

Troubleshooting

Quite a number of problems can be solved by deleting the Prefs or by retracing your steps. Things don't "suddenly" happen, as a rule, although they do at times. More often than not, a problem can be traced to another application's being installed, a change of hardware, or even a setting that was changed and then forgotten about. Some of the common culprits to look out for are the following:

- Corrupt fonts or system permissions, or bad RAM or hard drive.

- Locked folders.

- Saving to a CD/DVD or a network drive.

- Outdated video display drivers. (Windows users can try decreasing the video hardware acceleration to see whether the problem disappears).

- Too much RAM allocated to Photoshop.

- Plug-ins conflicting. Solution: Disable all plug-ins by inserting a ~ character in front of the plug-ins folder name and then starting Photoshop. If the problem disappears, enable plug-ins one at a time.

- Lack of user privileges. Solution: Log in as administrator or see your administrator.

Also note that when you're troubleshooting, it's worth unplugging external drives, scanners, pens and tablets, and the like.

In addition to those general troubleshooting ideas, here are some specific user-focused problems that occur quite frequently, and here's how you can deal with them.

- **How do I get rid of the 01 figure in the top-left corner?** This figure, along with an icon, appears when you select the Slice Select tool. The figure indicates the number for a rectangular slice, and the icon indicates that the slice contains image content. You can hide the figure and the icon by choosing View ➜ Show ➜ Slices, or ignore it because it is nonprintable.

- **I can't save actions because the save item is grayed out in the menu.** To save an action, you need to select an *action set* and not an individual action. Highlight the folder name and try again.

- **The Eyedropper tool keeps selecting the background color.** In the Color Palette, make sure that the foreground color box is highlighted with a black outline. To do so, click the box outline gently. It helps to see the outline more clearly if the foreground color is not white.

- **The crop command always crops larger than the marquee.** Make sure that the selection is not feathered: Select the Rectangular Marquee tool and then enter a zero value for Feather in the options bar.

- **The crop tool is taking ages to crop an image.** Make sure that you, or colleagues playing tricks, have not inadvertently entered values in the Width, Height, and Resolution text fields in the options bar. The tool can act as an image size command when the text fields contain values.

- **Why has a curled page icon appeared on my thumbnail in Bridge?** It simply indicates that the file is open and that you cannot perform any modifications to it in Bridge while it is open.

- **My cursor keeps turning to a crosshair.** This usually happens when the Caps Lock key is in the on position. It's a neat keyboard shortcut for switching icons but can frustrate you if you are unaware of the shortcut.

- **I can't fill the layer with color.** In the Layers palette, make sure that transparency is not locked and Fill is not turned to zero. Click the Lock Transparent Pixels icon to unlock the layer or raise the value in the Fill text box. Check that the blend mode is set to Normal and, if you're using the Fill command, the Preserve Transparency option is not selected (located at the base of the dialog box).

- **When I open a file, I cannot access icons and menu items.** Make sure that your image is not a GIF or a PNG-8. Those formats support limited editing. If it is a GIF or PNG-8, the title bar should state that it's in Index mode and the layer will be named Index. To make edits to an image in Indexed Color mode, convert it to RGB, make the edits, and then convert it back to Indexed Color mode.

- **Where has my palette well gone?** The palette well is supported only by a screen resolution greater than 800 × 600 pixels. A minimum resolution of 1024 × 768 pixels is recommended.

■ **Photoshop won't let me transform a selection.** If you have been working with paths and then decide to transform a selected area, as long as a path is active, Photoshop thinks that you want to transform the path, even though the selection was made afterward and is current. Deselect the path by clicking in an empty area of the Paths palette and then invoke the transform command again. The focus should now be on the selection, making the transform possible.

■ **When I convert to CMYK mode, why do RGB sliders persist in the Color palette?** The palette display is not mode dependent. Select CMYK Sliders from the palette menu to change the display and, if you wish, CMYK Spectrum to change the color field at the bottom of the palette. You can also change the readout in the Info palette to display CMYK values by clicking the eyedropper icons and choosing CMYK Color from the pop-up menu.

■ **When I save using Save for Web, my images look dull.** The remedy is to convert the document to sRGB using the Convert to Profile command before entering Save for Web. By default, the dialog box shows you how the browsers will interpret your image. If it is in a color space wider than sRGB, for example, Adobe RGB (1998) or ProPhoto RGB, there will be a perceived color shift.

■ **I can't save a file as a JPEG.** This often happens when working on a raw file that has been brought into Photoshop in 16-Bits/Channel mode or scanned in 16-Bits/Channel mode. The JPEG file format supports only 8-Bits/Channel. Therefore, the remedy is to change modes from the Image menu.

■ **Why don't the tools do what they're supposed to do?** If your tools start to behave erratically, before taking any drastic action, right-click (Windows), Ctrl-click (Mac OS) on the tool's icon in the options bar and then choose Reset Tool. If that fails, shut down Photoshop. Hold down Ctrl+Alt+Shift (Windows), ⌘+Opt+Shift (Mac OS) and launch Photoshop again. When you're asked to delete the Photoshop Settings file, click the Yes button. Photoshop will replace the settings files with factory defaults. Note that any custom settings will be lost.

■ **The Zoom tool always zooms out, instead of zooming in.** The remedy is to change the Zoom tool's option on the options bar from Zoom In to Zoom Out; select the icon with the plus sign.

■ **The Clone Stamp and Healing Brush tools won't work.** To clone or heal, you need to define a source (not applicable to the Spot Healing Brush). To do that, you need to hold down Alt (Windows), Opt (Mac OS) and click in the current or another open document in the same color space and mode. If another application has taken over the key, you will not be able to use the tools. You probably installed another application recently that has taken over the key or remapped your keyboard. Either remove the program or remap the keyboard.

- **The Pen tool keeps drawing shapes instead of paths.** If you have been using the Pen tool to draw paths and then you switch to a shape tool and set its option to draw Shape layers, when you come back to the Pen tool, its options will have been changed to Shape layers, too. This is the default behavior: Options for the Pen tools affect the shape tools, and vice versa. The remedy is to reset the Pen tools options to draw Paths each time you switch between tools by clicking the second icon on the options bar, not counting the tool icon.

- **I can't find the Airbrush tool.** The Airbrush tool is integrated into the brush tools and can be accessed from the options bar after a brush tool has been selected. It's available as a modal tool for the Brush, History Brush, and Eraser tools (provided that the latter is set to Brush mode).

- **The Rectangular Marquee tool always creates a 600 × 450 px marquee.** Change the tool's style from Fixed Size to Normal on the options bar.

- **Why can't I cycle through my tools?** If you cannot cycle through your tools by using a key, for example, L for Lasso tools, make sure that Use Shift Key for Tool Switch is not selected in the General screen of Preferences.

- **Type keeps typing over itself when I use the Type tool.** This happens when the Leading has been set too low in the Character palette for the Type tool. Select Reset Character from the palette menu to restore the Leading to default.

- **Type keeps typing over itself when I run an old action.** The Type tool is resolution dependent. Either run the action on a file that has the same resolution as the one used to create the action, or rerecord the action. Before creating your action, set the Units & Rulers in Prefs to read Rulers: Percentage and Type: Pixels.

- **Even though I have set the font size to 6 points, the type is still huge.** This can happen when a scan has been brought into Photoshop at the scanner's resolution. Because the Type tool is resolution dependent, the point size can appear huge. In Image Size, deselect Resample Image and then change the Resolution to something more practical, such as 72 pixels/inch or 300 pixels/inch.

Adobe has links to top issues for Photoshop and Bridge on the Adobe Photoshop Support page. To keep abreast, it's worth the occasional visit to the site: www.adobe.com/support/products/photoshop.html.

Index

F

Continued

441

Continued

How to take it to the Extreme.

If you enjoyed this book, there are many others like it for you. From *Podcasting* to *Hacking Firefox*, ExtremeTech books can fulfill your urge to hack, tweak and modify, providing the tech tips and tricks readers need to get the most out of their hi-tech lives.